Review Text in

FRENCH THREE YEARS

SECOND EDITION

Eli Blume

Former Chairman of the Foreign Language Department,
Forest Hills High School,
New York City

Other Books by Eli Blume
French First Year
French Two Years
Cours Supérieur de Français
Douze Contes de Maupassant

When ordering this book, please specify:
either R 194 P
or REVIEW TEXT IN FRENCH THREE YEARS: SECOND EDITION

AMSCO SCHOOL PUBLICATIONS, INC.
315 Hudson Street New York, N.Y. 10013

ISBN 0-87720-471-3

Printed in the United States of America

Preface

This carefully planned *Review Text in French Three Years* (Second Edition) is designed to give the student a thorough understanding and review of the elements of the French language and the highlights of the culture of France. The multiplicity and variety of exercises will assist both student and teacher in evaluating mastery of each phase of the work.

For logical study and for reference purposes, the book is divided into units, namely, Verbs, Structure, Idioms, Composition, and Civilization. Each lesson in these units deals fully with one significant aspect. Thus, the comprehensive treatment of each topic is presented as an integrated whole, rather than in the fragmentary fashion generally found in textbooks.

Much of the material is in French to help the student think in the foreign language. The chapters on Civilization and the exercises based on them, as well as the cultural vignettes interspersed throughout the book, are entirely in French. Each passage in the section on Reading Comprehension is tested through the use of multiple-choice exercises in French.

An attempt is made to set a standard for the student in the writing of a guided composition. In the exercises, several types of compositions have been suggested to provide for a variety of tastes.

Review Quizzes and Mastery Drills give ample opportunity for the testing of broader aspects of language and culture.

It is hoped that this review text, with its clear explanations, varied and attractive drills, significant vocabulary, and comprehensive reviews, will aid the student in the acquisition of communication skills as well as give insights into the culture of the French people.

The author wishes to express his earnest appreciation to the French Embassy Press & Information Division for its kind cooperation in furnishing the pictures from which most of the cultural vignettes were drawn by our artists. The author is indebted also to the French Government Tourist Office for providing the cover photograph of the Eiffel Tower.

Contents

Part I. Verbs

Part II. Structures

Part III. Idioms

Part IV

Part V. Civilization

Part I—*Verbs*

1. THE PRESENT INDICATIVE AND IMPERATIVE OF REGULAR VERBS

PRESENT INDICATIVE

FIRST CONJUNCTION: VERBS IN *-er*

expliqu***er***, to explain

AFFIRMATIVE	INTERROGATIVE
I explain, I am explaining, I do explain	*am I explaining? do I explain?*
j'expliqu***e***	***est-ce que*** j'explique?
tu expliqu***es***	expliques-tu?
il (elle) expliqu***e***	explique-***t***-il (elle)?
nous expliqu***ons***	expliquons-nous?
vous expliqu***ez***	expliquez-vous?
ils (elles) expliqu***ent***	expliquent-ils (elles)?

SECOND CONJUGATION: VERBS IN *-ir*

réuss***ir***, to succeed

AFFIRMATIVE	NEGATIVE
I succeed, I am succeeding, I do succeed	*I am not succeeding, I do not succeed*
je réuss***is***	je ***ne*** réussis ***pas***
tu réuss***is***	tu ***ne*** réussis ***pas***
il (elle) réuss***it***	il (elle) ***ne*** réussit ***pas***
nous réuss***issons***	nous ***ne*** réussissons ***pas***
vous réuss***issez***	vous ***ne*** réussissez ***pas***
ils (elles) réuss***issent***	ils (elles) ***ne*** réussissent ***pas***

THIRD CONJUGATION: VERBS IN *-re*

défend***re***, to defend

AFFIRMATIVE

I defend, I am defending,
I do defend

je défend***s***
tu défend***s***
il (elle) défend
nous défend***ons***
vous défend***ez***
ils (elles) défend***ent***

NEGATIVE INTERROGATIVE

am I not defending? do I not defend?

est-ce que je ***ne*** défends ***pas?***
ne défends-tu ***pas?***
ne défend-il (elle) ***pas?***
ne défendons-nous ***pas?***
ne défendez-vous ***pas?***
ne défendent-ils (elles) ***pas?***

Note

1. The present tense **(le présent)** of the indicative of regular verbs can be found by dropping the infinitive ending and adding the personal endings:

   for **-er** verbs: **-e, -es, -e, -ons, -ez, -ent**
   for **-ir** verbs: **-is, -is, -it, -issons, -issez, -issent**
   for **-re** verbs: **-s, -s, -, -ons, -ez, -ent**

   However, the third person singular of **rompre** and **interrompre** ends in **-t**: il **rompt**, il **interrompt**.

2. **Est-ce que,** regularly used with the pronoun **je,** may also be used before any other subject to change a statement into a question.

Est-ce que ses amis nous accompagnent?	Are his friends accompanying us?
Est-ce que vous ne m'entendez pas?	Don't you hear me?

3. If the verb ends with a vowel in the third person singular, a **-t-** is inserted before **il, elle,** and **on** in the inverted question form.

   Pleure-***t***-elle souvent? — Does she cry often?
   Pourquoi me blâme-***t***-on? — Why do they blame me?

4. In a question with a noun as subject, the noun precedes the inverted verb and pronoun.

   Où ***le fermier*** travaille-t-il? — Where is the farmer working?
   Vos cousines patinent-elles bien? — Do your cousins skate well?

5. The negative is formed by placing **ne (n')** before the verb and **pas** after the verb or, in the inverted question form, after the pronoun.

IMPERATIVE

	FAMILIAR	POLITE	
expliqu*er*	expliqu*e*, explain	expliqu*ez*, explain	expliqu*ons*, let us explain
réuss*ir*	réuss*is*, succeed	réuss*issez*, succeed	réuss*issons*, let us succeed
défend*re*	défend*s*, defend	défend*ez*, defend	défend*ons*, let us defend

Note

1. The forms of the imperative **(l'impératif)** of regular verbs are the same as the corresponding forms of the present indicative except for the omission of the subject pronouns **tu, vous,** and **nous.**
2. The exception is the familiar form of **-er** verbs, which drops the final **s: sonne.**

VOCABULAIRE: VERBES RÉGULIERS

Première Conjugaison

accompagner, to accompany
aider, to help
aimer, to like, love
ajouter, to add
allumer, to light, turn on
apporter, to bring
arracher, to pull out
arrêter, to stop, arrest
attraper, to catch
baigner, to bathe
baisser, to lower
bavarder, to chatter
blâmer, to blame
blesser, to wound, hurt
briller, to shine
briser, to break, smash
brosser, to brush
brûler, to burn
cacher, to hide
casser, to break
causer, to chat
cesser, to stop

chanter, to sing
chasser, to hunt, chase
chauffer, to warm, heat
chercher, to look for
commander, to command, order
compter, to count, intend
conseiller, to advise
couper, to cut
coûter, to cost
crier, to shout
danser, to dance
déchirer, to tear
déjeuner, to breakfast, lunch
demander, to ask (for)
demeurer, to live
dépenser, to spend (money)
désirer, to wish, want
dessiner, to draw
dîner, to dine
diviser, to divide
donner, to give
douter, to doubt
durer, to last
échouer, to fail
éclater, to burst
écouter, to listen (to)
embrasser, to kiss
empêcher, to prevent
emprunter, to borrow
enchanter, to delight
enseigner, to teach
entourer, to surround
entrer, to enter
envelopper, to wrap
épouser, to marry
éternuer, to sneeze
étonner, to astonish
étudier, to study
éveiller, to wake (up)
éviter, to avoid
expliquer, to explain
exprimer, to express
fabriquer, to manufacture
fatiguer, to tire
féliciter, to congratulate
fermer, to close
frapper, to strike, knock
frotter, to rub
fumer, to smoke
gagner, to earn, win
garder, to keep
gaspiller, to waste
gâter, to spoil
glisser, to slip, slide
goûter, to taste
gronder, to scold
habiter, to live in
hésiter, to hesitate
ignorer, not to know, be unaware of
intéresser, to interest
jouer, to play
jurer, to swear
laisser, to leave, let
laver, to wash
louer, to praise, hire, rent
manquer, to lack, miss
marcher, to walk, go
mêler, to mix
mériter, to deserve
monter, to go (come) up
montrer, to show
nommer, to name
ordonner, to order
oser, to dare
ôter, to remove, take off
oublier, to forget
pardonner, to forgive
parler, to speak, talk
passer, to pass, spend (time)
patiner, to skate
peigner, to comb
penser, to think
pleurer, to cry
porter, to carry, wear
poser, to put, place
pousser, to push, grow, utter
présenter, to introduce
prêter, to lend
prier, to pray, beg
prouver, to prove

quitter, to leave
raconter, to relate, tell
ramasser, to pick up, collect
regarder, to look (at)
regretter, to be sorry
remarquer, to notice
remercier, to thank
rencontrer, to meet
rentrer, to go in again, return (home)
repasser, to review, iron
rester, to remain, stay
retourner, to go back, return
retrouver, to find (again)
réveiller, to wake (up)
rêver, to dream
saluer, to greet
sauter, to jump
sauver, to save
sembler, to seem
siffler, to whistle
signifier, to mean
soigner, to take care of
sonner, to ring
souhaiter, to wish
souligner, to underline
stationner, to park
tâcher, to try
téléphoner, to telephone
terminer, to end, finish
tirer, to pull
tomber, to fall
tourner, to turn
tousser, to cough
travailler, to work
traverser, to cross
tremper, to soak, dip
tromper, to deceive
trouver, to find
tuer, to kill
voler, to fly, steal, rob

Deuxième Conjugaison

accomplir, to accomplish
agir, to act
applaudir, to applaud
bâtir, to build
bénir, to bless
choisir, to choose
désobéir (à), to disobey
établir, to establish
finir, to finish
grandir, to grow
guérir, to cure, heal
jouir (de), to enjoy
nourrir, to nourish, feed
obéir (à), to obey
punir, to punish
ravir, to delight
réfléchir, to think, reflect
remplir, to fill
réussir, to succeed
rougir, to blush
saisir, to seize
trahir, to betray

Troisième Conjugaison

attendre, to wait (for)
défendre, to defend, forbid
descendre, to go (come) down
entendre, to hear
interrompre, to interrupt
perdre, to lose
rendre, to give back, return
répondre (à), to answer
rompre, to break
vendre, to sell

EXERCICES

A. Remplacer l'infinitif en italique par la forme convenable du présent:

1. Nous *allumer* la lampe à sept heures.
2. Les Américains *nourrir* bien leurs enfants.
3. Je *compter* cent personnes dans la foule.
4. Il ne *perdre* jamais courage.
5. Qu'est-ce que tu *emprunter?*
6. Je *réfléchir* avant de donner mon opinion.
7. Ces hommes ne *fumer* pas.
8. Pourquoi *punir*-vous cet enfant?
9. Sa sœur *interrompre* souvent notre conversation.
10. Que *signifier* ce mot?
11. Vous *répondre* toujours bien à ses questions.
12. Où l'oiseau *voler*-il?
13. Nous ne *trahir* pas nos amis!
14. Je *rendre* visite à mon oncle.
15. Que *bâtir*-on là-bas?

B. Répéter chaque phrase en substituant la forme convenable du verbe entre parenthèses:

1. (entendre) Rencontre-t-elle souvent ses voisins?
2. (blâmer) Ne punis pas le pauvre élève.
3. (agir) Vous parlez d'une manière étrange.
4. (rompre) Joseph ne demande jamais rien.
5. (remplir) Lavons votre verre et le mien.
6. (saisir) Tout à coup, je coupe la corde.
7. (siffler) Qu'est-ce que tu accomplis?
8. (obéir) Ces chiens intelligents aiment leur maître.
9. (rentrer) A quelle heure le médecin descend-il dans la salle d'opération?
10. (ravir) Cette idée m'étonne.

C. Donner l'équivalent en français:

1. He forgets.
2. Am I forgetting?
3. Do not forget (*fam.*).
4. Let us forget.
5. Aren't they forgetting?
6. I do not disobey.
7. Do we disobey?
8. Who disobeys?
9. Do Paul and Henry disobey?

10. Do not disobey.*

11. They are coming down.
12. Why doesn't Anne come down?
13. Don't come down now.
14. Are you coming down, John?
15. Yes, I'm coming down.

D. Compléter la réponse avec la forme convenable du verbe:

1. Qui demeure dans cette maison?	M. et Mme Durand y ______.
2. Est-ce que je réussis?	Oui, vous ______.
3. Que cachez-vous?	Je ne ______ rien.
4. Qui désire me parler?	Georges et moi, nous ______ vous parler.
5. Où est-ce que je vous attends?	______ -moi ici.
6. Qui soigne le malade?	Sa femme le ______.
7. Combien de billets est-ce que je garde?	Tu ______ trois billets.
8. Que vendez-vous?	Je ______ ma machine à écrire.
9. Quand finissez-vous vos devoirs?	Nous les ______ vers dix heures.
10. Qui joue au tennis?	Mes cousins ______ au tennis.

E. Répondre à chaque question par une phrase complète en français:

1. Enseignez-vous le français?
2. Qui frappe à la porte?
3. Est-ce que je danse bien?
4. Jouissez-vous d'une bonne santé?
5. Quand applaudit-on au théâtre?
6. Qui attends-tu?
7. Où vos amis dînent-ils?
8. Est-ce que je rougis facilement?
9. Qu'est-ce que nous entendons?
10. Les petites écoutent-elles quand vous parlez?

*In all exercises in this book, the word *you* should be translated by the polite form **vous**, unless the question specifically indicates that the familiar form **tu** is required.

2. THE PRESENT INDICATIVE AND IMPERATIVE OF IRREGULAR VERBS

PRESENT INDICATIVE

aller, to go:

je vais, tu vas, il va, nous allons, vous allez, ils vont

s'asseoir, to sit (down):

je m'assieds, tu t'assieds, il s'assied, nous nous asseyons, vous vous asseyez, ils s'asseyent

avoir, to have:

j'ai, tu as, il a, nous avons, vous avez, ils ont

battre, to beat:

je bats, tu bats, il bat, nous battons, vous battez, ils battent
Like battre: **se battre**, to fight

boire, to drink:

je bois, tu bois, il boit, nous buvons, vous buvez, ils boivent

conduire, to lead, drive:

je conduis, tu conduis, il conduit, nous conduisons, vous conduisez, ils conduisent
Like conduire: **construire**, to construct; **produire**, to produce; **traduire**, to translate

connaître, to know, be acquainted with:

je connais, tu connais, il connaît, nous connaissons, vous connaissez, ils connaissent
Like connaître: **reconnaître**, to recognize; **paraître**, to appear; **disparaître**, to disappear

courir, to run:

je cours, tu cours, il court, nous courons, vous courez, ils courent

craindre, to fear:

je crains, tu crains, il craint, nous craignons, vous craignez, ils craignent
Like craindre: **plaindre**, to pity
atteindre, to reach, attain
éteindre, to extinguish, turn off
peindre, to paint
joindre, to join

croire, to believe:

je crois, tu crois, il croit, nous croyons, vous croyez, ils croient

devoir, to owe, have to, be (supposed) to:

je dois, tu dois, il doit, nous devons, vous devez, ils doivent

dire, to say, tell:

je dis, tu dis, il dit, nous disons, vous dites, ils disent

dormir, to sleep:

je dors, tu dors, il dort, nous dormons, vous dormez, ils dorment
Like dormir: **s'endormir**, to fall asleep; **mentir**, to lie; **partir**, to go away, leave; **sentir**, to feel, smell; **servir**, to serve; **sortir**, to go out, leave

écrire, to write:

j'écris, tu écris, il écrit, nous écrivons, vous écrivez, ils écrivent
Like écrire: **décrire**, to describe

envoyer, to send:

j'envoie, tu envoies, il envoie, nous envoyons, vous envoyez, ils envoient

être, to be:

je suis, tu es, il est, nous sommes, vous êtes, ils sont

faire, to do, make:

je fais, tu fais, il fait, nous faisons, vous faites, ils font

falloir, to be necessary:

il faut

lire, to read:

je lis, tu lis, il lit, nous lisons, vous lisez, ils lisent

mettre, to put, put on:

je mets, tu mets, il met, nous mettons, vous mettez, ils mettent
Like mettre: **permettre**, to permit; **promettre**, to promise; **remettre**, to put back, postpone, deliver

mourir, to die:

je meurs, tu meurs, il meurt, nous mourons, vous mourez, ils meurent

ouvrir, to open:

j'ouvre, tu ouvres, il ouvre, nous ouvrons, vous ouvrez, ils ouvrent
Like ouvrir: **couvrir**, to cover; **découvrir**, to discover, uncover; **offrir**, to offer; **souffrir**, to suffer

plaire, to please:

je plais, tu plais, il plaît, nous plaisons, vous plaisez, ils plaisent

pleuvoir, to rain:

il pleut

pouvoir, to be able:

je peux (puis), tu peux, il peut, nous pouvons, vous pouvez, ils peuvent

prendre, to take:

je prends, tu prends, il prend, nous prenons, vous prenez, ils prennent
Like prendre: **apprendre**, to learn, teach
comprendre, to understand, include
reprendre, to take back
surprendre, to surprise

recevoir, to receive:

je reçois, tu reçois, il reçoit, nous recevons, vous recevez, ils reçoivent

rire, to laugh:

je ris, tu ris, il rit, nous rions, vous riez, ils rient
Like rire: **sourire**, to smile

savoir, to know:

je sais, tu sais, il sait, nous savons, vous savez, ils savent

suivre, to follow:

je suis, tu suis, il suit, nous suivons, vous suivez, ils suivent

se taire, to be silent, keep quiet:

je me tais, tu te tais, il se tait, nous nous taisons, vous vous taisez, ils se taisent

tenir, to hold:

je tiens, tu tiens, il tient, nous tenons, vous tenez, ils tiennent
Like tenir: **appartenir à**, to belong to
devenir, to become
obtenir, to obtain
retenir, to hold back
revenir, to come back
venir, to come

valoir, to be worth:

je vaux, tu vaux, il vaut, nous valons, vous valez, ils valent

vivre, to live, be alive:

je vis, tu vis, il vit, nous vivons, vous vivez, ils vivent

voir, to see:

je vois, tu vois, il voit, nous voyons, vous voyez, ils voient
Like voir: **revoir**, to see again

vouloir, to wish, want:

je veux, tu veux, il veut, nous voulons, vous voulez, ils veulent

Note

1. The first person plural of irregular verbs ends in **-ons**, except: **nous sommes.**
2. The second person plural ends in **-ez**, except: **vous dites, vous êtes, vous faites.**
3. The third person plural ends in **-ent**, except: **ils vont, ils ont, ils sont, ils font.**

IMPERATIVE

The imperative of irregular verbs generally follows the same pattern as regular verbs.

aller: va, allez, allons
dire: dis, dites, disons
ouvrir: ouvre, ouvrez, ouvrons
recevoir: reçois, recevez, recevons

Note

1. Irregular **-er** verbs, and verbs conjugated like **-er** verbs in the present indicative, drop the final **s** in the familiar imperative. However, when linked to the pronouns **y** and **en**, all verbs, regular and irregular, retain the **s.**

***Manges*-en** la moitié.	Eat half of it.
***Vas*-y** vite.	Go there quickly.

2. The verbs **avoir, être,** and **savoir** have exceptional imperatives.

avoir: aie, ayez, ayons
être: sois, soyez, soyons
savoir: sache, sachez, sachons

3. The pronoun object of a reflexive verb follows the verb in the affirmative imperative but precedes it in the negative imperative.

s'asseoir

AFFIRMATIVE IMPERATIVE	NEGATIVE IMPERATIVE
assieds-toi	ne t'assieds pas
asseyez-vous	ne vous asseyez pas
asseyons-nous	ne nous asseyons pas

EXERCICES

A. Compléter chaque phrase avec la forme convenable du présent ou de l'impératif:

1. (faire) Ils ______ deux choses à la fois.
2. (courir) Il ______ par la pluie.
3. (boire) Nous ______ du jus de tomate.
4. (apprendre) ______ à faire face à vos difficultés avec courage!
5. (servir) On ______ le dîner.
6. (sortir) Elles ______ malgré le mauvais temps.
7. (mourir) Cette plante ______ sans eau.
8. (être) Nous ______ en bonne santé.
9. (tenir) Elle ______ une rose entre les dents.
10. (aller) Mes sœurs ______ au concert.
11. (conduire) Le guide les ______ à travers les salles du palais.
12. (voir) Tout le monde ______ la faute.
13. (valoir) Il ______ la peine d'étudier les langues étrangères.
14. (construire) Qu'est-ce que vous ______?
15. (vivre) C'est un animal qui ______ aux plus basses températures.
16. (s'endormir) Le bébé ______ dans son lit.
17. (plaire) Est-ce que le cadeau lui ______?
18. (savoir) ______, messieurs, que je n'ai pas l'habitude de répéter mes questions!
19. (suivre) Je crois que quelqu'un me ______.
20. (connaître) Leur oncle ______ plusieurs avocats.

B. Mettre au pluriel les mots en italique:

1. *Elle veut* acheter des meubles.
2. *J'envoie* ces lettres par avion.
3. *Ne sois pas* si paresseux!
4. *Assieds-toi* près de nous.
5. *Je connais* le chemin de Chamonix.
6. *Aie* la bonté d'éteindre la lumière.
7. *Elle reçoit* beaucoup de bonnes notes.
8. *Ne vois-tu pas* toutes les étoiles?
9. *Il peint* des portraits.
10. *Il prend* un repas léger.

C. Demander à un petit cousin:

1. de se taire
2. de ne pas aller près de l'eau
3. pourquoi il ouvre le tiroir
4. s'il sait patiner

Dire à une connaissance:

5. de vous lire le télégramme
6. de ne pas boire cette eau
7. que vous courez à la poste
8. que vous plaignez la pauvre femme
9. que vous vivez à la campagne
10. que vous partez de bonne heure demain

D. Compléter la phrase avec la forme convenable du verbe:

1. Où allez-vous?	Je ______ au supermarché.
2. Qui sait l'alphabet?	Tous les élèves le ______.
3. Est-ce que je la connais?	Non, vous ne la ______ pas.
4. Que voulez-vous?	Je ne ______ rien.
5. Est-ce que je lis bien?	Oui, mais ______ plus haut, s'il vous plaît.
6. Qui comprend l'espagnol?	Nos cousines le ______.
7. Quelle voiture conduisez-vous?	Je ______ une Citroën.
8. Que faites-vous?	Nous ______ les exercices.
9. Suivez-vous mon exemple?	Oui, je le ______.
10. Qui traduit le paragraphe?	Paul et Alain le ______.

E. Dans chaque série, changer la première phrase en substituant les mots indiqués. Faire tous les autres changements nécessaires:

1. Vous prenez des œufs, vous les battez, et vous les mettez dans une casserole. On ______.
2. Pouvez-vous être heureux si vous ne riez guère? ______-elles ______?
3. Nous lui envoyons l'argent que nous lui devons. Ils ______.
4. Tu ne le crains pas parce que tu le connais. Nous ______.
5. Ne mens pas; sois franc et dis la vérité. ______ disons ______.

F. Répondre à chaque question par une phrase complète en français:

1. Combien de verres de lait buvez-vous par jour?
2. Est-ce que je peux t'accompagner ce soir?
3. Est-ce qu'on doit mentir?
4. Prenez-vous des photos en couleurs?
5. Où ces enfants courent-ils?
6. Que craignez-vous?
7. Que fait le poète?
8. Vous taisez-vous quand vous dormez?
9. En quel mois pleut-il souvent?
10. Croyez-vous ce que je vous dis?

3. THE *PASSÉ COMPOSÉ*

VERBS CONJUGATED WITH *AVOIR*

expliqu*er*	réuss*ir*	défend*re*
I explained, *I have explained,* *I did explain*	*I succeeded,* *I have succeeded,* *I did succeed*	*I defended,* *I have defended,* *I did defend*
j'***ai*** expliqu*é* tu ***as*** expliqu*é* il (elle) ***a*** expliqu*é* nous ***avons*** expliqu*é* vous ***avez*** expliqu*é* ils (elles) ***ont*** expliqu*é*	j'***ai*** réuss*i* tu ***as*** réuss*i* il (elle) ***a*** réuss*i* nous ***avons*** réuss*i* vous ***avez*** réuss*i* ils (elles) ***ont*** réuss*i*	j'***ai*** défend*u* tu ***as*** défend*u* il (elle) ***a*** défend*u* nous ***avons*** défend*u* vous ***avez*** défend*u* ils (elles) ***ont*** défend*u*

Note

1. The **passé composé** (past indefinite) of most verbs is formed by combining the present tense of **avoir** and the past participle of the verb.
2. The endings of past participles of regular verbs are **é** (for **-er** verbs), **i** (for **-ir** verbs), and **u** (for **-re** verbs).
3. The following irregular verbs, and the verbs conjugated like them (see Verb Lesson 2), have irregular past participles:

asseoir, *assis*
avoir, *eu*
boire, *bu*
conduire, *conduit*
connaître, *connu*
courir, *couru*
craindre, *craint*
croire, *cru*
devoir, *dû* (*f.* *due*)
(*pl.* *dus, dues*)
dire, *dit*
écrire, *écrit*
être, *été*
faire, *fait*
falloir, *fallu*
lire, *lu*
mettre, *mis*
ouvrir, *ouvert*
plaire, *plu*
pleuvoir, *plu*
pouvoir, *pu*
prendre, *pris*
recevoir, *reçu*
rire, *ri*
savoir, *su*
suivre, *suivi*
taire, *tu*
tenir, *tenu*
valoir, *valu*
vivre, *vécu*
voir, *vu*
vouloir, *voulu*

VERBS CONJUGATED WITH *ÊTRE*

tomb***er***, to fall

I fell, I have fallen, I did fall

MASCULINE SUBJECTS	FEMININE SUBJECTS
je ***suis*** tomb***é***	je ***suis*** tomb***ée***
tu ***es*** tomb***é***	tu ***es*** tomb***ée***
il ***est*** tomb***é***	elle ***est*** tomb***ée***
nous ***sommes*** tomb***és***	nous ***sommes*** tomb***ées***
vous ***êtes*** tomb***é(s)***	vous ***êtes*** tomb***ée(s)***
ils ***sont*** tomb***és***	elles ***sont*** tomb***ées***

Note

1. Sixteen common verbs are conjugated with **être** in the **passé composé**:

INFINITIVE	PAST PARTICIPLE
aller, to go	***allé***
venir, to come	***venu***
arriver, to arrive	***arrivé***
partir, to leave, go away	***parti***
entrer, to go (come) in, enter	***entré***
sortir, to go out, leave	***sorti***
monter, to go (come) up	***monté***
descendre, to go (come) down	***descendu***
revenir, to come back, return	***revenu***
retourner, to go back, return	***retourné***
rentrer, to go in again, return (home)	***rentré***
tomber, to fall	***tombé***
rester, to remain, stay	***resté***
devenir, to become	***devenu***
naître, to be born	***né***
mourir, to die	***mort***

2. Like adjectives, past participles conjugated with **être** agree in gender and number with the *subject.*

Quand sont-**ils** ***sortis?***	When did they leave?
Sa femme est ***née*** en Afrique.	His wife was born in Africa.

3. In the **passé composé,** the present of **avoir** or **être** is treated as the main verb, and the past participle is added to it. Thus,

   a. in the *negative*, the present tense of the auxiliary verb is made negative.

   Elles ***ne sont pas*** descendues.

   b. in the *interrogative*, the present tense of the auxiliary is changed to the interrogative.

   A-t-il plu?

EXERCICES

A. Compléter chaque phrase avec la forme convenable du participe passé:

1. (laisser) Son grand-père lui a ______ une fortune.
2. (dormir) J'ai ______ pendant huit heures.
3. (venir) Elle est ______ me voir.
4. (savoir) Nous n'avons pas ______ le faire.
5. (ravir) Cela m'a ______.
6. (asseoir) Il s'est ______ devant la classe.
7. (pouvoir) N'ont-ils pas ______ y arriver à l'heure?
8. (défendre) L'armée a-t-elle ______ la forteresse?
9. (retourner) Les voyageurs sont ______ au Mexique.
10. (taire) En voyant sa femme, le mari s'est ______.

B. Mettre les phrases au passé composé:

1. Je dois rire.
2. Épouse-t-il une belle dame?
3. Nous saisissons l'occasion.
4. Connaissez-vous sa nouvelle adresse?
5. Elle monte jusqu'au deuxième étage de la tour.
6. Que craignez-vous?
7. Il faut partir tout de suite.
8. Croit-on ses mensonges?
9. Bien entendu, nous arrivons de bonne heure.
10. Cette ville vaut une visite.
11. Les vaches malades ne meurent pas.
12. A quelle heure rentrez-vous, Bernard?
13. Le médecin découvre une nouvelle technique d'inoculation.
14. Elles font un voyage en Afrique.
15. La mère conduit son fils à l'école.

C. Compléter les phrases en anglais:

1. J'en ai eu assez.	I ______ enough.
2. Le géant a rompu les branches.	The giant ______ the branches.
3. Elle est devenue infirmière.	She ______ a nurse.
4. As-tu apporté ta raquette?	______ your tennis racket?
5. Nous sommes restés dans la salle d'attente.	We ______ in the waiting room.
6. La cuisine lui a plu.	The cooking ______ him.
7. Ne sont-ils pas revenus du musée?	______ from the museum?
8. Il n'a pas voulu entrer.	He ______ come in.
9. Le paysan a vécu longtemps.	The peasant ______ a long time.
10. N'a-t-il pas plu hier soir?	______ last night?

D. Donner l'équivalent en français:

1. Where did she go?
2. I put it on the desk.
3. Which book did you (*fam.*) take?
4. We opened the drawer.
5. How much have they read?
6. I held his books.
7. Who came in?
8. They have not been to Paris.
9. How did he do it?
10. Why didn't you run?
11. What did she say?
12. At what time did he go out?
13. We didn't see the garden.
14. Whom did he bless?
15. When did they go down?

E. Répondre à chaque question par une phrase complète en français:

1. Qu'est-ce qu vous avez bu ce matin?
2. Est-ce que la nuit est déjà tombée?
3. Quand ont-ils reçu le télégramme?
4. As-tu suivi cette année un cours de musique?
5. Qui a écrit les phrases au tableau?
6. Est-ce que j'ai gagné le prix?
7. Dans quel pays êtes-vous né(e)?
8. A quelle heure sont-ils partis?
9. A-t-on ri quand Claire a chanté?
10. Avez-vous couvert votre livre de français?

4. THE IMPERFECT INDICATIVE

FORMS OF THE IMPERFECT

expliqu*er*	réuss*ir*	défend*re*
I was explaining, *I used to explain,* *I explained*	*I was succeeding,* *I used to succeed,* *I succeeded*	*I was defending,* *I used to defend,* *I defended*
j'expliqu***ais*** tu expliqu***ais*** il (elle) expliqu***ait*** nous expliqu***ions*** vous expliqu***iez*** ils (elles) expliqu***aient***	je réussiss***ais*** tu réussiss***ais*** il (elle) réussiss***ait*** nous réussiss***ions*** vous réussiss***iez*** ils (elles) réussiss***aient***	je défend***ais*** tu défend***ais*** il (elle) défend***ait*** nous défend***ions*** vous défend***iez*** ils (elles) défend***aient***

Note

1. The imperfect **(l'imparfait)** indicative of regular verbs can be found by dropping the **-ons** from the "**nous**" form of the present tense and adding the personal endings: **-ais, -ais, -ait, -ions, -iez, -aient.**

2. The imperfect of irregular verbs, with few exceptions, can be found in the same way. For example:

INFINITIVE	"**nous**" FORM OF PRESENT	IMPERFECT
boire	**buvons**	je ***buvais***
craindre	**craignons**	je ***craignais***
faire	**faisons**	je ***faisais***
voir	**voyons**	je ***voyais***

3. The forms of **être** and the impersonal verbs are as follows:

être: j'***étais*** **falloir**: il ***fallait*** **pleuvoir**: il ***pleuvait***

4. Verbs that end in **-ions** in the present indicative have forms ending in **-iions** and **-iiez** in the imperfect: **nous étudiions, vous étudiiez; nous riions, vous riiez.**

USES OF THE IMPERFECT

The imperfect tense is used for two kinds of past action: *continuous* and *repeated.* Thus, the signs of this tense in English are usually the words *was . . . -ing, were . . . -ing, used to.*

Philippe ***écoutait*** quand vous ***lisiez.***	Philip was listening when you were reading.
Il me ***rendait*** visite tous les jours.	He used to visit me every day.

The form *I worked* is translated by **je travaillais** only if we can substitute *I was working* or *I used to work* for *I worked.*

Elle préparait le repas pendant que je ***travaillais.***	She was preparing the meal while I worked (= was working).
Je ***travaillais*** toujours dans ma chambre.	I always worked (= used to work) in my room.

If the word *would* means *used to*, it is translated by the imperfect.

Le matin nous ***faisions*** une longue promenade.	In the morning we would (= used to) take a long walk.

The imperfect of **avoir** is generally translated by *had*, and the imperfect of **être** by *was* or *were*; the imperfect of **pouvoir** is often translated by *could.*

j'avais = I had
vous étiez = you were
ils pouvaient = they could (were able)

While the **passé composé** expresses the completion of an action, the imperfect stresses the *continuity* of an action.

Quand elle y ***est arrivée***, il ***pleuvait.***	When she arrived there, it was raining.
Nous ***dînions*** lorsque vous ***avez téléphoné.***	We were having dinner when you telephoned.

Since it stresses continuity, the imperfect is the tense for *description* in the past.

Il ***faisait*** du vent et la neige ***couvrait*** la terre.	It was windy and the snow covered the earth.

EXERCICES

A. Donner la forme convenable de l'imparfait:

1. *battre:*	ils ______	6. *valoir:*	cela ______
2. *craindre:*	je ______	7. *mourir:*	elles ______
3. *hésiter:*	tu ______	8. *mentir:*	vous ______
4. *grandir:*	il ______	9. *vivre:*	il ______
5. *ouvrir:*	nous ______	10. *plaire:*	elle ______

B. Mettre à l'imparfait:

1. Il met le timbre sur l'enveloppe.
2. Nous recevons nos amis dans la salle de séjour.
3. Étudiez-vous seulement le commencement de la leçon?
4. L'eau devient de la glace.
5. N'a-t-il pas une voiture européenne?
6. Qu'est-ce que je dois faire?

7. Je le tiens par la main.
8. Ils boivent du cidre normand.
9. Le professeur lit distinctement quand il nous donne une dictée.
10. Ne connais-tu pas cette actrice?

C. Compléter les phrases en anglais:

1. C'était une nuit sans lune.	______ a moonless night.
2. Je ne pouvais pas retenir mes larmes.	______ hold back my tears.
3. Nous suivions toujours ses conseils.	We always ______ his advice.
4. Fallait-il tuer le pauvre cheval?	______ to kill the poor horse?
5. Ils avaient un beau magnétophone.	______ a beautiful tape recorder.
6. Ne pensiez-vous pas lorsque vous l'avez dit?	______ when ______ it?
7. Qui voulait faire ma connaissance?	Who ______ to meet me?
8. Ce pays produisait beaucoup de blé.	That country ______ much wheat.
9. Nous causions quand nous avons entendu le bruit.	______ when ______ the noise.
10. Il perdait souvent son portefeuille.	He often ______ his wallet.

D. Mettre au passé en employant le passé composé et l'imparfait:

Exemple: Je vois les enfants qui jouent dans la rue.
J'ai vu les enfants qui jouaient dans la rue.

1. Le téléphone sonne pendant que j'écris une lettre.
2. Lorsque nous arrivons à la gare, nos amis nous y attendent.
3. Je remarque que vous souriez.
4. Quand elle sort du théâtre, elle a faim.
5. Tu entres dans la bibliothèque pendant que nous lisons.
6. Ouvre-t-on la boîte qui est sur la table?
7. Quand elles reviennent, il ne pleut plus.
8. Reconnaissez-vous le musicien qui joue de la guitare?
9. Je vais chez mon ami parce que je lui dois un livre.
10. Mme Lejeune rencontre des amies pendant qu'elle choisit un manteau.

E. Compléter chaque phrase en donnant l'équivalent des mots entre parenthèses:

1. (You used to help) ______ tes voisins.
2. (knew) Tout le monde ______ qu'ils étaient fiancés.
3. (she would blush) A l'âge de quinze ans, ______ fréquemment.
4. (were you translating) Quel poème ______?
5. (they used to run) Le matin ______ à l'école.
6. (one could) Chaque nuit de l'été passé, ______ voir les étoiles dans le ciel.
7. (wasn't he learning) Pourquoi ______ à danser?
8. (We believed) ______ qu'elle avait raison.
9. (used to send) Je leur ______ un cadeau tous les ans.
10. (They weren't accomplishing) ______ tout ce qu'ils voulaient.

F. Répondre à chaque question par une phrase complète en français:

1. Où étais-tu quand le téléphone a sonné?
2. Quelle chanson chantaient-ils?
3. Quand vous étiez jeune, obéissiez-vous à votre mère?
4. Y avait-il beaucoup de gens dans le théâtre?
5. Où alliez-vous, toi et Eugène, quand il est tombé?
6. Que faisaient-ils pendant que nous travaillions?
7. Pouvait-on comprendre tout ce que vous disiez?
8. Qu'est-ce que je faisais quand vous m'avez vu dans le musée?
9. Pourquoi l'enfant pleurait-il?
10. Quel temps faisait-il ce matin lorsque vous avez quitté la maison?

5. THE FUTURE AND THE CONDITIONAL

THE FUTURE

expliqu*er*	réuss*ir*	défend*re*
I shall (will) explain	*I shall (will) succeed*	*I shall (will) defend*
j'expliquer***ai*** tu expliquer***as*** il (elle) expliquer***a*** nous expliquer***ons*** vous expliquer***ez*** ils (elles) expliquer***ont***	je réussir***ai*** tu réussir***as*** il (elle) réussir***a*** nous réussir***ons*** vous réussir***ez*** ils (elles) réussir***ont***	je défendr***ai*** tu défendr***as*** il (elle) défendr***a*** nous défendr***ons*** vous défendr***ez*** ils (elles) défendr***ont***

THE CONDITIONAL

expliqu*er*	réuss*ir*	défend*re*
I would explain	*I would succeed*	*I would defend*
j'expliquer***ais*** tu expliquer***ais*** il (elle) expliquer***ait*** nous expliquer***ions*** vous expliquer***iez*** ils (elles) expliquer***aient***	je réussir***ais*** tu réussir***ais*** il (elle) réussir***ait*** nous réussir***ions*** vous réussir***iez*** ils (elles) réussir***aient***	je défendr***ais*** tu défendr***ais*** il (elle) défendr***ait*** nous défendr***ions*** vous défendr***iez*** ils (elles) défendr***aient***

Note

1. The future **(le futur)** and the conditional **(le conditionnel)** are formed by adding the personal endings to the infinitive. In **-re** verbs, the final **e** is dropped before the endings are added.

2. *a.* The endings for all verbs in the future are related to the present tense of **avoir**:

   -ai, -as, -a, -ons, -ez, -ont.

   b. The endings of the conditional are the same as those of the imperfect indicative:

   -ais, -ais, -ait, -ions, -iez, -aient.

3. Some verbs have an irregular stem in the future and conditional:

INFINITIVE	FUTURE	CONDITIONAL
aller	j'*irai*	j'*irais*
s'asseoir	je *m'assiérai* / je *m'assoirai*	je *m'assiérais* / je *m'assoirais*
avoir	j'*aurai*	j'*aurais*
courir	je *courrai*	je *courrais*
devoir	je *devrai*	je *devrais*
envoyer	j'*enverrai*	j'*enverrais*
être	je *serai*	je *serais*
faire	je *ferai*	je *ferais*
falloir	il *faudra*	il *faudrait*
mourir	je *mourrai*	je *mourrais*
pleuvoir	il *pleuvra*	il *pleuvrait*
pouvoir	je *pourrai*	je *pourrais*
recevoir	je *recevrai*	je *recevrais*
savoir	je *saurai*	je *saurais*
tenir	je *tiendrai*	je *tiendrais*
valoir	je *vaudrai*	je *vaudrais*
venir	je *viendrai*	je *viendrais*
voir	je *verrai*	je *verrais*
vouloir	je *voudrai*	je *voudrais*

4. Although the sign of the conditional in English is generally *would*, it may also be *should* in the sense of *would*.

   Je le ***reconnaîtrais*** si je le voyais. — I should (would) recognize him if I saw him.

5. In addition to the usual translation, certain conditional forms have other frequent translations.

   je devrais = I ought, I should (in the sense of obligation)
   je pourrais = I could
   je voudrais = I would like

EXERCICES

A. Mettre au temps indiqué:

AU FUTUR:

1. Porte-t-elle les chemises à la blanchisserie?
2. Ils veulent visiter le palais.
3. Les voyez-vous souvent?
4. Il faut partir à midi.
5. Nous arrivons au Havre et de là nous allons à Paris.

AU CONDITIONNEL:

6. Tu dois éviter le danger.
7. Vaut-il mieux attendre?
8. Je tiens à payer mes dettes.
9. Au lieu de gâteau, nous prenons un morceau de fromage.
10. Sait-elle le faire?

B. Compléter les phrases en anglais:

1. Nous croyions qu'il pleuvrait.	We thought that ______.
2. Le médecin a dit qu'elle ne mourrait pas.	The doctor said that ______.
3. Nous ne vendrons pas la peau d'ours.	______ the bearskin.
4. Elle était certaine que nous pourrions attraper le train.	She was certain that ______ catch the train.
5. Je devrai mettre de l'huile dans la machine.	______ put oil into the machine.
6. La dactylo lui enverra une lettre.	The typist ______ him a letter.
7. Nous voudrions demeurer dans cet immeuble.	______ to live in that apartment house.
8. Iront-elles chez le couturier cet après-midi?	______ to the dressmaker's this afternoon?
9. Vous ne le guérirez pas de sa peur.	______ him of his fear.
10. Je croyais qu'ils ne me verraient jamais.	I thought that ______ me.

C. Remplacer l'infinitif en italique par la forme convenable du verbe:

1. (conditionnel)	Ils *être* ravis de faire votre connaissance.
2. (conditionnel)	Nous ne *courir* pas même s'il était tard.
3. (futur)	J'espère que tu *faire* de ton mieux.
4. (conditionnel)	Il *falloir* partir à midi précis.
5. (conditionnel)	On *dire* qu'il va pleuvoir.
6. (futur)	Les petites filles *embrasser* leur père.
7. (futur)	Je *tenir* mes promesses.
8. (conditionnel)	Lui *envoyer*-vous le colis?
9. (conditionnel)	Il a dit qu'il *aller* à un hôtel.
10. (futur)	Quand *avoir*-vous le temps de me parler?

D. Répéter la phrase en remplaçant l'expression en italique par le futur:

Exemple: Nous *allons l'inviter* à la soirée.
Nous l'inviterons à la soirée.

1. Je ne sais pas ce que le concierge *va faire*.
2. *N'allez-vous pas être* à Paris au printemps?

3. Je crois qu'il *va pleuvoir* ce matin.
4. Combien d'argent *vas-tu dépenser* en livres?
5. Nous *allons savoir* sa réponse avant lundi.
6. Vincent lui promet que son amour *va grandir* de jour en jour.
7. Je *ne vais pas répondre* à une telle question!
8. *Ne vont-elles pas venir* avec nous à la banque?
9. Après la promenade, nous *allons nous asseoir* dans le parc.
10. Je suis sûr qu'ils *ne vont pas punir* une personne innocente.

E. Répondre à chaque question par une phrase complète en français:

1. Pourrez-vous m'aider demain matin?
2. A-t-il dit qu'il accepterait le cadeau ou qu'il le refuserait?
3. Voudriez-vous aller en France l'été prochain?
4. Qui viendra avec nous au magasin?
5. Quand est-ce que je recevrai votre réponse?
6. Y aurait-il assez de place dans la salle pour un piano?
7. Combien de temps passeront-ils à la campagne?
8. Que ferions-nous samedi s'il pleuvait?
9. Est-ce que le dentiste devra arracher la dent?
10. Quelle viande commanderas-tu si nous allons au restaurant?

Rose de portail

Pour orner les églises gothiques et y laisser pénétrer la lumière du jour, les artistes français construisaient des vitraux contenant des panneaux de verre coloré. Cette rose—une baie circulaire garnie de vitraux en compartiments—se trouve au-dessus du portail d'une cathédrale. Il n'est guère possible de reproduire la richesse des couleurs de ces admirables vitraux du Moyen Age.

6. THE *PASSÉ SIMPLE*

REGULAR VERBS

expliqu***er***	réuss***ir***	défend***re***
I explained	*I succeeded*	*I defended*
j'expliqu***ai*** tu expliqu***as*** il (elle) expliqu***a***	je réuss***is*** tu réuss***is*** il (elle) réuss***it***	je défend***is*** tu défend***is*** il (elle) défend***it***
nous expliqu***âmes*** vous expliqu***âtes*** ils (elles) expliqu***erent***	nous réuss***îmes*** vous réuss***îtes*** ils (elles) réuss***irent***	nous défend***îmes*** vous défend***îtes*** ils (elles) défend***irent***

Note

The forms of the **passé simple** (past definite) are found by dropping the ending of the infinitive and adding the following personal endings:

a. for all **-er** verbs: **-ai -as, -a, -âmes, -âtes, -èrent.**
b. for regular **-ir** and **-re** verbs: **-is, -is, -it, -îmes, -îtes, -irent.**

IRREGULAR VERBS

Verbs with irregular stems in the **passé simple** have the endings: **-s, -s, -t, -ˆmes, -ˆtes, -rent.** The stems generally end in **i** or **u**. For example:

faire: je fis, tu fis, il fit, nous fîmes, vous fîtes, ils firent
boire: je bus, tu bus, il but, nous bûmes, vous bûtes, ils burent
tenir: je tins, tu tins, il tint, nous tînmes, vous tîntes, il tinrent

The following irregular verbs, and the verbs conjugated like them (see Verb Lesson 2), have irregular stems in the **passé simple**:

INFINITIVE	PASSÉ SIMPLE	INFINITIVE	PASSÉ SIMPLE
s'asseoir	je m'***assis***	**craindre**	je ***craignis***
avoir	j'***eus***	**croire**	je ***crus***
boire	je ***bus***	**devoir**	je ***dus***
conduire	je ***conduisis***	**dire**	je ***dis***
connaître	je ***connus***	**écrire**	j'***écrivis***
construire	je ***construisis***	**être**	je ***fus***
courir	je ***courus***	**faire**	je ***fis***

INFINITIVE	PASSÉ SIMPLE	INFINITIVE	PASSÉ SIMPLE
falloir	il ***fallut***	**recevoir**	je ***reçus***
joindre	je ***joignis***	**rire**	je ***ris***
lire	je ***lus***	**savoir**	je ***sus***
mettre	je ***mis***	**suivre**	je ***suivis***
mourir	il ***mourut***	**se taire**	je me ***tus***
naître	je ***naquis***	**tenir**	je ***tins***
paraître	je ***parus***	**traduire**	je ***traduisis***
plaindre	je ***plaignis***	**valoir**	je ***valus***
plaire	je ***plus***	**venir**	je ***vins***
pleuvoir	il ***plut***	**vivre**	je ***vécus***
pouvoir	je ***pus***	**voir**	je ***vis***
prendre	je ***pris***	**vouloir**	je ***voulus***

Note

The **passé simple** is used in *historical* and *literary* writing to express an action completed in the past.

Jeanne d'Arc ***naquit*** en Lorraine.	Joan of Arc was born in Lorraine.
Les mousquetaires ***arrivèrent*** à Calais.	The musketeers arrived in Calais.

In conversation and informal writing, such past action is expressed by the **passé composé.**

EXERCICES

A. Compléter chaque phrase en choisissant un des verbes suivants:

arrivèrent	**dus**	**fut**	**passâmes**	**prirent**
dura	**fit**	**mis**	**naquit**	**saisit**

1. Le renard ______ le fromage.
2. Guillaume le Conquérant ______ la conquête de l'Angleterre en 1066.
3. Pour traverser le fleuve, nous ______ sur le pont.
4. Tu ______ de côté beaucoup d'argent.
5. Après la révolte, la France ______ plus forte que jamais.
6. Enfin ils ______ à la côte de la Méditerranée.
7. Napoléon ______ en Corse.
8. Pour l'attraper, je ______ courir vite.
9. Les mousquetaires ______ le chemin de Paris.
10. La soirée ______ jusqu'à deux heures du matin.

B. Mettre les phrases au style de la conversation:

1. Mardi il fit du soleil; le lendemain il plut à verse.
2. Tout le jour nous suivîmes le cours du fleuve.
3. Lorsque l'actrice parut, la salle éclata en applaudissements.
4. Alors je retournai chez moi puisque je tenais à revoir mon village.
5. Tout lui causa du chagrin; rien ne lui plut.
6. Enfin, quand tu la vis, tu la reconnus.
7. On construisit une grande tour pour pouvoir arriver au ciel.
8. Tout à coup nous entendîmes un cri perçant; tout le monde courut vers le porte.
9. Puis les cosmonautes sortirent et travaillèrent hors de la cabine.
10. Pour aider le diplomate, l'interprète traduisit le discours du sénateur.

C. Mettre les verbes en italique au passé simple:

1. L'oiseau *a volé* vers son nid.
2. Ils *ont habité* dans une belle maison.
3. Quand *j'ai lu* le télégramme, *j'ai rougi.*
4. Jacques Cartier *a découvert* le Saint-Laurent.
5. Les artistes *sont revenus* d'Italie avec des idées nouvelles.
6. Tu *as entendu* la mauvaise nouvelle.
7. Elles *ont eu* une longue conversation.
8. Jeanne d'Arc *est morte* en 1431.
9. Ils *ont fait* une contribution à la science.
10. Elle *a reçu* le collier de perles.

D. Compléter chaque phrase avec la forme convenable du passé simple:

1. (écrire) Corneille ______ des tragédies.
2. (crier) Je ______ pour appeler mes camarades.
3. (établir) Ils ______ l'identité de l'homme.
4. (exprimer) Tu ______ les sentiments de tout le monde.
5. (vouloir) Il ______ faire de la France un grand pays.
6. (voir) Nous ______ les villages anciens.
7. (rendre) Le juge ______ la justice.
8. (falloir) Il nous ______ terminer nos études.
9. (travailler) Le ministre ne ______ que pour la gloire.
10. (gagner) Les ennemis ______ la bataille.

E. Donner l'équivalent en anglais:

1. Le domestique alluma le feu.
2. Socrate but le poison et mourut avec courage.
3. De grands écrivains vécurent en France au temps de Louis XIV.
4. Ils essayèrent de me faire parler, mais je me tus.
5. Lorsqu'elle vit ses enfants, elle sourit fièrement.

6. Pascal inventa la presse hydraulique.
7. Le résultat lui parut si ridicule qu'il n'osa pas le mentionner.
8. Ils joignirent leurs efforts aux nôtres.
9. Le cardinal Richelieu, qui fut le créateur de l'absolutisme royal, fonda l'Académie française.
10. On put voir partout les monuments magnifiques des Romains.
11. Elle promit de me rendre mon cahier au bout de quinze jours.
12. La sculpture gothique naquit en Ile-de-France.
13. Ils passèrent leur enfance à Paris, où ils reçurent une bonne éducation.
14. Le général Washington battit les Anglais à Yorktown.
15. Henri IV promulgua l'édit de Nantes et rendit au peuple français sa prospérité passée.

Monument Jeanne d'Arc à Rouen

Ce monument se trouve sur la place du Vieux-Marché, où Jeanne d'Arc fut brûlée en 1431. Rouen, grand port en Normandie, est une ville d'art et un centre industriel très important.

7. SPELLING CHANGES IN CERTAIN *-ER* VERBS

Verbs ending in **-cer** change **c** to **ç** before **a** or **o** to keep the soft **c** sound.

pronon*cer*, to pronounce		
PRESENT INDICATIVE	IMPERFECT INDICATIVE	PASSÉ SIMPLE
je prononce tu prononces il prononce	je pronon*ç*ais tu pronon*ç*ais il pronon*ç*ait	je pronon*ç*ai tu pronon*ç*as il pronon*ç*a
nous pronon*ç*ons vous prononcez ils prononcent	nous prononcions vous prononciez ils pronon*ç*aient	nous pronon*ç*âmes vous pronon*ç*âtes ils prononcèrent

Verbs ending in **-ger** insert mute **e** between **g** and **a** or **o** to keep the soft **g** sound.

voya*ger*, to travel		
PRESENT INDICATIVE	IMPERFECT INDICATIVE	PASSÉ SIMPLE
je voyage tu voyages il voyage	je voyag*e*ais tu voyag*e*ais il voyag*e*ait	je voyag*e*ai tu voyag*e*as il voyag*e*a
nous voyag*e*ons vous voyagez ils voyagent	nous voyagions vous voyagiez ils voyag*e*aient	nous voyag*e*âmes vous voyag*e*âtes ils voyagèrent

Verbs ending in **-yer** change **y** to **i** before mute **e**.

emplo*yer*, to use		
PRESENT INDICATIVE	FUTURE	CONDITIONAL
j'emplo*i*e tu emplo*i*es il emplo*i*e	j'emplo*i*erai tu emplo*i*eras il emplo*i*era	j'emplo*i*erais tu emplo*i*erais il emplo*i*erait
nous employons vous employez ils emplo*i*ent	nous emplo*i*erons vous emplo*i*erez ils emplo*i*eront	nous emplo*i*erions vous emplo*i*eriez ils emplo*i*eraient

However, verbs ending in **-ayer** may or may not change the **y** to **i**.

payer, to pay   elle ***paye*** *or* elle ***paie***, she pays

Verbs with mute **e** in the syllable before the infinitive ending change mute **e** to **è** when the next syllable contains another mute **e**.

m*ener*, to lead		
PRESENT INDICATIVE	FUTURE	CONDITIONAL
je m**è**ne tu m**è**nes il m**è**ne nous menons vous menez ils m**è**nent	je m**è**nerai tu m**è**neras il m**è**nera nous m**è**nerons vous m**è**nerez ils m**è**neront	je m**è**nerais tu m**è**nerais il m**è**nerait nous m**è**nerions vous m**è**neriez ils m**è**neraient

Two verbs with mute **e, appeler** and **jeter,** and compounds of these verbs, double the consonant instead of adding the grave accent.

app*eler*, to call		
PRESENT INDICATIVE	FUTURE	CONDITIONAL
j'appe*ll*e tu appe*ll*es il appe*ll*e nous appelons vous appelez ils appe*ll*ent	j'appe*ll*erai tu appe*ll*eras il appe*ll*era nous appe*ll*erons vous appe*ll*erez ils appe*ll*eront	j'appe*ll*erais tu appe*ll*erais il appe*ll*erait nous appe*ll*erions vous appe*ll*eriez ils appe*ll*eraient

Verbs with **é** in the syllable before the infinitive ending change **é** to **è** only before the mute endings **-e, -es, -ent**. The future and conditional remain unchanged.

esp*érer*, to hope	
PRESENT INDICATIVE	
j'esp**è**re	nous espérons
tu esp**è**res	vous espérez
il esp**è**re	ils esp**è**rent

COMMON -*CER* VERBS

annoncer, to announce
avancer, to advance; be fast (of clocks and watches)
commencer, to begin
effacer, to erase, efface
lancer, to hurl, launch
menacer, to threaten
placer, to place, set
prononcer, to pronounce
remplacer, to replace

COMMON -*GER* VERBS

arranger, **ranger** } to set in order
changer, to change
corriger, to correct
déranger, to disturb
manger, to eat
nager, to swim
neiger, to snow
obliger, to oblige, compel
partager, to share, divide
plonger, to plunge, dive
songer, to think
voyager, to travel

COMMON -*YER* VERBS

employer, to use
ennuyer, to bore
essayer, to try, try on
essuyer, to wipe
nettoyer, to clean
payer, to pay, pay for

COMMON VERBS WITH MUTE *E* IN STEM

MUTE *E* CHANGES TO *È*

acheter, to buy
achever, to complete
amener, to bring, lead to
élever, to bring up, raise
emmener, to lead away, take away
enlever, to remove, take off
geler, to freeze
lever, to raise, lift
mener, to lead, take
peser, to weigh
se promener, to take a walk

CONSONANT DOUBLES

appeler, to call
jeter, to throw
rappeler, to recall, call again

COMMON VERBS WITH *É* IN STEM

célébrer, to celebrate
espérer, to hope
posséder, to possess, own
préférer, to prefer
protéger, to protect
répéter, to repeat

EXERCICES

A. Mettre au pluriel les mots en italique:

1. *Répète* ce que je dis.
2. *Je place* les invités à table.
3. *Tu corrigeais* mes fautes.
4. *Emploie* un bon remède.
5. *L'oiseau annonça* l'arrivée du printemps.
6. *Il mènera* les affaires de l'état.
7. *Je paie* tout par chèque.
8. *Tu possèdes* une très belle maison.
9. *Ne jette pas* cette pierre!
10. *Je plongeai* dans l'eau.

B. Remplacer l'infinitif en italique par la forme convenable du verbe:

1.	(imparfait)	Où *voyager*-ils quand tu les as rencontrés?
2.	(présent)	Elle *peser* dix livres de trop.
3.	(passé simple)	Un grand danger les *menacer.*
4.	(conditionnel)	Je *payer* la note si j'avais assez d'argent.
5.	(présent)	Le sculpteur *espérer* achever bientôt son ouvrage.
6.	(imparfait)	Elle *effacer* les autres actrices par sa beauté.
7.	(futur)	Je le *rappeler* au téléphone.
8.	(passé simple)	Tout à coup, l'image *changer.*
9.	(conditionnel)	On le *jeter* en prison.
10.	(futur)	L'agent de police *lever* son bâton.

C. Former des phrases au présent et au futur avec les sujets indiqués:

Exemple: guérir vite *(il)* Il guérit vite. Il guérira vite.

			PRÉSENT	FUTUR
1.	acheter un réfrigérateur	*(tu)*	------	------
2.	ne pas jeter de pierres	*(nous)*	------	------
3.	employer un système électronique	*(ils)*	------	------
4.	célébrer mon anniversaire	*(je)*	------	------
5.	achever ses vacances en Suisse	*(la voyageuse)*	------	------

D. Former des phrases à l'imparfait et au passé simple avec les sujets indiqués:

			IMPARFAIT	PASSÉ SIMPLE
1.	l'obliger à faire de son mieux	*(le savant)*	------	------
2.	lancer plusieurs satellites	*(nous)*	------	------

3. ne pas prononcer toutes les lettres *(les étrangers)* ______ ______
4. manger des légumes frais *(je)* ______ ______
5. remplacer son mari pendant sa maladie *(la femme)* ______ ______

E. Compléter les phrases en français:

1. They are celebrating Mother's Day. ______ le Jour des Mères.
2. Let us pronounce the words slowly. ______ lentement les mots.
3. The army will protect the government. L'armée ______ le gouvernement.
4. Who will clean the room? Qui ______ la salle?
5. We eat on the terrace of the café. ______ sur la terrasse du café.
6. The cold will freeze the water in the sink. Le froid ______ l'eau dans l'évier.
7. They were announcing the departure of the plane. On ______ le départ de l'avion.
8. Walter is trying on his new sweater. Gautier ______ son nouveau pull.
9. Would you buy that vacuum cleaner? ______ cet aspirateur?
10. When she went out, it was snowing. Quand elle est sortie, ______.

F. Répéter chaque phrase en substituant la forme convenable du verbe entre parenthèses:

1. Ils désirent rester ici. (préférer)
2. Elles voudraient rester chez elles. (préférer)
3. Quand le ferais-tu? (achever)
4. Nous lavons les assiettes. (essuyer)
5. Elle ne laverait pas toutes ces assiettes. (essuyer)
6. Pourquoi éviteriez-vous le médecin? (rappeler)
7. Le président remercie l'ambassadeur. (rappeler)
8. M. Durand conduit sa famille à la campagne. (emmener)
9. Vous avez deux belles enfants, madame. (élever)
10. On y bâtirait un gratte-ciel. (élever)

G. Donner le verbe qui manque:

1. Qu'est-ce que vous effacez? Nous ______ des traces de crayon.
2. Préférez-vous réussir ou échouer? Je ______ réussir.
3. Est-ce que j'essuie les meubles? Oui, vous les ______.
4. Qui arrange les affaires? Raoul et moi, nous les ______.
5. Que jetez-vous dans la corbeille? J'y ______ du papier.
6. Où vous promenez-vous? Nous nous ______ autour du lac.

7. Lanciez-vous la balle? — Non, Philippe la ______.
8. Qui dérangea la machine? — Les saboteurs la ______.
9. Nettoyez-vous souvent vos chaussures? — Oui, je les ______ tous les jours.
10. Qu'est-ce que vous enlevez? — J' ______ la peau de l'orange.

H. Donner l'équivalent en français:

1. she is cleaning, she used to clean, she did clean, she would clean
2. let us swim, we used to swim, he was swimming, he swam (*passé simple*)
3. I lead, I have led, I would lead, I will lead
4. we are beginning, they will begin, they were beginning, we began (*passé simple*)
5. let us call, you will call, I didn't call, he would call

I. Répondre à chaque question par une phrase complète en français:

1. Est-ce que vos livres pèsent beaucoup ou peu?
2. Quand espérez-vous nous rendre visite, Édouard?
3. Combien d'ouvriers emploie-t-on dans cette fabrique?
4. Est-ce que nous avançons bien dans nos études, M. le professeur?
5. A quoi songiez-vous?
6. Qui amènera l'enfant à l'école?
7. Messieurs, est-ce que vous partagez mes idées?
8. Achetez-vous les meilleurs disques haute-fidélité?
9. Est-ce que je vous ennuierai si je joue du piano?
10. Qui appelez-vous quand vous êtes malade?

La place Stanislas à Nancy

Stanislas Ier, ancien roi de Pologne, beau-père de Louis XV, et souverain de la Lorraine, a donné son nom à cette belle place. Les élégantes grilles de la place Stanislas sont l'œuvre de Jean Lamour, serrurier d'art de Nancy du XVIIIe siècle.

8. REFLEXIVE VERBS

In a reflexive verb, the action is performed by the subject on itself. Thus, the subject and the pronoun object refer to the same person(s): *he hurt himself; we will enjoy ourselves.*

s'amuser, to enjoy oneself

PRESENT INDICATIVE

I enjoy (am enjoying, do enjoy) myself

je ***m'amuse***	nous ***nous amusons***
tu ***t'amuses***	vous ***vous amusez***
il (elle) ***s'amuse***	ils (elles) ***s'amusent***

IMPERFECT INDICATIVE:	je ***m'amusais***	I was enjoying (used to enjoy) myself
FUTURE:	je ***m'amuserai***	I will enjoy myself
CONDITIONAL:	je ***m'amuserais***	I would enjoy myself
PASSÉ SIMPLE:	je ***m'amusai***	I enjoyed myself

IMPERATIVE

AFFIRMATIVE

amuse-toi, enjoy yourself
amusez-vous, enjoy yourself (-selves)
amusons-nous, let us enjoy ourselves

NEGATIVE

ne t'amuse pas, do not enjoy yourself
ne vous amusez pas, do not enjoy yourself (-selves)
ne nous amusons pas, let us not enjoy ourselves

Note

1. The reflexive pronouns **me, te, se, nous,** and **vous,** like other personal pronoun objects, normally precede the verb. In the affirmative, they follow the verb. After the verb, **toi** is used instead of **te.**

2. The reflexive pronoun is not always a direct object. It may be an indirect object, with or without a direct object expressed in the sentence.

Se parle-t-il souvent?	Does he talk to himself often?
Nous allons nous laver les mains.	We're going to wash our hands.
Je ne me rappelle pas son adresse.	I don't remember his address.
Elle s'achetait un chapeau.	She was buying herself a hat.

N.B. Any French verb that takes an object, direct or indirect, may be made reflexive by adding a personal pronoun object that refers back to the subject.

3. A verb that is reflexive in French need not be reflexive in English.

Vous vous trompez.	You are mistaken.
Qu'est-ce qui se passe?	What is happening?

4. Reflexive verbs used in the plural may show *reciprocal* force, that is, action of one part of the subject on another part.

Nous nous aidons.	We help one another.
Ils ne s'écrivent pas.	They do not write to each other.

COMMON REFLEXIVE VERBS

s'amuser, to enjoy oneself, have a good time
s'appeler, to be called
s'arrêter, to stop
s'asseoir, to sit (down)
se battre, to fight
se blesser, to hurt oneself, get hurt
se brosser, to brush oneself
se coucher, to lie down, go to bed, set
se dépêcher, to hurry
se déshabiller, to get undressed
s'en aller, to go away
s'endormir, to fall asleep
s'ennuyer, to get bored
se fâcher, to get angry
s'habiller, to dress (oneself), get dressed
se laver, to wash (oneself), get washed
se lever, to get up, rise
se marier, to marry, get married
se passer, to happen
se plaindre, to complain
se porter, to feel (of health)
se promener, to take a walk
se rappeler, to recall, remember
se raser, to shave (oneself)
se reposer, to rest
se réveiller, to wake up
se sentir, to feel
se souvenir de, to remember
se taire, to be silent, keep quiet
se tromper, to be mistaken, make a mistake
se trouver, to be, be situated

EXERCICES

A. Remplacer l'infinitif en italique par la forme convenable du verbe:

1. (présent) *Se souvenir*-vous de ce qu'il vous a dit?
2. (imparfait) Ne *se raser*-il pas chaque matin?
3. (futur) Je *s'en aller* tout à l'heure.
4. (présent) Cette femme *se plaindre* sans cesse.
5. (conditionnel) Tu *s'ennuyer* si tu étais tout seul.
6. (passé simple) Elle *se regarder* dans la glace.
7. (impératif) *Se dépêcher*, mes enfants!
8. (futur) Nous *s'habiller* vite.
9. (présent) Elle ne *se rappeler* pas le nom du livre.
10. (impératif) *Se reposer* avant de te laver.

B. Compléter les phrases en anglais:

1. Qu'est-ce qui se passait? What ______?
2. Le vieillard s'assied dans le fauteuil pour se reposer. The old man ______ in the armchair to ______.
3. Te laves-tu les mains avec de l'eau chaude et du savon? ______ with warm water and soap?
4. Il ne se blessera pas s'il ne se bat pas. ______ if ______.
5. Il me semble que vous vous trompez. It seems to me that ______.
6. Va-t'en, méchant garçon! ______, naughty boy!
7. Nous nous léverions de bonne heure s'il faisait beau. ______ early if the weather was nice.
8. Le petit se déshabilla, se coucha, et s'endormit tout de suite. The child ______, ______ and ______ immediately.
9. Je m'arrêtais chaque jour devant le kiosque. ______ each day in front of the newsstand.
10. Pourquoi les deux sœurs se grondaient-elles? Why ______?

C. Employer une phrase complète pour:

1. dire où vous vous trouviez quand il a commencé à neiger.
2. demander à quelqu'un où il se promènerait s'il faisait beau cet après-midi.
3. dire à des amis de ne pas s'en aller si tôt.
4. dire que vous et Françoise, vous vous voyez souvent.
5. dire à Mme Lejeune que vous ne vous fâcherez pas si elle se trompe.
6. demander à un ami s'il ne se porte pas bien aujourd'hui.
7. demander à M. Martin s'il va se marier en juin ou en juillet.
8. demander à une connaissance si elle s'ennuie quand il n'y a rien à faire.
9. dire à un(e) camarade de classe de se taire quand le professeur parle.
10. dire que vous vous dépêcheriez si vous étiez en retard.

D. Donner l'équivalent en français:

1. Do not get angry.

2. I was getting up.
3. Let us go away.
4. What is her name?
5. Aren't they taking a walk?
6. Enjoy yourselves.
7. He would not be mistaken.
8. Let's not stop.
9. Do not get hurt. (*fam.*)
10. She was washing her face.

E. Répondre à chaque question par une phrase complète en français:

1. Vous sentez-vous triste ou heureux (heureuse) aujourd'hui?
2. Dans quel continent se trouvent les États-Unis?
3. Préférez-vous vous promener en été au soleil ou à l'ombre?
4. Lequel se plaindrait des devoirs, l'élève paresseux ou l'élève travailleur?
5. Te souviens-tu de la date de la prise de la Bastille?
6. Est-ce que je m'amuserai si je vais en France?
7. Vous brossez-vous les dents avant ou après le petit déjeuner?
8. Comment s'appelle votre professeur d'anglais?
9. A quelle heure est-ce que le soleil se couche?
10. Pourquoi vous dépêchez-vous, mes amis?

9. COMPOUND TENSES; AGREEMENT OF PAST PARTICIPLES

Compound tenses are formed with the auxiliary verb **avoir** or **être** and the past participle.

PASSÉ COMPOSÉ (SEE VERB LESSON 3.)

(present of the auxiliary + the past participle)

j'**ai travaillé**, I worked (have worked, did work)
je **suis parti(e)**, I left (have left, did leave)

s'amuser, to enjoy oneself

I enjoyed (have enjoyed, did enjoy) myself

je me ***suis*** amus***é***(***e***)	nous nous ***sommes*** amus***é***(***e***)***s***
tu t'***es*** amus***é***(***e***)	vous vous ***êtes*** amus***é***(***e***)(***s***)
il s'***est*** amus***é***	ils se ***sont*** amus***és***
elle s'***est*** amus***ée***	elles se ***sont*** amus***ées***

PLUPERFECT (LE PLUS-QUE-PARFAIT)

(imperfect of the auxiliary + the past participle)

j'***avais*** travaillé, I had worked
j'***étais*** part***i***(***e***), I had left
je m'***étais*** amus***é***(***e***), I had enjoyed myself

FUTURE PERFECT (LE FUTUR ANTÉRIEUR)

(future of the auxiliary + the past participle)

j'***aurai*** travaillé, I shall have worked
je ***serai*** part***i***(***e***), I shall have left
je me ***serai*** amus***é***(***e***), I shall have enjoyed myself

PAST CONDITIONAL (LE CONDITIONNEL PASSÉ)

(conditional of the auxiliary + the past participle)

> j'***aurais*** travaillé, I would have worked
> je ***serais*** part***i(e)***, I would have left
> je me ***serais*** amus***é(e)***, I would have enjoyed myself

Note

1. Reflexive verbs are conjugated with the auxiliary **être**.
2. In forming the negative and interrogative of compound tenses, only the auxiliary verb is affected.
   a. In the *negative*, the auxiliary is made negative.
   b. In the *interrogative*, the auxiliary is changed to the interrogative.

   nous ***n'avions pas*** travaillé, we hadn't worked
   serait-elle partie? would she have left?
   ne se sont-ils pas amusés? didn't they enjoy themselves?

AGREEMENT OF PAST PARTICIPLES

Past participles conjugated with **avoir** agree in gender and number with the *preceding direct object* (if there is one).

Elle nous a écrit. Elle **nous** a ***punis.***	She wrote to us. She punished us.
Il avait traduit la phrase. Il **l'**avait ***traduite.***	He had translated the sentence. He had translated it.
Quelle **bouteille** as-tu ***cassée?***	Which bottle did you break?
Avez-vous vu les cravates **que** j'ai ***achetées?***	Have you seen the ties I bought?

Past participles conjugated with **être** agree in gender and number with the *subject.*

Ils sont ***restés*** à la campagne.	They stayed in the country.
Leur **chèvre** était ***morte.***	Their goat had died.

Past participles of reflexive verbs agree in gender and number with the *preceding direct object* (if there is one).

Ils **se** sont ***arrêtés*** court.	They stopped short.
Où sont les cravates **qu'**il s'est ***achetées?***	Where are the ties he bought for himself?

Elle s'est ***brossée.***	She brushed herself.
But:	
Elle s'est brossé les cheveux.	She brushed her hair.
Nous nous serions écrit.	We would have written to each other.
Ils ne se sont pas rappelé la rue.	They didn't remember the street.

Past participles used as adjectives agree with the noun they modify.

Les **bijoux** étaient ***cachés.***	The jewels were hidden.
Je dis que le latin n'est pas une **langue *morte.***	I say Latin is not a dead language.

EXERCICES

A. Donner le mot français qui manque:

1.	it had rained	il ______ plu
2.	they would have lived	ils ______ vécu
3.	I made a mistake	je me ______ trompé
4.	she had returned	elle ______ revenue
5.	we had a good time	nous nous ______ amusés
6.	they will have become	ils seront ______
7.	the dead animals	les animaux ______
8.	we had gone	nous ______ allés
9.	you will have had	vous ______ eu
10.	spoken languages	des langues ______
11.	I would have stopped	je me ______ arrêté
12.	you had been	tu ______ été
13.	he would have stayed	il ______ resté
14.	the promised land	la terre ______
15.	you had complained	vous vous ______ plaint

B. Compléter chaque phrase avec la forme convenable du participe passé:

1.	(asseoir)	Elle était ______ à l'ombre.
2.	(ramasser)	Quels fruits avez-vous ______ sous l'arbre?
3.	(brosser)	Elle s'est ______ les dents.
4.	(battre)	Avait-il ______ ses chiens? Oui, il les avait ______.
5.	(étonner)	Les savants étaient ______ de ce qu'ils avaient vu.
6.	(recevoir)	Où sont les cadeaux que tu as ______?
7.	(ouvrir)	Il regardait par la fenêtre ______.
8.	(promener)	Nous nous étions ______ vers le ruisseau.

9. (acheter) Voici les livres qu'elle s'est ______.
10. (parler) Nous nous sommes ______ au téléphone.

C. Répéter chaque phrase en substituant la forme convenable du verbe entre parenthèses:

1. (se réveiller) Catherine avait téléphoné à deux heures.
2. (naître) N'ont-ils pas été au Canada?
3. (se battre) Bien entendu, j'aurais hésité.
4. (se lever) Leur mère aura déjeuné avant eux.
5. (sortir) Nous n'aurions pas menti.
6. (se blesser) Comment les vaches étaient-elles mortes?
7. (se passer) Qu'est-ce qui a sonné?
8. (disparaître) Tu étais déjà montée.
9. (s'amuser) Auraient-elles pleuré?
10. (rentrer) Pourquoi avez-vous déjeuné si tard?

D. Compléter la phrase en anglais:

1. Quelqu'un avait dérangé les journaux. Someone ______ the newspapers.
2. Quelle couleur aurais-tu choisie? What color ______?
3. S'est-elle brossé les cheveux? ______ her hair?
4. Il l'aura fini avant son départ. ______ before his departure.
5. Si je ne l'avais pas aidée, elle serait tombée. If ______, she ______.
6. Qu'est-ce qu'ils avaient fait? What ______?
7. Hier soir nous avons joué aux dames. Last night ______ checkers.
8. A huit heures le soleil se sera couché. At eight o'clock the sun ______.
9. Elle ne se serait pas ennuyée au concert. ______ at the concert.
10. N'auriez-vous pas cassé les œufs aussi? ______ the eggs, too?

E. Compléter la phrase en français:

1. Elle avait mangé les pommes de terre. Elle les avait ______.
2. S'est-elle blessée? Elle s'est ______ la main.
3. Qu'est-ce que vous avez vendu? J'ai ______ ma montre.
4. Qui est rentré? Suzanne est ______.
5. J'ai étudié le français. Quelle autre langue avez-vous ______?
6. A-t-il écrit à ses amis? Oui, il leur a ______.
7. Qui s'est amusé à la fête? Marcel et moi, nous nous y sommes ______.
8. Où as-tu mis la tasse de thé? Je l'ai ______ sur la table.
9. Est-ce que le médecin a guéri votre mére? Non, il ne l'a pas encore ______.
10. Avez-vous traduit la phrase? Non, Renée l'a ______.

F. Donner l'équivalent en français:

1. We had not looked for her.
2. When were you born?
3. Here is the silk that you gave me.
4. I would have shaved.
5. They had heard us.
6. Didn't she rest?
7. We would have been absent.
8. Who had said it?
9. Which novels has he read?
10. Would you have done it?
11. He had fallen asleep.
12. They would not have been able to come.
13. He got dressed.
14. Would she have died?
15. They did not hurry.

G. Répondre à chaque question par une phrase complète en français:

1. Quand se sont-ils mariés?
2. S'est-elle fâchée quand elle vous a reconnus?
3. A quelle heure seriez-vous arrivés à Paris si l'avion avait quitté New York à midi?
4. L'enfant s'était-il lavé les mains avant le dîner?

Dans les réponses aux questions suivantes, remplacer les mots en italique par des pronoms:

5. Qui a raconté *l'histoire?*
6. Avez-vous vu *mes gants?*
7. Quand aura-t-elle fini *le travail?*
8. Avaient-ils pris *les clefs?*
9. Votre sœur avait-elle parlé *à la bonne?*
10. Aurait-il fermé *la fenêtre* s'il avait plu?

10. CONDITIONAL SENTENCES

A conditional sentence consists of two parts:

1. the condition or "**si**" clause;
2. the main or result clause.

Either clause may come first in the sentence. The tense used in the main clause is the same in both languages.

When the verb in the main clause is in the future, present, or imperative, the present indicative is used in the "**si**" clause.

S'il ***pleut***, { nous ne ***sortirons*** pas. / nous ne ***sortons*** pas. / ne ***sortez*** pas. }	If it rains, { we shall not go out. / we do not go out. / do not go out. }

When the main clause is in the present conditional, the imperfect is used in the "**si**" clause.

S'il ***pleuvait***, nous ne ***sortirions*** pas.	If it rained (were to rain), we would not go out.

The same sequence of tenses applies in compound tenses, with the auxiliary considered as the verb. Thus, if the past conditional is used in the main clause, the pluperfect is used in the "**si**" clause.

S'il ***avait plu***, nous ***ne serions pas sortis.***	If it had rained, we would not have gone out.

Note

1. In conditional sentences, **si** always means *if*. The **i** of **si** is dropped only before **il** and **ils**.
2. The imperfect tense after **si** is translated by a simple past tense or by *were to*.

   si vous finissiez = if you finished, if you were to finish

3. The only tenses used in "**si**" clauses are the *present indicative*, the *imperfect*, and the *pluperfect*.

SUMMARY OF TENSES

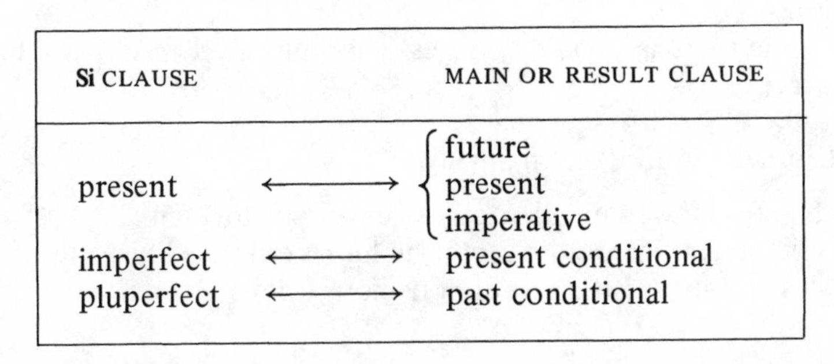

Si CLAUSE		MAIN OR RESULT CLAUSE
present	⟷	future / present / imperative
imperfect	⟷	present conditional
pluperfect	⟷	past conditional

When **si** means *whether*, it may be followed by any tense, just as in English.

Savez-vous **si** elle le ***fera?***	Do you know whether she will do it?
Nous ne savions pas **si** elle le ***ferait.***	We didn't know whether she would do it.
Je ne sais pas **si** elle l'***a fait.***	I don't know whether she did it.

EXERCICES

A. Compléter chaque phrase avec la forme convenable du verbe:

1. (demander) S'ils me ______ pardon, je les excuserais.
2. (prendre) Tu ne dormiras pas bien si tu ______ trop de café.
3. (acheter) Si elle préfère les choux de Bruxelles, nous en ______.
4. (vouloir) Nous ne l'aurions pas retenu s'il ______ partir.
5. (voir) Si vous ______ mon chien, dites-le-moi.
6. (nager) J'irais avec eux à la piscine si je ______ bien.
7. (finir) René ______ la lecture s'il avait eu plus de temps.
8. (attendre) Asseyez-vous un moment si vous ______ le dentiste.
9. (se souvenir) ______-vous de son nom si je le mentionnais?
10. (mourir) Si ses parents ______ dans l'accident, cet enfant aurait été orphelin.
11. (envoyer) Savez-vous s'ils ______ le colis hier?
12. (sentir) Si cette dame ______ des fleurs, elle éternue.

B. Dans chaque série, changer la première phrase en substituant les mots indiqués. Faire tous les autres changements nécessaires:

1. Si vous vous levez de bonne heure, nous irons à la pêche. ______ étiez levé ______.
2. Ils applaudiraient si l'acteur jouait bien. ______ applaudiront ______.
3. Si les vases ne me plaisent pas, je ne les achèterai pas. ______ achèterais ______.
4. Catherine serait allée à la plage s'il avait fait du soleil. ______ faisait ______.
5. Si nous offrons le billet à Jules, l'acceptera-t-il? ______, l'aurait-il accepté?

C. Donner l'équivalent en anglais:

1. S'ils refusent de s'en aller, qu'est-ce que je dois faire?
2. Si elle pouvait garder un secret, je lui raconterais l'histoire.
3. Qu'est-ce qui serait arrivé si nous nous étions plaints?

4. Je me demande s'ils assisteront à la réunion.
5. Si l'on dort bien pendant la nuit, le lendemain on a beaucoup d'énergie.
6. Si tu avais pris de l'aspirine, tu n'aurais pas eu mal à la tête.
7. Je vous en saurais bon gré si vous arrangiez ces fleurs.
8. S'il avait fait beau, nous aurions fait une promenade en bateau.
9. Mettez un tricot si vous avez tellement froid.
10. S'il osait me tromper, je ne lui parlerais pas.

D. Répondre à chaque question par une phrase complète en français:

1. Est-ce que vous chanteriez si je jouais du piano?
2. Sa grand-mère sort-elle s'il fait du vent?
3. Savez-vous si le paquebot est déjà arrivé?
4. Si elle était tombée malade pendant le voyage, qu'aurait-elle fait?
5. Qui se fâcherait si vous ne réussissiez pas à l'école?
6. Si nous voulons voir la Sainte-Chapelle, à quelle ville devons-nous aller?
7. A quelle heure te lèverais-tu si tu n'avais rien à faire?
8. Si je lui avais demandé de danser avec moi, aurait-elle accepté?
9. Me laisserez-vous porter votre nouveau chapeau si l'on m'invite à la soirée?
10. Est-ce que les Français riraient s'ils nous entendaient parler français?

E. Donner l'équivalent en français:

1. If you write me a letter, I shall answer you.
2. I would answer you if you wrote me a letter.
3. If you had written me a letter, I would have answered you.
4. What would they say if he were to hurt himself?
5. If they tell the truth, they will not regret it.
6. We do not know whether he plays tennis.
7. If I had money, I would lend you some.
8. You would have laughed if you had seen his face.
9. If she begins to chatter, we keep quiet.
10. He didn't know whether I would scold him.

11. SPECIAL USES OF CERTAIN TENSES

THE PRESENT WITH *DEPUIS*

The present tense is used in French to express an action begun in the *past* and continuing up to the *present.* In this construction,

depuis quand? *or* **combien de temps y a-t-il que?** = how long?
depuis *or* **il y a (voici, voilà) . . . que** = for

Depuis quand le ***cherchez***-vous? **Combien de temps y a-t-il que** vous le ***cherchez?***	How long have you been looking for him?
Je le ***cherche*** **depuis** vingt minutes. **Il y a (Voici, Voilà)** vingt minutes **que** je le ***cherche.***	I have been looking for him for twenty minutes.

Note: In the equivalent English construction, the present perfect tense, generally progressive, is used.

THE IMPERFECT WITH *DEPUIS*

The imperfect tense is used in French to express an action begun in the *past* and continuing up to another point in the *past.* In this construction,

depuis quand? *or* **combien de temps y avait-il que?** = how long?
depuis *or* **il y avait (voici, voilà) . . . que** = for

Depuis quand le ***cherchiez***-vous? **Combien de temps y avait-il que** vous le ***cherchiez?***	How long had you been looking for him?
Je le ***cherchais*** **depuis** vingt minutes. **Il y avait (Voici, Voilà)** vingt minutes **que** je le ***cherchais.***	I had been looking for him for twenty minutes.

Note: In the equivalent English construction, the pluperfect tense, generally progressive, is used.

OTHER VERBAL EXPRESSIONS WITH DURATION OF TIME

For other verbal expressions that show duration of time, **combien de temps?** (*how long?*) and **pendant** (*for*) are used. In the future, however, **pour** (*for*) is generally used. **Pendant** and **pour,** like *for* in English, may be omitted.

Combien de temps travaille-t-il chaque jour?	How long does he work each day?
Il travaille **pendant** huit heures.	He works for eight hours.
Combien de temps a-t-il travaillé?	How long did he work?
Il a travaillé **(pendant)** huit heures.	He worked (for) eight hours.
Nous resterons en France **(pour)** un mois.	We will stay in France (for) a month.

THE FUTURE WITH *QUAND*

After **quand** (*when*), **lorsque** (*when*), **aussitôt que** (*as soon as*), **dès que** (*as soon as*), and **après que** (*after*), if the action refers to the *future*, French uses the future or, less frequently, the future perfect.

Donnez-lui mes amitiés **lorsque** vous la ***verrez***.	Give her my regards when you see her.
Aussitôt qu'ils ***arriveront***, nous partirons.	As soon as they arrive, we shall leave.
Le ferez-vous **après que** nous ***reviendrons*** (***serons revenus***)?	Will you do it after we return?

In all other cases, the tense used after these conjunctions is similar to the English tense.

Quand elle est heureuse, elle sourit.	When she is happy, she smiles.
Je l'ai remarqué dès que je suis entré.	I noticed it as soon as I came in.

EXERCICES

A. Choisir la réponse convenable:

1. (Combien de temps, Depuis quand) a-t-il plu?
2. As-tu besoin de lunettes lorsque tu (lis, liras)?
3. Vos cousins habitent en Provence? (Combien de temps, Depuis quand) y habitent-ils?
4. Ils y habitent (depuis, pendant) longtemps.
5. Où habiteront-ils après qu'on (vend, vendra) la maison?
6. Portez-vous un parapluie quand il (pleut, pleuvra)?
7. J'ouvrirai mon parapluie (s'il, quand il) pleut.
8. Depuis quand (a-t-il plu, pleuvait-il)?
9. Il a lu la revue (pendant, pour) une heure.
10. (Depuis quand, Combien de temps) faites-vous du judo chaque jour?
11. (Combien de temps, Combien de temps y a-t-il que) vous faites du judo?
12. Aussitôt que vous vous (laverez, lavez), nous nous mettrons en route.

13. Madeleine étudiait le français (depuis, pour) trois ans quand elle a décidé d'aller en France.
14. M. et Mme Marais iront à Nice (pendant, pour) une semaine.
15. (Il y a, Il y avait) un quart d'heure qu'il se reposait.

B. Donner l'équivalent en anglais:

1. Combien de temps a-t-elle souffert? Elle a souffert pendant huit jours.
2. Cette forêt brûle depuis longtemps.
3. Dès que nous verrons un poste d'essence, nous nous arrêterons.
4. Le satellite restera dans le ciel pour dix mois.
5. Combien de temps y a-t-il qu'elle a de la fièvre?
6. Quand nous avons vu les nuages noirs, nous savions qu'il allait neiger.
7. Depuis quand vos cousins demeuraient-ils à Cannes lorsque vous leur avez rendu visite?
8. Combien de temps cette tempête durera-t-elle?
9. Il y avait des années que je me servais d'un rasoir électrique.
10. Nous partirons aussitôt que vous aurez payé l'addition.

C. Compléter chaque phrase avec la forme convenable du verbe:

1.	(voir)	Tournez à gauche dès que vous ______ l'école rouge.
2.	(causer)	Nous ______ hier pendant plusieurs heures.
3.	(mourir)	Voulez-vous dîner? Oui, je ______ de faim depuis une heure.
4.	(rencontrer)	Elle ne me reconnaît jamais lorsqu'elle me ______.
5.	(réfléchir)	Il y a déjà vingt minutes que vous ______.
6.	(mener)	Le professeur parlera à M. Périer quand celui-ci ______ son fils à l'école.
7.	(se sentir)	Venez chez moi aussitôt que vous ______ mieux.
8.	(jouer)	Quand j'étais jeune, je ______ beaucoup à la balle.
9.	(chercher)	Combien de temps y avait-il que vous ______ la boutique?
10.	(dépenser)	Comment vivront-ils après qu'ils ______ tout leur argent?

D. Pour chacune des phrases suivantes, donner une phrase équivalente avec *depuis:*

1. Combien de temps y a-t-il que vous lisez le journal?
2. Il y a quinze jours que je suis ici.
3. Voilà longtemps que les deux garçons patinent.
4. Combien de temps y avait-il qu'ils suivaient cette route?
5. Il y avait une heure que nous mangions.

E. Donner la (une) question qu'on pose pour obtenir chacune des réponses suivantes:

Exemple: Elle attend le médecin depuis dix minutes.
Depuis quand attend-elle le médecin?

1. Il y a une demi-heure qu'ils écoutent la radio.
2. Ils écoutaient la radio depuis une demi-heure.
3. Ils ont écouté la radio pendant une demi-heure.
4. Ils écoutent la radio depuis une demi-heure.
5. Ils écoutent la radio une demi-heure chaque matin.

F. Répondre à chaque question par une phrase complète en français:

1. Qui lui dira la mauvaise nouvelle quand il reviendra?
2. Combien de temps ont-elles parlé au téléphone hier soir?
3. Depuis quand cette jolie infirmière travaille-t-elle dans cet hôpital?
4. Où irez-vous après que nous partirons?
5. Combien de temps est-ce que je pourrai garder ce livre?
6. Est-ce que le soleil se lève ou se couche quand la journée commence?
7. Depuis quand l'attendiez-vous lorsqu'elle est rentrée?
8. Combien de temps y a-t-il que le mécanicien répare votre automobile?
9. Que feras-tu dès que les grandes vacances seront arrivées?
10. Combien de temps y avait-il que vous écriviez quand la cloche a sonné?

G. Donner l'équivalent en français:

1. How long have you been working? I have been working for three weeks.
2. How long do they study? They study for two hours.
3. How long did he stay in Europe? He stayed there for six months.
4. How long had she been singing? She had been singing for ten minutes.
5. How long will you swim? I will swim for a half hour.

12. THE PRESENT PARTICIPLE; CONSTRUCTIONS WITH *EN* AND *APRÈS*

PRESENT PARTICIPLE

The present participle, ending in *-ing* in English, ends in **-ant** in French.

Sa sœur, ***étant*** fatiguée, ne l'a pas accompagnée.	Her sister, being tired, did not go with her.
Ayant parlé, je me suis assis.	Having spoken, I sat down.
Le Père Noël y est arrivé, ***portant*** de beaux cadeaux.	Santa Claus arrived there, carrying beautiful presents.

The French stem is similar to that of the "**nous**" form of the present tense. For example:

INFINITIVE	"**nous**" FORM	PRESENT PARTICIPLE
bâtir	**bâtissons**	***bâtissant***, building
commencer	**commençons**	***commençant***, beginning
devoir	**devons**	***devant***, owing
faire	**faisons**	***faisant***, doing
lire	**lisons**	***lisant***, reading
plaindre	**plaignons**	***plaignant***, pitying

Verbs with irregular present participles are:

avoir	***ayant***, having
être	***étant***, being
savoir	***sachant***, knowing

When the French present participle is used as an adjective, it agrees in gender and number with the noun or pronoun it modifies.

Henri a raconté une **anecdote** ***amusante***.	Henry told an amusing anecdote.
Vous faites des **progrès** ***étonnants***.	You are making amazing progress.
Elles sont tout à fait ***charmantes***.	They are quite charming.

EN + THE PRESENT PARTICIPLE

The preposition **en** (*while, by, in, on, upon*) is followed by the present participle.

Il lisait le journal ***en*** s'***habillant***.	He was reading the newspaper while dressing.
En voyageant, on apprend beaucoup.	By traveling, you learn a great deal.
En entendant le tonnerre, j'ai regardé par la fenêtre.	On hearing the thunder, I looked out the window.

The word **tout** is sometimes used with **en** and the present participle to add emphasis. It may be omitted in English or translated by *still.*

Il a disparu ***tout* en courant**.	He disappeared while (still) running.
***Tout* en travaillant**, elle tomba malade.	While (still) working, she took sick.

APRÈS + THE PAST INFINITIVE

The preposition **après** (*after*) is followed by the past infinitive, that is, the infinitive of **avoir** or **être** plus the past participle.

Après avoir dîné, ils faisaient une promenade.	After dining, they used to take a walk.
Après les ***avoir achetés***, il l'a regretté.	After buying them, he was sorry.
Après y ***être restées*** longtemps, elles ont décidé de partir.	After staying there for a long time, they decided to leave.
Après nous être reposés, nous dînerons.	After resting, we will have dinner.

Note: Past participles in this construction follow the regular rules for agreement. (See Verb Lesson 9.)

EXERCICES

A. Compléter chaque phrase avec la forme convenable du verbe:

1. (ouvrir) Qu'est-ce qu'ils ont trouvé en ______ le colis?
2. (manger) Après ______ du poisson, je suis tombé malade.
3. (faire) Je l'ai rencontré dans le magasin en ______ mes emplettes de Noël.
4. (se brosser) Après ______ les dents, elle est sortie.
5. (porter) Jean est entré ______ deux valises lourdes.
6. (effacer) J'ai fait la correction en ______ une lettre.
7. (venir) Après ______ à l'école, nous faisons nos études.
8. (suivre) Vous vous sentirez mieux après ______ un cours de culture physique.
9. (pouvoir) N'en ______ plus, nous nous sommes assis.
10. (éteindre) Après ______ la lampe, il s'est endormi.
11. (rougir) Tout en ______, il éclata de rire.
12. (avoir) ______ mal à la gorge, je ne voulais pas parler.
13. (se marier) Après _______, ils partiront pour le Canada.
14. (se battre) Il mourut en ______.
15. (voyager) On apprend beaucoup en ______.

B. Donner l'équivalent en français:

1. after disappearing
2. while swimming
3. in writing the address
4. after washing ourselves
5. by beginning early
6. upon drinking the tea
7. after entering the house, she . . .
8. while pitying him
9. by knowing the lesson
10. after enjoying herself
11. while laughing
12. on receiving the prize
13. after seeing her
14. by punishing them
15. while shaving myself

C. Compléter les phrases en anglais:

1. Il aime à chanter en prenant sa douche. He likes to sing ______ his shower.
2. Y a-t-il de l'eau courante dans toutes les chambres? Is there ______ in all the rooms?
3. Après avoir déchiré la lettre, elle l'a jetée. ______ the letter, she threw it away.
4. En voyant le feu rouge, le chauffeur s'est arrêté. ______ the red light, the driver stopped.
5. C'est une femme charmante et très obligeante. She is a ______ woman.
6. Après y être restées longtemps, elles ont décidé de quitter la ville. ______, they decided to leave the city.
7. Étant malade, je ne pouvais pas les accompagner. ______, I couldn't go with them.
8. Nous avons vu le chat courant après les oiseaux. We saw the cat ______.
9. Après avoir atteint son but, il était content de se reposer sur ses lauriers. ______ his goal, he was satisfied to rest on his laurels.
10. Tout en pleurant, elle a couru vers moi. ______, she ran toward me.
11. Sachant que tu viendrais, nous t'avons attendu. ______, we waited for you.
12. Après nous être reposés, nous ferons du ski nautique. ______, we shall go water-skiing.
13. En travaillant dur, on fait des progrès. ______, we make progress.

14. Ayant terminé son discours, le sénateur s'est assis. ______ his speech, the senator sat down.
15. En assistant aux derniers Jeux Olympiques d'hiver, elle s'est cassé le bras. ______ the last winter Olympics, she broke her arm.

D. Relier les deux phrases en remplaçant le premier verbe par *en* et le participe présent:

Exemple: J'allais chez le coiffeur. J'ai remarqué les avions.
En allant chez le coiffeur, j'ai remarqué les avions.

1. Antoine change de vêtements. Il laisse tomber sa montre.
2. Nous remplissions la bouteille. Nous l'avons cassée.
3. Je raconterai l'incident. Je ne mentirai pas.
4. Elle sortait de chez elle. Elle a appelé un taxi.
5. Tu annonces la bonne nouvelle. Tu ne pouvais t'empêcher de sourire.

E. Compléter chaque phrase en donnant l'équivalent des mots entre parenthèses:

1. (After discovering) ______ l'Amerique, Christophe Colomb retourna en Espagne.
2. (interesting and amusing) Son histoire est sans doute ______.
3. (On hearing) ______ le tonnerre, nous croyions qu'il allait pleuvoir.
4. (after getting dressed) Je suis descendu ______.
5. (Taking off) ______ son chapeau, le marchand nous a salués.
6. (After waking up) ______, elle prend le petit déjeuner.
7. (astonishing) Que vous avez une mémoire ______!
8. (while still eating) Il s'est levé ______.
9. (After going out) ______, ils ont remarqué qu'il neigeait.
10. (holding) Une femme, ______ un livre sous le bras, est entrée dans la bibliothèque.

F. Répondre à chaque question par une phrase complète en français:

1. Sifflez-vous en travaillant?
2. Qu'est-ce que le boucher fait de la viande après l'avoir coupée?
3. Quand tu étais jeune, étais-tu un(e) enfant obéissant(e)?
4. Où sont-ils allés après être sortis du théâtre?
5. Qui est cet homme là-bas patinant sur la glace?

13. THE INFINITIVE

The infinitive is used principally after another verb or after a preposition.

Some verbs are followed directly by the infinitive, without a preposition.

aimer mieux } to prefer	**faire**, to make, have, cause
préférer }	**falloir**, to be necessary
aller, to go	**laisser**, to let, allow
compter, to intend	**oser**, to dare
croire, to believe	**pouvoir**, to be able
désirer } to wish, want	**savoir**, to know how
vouloir }	**valoir mieux**, to be better
devoir, to have to, be (supposed) to	**venir**, to come
entendre, to hear	**voir**, to see
espérer, to hope	

Comptez-vous visiter la Bretagne?	Do you intend to visit Brittany?
Je ***dois*** acheter de l'essence.	I must buy some gasoline.
Nous ***avons entendu*** chanter les oiseaux.	We heard the birds singing.
Ils ***viennent*** nous voir.	They are coming to see us.

Some verbs require **à** before the following infinitive.

aider à, to help	**continuer à**, to continue
aimer (à), to like	**enseigner à**, to teach
s'amuser à, to enjoy, amuse oneself by	**hésiter à**, to hesitate
apprendre à, to learn	**inviter à**, to invite
avoir à, to have to	**réussir à**, to succeed in
commencer à } to begin	**tenir à**, to be anxious, insist on
se mettre à }	**venir à**, to happen to

Joséphine ***s'amuse à*** lire.	Josephine enjoys reading.
Je lui ***ai enseigné à*** le faire.	I taught him to do it.
Si tu ***viens à*** la voir, dis-le-moi.	If you happen to see her, tell me.

Note: The **à** is often omitted with **aimer**.

Nous ***aimons*** (à) patiner.	We like to skate.

Some verbs require **de** before the following infinitive.

cesser de, to stop	**oublier de,** to forget
craindre de, to fear, be afraid	**prier de,** to beg
décider de, to decide	**refuser de,** to refuse
empêcher de, to prevent	**regretter de,** to regret
essayer de } to try	**remercier de,** to thank for
tâcher de } to try	**se souvenir de,** to remember
finir de, to finish	**venir de,** to have just

conseiller (à quelqu'un) de, to advise (someone) to
défendre (à quelqu'un) de, to forbid (someone) to
demander (à quelqu'un) de, to ask (someone) to
dire (à quelqu'un) de, to tell (someone) to
ordonner (à quelqu'un) de, to order (someone) to
permettre (à quelqu'un) de, to permit (someone) to
promettre (à quelqu'un) de, to promise (someone) to

Il ***craint de*** perdre son portefeuille.	He is afraid of losing his wallet.
Essayez de venir à l'heure.	Try to come on time.
Je ***viens de*** les rencontrer.	I have just met them.
Elle lui ***a demandé de*** ne pas fumer.	She asked him not to smoke.

Most adjectives and nouns are followed by **de** before the infinitive.

Je suis ***content d'***apprendre la bonne nouvelle.	I am pleased to learn the good news.
Nous serons ***heureux de*** vous prêter un parapluie.	We shall be happy to lend you an umbrella.
Ayez la ***bonté de*** me passer le sel.	Please pass me the salt.
Ont-ils l'***intention de*** vendre l'usine?	Do they intend to sell the factory?
Défense de fumer.	No smoking.

Note: The adjective **prêt** (*ready*) is followed by **à**.

Elle n'est pas encore ***prête à*** partir.	She is not yet ready to leave.

Other prepositions followed by the infinitive are: **pour** (*to, in order to, for the purpose of*), **afin de** (*in order to*), **avant de** (*before*), **sans** (*without*), **au lieu de** (*instead of*).

Il a emprunté de l'argent ***pour*** (***afin de***) payer ses dettes.	He borrowed money to (= in order to) pay his debts.
Je me lave ***avant de*** manger.	I wash before eating.
Ils sont sortis ***sans*** me parler.	They left without speaking to me.
Au lieu de pleurer, elle a ri.	Instead of crying, she laughed.

The preposition **par** (*by*) is used only after **commencer** and **finir.** In other cases, *by* + a verb is translated by **en** + the present participle.

Il ***a commencé par*** lire à haute voix.	He began by reading aloud.
J'***ai fini par*** le faire.	I ended up by doing it (I finally did it).

But:

En mentant, il a perdu ses amis.	By lying, he lost his friends.

An infinitive that is passive in meaning is preceded by **à**.

Y a-t-il quelque chose ***à voir?***	Is there anything to see (= to be seen)?
Cette chanson est facile ***à chanter.***	This song is easy to sing (= to be sung).
Voilà un appartement ***à louer.***	There is an apartment for rent (= to be rented).
Ils sont ***à plaindre.***	They are to be pitied.

Impersonal expressions composed of **il** + **être** + *adjective* require **de** before the infinitive. In this case, the infinitive is really the subject.

Il est bon de dire la vérité.	It is good to tell the truth. (= To tell the truth is good.)
Il n'est pas facile de réussir.	It is not easy to succeed. (= To succeed is not easy.)

Note

1. Notice the difference in the use of the prepositions before the infinitives in the following French sentences.

Il est difficile ***d'***apprendre le chinois.	It is difficult to learn Chinese. (impersonal)
Le chinois est difficile ***à*** apprendre.	Chinese is difficult to learn. (passive)

2. French makes clear the meaning of *it* by two distinct constructions. The translations of these sentences into English, although identical, have two different meanings.

Il est intéressant de lire.	It is interesting to read. (= Reading is interesting.)
C'est intéressant à lire.	It is interesting to read. (= The book, The letter, etc., is interesting to read.)

Memorize:

Il est bon ***de***	***C'est*** bon ***à*** . . . .

EXERCICES

A. Donner la préposition convenable, s'il en faut une:

1. C'est impossible ______ comprendre.

2. Il n'est pas nécessaire ______ fumer.
3. Pourquoi hésitez-vous ______ me répondre?
4. Elle a promis ______ ne pas gâter notre plaisir.
5. ______ vendant les bijoux, il a gagné beaucoup d'argent.
6. Voilà un magasin ______ louer.
7. Vous avez l'air ______ vous ennuyer.
8. Je l'ai prié ______ me rendre un service.
9. ______ réussir, il faut travailler dur.
10. Il lui a demandé ______ baisser la voix.
11. Ce savant va ______ étudier les virus des animaux domestiques.
12. Vous amusez-vous ______ écouter la bonne musique?
13. S'est-il souvenu ______ lui envoyer la carte?
14. Je me suis frotté les mains ______ me chauffer.
15. L'aviateur espérait ______ accomplir la mission avec succès.
16. Il est bon ______ savoir plusieurs langues.
17. La pluie m'a empêché ______ partir.
18. J'essaie ______ travailler dans une pièce tranquille, loin du bruit.
19. Elle était enchantée ______ faire sa connaissance.
20. Il vaut mieux ______ prendre le métro.

B. Dans chaque série, changer la première phrase en substituant les mots indiqués. Faire tous les autres changements nécessaires:

1. Elle n'aime pas à se plaindre. ______ oserait ______.
2. J'ai bien réfléchi en le disant. ______ avant ______.
3. As-tu fini de le faire? ______ par ______?
4. Laissez-moi ranger cette chambre. Aidez ______.
5. Il est très facile d'oublier. C'est ______.
6. Nous sommes prêts à vous suivre. ______ contents ______.
7. L'avez-vous empêchée de sortir? ______ entendue ______?
8. Nous l'avons invité à partager notre repas. ______ permis ______.

9. Au lieu d'étudier, Louis jouait avec ses amis. Après ______.
10. N'a-t-il pas conseillé à son fils de téléphoner à la police? ______ prié ______?

C. Donner l'équivalent en anglais:

1. Il aimait s'asseoir pour regarder jouer les enfants.
2. Je vous ai dit de ne pas me déranger!
3. Défense de stationner.
4. Il faut aller en France pour obtenir une image complète de la vie intellectuelle.
5. Je tiens à devenir écrivain.
6. Nous avons mille choses à faire.
7. Pour se faire couper les cheveux sans attendre longtemps, il faut venir de bonne heure.
8. Si vous venez à le voir, soyez sûr de le féliciter.
9. Pouvez-vous nous donner quelques conseils pour nous aider à vivre heureux?
10. Il regrette d'avoir à refuser notre offre.
11. Rien n'est plus facile à laver.
12. Il est inutile d'essayer de l'arrêter.
13. On a besoin de prendre de l'exercice tous les jours.
14. Nous avons vu briller le soleil dans le ciel.
15. Pour faire du vert, il faut mêler ensemble du jaune et du bleu.

D. Remplacer les mots en italique par une expression équivalente:

1. *Ils ont l'intention de* nous surprendre.
2. *Permettez-moi de* finir cette lettre.
3. *Je n'ai jamais peur de* dire la vérité.
4. *Ayez la bonté d'entrer.*
5. Mon frère m'a emprunté mille francs *afin de* payer la note.
6. *Tâchez de* couper l'herbe avec soin.
7. *Nous désirons* établir un équilibre entre les deux.
8. L'étoile *se mettait à* paraître sur l'horizon.
9. *Enfin il a vendu* le restaurant.
10. *Aimez-vous mieux* demeurer au rez-de-chaussée?

E. Répondre à chaque question par une phrase complète en français:

1. Êtes-vous heureux (heureuse) de me revoir?
2. A quel âge a-t-il appris à nager?
3. Est-il possible de changer les lois de la gravitation?
4. Qu'est-ce que vous me conseillez de faire s'il fait mauvais cet après-midi?
5. A quelle heure faut-il quitter la maison pour ne pas manquer le train?

6. Avez-vous peur de trop manger?
7. Que fera-t-il au lieu d'aller à l'université?
8. Le français est-il facile ou difficile à apprendre?
9. Aurez-vous le temps de repasser le poème avant de le réciter?
10. Quand est-ce que je dois être prêt à partir?
11. Qu'est-ce que tu viens de voir?
12. Pourquoi ont-ils fait venir le médecin?
13. Croyez-vous avoir appris tout ce qu'il y a à savoir?
14. De quoi a-t-on besoin pour vivre?
15. Vos parents vous ont-ils enseigné à être prompt(e)?

F. Construire de nouvelles phrases en employant les verbes entre parenthèses:

Exemple: (espérer) L'artiste achève le portrait.
L'artiste espère achever le portrait.

1. (préférer) Il vit comme un poisson dans l'eau.
2. (cesser) Quand pleuvra-t-il?
3. (vouloir) Le cycliste changeait de direction.
4. (réussir) Je me tais.
5. (devoir) Combien d'argent laisse-t-on comme pourboire?
6. (décider) Nous remettons la réunion au lendemain.
7. (continuer) Elle a toussé toute la nuit.
8. (oublier) Robert s'est rasé.
9. (tenir) Pourquoi répétez-vous cette anecdote?
10. (ne pas pouvoir) On dépense l'argent qu'on n'a pas.

G. Donner l'équivalent en français:

1. Why do you refuse to speak to me?
2. Do not leave without speaking to me.
3. He came to see them.
4. He has just seen them.
5. We began to applaud the actors.
6. We began by applauding the actors.
7. By applauding the actors, we helped them.
8. What is there to read?
9. He forbids them to speak about it.
10. They are supposed to leave tonight.
11. It is useful to know how to draw.
12. I enjoy chatting with you.
13. Is that lesson hard to study?
14. In order to be able to do it, one must be intelligent.
15. Have you had the opportunity to visit the Louvre?

14. SPECIAL USES OF *DEVOIR, FALLOIR, POUVOIR, SAVOIR,* AND *VOULOIR*

A few French verbs, when followed by the infinitive, act as auxiliary verbs, helping to form with the infinitive a complete verbal phrase. The meaning varies with the tense.

devoir, to have to, be (supposed) to

Je ***dois*** partir.	I have to leave. I must leave. I am (supposed) to leave.
Je ***devais*** partir.	I had to leave. I was (supposed) to leave.
Je ***devrai*** partir.	I will have to leave.
Je ***devrais*** partir.	I ought to leave. I should (= ought to) leave.
J'***ai dû*** partir.	I had to leave. I have had to leave. I must have left.
J'***aurais dû*** partir.	I ought to have left. I should (= ought to) have left.

Note

1. In addition to *obligation,* **devoir** also expresses *probability* or *supposition.*

Il ***doit*** être malade.	He must be sick (= He is probably sick).
Il ***a dû*** être malade.	He must have been sick (= I suppose he was sick).

2. The past participle of **devoir** has a circumflex accent only in the masculine singular: **dû, due, dus, dues.**

falloir, to be necessary

The impersonal verb **falloir** may be used:

a. with the infinitive.

Il faut le *faire.*	It is necessary to do it. One must do it.
Il ne faut pas *dire* cela.	We must not say that.

b. with an indirect object pronoun and the infinitive.

Il *lui* faut le faire.	He must do it.
Il *me* faudra partir.	I will have to leave.

c. with the subjunctive.

Il faut qu'il le ***fasse.***	He must do it.
Il faudra que je ***parte.***	I will have to leave.

Note

1. **Falloir** shows *necessity*. It is stronger than **devoir.**
2. **Falloir** and **devoir** often express the same idea.

Vous ***devez*** étudier. ***Il faut que*** vous étudiiez. ***Il vous faut*** étudier.	You must study.

3. When followed by a noun, ***devoir*** means *to owe;* **falloir,** *to need.*

Ils lui ***doivent*** **cent dollars.**	They owe him a hundred dollars.
Il me ***faut*** **l'argent** que vous me devez.	I need the money you owe me.
Il lui ***faut*** **de l'énergie.**	She needs energy.

pouvoir, to be able (physically), be permitted to

Il ne ***peut*** pas nager aujourd'hui; il s'est cassé le bras.	He cannot swim today; he has broken his arm.
Peux-tu lire sans lunettes?	Can you read without glasses?
Puis-je le voir?	May I see it?
Pouviez-vous le faire?	Could you (= Were you able to) do it?
Pourriez-vous le faire?	Could you (= Would you be able to) do it?
Auriez-vous pu le faire?	Could you have done it?

Note

Pouvoir may express *possibility*.

Il ***peut*** être malade.	He may be sick.
Ils ***auraient pu*** le perdre.	They might have lost it.

savoir, to be able (mentally), to know how

Il ne ***sait*** pas nager.	He cannot (= He does not know how to) swim.
Elle est trop jeune pour **savoir** lire.	She is too young to be able to read.

Idiomatic use of the conditional:

Sauriez-vous me dire où il demeure?	Can you tell me where he lives?
Je ***ne saurais*** vous le dire.	I cannot tell you.

vouloir, to wish, want, will

The form **je veux** generally shows strong will, similar to a command.

–***Je veux*** le faire, dit le roi.	"I will do it," the king said.
Je ne ***veux*** pas vous écouter.	I will not (do not want to) listen to you.

Thus, the conditional **je voudrais,** a courteous form, often replaces the present.

Je voudrais lui parler.	I wish (would like) to speak to him.

The imperative form **veuillez** is used with the infinitive to express a polite command.

Veuillez fermer la porte.	Kindly close the door.
Veuillez nous excuser.	Please excuse us.

Idiomatic use: **vouloir bien,** to be willing, be good enough to.

Je veux bien partir maintenant.	I am willing to leave now.
Voulez-vous bien m'attendre?	Will you be good enough to wait for me?

EXERCICES

A. Compléter la phrase en anglais:

1. Nous devons nous dépêcher. ______ hurry.
2. Il lui faut du courage. ______ courage.
3. Pourra-t-elle oublier sa tristesse? ______ to forget her sadness?
4. Veuillez vous asseoir. ______ sit down.
5. Il ne faut pas regarder le tableau. ______ look at the board.
6. Sais-tu jouer au golf? ______ play golf?
7. Je ne pouvais pas comprendre le dialogue du film. ______ understand the dialogue of the film.
8. Ils ont dû être très riches. ______ very wealthy.
9. Il faudra que nous lui envoyions un télégramme. ______ send him a telegram.
10. Sauriez-vous nous indiquer le palais du président? ______ point out to us the President's palace?

B. Donner une phrase équivalente en employant le verbe entre parenthèses:

Exemple: (devoir) Ils sont sans doute sincères.
Ils doivent être sincères.

1. (falloir) Nous avons besoin de temps.
2. (pouvoir) Est-il possible que vous m'aidiez?
3. (devoir) Après cette longue promenade, tu es probablement très fatiguée.
4. (falloir) Simone devra étudier pour réussir.
5. (vouloir) Je refuse de suivre la foule.
6. (devoir) Serez-vous obligés de partir de bonne heure?
7. (falloir) Je dois travailler ce soir.
8. (pouvoir) Ont-ils la permission de vous accompagner?
9. (vouloir) Asseyez-vous, s'il vous plaît.
10. (falloir) Est-il nécessaire de téléphoner pour retenir une place dans le train?

C. Donner l'équivalent en anglais:

1. Je ne veux pas me taire!
2. Il leur faut suivre un cours de musique.
3. Ceux qui gouvernent peuvent se tromper.
4. Je ne saurais vous le dire.
5. Il lui fallait des lunettes pour pouvoir lire.
6. J'ai reçu les cinq mille francs qu'il m'avait dus.
7. Veut-il bien partager la vie de famille?
8. Où peut-elle être? Elle peut être en ville.
9. Il faut que je vous rende votre dictionnaire.
10. Le dentiste a dû arracher la dent; il ne pouvait pas la sauver.

D. Donner *deux* traductions de chaque phrase en anglais ou en français:

1. Elle doit chanter au concert.
2. Je devrais nettoyer ces gants.
3. Nous devions y être à midi.
4. Ils ont dû le vendre.
5. Vous auriez dû lire l'article.
6. Il faut manger pour vivre.
7. I must cover the book.
8. Can you swim?
9. Could he see them?
10. Please thank your brother.

E. Répondre à chaque question par une phrase complète en français:

1. Savez-vous danser?
2. Pourquoi Georges ne peut-il pas danser cette semaine?
3. Est-ce que je peux me reposer ici quelques minutes?
4. Voulez-vous bien vous lever de bonne heure samedi?
5. Qu'est-ce qu'il me faudra faire pour réussir?

6. Où devons-nous mettre votre malle, madame?
7. Combien d'argent vous faut-il pour acheter cette montre-bracelet?
8. Est-ce qu'un garçon de dix ans est trop jeune pour savoir écrire?
9. Sauriez-vous me dire qui a pris mon cahier?
10. Est-ce que j'aurais dû leur dire la vérité?

F. Donner l'équivalent en français:

1. They must be unhappy.
2. They must have been unhappy.
3. You ought to write to him.
4. You should have written to him.
5. It is necessary to think of the future.
6. We cannot work today.
7. Will you be good enough to erase the board?
8. She might have fallen.
9. He is to spend a month at our house.
10. Could you finish if you had more time?

Strasbourg

Dans cette ancienne capitale de l'Alsace, celebre par son pâté de foie gras, on peut voir des maisons d'une architecture charmante. Un pont de Strasbourg, traversant le Rhin, relie la France à l'Allemagne.

15. THE PASSIVE

The passive is formed by combining any tense of **être** with the past participle of the verb. Since the past participle is conjugated with **être**, it agrees with the subject in gender and number.

Elle ***a été blessée*** par une voiture.	She was hurt by a car.
Les chaises ***seront couvertes.***	The chairs will be covered.
Cette église ***fut construite*** au XVe siècle.	That church was built in the 15th century.
La maison ***avait été vendue.***	The house had been sold.
Il ***aurait été puni.***	He would have been punished.

The passive is generally avoided in French by using an active construction: the pronoun **on** followed by the third person singular of the verb.

Ici ***on parle*** anglais.	English is spoken here.
Est-ce qu'***on a*** tout ***fait?***	Has everything been done?
On avait vendu la maison.	The house had been sold.
On entendra la cloche.	The bell will be heard.
Peut-on le guérir?	Can he be cured?

The passive construction is less frequently replaced by a reflexive verb.

Est-ce que les billets ***se vendent*** ici?	Are tickets sold here?
Il ***s'appelle*** Alain.	He is called Allen.
Le français ***se parle*** en Belgique.	French is spoken in Belgium.
Beaucoup d'arbres ***se voyaient*** le long de la route.	Many trees were seen along the road.
Tout à coup la porte ***s'est ouverte.***	Suddenly the door was opened.

EXERCICES

A. Compléter la phrase en anglais:

1. Le pot à fleurs avait été posé sur la table. The flower pot ______ on the table.
2. On l'invitera à la soirée. He ______ to the party.
3. Cela s'explique facilement. That ______.
4. Rien n'y a été ajouté. Nothing ______ to it.
5. Il fut étonné de ce qu'il voyait. He ______ at what he saw.
6. Le gâteau se fait avec de la farine. Cake _______ with flour.
7. Un motel de style américain sera construit près du rond-point. An American-style motel ______ near the traffic circle.

8. On a souligné les mots importants. The important words ______.
9. L'eau était amenée à la ville par un aqueduc. Water ______ to the city by an aqueduct.
10. Il est défendu de stationner devant l'hôtel. It ______ to park in front of the hotel.

B. Remplacer chaque phrase par une phrase équivalente avec *on:*

1. Comment se prononce ce nom?
2. Les malades seront guéris.
3. Une tranche de jambon avait été coupée.
4. Cela ne se fait pas.
5. Cette lettre doit être portée à la poste.
6. Le papier a été jeté sous le canapé.
7. Quelle langue se parle au Mexique?
8. Ses poèmes ne seront jamais oubliés.
9. Les repas se préparent dans la cuisine.
10. Le voleur n'a pas été tué.

C. Traduire en français les mots en italique en employant la construction indiquée:

LE PASSIF:

1. Ces parfums *will be sent* aux quatre coins de la terre.
2. La fenêtre *had been closed* par mon père.
3. Par qui ce gratte-ciel *has it been built?*
4. Votre temps *would not have been wasted.*
5. L'Amérique *had been discovered!*

ON:

6. *It is said* que vous êtes le premier de la classe.
7. *A tip was given* au garçon.
8. En Bretagne *wooden shoes are worn.*
9. *A prize will be offered* au meilleur artiste.
10. *The cake had been divided* en six morceaux.

VERBE RÉFLÉCHI:

11. Beaucoup de livres *are lost* à l'école.
12. *She was called* Yvette.
13. Plusieurs cafés *are found* sur la place.
14. Comment *is that word written?*
15. Rien ne *is ever lost.*

D. Répondre à chaque question par une phrase complète en français:

1. Qu'est-ce qu'on a volé dans le musée?
2. Par qui ce beau vase a-t-il été cassé?
3. Quelle église de Montmartre se voit de loin?
4. Peut-on vous tromper facilement?
5. Serait-il puni s'il n'étudiait pas?
6. A-t-on déjà annoncé la date de leur mariage?
7. A quelle distance est-ce que les cloches de la cathédrale s'entendent?
8. En quelle année votre dernière photo a-t-elle été prise?
9. A qui a-t-on vendu le tapis oriental?
10. Est-ce que la viande sera servie chaude ou froide?

Tirage de sérums à l'Institut Pasteur

Il est impossible de compter les vies que l'Institut Pasteur a sauvées depuis sa création. L'Institut a contribué à arrêter toutes les grandes épidémies qui ravageaient encore le monde il y a moins d'un siècle. L'Institut possède des filiales en France, dans les territoires d'outre-mer, et à l'étranger.

16. THE PRESENT SUBJUNCTIVE; THE SUBJUNCTIVE WITH IMPERSONAL EXPRESSIONS

The subjunctive **(le subjonctif)** is the mood of uncertainty and emotion. Verbs in the subjunctive mood are generally used in a dependent clause introduced by **que** (*that*).

REGULAR VERBS

expliqu*er*	réuss*ir*	défend*re*
que j'expliqu*e*	que je réussiss*e*	que je défend*e*
que tu expliqu*es*	que tu réussiss*es*	que tu défend*es*
qu'il (elle) expliqu*e*	qu'il (elle) réussiss*e*	qu'il (elle) défend*e*
que nous expliqu***ions***	que nous réussiss***ions***	que nous défend***ions***
que vous expliqu***iez***	que vous réussiss***iez***	que vous défend***iez***
qu'ils (elles) expliqu***ent***	qu'ils (elles) réussiss***ent***	qu'ils (elles) défend***ent***

Note

1. The present subjunctive is found by dropping the **-ant** of the present participle and adding the endings: **-e, -es, -e, -ions, -iez, -ent**. These endings are the same for all verbs except **avoir** and **être**.
2. Verbs with spelling changes, such as **employer, mener, appeler**, and **espérer** (see Verb Lesson 7), have the same changes in the present subjunctive as in the present indicative. For example:

que j'emploie	**qu'il appelle**
qu'elle mène	**qu'elles espèrent**

SUBJUNCTIVE AFTER IMPERSONAL EXPRESSIONS

The subjunctive is used after impersonal expressions (except those that show certainty or probability). Common impersonal expressions followed by the subjunctive are:

il faut, it is necessary, must
il est nécessaire, it is necessary
il est bon, it is good
il est important, it is important
il est possible } it is possible,
il se peut } it may be
il est impossible, it is impossible
il est juste, it is right
il est (c'est) dommage, it is a pity, it is a shame
il est temps, it is time
il semble, it seems
il vaut mieux, it is better

Il faut que vous y ***arriviez*** à l'heure.	You must (It is necessary that you) get there on time.
Est-il possible qu'elle ***finisse*** demain?	Is it possible for her to finish tomorrow?
Il se peut que tu te ***trompes.***	You may be mistaken.
Il vaudra mieux que nous ***travaillions.***	It will be better for us to work.

Note

1. There is no future tense in the subjunctive. The present tense is used to express both present and future actions.
2. The subjunctive in French is often translated by an infinitive in English.

EXERCICES

A. Faire une seule phrase en reliant les deux phrases données:

Exemple: Je le prouverai. C'est impossible.
Il est impossible que je le prouve.

1. Les étudiants réfléchiront avant de répondre. C'est nécessaire.
2. Tu perds ton temps. C'est dommage.
3. François agit en homme d'honneur. C'est bon.
4. Nous mangeons tous ces desserts. Ce n'est pas possible.
5. Elles partageront leurs idées avec nous. C'est juste.
6. On choisira la reine de la fête. C'est important.
7. Vous vous ennuyez si facilement. Est-ce possible?
8. Le médecin les guérira tout de suite. C'est impossible.
9. Vous pesez vos mots. C'est important.
10. J'attends longtemps. Est-ce nécessaire?

B. Construire des phrases selon le modèle en employant le vocabulaire donné:

Modèle: il semble/ Richard/ ne pas entendre/ téléphone
Il semble que Richard n'entende pas le téléphone.

1. il faudra/ nous/ finir/ travail/ demain
2. il sera nécessaire/ on/ vendre/ peintures
3. est-il temps/ soleil / se lever
4. il est dommage/ vous / ne pas nager
5. il n'est pas juste/ on / punir / innocents
6. faut-il / je / répéter / question
7. il se peut / vous / s'amuser / théâtre
8. il semble/ tu / ignorer / ce qui / se passer
9. il vaut mieux / nous / effacer / fautes
10. se peut-il / énergie / coûter / plus cher / année prochaine

IRREGULAR VERBS

The stem of most irregular verbs, as with regular verbs, can be found by dropping the **-ant** of the present participle. For example:

INFINITIVE	PRESENT PARTICIPLE	PRESENT SUBJUNCTIVE
s'asseoir	**s'asseyant**	je ***m'asseye***
conduire	**conduisant**	je ***conduise***
connaître	**connaissant**	je ***connaisse***
courir	**courant**	je ***coure***
craindre	**craignant**	je ***craigne***
écrire	**écrivant**	j'***écrive***
rire	**riant**	je ***rie***
vivre	**vivant**	je ***vive***

A few irregular verbs have a *single irregular* stem:

faire: je ***fasse***, tu ***fasses***, il ***fasse***, nous ***fassions***, vous ***fassiez***, ils ***fassent***
falloir: il ***faille***
pouvoir: je ***puisse***, tu ***puisses***, il ***puisse***, nous ***puissions***, vous ***puissiez***, ils ***puissent***
savoir: je ***sache***, tu ***saches***, il ***sache***, nous ***sachions***, vous ***sachiez***, ils ***sachent***

A number of irregular verbs have *two* stems in the present subjunctive, one stem for the **nous** and **vous** forms (which is identical with the stem of the **nous** and **vous** forms of the present indicative), and one for the other forms:

aller: j'***aille***, tu ***ailles***, il ***aille***, nous allions, vous alliez, ils ***aillent***
boire: je ***boive***, tu ***boives***, il ***boive***, nous buvions, vous buviez, ils ***boivent***
croire: je ***croie***, tu ***croies***, il ***croie***, nous croyions, vous croyiez, ils ***croient***
devoir: je ***doive***, tu ***doives***, il ***doive***, nous devions, vous deviez, ils ***doivent***
envoyer: j'***envoie***, tu ***envoies***, il ***envoie***, nous envoyions, vous envoyiez, ils ***envoient***
mourir: je ***meure***, tu ***meures***, il ***meure***, nous mourions, vous mouriez, ils ***meurent***
prendre: je ***prenne***, tu ***prennes***, il ***prenne***, nous prenions, vous preniez, ils ***prennent***
recevoir: je ***reçoive***, tu ***reçoives***, il ***reçoive***, nous recevions, vous receviez, ils ***reçoivent***
tenir: je ***tienne***, tu ***tiennes***, il ***tienne***, nous tenions, vous teniez, ils ***tiennent***
valoir: je ***vaille***, tu ***vailles***, il ***vaille***, nous valions, vous valiez, ils ***vaillent***

venir: je ***vienne***, tu ***viennes***, il ***vienne***, nous venions, vous veniez, ils ***viennent***
voir: je ***voie***, tu ***voies***, il ***voie***, nous voyions, vous voyiez, ils ***voient***
vouloir: je ***veuille***, tu ***veuilles***, il ***veuille***, nous voulions, vous vouliez, ils ***veuillent***

The only verbs with irregular endings are **avoir** and **être**:

avoir		**être**	
j'***aie***	nous ***ayons***	je ***sois***	nous ***soyons***
tu ***aies***	vous ***ayez***	tu ***sois***	vous ***soyez***
il (elle) ***ait***	ils (elles) ***aient***	il (elle) ***soit***	ils (elles) ***soient***

OTHER IMPERSONAL EXPRESSIONS

After impersonal expressions of certainty or probability, the indicative is used. Some common expressions of this type are:

il est certain, it is certain	**il est probable**, it is probable
il est clair, it is clear	**il est vrai**, it is true
il est évident, it is evident	**il paraît**, it appears

Il est évident que vous *savez* la leçon. — It is evident that you know the lesson.
Il est probable qu'ils ***viendront*** demain. — It is probable that they will come tomorrow.

However, when these expressions are used negatively or interrogatively, they generally express doubt and take the subjunctive.

Il n'est pas certain qu'il ***vienne*** demain. — It is not certain that he will come tomorrow.
Est-il vrai qu'on ***bâtisse*** une nouvelle école? — Is it true that they are building a new school?

EXERCICES

C. Mettre au pluriel les mots en italique:

1. Il est important que *j'aille* à la gare prendre un billet.
2. Il semble que *tu sois* très paresseux.
3. Il n'est pas nécessaire que *tu étudies* à cette heure.
4. Vaut-il mieux que *j'enlève* ce fauteuil?

5. Il se peut que *je vienne* vous voir demain.
6. Il est bon que *tu boives* beaucoup de lait.
7. Il faut que *je m'asseye* un instant.
8. Est-il possible que *tu doives* tant d'argent?
9. Il est dommage que *tu ne puisses pas* nous accompagner.
10. Est-il temps que *j'envoie* le chèque à la banque?

D. Donner l'équivalent en anglais:

1. Il est temps qu'il apprenne la vérité.
2. Est-il nécessaire que je le fasse tout de suite?
3. C'est dommage que tu ne saches pas danser.
4. Se peut-il que cette femme craigne une petite souris?
5. Est-il impossible que vous vous taisiez?
6. Il faudra que nous voyions les rideaux avant de les acheter.
7. Est-il vrai qu'elle veuille me présenter à son amie?
8. Il n'est pas juste qu'on jette des pierres au pauvre animal.
9. Ne faut-il pas que je mette de l'huile dans le moteur?
10. Est-il possible que vous croyiez tout ce qu'il vous dit?

E. Compléter chaque phrase avec la forme convenable du verbe:

1. (écrire) Il faut qu'un poète ______ des poèmes.
2. (tenir) Il est bon que cette voiture ______ bien la route.
3. (mourir) Est-il possible que le blessé ______?
4. (avoir) Il est clair que la Terre ______ sa propre atmosphère.
5. (s'ennuyer) Est-il certain qu'ils ______ s'ils vont à la réunion?
6. (suivre) Il est juste que le pilote ______ ses ordres.
7. (neiger) Il paraît qu'il ______ demain.
8. (pleuvoir) Il se peut qu'il ______ ce soir.
9. (se promener) Il vaut mieux que vous ______ le long du quai.
10. (réussir) Il est très important que je ______.
11. (valoir) C'est dommage que ce diamant ______ si peu.
12. (répéter) Sera-t-il nécessaire que je ______ la question?
13. (se souvenir) Il n'est pas certain qu'elle ______ de la rue.
14. (connaître) Il semble que tu ______ ce journaliste.
15. (vivre) Est-il vrai que cet artiste ______ sur sa réputation?

F. Répondre à chaque question par une phrase complète en français:

1. Pourquoi est-il important que vous ayez de bonnes notes?
2. Est-il nécessaire que je sache nager?
3. Quel paragraphe faut-il que nous traduisions?
4. Est-il temps que vous alliez chez le dentiste?
5. A quelle heure faut-il que je prenne le train?

G. Donner l'équivalent en français:

1. It is time for us to leave.
2. It's a pity that the weather is cold.
3. It is true that he reads well.
4. Is it true that he understands French?
5. You must obey your teachers.
6. It is better that they go to London.
7. It seems that there is an error in the sentence.
8. It is possible that he will receive your card.
9. It isn't right for you to deceive me.
10. It's important that she be here.
11. It is evident that they will not arrive on time.
12. Is it possible that I am wrong?
13. It is impossible for him to finish before noon.
14. Must you (*fam.*) always complain?
15. It is probable that you will see them.

Les caves de Roquefort

Au sud du Massif Central, la petite ville de Roquefort s'est acquis une réputation mondiale. C'est d'ici que provient le roquefort—le plus célèbre des fromages fabriqués avec du lait de brebis. Ce fromage est affiné dans des caves parcourues de courants d'air naturels, froids, et humides.

17. THE PERFECT SUBJUNCTIVE; THE SUBJUNCTIVE WITH EXPRESSIONS OF EMOTION, WISHING, AND DOUBT

THE PERFECT SUBJUNCTIVE

défendre

que j'aie défendu	que nous ayons défendu
que tu aies défendu	que vous ayez défendu
qu'il (elle) ait défendu	qu'ils (elles) aient défendu

tomber

que je sois tombé(e)	que nous soyons tombé(e)s
que tu sois tombé(e)	que vous soyez tombé(e)(s)
qu'il soit tombé	qu'ils soient tombés
qu'elle soit tombée	qu'elles soient tombées

s'amuser

que je me sois amusé(e)	que nous nous soyons amusé(e)s
que tu te sois amusé(e)	que vous vous soyez amusé(e)(s)
qu'il se soit amusé	qu'ils se soient amusés
qu'elle se soit amusée	que'elles se soient amusées

Note

1. The perfect subjunctive is formed by combining the present subjunctive of **avoir** or **être** and the past participle of the verb.
2. As the subjunctive equivalent of the **passé composé**, the perfect subjunctive is used to express an action that has already taken place.

C'est dommage qu'il n'***ait*** pas ***étudié***.	It is a pity that he didn't study.
Il semble qu'ils ***soient sortis***.	It seems they have gone out.

EXERCICES

A. Mettre au passé l'expression en italique:

1. Il est possible que *je perde* mon temps.
2. Il est juste que *vous receviez* le prix.
3. Est-il probable qu'*ils aillent* au café?
4. Il est impossible que *tu te coupes* avec ce canif.
5. Il se peut qu'*ils aient* une longue conversation.

6. Il est vrai que *ce savant contribue* à la conquête de l'espace.
7. Il est bon que *nous lui écrivions.*
8. Se peut-il que *Claude me reconnaisse?*
9. C'est dommage que *les employés souffrent.*
10. Il n'est pas possible que *l'oiseau vive* si longtemps.
11. Nous sommes désolés que *tu ne puisses pas* l'empêcher.
12. Il est dommage que *votre sœur ne vienne pas* avec nous.
13. Est-il vrai que *nous courions* un grand danger?
14. Il est évident qu'*ils lui pardonnent* le faux pas.
15. Est-il possible que *vous mettiez* tant de sucre dans votre thé?

THE SUBJUNCTIVE WITH EXPRESSIONS OF EMOTION, WISHING, AND DOUBT

The subjunctive is used in a dependent clause when the subject of the dependent clause is *different* from the subject of the main clause.

a. After expressions of *emotion* (joy, fear, sorrow), such as:

j'ai peur (. . . ne), I am afraid	**je suis désolé,** I am very sorry, I am distressed
je crains (. . . ne), I fear	**je suis heureux,** I am happy
je m'étonne, I am astonished	**je suis surpris,** I am surprised
je regrette, I am sorry	
je suis content, I am glad	

Je crains qu'elle **ne *tombe*.**	I fear she may fall.
Nous regrettons que vous ***ayez attendu*.**	We are sorry that you waited.

Note: Expressions of fear in declarative affirmative sentences generally take **ne** with the subjunctive. **Ne** is not used if the verb of fearing is negative or interrogative.

Je **ne crains pas** qu'elle ***tombe*.**	I'm not afraid that she will fall.

b. After expressions of *wishing* or *commanding*, such as:

j'aime mieux / **je préfère** } I prefer	**j'ordonne,** I order
je défends, I forbid	**je souhaite,** I wish
je désire, I wish, I want	**je veux,** I want, I wish
	je voudrais, I should like

Son père **défend** qu'elle ***devienne*** actrice.	Her father forbids her to become an actress.
Voulez-vous que je ***fasse*** de mon mieux?	Do you want me to do my best?

c. After expressions of *doubt*, such as:

je doute, I doubt	**croyez-vous?** do you believe?
je ne suis pas sûr (certain), I am not sure (certain)	**espérez-vous?** do you hope?
je ne crois pas, I do not believe	**je ne pense pas,** I do not think
	pense-t-il? does he think?

Elle doute qu'il ***finisse*** le travail. — She doubts that he will finish the work.

Croyez-vous qu'elle ***dise*** la vérité? — Do you think she is telling the truth?

Je ne pense pas que vous l'***ayez fait.*** — I don't think you did it.

Note: **Penser, croire,** and **espérer,** when used *negatively* or *interrogatively*, generally imply doubt and are followed by the subjunctive. Sometimes both the indicative and the subjunctive are possible, depending on the thought of the speaker. For example:

Je ne crois pas qu'elle ***viendra.*** (No doubt implied.)
Je ne crois pas qu'elle ***vienne.*** (Doubt implied.)
} I do not believe she will come.

When these verbs are used negatively *and* interrogatively, they are followed by the indicative since they suggest an affirmative answer with no doubt implied.

N'espérez-vous pas qu'il le ***fera?*** — Don't you hope he will do it?

Note

1. The infinitive is sometimes used in English where French uses the subjunctive.

   Je voudrais que vous ***restiez*** ici. — I would like you to stay here.

2. If both the main and dependent verbs have the *same* subject, the infinitive is generally used in French instead of the subjunctive.

   Avez-vous peur de ***rire?*** — Are *you* afraid *you* may laugh? (Are you afraid of laughing?)

   Nous préférons le ***croire.*** — We prefer to believe it.

   Croyez-vous ***avoir trouvé*** la réponse? — Do *you* think *you* have found the answer?

EXERCICES

B. Dans chaque série, changer la première phrase en substituant les mots indiqués. Faire tous les changements nécessaires:

1. Nous espérons qu'on rompra le silence. Nous défendons ______.
2. Il paraît que Jean-Pierre est déjà rentré. Il semble ______.
3. Elle croit qu'il pleuvra demain. Elle craint ______.
4. Êtes-vous certain que tous les avions soient équipés d'un radar? N'est-il pas évident ______?
5. Il est clair que la cravate ne vous plaît pas. Je regrette ______.
6. J'espère que vous prenez le temps de vivre. Il est bon ______.
7. Tout le monde dit que cette situation durera longtemps. On doute ______.
8. Vous savez qu'ils ont visité tous les pays du Marché Commun. Nous sommes heureux ______.
9. Je pense que ces dames sont nées en Belgique. Il est probable ______.
10. On dit que le Concorde a atteint deux fois la vitesse du son. Nous nous étonnons ______.

C. Ajouter à chaque phrase l'expression indiquée en faisant les changements nécessaires:

Exemple: Je défends mes idées.
Le professeur souhaite ______.
Le professeur souhaite que je défende mes idées.

1. Nous payerons d'avance. Aiment-ils mieux ______?
2. Il y a trop de pollution près des fabriques. Nous craignons ______.
3. Je les ai vus. Je pense ______.
4. Il fera chaud dimanche. Espères-tu ______?
5. Il s'agit d'une maladie imaginaire. Elle ne croit pas ______.
6. Vous vous êtes amusés au cirque. Nous sommes contents ______.
7. Tu ne les puniras pas. Ils croient ______.
8. Cette carte de crédit lui appartient. Je doute ______.
9. Charles a acheté une voiture de sport. Sa mère regrette ______.
10. Personne ne l'interrompra. M. Marchand préfère ______.

D. Répondre à chaque question par une phrase complète en français:

1. Doutez-vous que Michèle soit sincère?
2. Se peut-il qu'elle m'ait reconnu?
3. Quand voudriez-vous que je vous aide?
4. Voudriez-vous dîner avec nous?
5. Dans quelle pièce désire-t-elle que la domestique serve le repas?
6. Croyez-vous qu'il soit parti en avion?
7. Est-il possible que vous nous ayez menti?

8. Aimes-tu mieux que je sois ton ami ou ton ennemi?
9. Ont-ils peur que vous brisiez la glace?
10. Pensez-vous qu'elles se soient déjà réveillées?

E. Compléter la seconde phrase de chaque série:

1. Il veut que je conduise le camion. ______ the truck.
2. Je défends que vous riiez quand il chantera. ______ when he sings.
3. Elle croyait rêver. She ______.
4. Pensez-vous qu'ils aient pu l'obtenir? Do you think ______?
5. Pourquoi n'ordonnez-vous pas qu'ils s'arrêtent? Why don't you ______?
6. J'ai peur qu'on ne glisse sur cette peau de banane. ______ on that banana peel.
7. Ils souhaitent que vous restiez chez eux. ______ with them.
8. Es-tu surpris que ce petit garçon ait mangé deux tablettes de chocolat? ______ two bars of chocolate?
9. Que désirent-ils que je fasse? What ______?
10. Je doute qu'il vous faille une heure pour l'achever. ______ to finish it.
11. I'm afraid the house may burn. J'ai peur ______.
12. I'm afraid I may fall. J'ai peur ______.
13. They wish that she would come back. Ils souhaitent ______.
14. His father forbids him to smoke. Son père défend ______.
15. We hope we can try it. Nous espérons ______.
16. I'm terribly sorry that you hurt yourself. Je suis désolé ______.
17. Don't you think he will remember it? Ne crois-tu pas ______?
18. It's a shame that Delphine changed her mind. C'est dommage ______.
19. We're not certain that they have gone out. Nous ne sommes pas certains ______.
20. Do you want me to show you the bike? ______ le vélo?

18. OTHER USES OF THE SUBJUNCTIVE

a. The subjunctive is used after certain *conjunctions:*

afin que, **pour que** } in order that, so that
avant que, before
à moins que (. . . ne), unless
bien que, **quoique** } although
de crainte que (. . . ne), **de peur que (. . . ne)** } for fear that, lest
jusqu'à ce que, until
pourvu que, provided that
sans que, without

Je vous lirai l'histoire **à moins que** vous ne la ***connaissiez*** déjà.	I shall read you the story unless you know it already.
Il refuse de se reposer **bien qu'**il ***soit*** fatigué.	He refuses to rest although he is tired.
Elle réussira **pourvu qu'**elle ***fasse*** attention.	She will pass provided she pays attention.

Note

1. **A moins que, de crainte que**, and **de peur que** are generally followed by **ne** before the subjunctive verb.

2. When both the main and dependent verbs have the *same* subject, the corresponding preposition, if there is one, is generally used with the infinitive instead of the conjunction with the subjunctive.

Nous sommes partis de bonne heure **afin de (pour)** le ***voir.***	We left early in order to see him.
Je me lave **avant de *manger.***	*I* wash before *I* eat.

3. After the verb **attendre, que** alone is generally used to mean *until.*

Attendez *que* je le fasse.	Wait until I do it.

4. The following common conjunctions take the indicative:

après que, after	**pendant que**, while
aussitôt que, **dès que** } as soon as	**peut-être que**, perhaps
	puisque, since
parce que, because	**tandis que**, whereas, while

b. The subjunctive is used in a relative clause referring to an indefinite person or thing that is sought but not yet found.

Y a-t-il un peintre qui ***puisse*** faire mon portrait?	Is there a painter who can paint my portrait?

Nous cherchons un appartement qui ***soit*** grand.	We are looking for an apartment that is large.
Connaissez-vous un écrivain qui ***sache*** écrire mieux que lui?	Do you know a writer who can write better than he?

Note

If there is no doubt about the existence of the person or thing, the indicative is used.

Je connais un peintre qui ***peut*** faire votre portrait.	I know a painter who can paint your portrait.
Voici un appartement qui ***est*** grand.	Here is an apartment that is large.

c. The subjunctive is used after superlative expressions, generally showing opinion. Such superlatives include **le seul** (*the only*), **le premier** (*the first*), and **le dernier** (*the last*).

C'est **le meilleur café** qu'on ***puisse*** acheter.	That's the best coffee you can buy.
C'est **la seule fois** que je vous le ***dise***.	That's the only time I will tell it to you.
Ce sont **les plus beaux cadeaux** que j'***aie*** jamais ***vus***.	They are the most beautiful gifts I have ever seen.

d. The subjunctive is used in principal clauses to express a third-person imperative or a wish.

Qu'elle le ***fasse*** tout de suite!	Let her do it at once!
Qu'il ***entre!***	Let him come in!
Qu'ils ***réussissent!***	May they succeed!
Vive la France!	Long live France!

Note

These subjunctive clauses are really dependent on commands or wishes that are understood.

EXERCICES

A. Compléter chaque phrase avec la forme convenable du verbe:

1. (étudier) Bien que vous ______ beaucoup, vous ne recevez pas de bonnes notes.
2. (pouvoir) C'est le meilleur pain que vous ______ trouver.
3. (dormir) Sortons de la chambre afin que l'enfant ______.
4. (être) Y a-t-il un homme qui ______ parfait?
5. (tomber) Il marche très lentement de peur de ______.

6. (courir) Le train n'y sera pas à moins que nous ne ______.
7. (se sentir) Puisque vous ne ______ pas bien, reposez-vous un peu.
8. (être) Sylvie est fort diligente tandis que sa sœur ______ très paresseuse.
9. (connaître) C'est l'homme le plus riche que nous ______.
10. (partir) Qu'elle ______ immédiatement!
11. (essayer) Vous accomplirez beaucoup pourvu que vous ______.
12. (vivre) La foule cria: –Le roi est mort. ______ le roi!
13. (reconnaître) Il tourne la tête de crainte que je ne le _______.
14. (vouloir) Mme Fouchet connaît une femme qui ______ acheter votre piano.
15. (assister) Quoiqu'il ______ hier à l'accident, il refuse d'en parler.

B. Relier les deux phrases en employant *qui* ou *que:*

Exemple: On cherche un acteur. Il sait danser.
On cherche un acteur qui sache danser.

1. Y a-t-il un chapeau ici? Il me convient.
2. Je cherche une montre. Elle n'avancera pas.
3. Voici un stylo. Il écrit bien.
4. Avez-vous un stylo? Il écrit bien.
5. C'est le professeur le plus intelligent. Je le connais.
6. Connaissez-vous un enfant? Il sait lire mieux que Gérard.
7. Ce ne seront pas les seuls. Ils auront l'occasion de le féliciter.
8. Est-ce la plus belle langue? Vous l'avez étudiée.
9. J'ai trouvé une chaise. Elle me plaît.
10. C'est la meilleure histoire. Tu l'as racontée.

C. Compléter la seconde phrase de chaque série:

1. Elle cache ses bijoux de peur que quelqu'un ne les vole. She hides her jewels ______.
2. Avez-vous des conseils que je puisse suivre? Have you any advice ______?
3. C'est la pomme la plus délicieuse que j'aie jamais goûtée. This is the most delicious apple ______.
4. Quoiqu'il soit devenu à la télévision l'idole des familles américaines, il est très modeste. ______, he is very modest.
5. S'en iront-ils sans que je le sache? Will they go away ______?
6. Tu vas le répéter jusqu'à ce que tu l'apprennes. You're going to repeat it ______.
7. "Dieu vous bénisse!" dit-elle. ______, she said.

8. Ce fermier est assez gros bien qu'il fasse beaucoup d'exercice. That farmer is quite stout ______.

9. Je ne vous parlerai plus à moins que vous ne me répondiez. I won't speak to you anymore ______.
10. Qu'ils reviennent vers trois heures! ______ around three o'clock!
11. What happened after they left? Qu'est-ce qui est arrivé ______?
12. I will show it to you before we finish it. Je vous le montrerai ______.
13. Show it to me before you finish it. Montrez-le moi ______.
14. Let the pupils come in! Que ______!
15. She does not study without my helping her. Elle n'étudie pas ______.
16. Can one learn French without going to France? Peut-on apprendre le français ______?
17. Stay here until he returns; let's wait until he returns. Reste ici ______; attendons ______.
18. I will accompany you provided that you wait for me. Je vous accompagnerai ______.
19. Perhaps Philip will write us a letter. Peut-être ______.
20. I'll leave the newspaper here so that you may read it. Je laisserai le journal ici ______.

D. Répondre à chaque question par une phrase complète en français:

1. Pouvez-vous me donner un livre qui soit intéressant?
2. Iront-ils en ville ce soir quoiqu'il pleuve?
3. Que ferez-vous pendant que je finirai mon travail?
4. Veut-elle partir sans vous voir?
5. Peut-elle partir sans que vous la voyiez?
6. Est-ce le plus beau cheval que vous ayez jamais vu?
7. Connaissez-vous un médecin qui puisse me guérir?
8. Où mènerez-vous l'enfant pour qu'il voie des animaux sauvages?
9. Resteras-tu à Paris jusqu'à ce que nous arrivions?
10. Comptent-ils faire un pique-nique demain pourvu qu'il fasse beau?

VERB REVIEW QUIZZES

Épreuves A–J

Remplacer l'infinitif en italique par la forme convenable du verbe:

A

1. Nous étions au bord de la mer pendant qu'ils *voyager.*
2. Lavons-nous avant de *s'habiller.*
3. Après *être* longtemps à l'étranger, j'étais content de revenir.
4. Comment passerons-nous le temps jusqu'à ce qu'il *venir?*
5. Dès que vous *savoir* la réponse, dites-la-moi, s'il vous plaît.
6. En *faire* attention, on fait moins de fautes.
7. Depuis quand *se promener*-il quand l'accident a eu lieu?
8. Je regrette qu'il ne *pouvoir* pas nous accompagner.
9. *Aller*-vous visiter Versailles si vous étiez en France?
10. C'est la première pièce qu'il ait jamais *écrire.*

B

1. Il entra, s'assit, et *commencer* à écrire.
2. Toutes les fleurs étaient *mourir.*
3. *Avoir* la bonté de fermer la porte, monsieur.
4. Les Français *aimer* depuis longtemps les idées de justice et de liberté.
5. Si on *mentir* souvent, on perd tous ses amis.
6. Croyez-vous que ses œuvres *valoir* beaucoup par leur qualité littéraire?
7. Je le ferai de peur que vous ne *être* fâchée.
8. Puisqu'elle avait froid aux mains, elle *mettre* ses gants de laine.
9. Aussitôt que je *se sentir* mieux, nous nous mettrons en route.
10. En *produire* la bombe atomique, on exploite de nouvelles formes d'énergie.

C

1. Après les *voir,* il a décidé d'en acheter.
2. Lorsque vous *recevoir* le colis, ne l'ouvrez pas.
3. Je crois que Madeleine *aller* au musée demain matin.
4. L'ouvrier s'est blessé en *bâtir* l'édifice.
5. Voici dix minutes que je vous *attendre.*
6. C'est dommage que cette élève *craindre* tant les examens.
7. *Courir*-ils s'ils voyaient un tigre?
8. Y a-t-il un idiotisme qu'il n'*avoir* pas appris?
9. Voici les livres que nous *recevoir* hier comme prix.
10. *Faire* vos devoirs tout de suite!

D

1. S'il *battre* le tapis, il sera très fatigué.
2. La route est *couvrir* de glace.

3. *Nager*-il souvent quand il était jeune?
4. Je m'étonne que tu *oublier* de venir hier.
5. Elles se sont *parler* à la réunion.
6. Je ne sais pas s'ils nous *envoyer* leur nouvelle adresse quand ils y arriveront.
7. Où est Albert? Il *peindre* depuis une heure.
8. Je vous donnerai ma réponse quand je vous *revoir.*
9. Après *revenir,* nous avons rencontré nos voisins.
10. Je me suis coupé la joue en *se raser.*

E

1. Si le film vous *plaire*, faites-le-moi savoir.
2. Pourquoi a-t-elle honte de le *dire?*
3. Nous étions sur le quai quand ils *arriver.*
4. Après *ouvrir* la porte, il a remarqué le portrait.
5. Nous descendrons après qu'il *se lever.*
6. Je doute qu'il *boire* tout ce cidre hier.
7. En me *reconnaître*, il m'a salué.
8. Nous *étudier* depuis un quart d'heure quand le directeur est entré.
9. Tout ira bien pourvu que vous *faire* ce qu'il faut.
10. Elle s'est *brosser* les cheveux.

F

1. Il est important qu'elle *agir* ainsi.
2. L'hiver dernier, je les *voir* tous les jours.
3. Où sont les cravates qu'il s'est *acheter?*
4. Nous vous écrirons lorsque nous *devoir* partir.
5. N'*oublier* pas ton cahier, Gilbert.
6. Il est probable qu'il *pleuvoir* samedi prochain.
7. Ils *être* absents s'il avait fait du vent.
8. Après *rentrer*, elle n'avait plus envie de sortir.
9. Combien de temps y a-t-il que vous le *connaître?*
10. L'athlète est tombé en *lancer* la balle.

G

1. Elle avait cassé le vase sans le *savoir.*
2. En leur *présenter* son fils, il a loué ses talents.
3. On les *applaudir* cinq minutes au théâtre hier soir.
4. Depuis quand *dormir*-vous quand le réveille-matin a sonné?
5. Alice arrive en classe à l'heure de crainte que la maître ne la *punir.*
6. Après *se réveiller*, elles se lavent.
7. Donnez-moi un coup de téléphone dès que vous *revenir.*
8. Je voudrais que vous *apprendre* les paroles de ce cantique de Noël.
9. S'ils *recevoir* la lettre lundi, ils y répondront le même jour.
10. Jeanne d'Arc *naître* à Domremy et mourut à Rouen.

H

1. Après que la cloche avait sonné, les étudiants *s'asseoir.*
2. Nous aurions vu l'accident si nous *rentrer* plus tôt.
3. Y a-t-il des prunes qui *être* douces?
4. Je regardais par la fenêtre en *boire* mon café.
5. Quelle route avait-il *prendre?*
6. Madame, ne *se plaindre* pas tout le temps, s'il vous plaît.
7. Elle ne le fera pas sans que je la *voir.*
8. Quand j'*appeler* votre nom, répondez "présent."
9. Après *s'amuser*, nous avons fait nos devoirs.
10. Il y a un quart d'heure qu'on *entendre* la pluie sur le toit.

I

1. En *désobéir* à ses parents, il s'est fait mal.
2. Il *neiger* depuis longtemps quand elle a décidé de partir.
3. On n'a pas besoin d'être riche pour *lire* des livres.
4. Après *vendre* leurs meubles, ils l'ont regretté.
5. Voilà trois ans qu'il *vivre* seul ici.
6. Quoiqu'il *devenir* gros, il mange peu.
7. Nous visiterons Nice lorsque nous *être* au Midi de la France.
8. Si vous *vouloir* réparer l'horloge, je vous aurais aidé.
9. Il faut qu'ils *s'en aller* tout à l'heure.
10. Est-ce que les dames se *rencontrer* au cinéma hier?

J

1. Quand j'étais au camp, je me *plonger* dans le lac tous les matins.
2. La jeune fille s'est *laver* la figure.
3. Se peut-il qu'il *pleuvoir* hier?
4. C'est la voiture la plus confortable que j'aie jamais *conduire.*
5. La bonne ferma les fenêtres et *partir.*
6. En quittant ses enfants, la mère leur a dit, "*Être* sages."
7. Je pourrai vous l'expliquer si vous *se taire.*
8. A moins que vous ne *faire* de votre mieux, vous ne serez pas heureux.
9. Ils sont arrivés vers minuit après *se dépêcher.*
10. Aussitôt qu'elle *pouvoir* parler, nous apprendrons la vérité.

Épreuves K–M

Donner le mot qui manque:

K

1. Il nous faudra apprendre ______ ne pas gaspiller l'énergie.
2. –Dans quelle région voyagiez-vous? –Je ______ dans le Midi.
3. Quand on dort, on a les yeux ______.

4. Ils ont appelé une ambulance ______ conduire le malade à l'hôpital.
5. Si Micheline ______ gagné le prix, elle aurait crié de joie.
6. Ce volcan est actif ______ quinze jours.
7. Attendez ______ la pluie s'arrête.
8. Pourriez-vous me prêter un roman qui ______ intéressant?
9. La glace s'est cassée ______ tombant.
10. Il est difficile ______ savoir l'avenir.

L

1. Elle préfère s'en aller? ______ elle s'en aille!
2. Si tu te promenais, moi, je me ______ aussi.
3. Savez-vous si ces poissons sont bons ______ manger?
4. –La petite s'est lavée? –Elle s'est ______ seulement les mains.
5. Combien de temps faut-il ______ apprendre tous ces détails?
6. L'homme existe ______ longtemps sur la terre.
7. Nous avons le droit ______ habiter où il nous plaît.
8. Je crains qu'ils ______ viennent trop tard.
9. C'est le plus beau coucher du soleil que je (j') ______ jamais vu.
10. ______ nous le voyons, nous lui dirons la vérité.

M

1. –C'est vous qui avez pris mes clefs? –Non, c'est Bernard qui les a ______.
2. Voici les règles ______ observer.
3. Cette fenêtre est ouverte; veuillez la ______.
4. Si je lui avais demandé de danser avec moi, ______-elle accepté?
5. Il y avait un quart d'heure ______ nous causions dans la rue.
6. Il est dangereux ______ plonger dans cette rivière.
7. Peut-être ______ nous partirons en vacances au mois de juillet.
8. ______ être montés au sommet, nous pouvions voir l'océan à l'horizon.
9. J'espère avoir le plaisir ______ vous revoir bientôt.
10. Nous comptons aller au bord de la mer samedi pourvu qu'il ______ beau.

Épreuves N–O

Choisir la réponse qu'on *ne peut pas* substituer pour l'expression en italique:

N

1. Pourquoi Jeanne a-t-elle *refusé* de lui répondre?

   (*a*) cessé (*b*) essayé (*c*) hésité (*d*) décidé

2. Je *pris* l'enveloppe qui se trouvait sur le bureau.

   (*a*) lus (*b*) ramassai (*c*) remplis (*d*) vus

3. *Nous espérons* qu'ils ont marqué la date sur leur calendrier.

   (*a*) Il est bon (*b*) Je sais (*c*) Nous sommes sûrs (*d*) Elle croit

4. Ce monsieur *tient* à monter au haut de la montagne.

   (*a*) hésiterait (*b*) craint (*c*) a réussi (*d*) se mettait

5. Nous ne savons pas si *cela vous intéresse.*

   (*a*) nous pourrons stationner ici (*c*) elle soit de retour
   (*b*) la rivière a gelé (*d*) les clients s'en plaindraient

6. *C'est dommage* qu'on construise un gratte-ciel près du lac.

   (*a*) Il semble (*c*) Il n'est pas certain
   (*b*) Il se peut (*d*) Il est probable

7. *Allez*-vous révéler le secret?

   (*a*) Comptez (*b*) Regrettez (*c*) Devriez (*d*) Osez

8. Le client voulait lui donner un cadeau *pour* payer sa dette.

   (*a*) au lieu de (*b*) sans (*c*) après (*d*) avant de

9. Quand *doit-on* prendre leur photo?

   (*a*) sera-t-il possible (*c*) faudra-t-il
   (*b*) préférez-vous (*d*) espères-tu

10. Nous comptons rester ici *bien que* Victor se sente mieux.

    (*a*) jusqu'à ce que (*b*) puisque (*c*) afin que (*d*) quoique

O

1. Il nous avaient *reconnus.*

   (*a*) découverts (*b*) parlés (*c*) obéi (*d*) surpris

2. *Nous sommes heureux* de partir en week-end.

   (*a*) Nous sommes prêts (*c*) Rien ne nous empêchera
   (*b*) Nous n'avons pas l'intention (*d*) Nous tâcherons

3. *Regrettes-tu* qu'il ait obtenu la première place?

   (*a*) Ne crois-tu pas (*c*) Est-il possible
   (*b*) Espérez-vous (*d*) Es-tu surpris

4. Le pianiste leur avait *demandé* de chanter.

   (*a*) enseigné (*b*) permis (*c*) défendu (*d*) dit

5. Donnez-moi un coup de téléphone *quand* vous recevrez la bonne nouvelle.

   (*a*) après que (*b*) lorsque (*c*) dès que (*d*) si

6. Il paraît qu'il *neige*.

   (*a*) a plu (*b*) neigeait (*c*) pleuve (*d*) va neiger

7. *Il a dû* faire ses adieux.

(*a*) Elle n'a pas pu (*c*) Il vaudrait mieux
(*b*) Nous l'avons vue (*d*) Il a oublié

8. Si j'avis du temps, je vous *expliquerais le problème*.

(*a*) présenterais au directeur (*c*) amènerais à la plage
(*b*) montrais mon jardin (*d*) enverrais la musique

9. *Apprennent ils* à jouer au tennis?

(*a*) Ne s'amuse-t-il pas (*c*) Commence-t-elle
(*b*) Vous a-t-il enseigné (*d*) Aimez-vous mieux

10. *M. Lambert est* un avocat qui peut mettre en ordre nos affaires.

(*a*) Vous regardez (*c*) Nous cherchons
(*b*) Nous avons trouvé (*d*) Je connais

MASTERY VERB DRILL SHEET

This Verb Drill Sheet is designed to test your mastery of the forms and uses of the individual verbs studied. Complete each French sentence with the correct form of the verb you select, using the English as a guide.

	English	French
1.	We are ______-ing.	Nous ______.
2.	Doesn't he ______?	______-il ______?
3.	Do I ______?	______?
4.	They (You, We, People) are ______-ing.	On ______.
5.	Do not ______.	Ne (N') ______ pas.
6.	______ (imperative, familiar).	______.
7.	Let us ______.	______.
8.	You used to ______.	Vous ______.
9.	Were they ______-ing?	______-elles?
10.	She will ______.	Elle ______.
11.	Will they ______?	______-ils?
12.	He would ______.	Il ______.
13.	Would you ______?	______-vous?
14.	Who ______ yesterday?	Qui ______ hier?
15.	Didn't you ______?	______-vous ______?
16.	I had not ______.	Je ______.
17.	They would have ______.	Ils ______.
18.	We shall have ______.	Nous ______.
19.	He ______ (passé simple).	Il ______.
20.	They ______ (passé simple).	Elles ______.
21.	As soon as I ______, he will do it.	Aussitôt que je (j') ______, il le fera.

	English	French
22.	I shall do it when he ______.	Je le ferai quand il ______.
23.	How long did she ______?	Combien de temps ______?
24.	How long have you been ______-ing?	Depuis quand ______?
25.	They have been ______-ing for a long time.	Ils ______ depuis longtemps.
26.	How long had he been ______ -ing?	Depuis quand ______?
27.	We had been ______-ing for a long time.	Nous ______ depuis longtemps.
28.	If you ______, he will wait.	Si tu ______, il attendra.
29.	He would wait if I ______.	Il attendrait si je (j') ______.
30.	If she had ______, he would have waited.	Si elle ______, il aurait attendu.
31.	They are beginning to ______.	Ils commencent à ______.
32.	Must you ______?	Devez-vous ______.
33.	While ______-ing.	En ______.
34.	Without ______-ing.	Sans ______.
35.	After ______-ing.	Après ______.
36.	Before ______-ing.	Avant de (d') ______.
37.	George must ______.	Il faut que Georges ______.
38.	In order that you may ______.	Pour que tu ______.
39.	Unless they ______.	A moins qu'ils ne (n') ______.
40.	She fears we will ______.	Elle craint que nous ne (n') ______.
41.	I'm afraid I will ______.	J'ai peur de (d') ______.
42.	He wants you to ______.	Il veut que vous ______.
43.	I doubt that she will ______.	Je doute qu'elle ______.
44.	Do you think they may ______?	Croyez-vous qu'ils ______?
45.	We are sorry that he has ______.	Nous regrettons qu'il ______.
46.	It is possible that we have ______.	Il est possible que nous ______.
47.	It is probable that they have ______.	Il est probable qu'ils ______.
48.	It's the last time that I shall ______.	C'est la dernière fois que je (j') ______.
49.	Do you know anyone who may ______?	Connaissez-vous quelqu'un qui ______?
50.	Let him ______!	Qu'il ______!

PART II—*STRUCTURES*

1. DEFINITE AND INDEFINITE ARTICLES

FORMS OF THE ARTICLES

The definite article, *the*, has four forms: **le, la, l', les.**

	MASCULINE	FEMININE
SINGULAR	***le*** savant, the scientist ***l'***endroit, the place	***la*** cuiller, the spoon ***l'***horloge, the clock
PLURAL	***les*** savants, the scientists ***les*** endroits, the places	***les*** cuillers, the spoons ***les*** horloges, the clocks

The indefinite article, *a* (*an*), has two forms: **un** (masculine) and **une** (feminine).

un endroit, a place	***une*** cuiller, a spoon

Note

1. The article **l'** is used before a singular noun of either gender beginning with a vowel or silent **h.** Before aspirate **h,** the vowel of the article is retained: **le héros, la honte.**
2. The article is expressed in French before each noun, even though it may be omitted in English.

les fruits et ***les*** légumes	the fruits and vegetables
un oncle et ***une*** tante	an uncle and aunt

CONTRACTIONS WITH THE DEFINITE ARTICLE

The prepositions **à** and **de** contract with **le** and **les.**

à + le savant = ***au*** savant à + les endroits = ***aux*** endroits	de + le savant = ***du*** savant de + les endroits = ***des*** endroits

Note

There are no contractions with **la** or **l'**.

USES OF THE DEFINITE ARTICLE

In addition to meaning *the*, the definite article is used in French in the following cases:

a. With nouns used in a *general* or *abstract* sense:

L'acier est plus dur que ***le fer.***	Steel is harder than iron.
Nous approuvons ***les échanges*** culturels.	We approve of cultural exchanges.
Aime-t-elle ***la chimie?***	Does she like chemistry?
La honte est une émotion désagréable.	Shame is a disagreeable emotion.

b. With names of languages (except immediately after **parler**, after **en**, and in an adjective phrase with **de**):

Comprenez-vous ***le grec?***	Do you understand Greek?
Le russe n'est pas très facile.	Russian is not very easy.

But:

Ici on ***parle espagnol.***	Spanish is spoken here.
J'ai écrit la lettre ***en italien.***	I wrote the letter in Italian.
Où est votre livre ***de français?***	Where is your French book?

c. With parts of the body when the possessor is clearly indicated:

Il ne peut pas tourner ***la tête.***	He cannot turn his head.
Carmen tenait une fleur entre ***les dents.***	Carmen was holding a flower between her teeth.
Fermez ***les yeux.***	Close your eyes.
Je me suis fait mal ***au bras.***	I hurt my arm.

Note: In the above case, the definite article is used instead of the possessive adjective. When the possessor must be clarified, the possessive adjective is used.

Ses yeux me font peur.	His eyes frighten me.

d. With titles of rank or profession followed by a name (except in direct address):

le président Kennedy	President Kennedy
la reine Élisabeth	Queen Elizabeth
le général Leclerc	General Leclerc
le professeur Brunot	Professor Brunot

But:

Bonsoir, ***docteur*** Marais.	Good evening, Doctor Marais.

e. With proper nouns that are modified:

le Paris du XXe siècle	twentieth-century Paris
la belle Vénus	beautiful Venus

f. With days of the week in a plural sense. In English we add the word *on*.

Le samedi je me lève tard.	On Saturday(s) I get up late.
Nous allons à l'école ***le lundi.***	We go to school on Monday(s).

Note: If the day mentioned is one specific day, the article is omitted.

Le mariage a eu lieu ***dimanche.***	The marriage took place on Sunday.
Donnez-moi un coup de téléphone ***mardi.***	Give me a ring on Tuesday.

g. With names of seasons and colors:

Le printemps est une belle saison.	Spring is a beautiful season.
L'été avait déjà commencé.	Summer had already begun.
Aimez-vous ***le vert?***	Do you like green?
Moi, je préfère ***le bleu.***	I prefer blue.

h. With nouns of weight and measure to express *a*, *an*, or *per:*

Elle a payé **deux dollars *la douzaine.***	She paid two dollars a dozen.
Cette soie coûte **dix francs *le mètre.***	This silk costs ten francs per meter.

Note: With expressions indicating frequency of time, **par** is used:

On mange **trois fois *par jour.***	We eat three times a day.

i. In a number of common expressions, such as:

à l'école, to (in) school	**le matin**, in the morning
à l'église, to (in) church	**l'après-midi**, in the afternoon
à la maison, at home, home	**le soir**, in the evening

le mois prochain, next month
la semaine dernière, last week
l'année passée, last year

OMISSION OF THE ARTICLE

The article is omitted:

a. Before an unmodified predicate noun of nationality, occupation, or profession:

Est-il ***Espagnol?***	Is he a Spaniard?
Sa sœur aînée est ***actrice.***	Her older sister is an actress.
J'espère devenir ***ingénieur.***	I hope to become an engineer.

Note: The article must be used if the predicate noun is modified.

C'est ***un ingénieur bien connu.***	He is a well-known engineer.

b. Before nouns in apposition that serve merely to explain:

Rome, ***capitale*** de l'Italie	Rome, the capital of Italy
Debussy, ***grand compositeur*** français	Debussy, a great French composer

c. After the exclamatory adjective **quel, quelle, quels, quelles**:

Quelle prune délicieuse!	What a delicious plum!

d. Before the numbers **cent** and **mille**:

cent navires	a hundred ships
mille étoiles	a thousand stars

e. In numerical titles of monarchs:

Henri ***Quatre*** (Henri IV)	Henry the Fourth
Louis ***Quinze*** (Louis XV)	Louis the Fifteenth

EXERCICES

A. Compléter la phrase en français:

1. Il est allé chez le coiffeur pour se faire couper ______.

2. Ce vin coûte huit francs ______ bouteille.
3. La plus froide des quatre saisons de l'année est ______.
4. Nous allons à l'école cinq fois ______ semaine.
5. En Italie on parle ______.
6. Il y a ______ ans dans un siècle.
7. Le bleu, le blanc, et ______ sont les couleurs du drapeau français.
8. ______ est la langue officielle des États-Unis.
9. C'est dommage que vous n'ayez jamais fait la connaissance de ______ belle Hélène.
10. ______ mètres font un kilomètre.

B. Compléter la phrase en anglais:

1. Les vins français sont les meilleurs. ______ are ______.
2. Le mois passé nous avons dû faire venir le docteur Lebrun. ______ we had to send for ______.
3. On l'a emmené à la maison jeudi. He was taken ______.
4. L'argent ne fait pas le bonheur. ______ does not make ______.
5. Louis Quatorze, roi de France, fut le monarque le plus puissant d'Europe. ______, was the most powerful monarch in Europe.
6. Le dimanche on ne va pas à l'école. ______ we do not go ______.
7. C'est combien ce beurre? Je l'ai payé trois francs la livre. How much is this butter? ______.
8. Chenonceaux, château célèbre, se trouve sur la Loire. ______ is on the Loire.
9. Maurice étudie l'anglais, l'italien, la biologie, les mathématiques, et l'histoire. Maurice is studying ______.
10. J'aime marcher dans les rues du vieux Paris. I like to walk ______.
11. Il voulait être médecin, mais il devint écrivain pour payer ses études. He wanted to be ______, but he ______.
12. En Tunisie le français est enseigné à l'école primaire. In Tunisia ______.
13. Malgré le froid j'aime les sports d'hiver. ______, I like ______.
14. Son visage restera longtemps fixé dans ma mémoire. ______ will remain ______.
15. M. Reynaud, professeur de latin, parle plusieurs langues modernes. Quel homme intelligent! ______ speaks several modern languages. ______!

C. Compléter la phrase en français:

1. You have to lower your head to enter. On doit baisser ______ pour entrer.
2. Martha is very good in Russian. Marthe est très forte ______.
3. Autumn is my favorite season. ______ est ma saison favorite.
4. Is he an American or a Frenchman? Est-il ______ ou ______?
5. Your eyes are blue. Tu as ______ bleus.
6. Children like to play. ______ aiment à jouer.
7. General Washington slept here. ______ dormit ici.
8. Did you see him last week? No, but I'll see him Wednesday. L'avez-vous vu ______? Non, mais je le verrai ______.
9. We have a good time in our French class. Nous nous amusons dans ______.
10. Eggs cost four francs a dozen. ______ coûtent quatre francs ______.

D. Répondre à chaque question par une phrase complète en français:

1. Quelle couleur vous va le mieux?
2. Nommez deux métaux précieux.
3. Êtes-vous poète?
4. Jusqu'à quel jour puis-je garder votre livre?
5. Quelles langues comprenez-vous?
6. Étudiez-vous mieux l'après-midi ou le soir?
7. Quand un élève désire réciter en classe, que fait-il?
8. Quelle saison suit l'été?
9. Lequel préférez-vous: le poisson, la viande, ou le fromage?
10. Combien de fois par jour vous peignez-vous les cheveux?

E. Donner l'équivalent en français:

1. President Lincoln was a good lawyer.
2. What a lazy boy!
3. In the morning I brush my teeth.
4. Is she at home or in church?
5. We spent a hundred dollars Tuesday.
6. Life is beautiful.
7. Are you a dentist?
8. He answered me in Spanish.
9. King Henry was good to the people.
10. Next year I shall play tennis on Fridays.

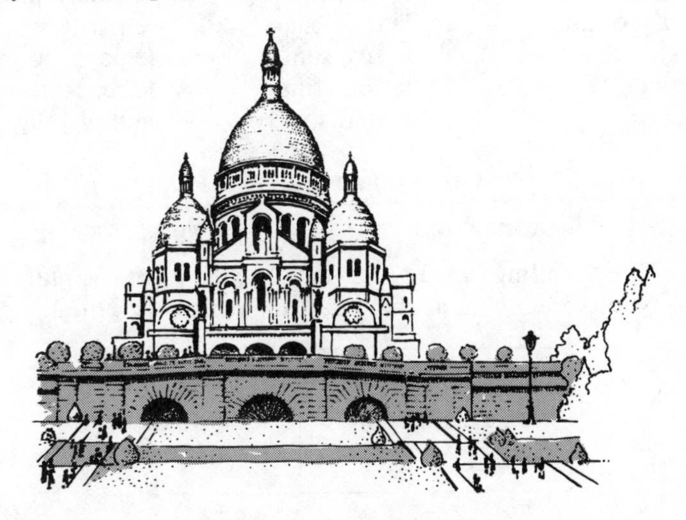

Le Sacré-Cœur

La silhouette blanche du Sacré-Cœur fait partie de l'horizon parisien. Située sur la butte Montmartre, cette église de style romano-byzantin domine tout Paris. On peut y monter à pied ou au moyen d'un funiculaire. La construction de l'église, commencée en 1875, fut achevée en 1914.

2. PLURAL OF NOUNS; FEMININE NOUNS

PLURAL OF NOUNS

The plural of most French nouns is formed by adding **s** to the singular:

SINGULAR	PLURAL
le musée, museum l'assiette (*f.*), plate la pomme, apple	les musée***s*** les assiette***s*** les pomme***s***

Nouns ending in **-s**, **-x**, or **-z** remain unchanged in the plural.

le mois, month le prix, price, prize le nez, nose	les mois les prix les nez

Other nouns ending in **-s**:

l'ananas (*m.*), pineapple
l'autobus (*m.*), bus
l'avis (*m.*), opinion
le bas, stocking
le bois, wood
le bras, arm
le colis, package
le corps, body
le dos, back
le fils, son
la fois, time
le héros, hero
le jus, juice
le palais, palace
le pardessus, overcoat
le pays, country
le repas, meal
le tapis, rug

Other nouns ending in **-x**:

la croix, cross
la voix, voice

Nouns ending in **-eau** and **-eu** add **x** to form the plural.
Nouns ending in **-al** change **-al** to **-aux** in the plural.

le drapeau, flag le neveu, nephew le métal, metal	les drapeau***x*** les neveu***x*** les mét***aux***

Other nouns ending in **-eau**:

le bateau, boat
le bureau, desk
le cadeau, gift, present
le chapeau, hat
le château, castle
le couteau, knife
l'eau (*f.*), water
le gâteau, cake
le manteau, coat, wrap
le morceau, piece
l'oiseau (*m.*), bird
la peau, skin
le rideau, curtain
le tableau, picture
le veau, calf

Other nouns ending in **-eu**:

le cheveu, hair **le feu**, fire **le jeu**, game **le lieu**, place

N.B. Since **le cheveu** refers to a single hair, the plural **les cheveux** is more commonly used.

Other nouns ending in **-al**:

l'animal (*m.*), animal **le général**, general **le journal**, newspaper
le cheval, horse **l'hôpital** (*m.*), hospital

A few nouns ending in **-ou** add **x** to form the plural.

le bijou, jewel	les bijou***x***
le caillou, pebble	les caillou***x***
le chou, cabbage	les chou***x***
le genou, knee	les genou***x***
le joujou, toy	les joujou***x***

Some nouns have irregular plurals.

le ciel, sky	les ***cieux***
l'œil (*m.*), eye	les ***yeux***
le travail, work	les ***travaux***
madame, Madam, Mrs.	***mesdames***
mademoiselle, Miss	***mesdemoiselles***
monsieur, gentleman, sir, Mr.	***messieurs***

Plurals of frequent compound nouns.

l'après-midi (*m.*), afternoon	les après-midi
le chef-d'œuvre, masterpiece	les chef***s***-d'œuvre
la grand-mère, grandmother	les grand-mère***s***
le grand-père, grandfather	les grand***s***-père***s***
le gratte-ciel, skyscraper	les gratte-ciel
la pomme de terre, potato	les pomme***s*** de terre
le rendez-vous, appointment	les rendez-vous
le réveille-matin, alarm clock	les réveille-matin

A few nouns are regularly used in the plural.

les ciseaux (*m.*), scissors **les mathématiques** (*f.*), mathematics
les lunettes (*f.*), eyeglasses **les vacances** (*f.*), vacation

FEMININE NOUNS

Some nouns have the same form in the masculine and the feminine.

un (une) artiste, artist	un (une) enfant, child
le (la) concierge, concierge	le (la) malade, patient
un (une) élève, pupil	le (la) touriste, tourist

Some feminine nouns are formed by adding **e** to the masculine.

l'ami	l'ami*e*, friend	l'Espagnol	l'Espagnol*e*, Spaniard
le client	la client*e*, customer	l'étudiant	l'étudiant*e*, student
le cousin	la cousin*e*, cousin	le voisin	la voisin*e*, neighbor

Other feminine nouns and their masculine equivalents are:

MASCULINE	FEMININE
l'acteur, actor	l'***actrice***, actress
le bouc, goat	la ***chèvre***, goat
le bœuf, ox le taureau, bull	la ***vache***, cow
le chat, cat	la ***chatte***, cat
le citoyen, citizen	la ***citoyenne***, citizen
le comte, count	la ***comtesse***, countess
le coq, rooster	la ***poule***, hen
le danseur, dancer	la ***danseuse***, dancer
le fils, son	la ***fille***, daughter
le frère, brother	la ***sœur***, sister
le garçon, boy	la ***jeune fille***, girl
l'homme, man	la ***femme***, woman
le mari, husband	la ***femme***, wife
le neveu, nephew	la ***nièce***, niece
l'oncle, uncle	la ***tante***, aunt
l'ouvrier, worker	l'***ouvrière***, worker
le paysan, peasant	la ***paysanne***, peasant
le père, father	la ***mère***, mother
le prince, prince	la ***princesse***, princess
le roi, king	la ***reine***, queen
le vendeur, salesman	la ***vendeuse***, saleslady
le vieillard, old man	la ***vieille***, old lady
le voyageur, traveler	la ***voyageuse***, traveler

Some nouns have two genders, each with a different meaning.

le livre, book	***la*** livre, pound
le tour, turn, trip, trick	***la*** tour, tower

A few nouns are always feminine, whether applied to a male or a female.

la connaissance, acquaintance **la personne**, person

Note

A *noun* of nationality is written with a *capital* letter, while an *adjective* of nationality is written with a *small* letter.

Les ***Français*** aiment la cuisine ***française***.	French people like French cooking.

EXERCICES

A. Mettre au pluriel:

1. le travail
2. le genou
3. le nez
4. l'après-midi
5. le cheveu
6. madame
7. le bateau
8. le rendez-vous
9. le bras
10. l'hôpital
11. la grand-mère
12. l'autobus
13. le morceau
14. la croix
15. le réveille-matin
16. le caillou

B. Donner les équivalents féminins des mots en italique:

1. Les *voyageurs* sont sur le point de partir.
2. Elle joue avec *le chat*.
3. Ce n'est qu'*un enfant*.
4. Comment va *l'acteur?*
5. *Le paysan* était dans le champ.
6. Ces *ouvriers* travaillent huit heures par jour.
7. *Le taureau* mange de l'herbe.
8. Vive *le roi!*
9. Où est *le malade?*
10. C'est *un citoyen* des États-Unis.
11. *Le vieillard* mange peu.
12. Est-ce *le prince* qui arrive?
13. L'artiste est *Espagnol*.
14. *Le concierge* ouvrira la porte.
15. Est-ce que *le vendeur* est dans le magasin?

C. Mettre la phrase entière au pluriel:

1. Le feu brûle.
2. Connais-tu le monsieur?
3. L'enfant aime le joujou.
4. Il ne veut pas manger la pomme de terre.
5. Où est le corps?
6. L'oiseau vole.
7. La jeune fille a gagné le prix.
8. Voici le chou.
9. Le héros est revenu.
10. Le rideau couvrait la fenêtre.
11. Je regardais le chef-d'œuvre.
12. Le général commande l'armée.
13. Elle cherche le bijou.
14. Entends-tu la voix?
15. J'ai visité le palais.

D. Donner le mot qui manque:

1. Louis XVI était le ______ de Marie-Antoinette.
2. La sœur de notre cousin est notre ______.
3. Quatre ______ cinq font vingt.
4. Les ______ américain et français ont les trois mêmes couleurs.
5. Je prends trois ______ par jour: le petit déjeuner, le déjeuner, et le dîner.
6. Les fils de mon frère sont mes ______.
7. Les chevaux et les bœufs sont des ______ domestiques.
8. Les bâtiments à très grand nombre d'étages s'appellent des ______.
9. Nous avons fait ______ tour de la ville.
10. L'astronome étudiait les étoiles qui brillaient dans les ______.
11. Le ______ est le mâle de la chèvre.
12. Sait-elle danser? Mais oui, c'est une ______ excellente.
13. Le père de ma mère et le père de mon père sont mes ______.
14. La femme d'un comte s'appelle une ______.
15. Alexandre n'est pas un de mes amis; c'est ______ de mes connaissances.
16. L'arithmétique, l'algèbre, et la géométrie sont des parties des ______.
17. C'est Eiffel qui a bâti ______ célèbre tour de Paris.
18. La femelle du coq est la ______.
19. Avez-vous coupé le papier avec un couteau? Non, je l'ai coupé avec des ______.
20. Le fer, l'or, l'acier, et le cuivre sont des ______ utiles.
21. Les ______ sont les petits de la vache.
22. Elle vient d'acheter ______ livre de café.

23. Jacques est un mauvais étudiant; sa sœur, au contraire, est une bonne ______.
24. Le bridge et la canasta sont des ______ de cartes.
25. M. Charpentier est ______ personne aimable.

E. Répondre à chaque question par une phrase complète en français:

1. Combien de fils cette femme a-t-elle?
2. Où comptez-vous passer les vacances de Noël?
3. Qui a envoyé tous ces beaux cadeaux aux nouveaux mariés?
4. Quels journaux lisez-vous?
5. Votre père se sert-il de lunettes pour lire?
6. Où sont les plus beaux châteaux de France?
7. Avez-vous les yeux clairs ou foncés?
8. Combien de paires de bas y a-t-il dans cette boîte, mademoiselle?
9. Quels sont les mois de l'année que vous aimez le mieux?
10. Nommez trois lieux intéressants que voùs voudriez visiter en France.

Le tourisme à Paris

Ses richesses naturelles et artistiques font de la France un grand pays de tourisme. L'ensemble des activités concernant l'accueil des touristes étrangers en France joue un rôle important dans la vie économique du pays.

3. ADJECTIVES: FORMS; AGREEMENT; POSITION

FORMS

a.

SINGULAR		PLURAL		MEANING
MAS.	FEM.	MAS.	FEM.	
étroit	étroit*e*	étroit*s*	étroit*es*	narrow
faible	faible	faible*s*	faible*s*	weak
curieux	curieu*se*	curieux	curieu*ses*	curious
neuf	neu*ve*	neuf*s*	neu*ves*	new
premier	premi*ère*	premier*s*	premi*ères*	first
gris	gris*e*	gris	gris*es*	gray
égal	égal*e*	ég*aux*	égal*es*	equal

Note

1. The feminine singular of adjectives is regularly formed by adding **e** to the masculine singular. If the masculine already ends in mute **e**, the feminine is the same: **faible, faible.**
2. The feminine of adjectives ending in **-x, -f,** and **-er** is formed by changing **-x** to **-se, -f** to **-ve,** and **-er** to **-ère: curieux, curieuse; neuf, neuve; premier, première.**
3. The plural is regularly formed by adding **s** to the singular. If the masculine singular ends in **-s** or **-x,** the masculine plural is the same: **gris, gris; curieux, curieux.**
4. Most masculine adjectives ending in **-al** in the singular end in **-aux** in the plural: **égal, égaux.**

OTHER FREQUENTLY USED ADJECTIVES

like *étroit:*

allemand, German
américain, American
bleu, blue
blond, blond
brun, brown
carré, square
certain, certain
charmant, charming
chaud, warm, hot
clair, clear, light (in color)
content, glad, pleased
court, short
délicat, delicate
différent, different
diligent, industrious
droit, right
espagnol, Spanish
fatigué, tired
foncé, dark
fort, strong
froid, cold
gai, gay

grand, great, large, tall
haut, high
humain, human
intelligent, intelligent
intéressant, interesting
joli, pretty
laid, ugly
lent, slow
lourd, heavy
méchant, naughty, wicked, bad
mouillé, wet
noir, black
parfait, perfect
petit, small, little
plein, full
poli, polite
prêt, ready
prochain, next
profond, deep
pur, pure
reconnaissant, grateful
rond, round
seul, alone, only
sourd, deaf
sûr, sure
vert, green
vilain, ugly
vrai, true

like ***faible:***

agréable, pleasant
aimable, kind
autre, other
aveugle, blind
bizarre, peculiar, odd
brave, brave, fine
célèbre, famous
chauve, bald
coupable, guilty
difficile, difficult
drôle, funny, odd
énorme, enormous
étrange, strange
facile, easy
fidèle, faithful
formidable, teriffic
gauche, left
grave, serious, solemn
honnête, honest, polite
illustre, illustrious
inutile, useless
jaune, yellow
jeune, young
juste, just, right
large, wide
libre, free
magnifique, magnificent
maigre, thin, lean
malade, sick
mince, thin, slender
moderne, modern
nécessaire, necessary
pâle, pale
pauvre, poor
proche, near
propre, clean, own
rapide, fast, rapid
riche, rich
rose, pink
rouge, red
russe, Russian
sage, wise, well-behaved
sale, dirty
sauvage, wild
semblable, similar
sincère, sincere
timide, timid
triste, sad
utile, useful
vide, empty

like ***curieux:***

affreux, frightful
dangereux, dangerous
délicieux, delicious, delightful
ennuyeux, boring
furieux, furious
généreux, generous
heureux, happy

	jaloux, jealous **joyeux**, merry **malheureux**, unhappy **merveilleux**, marvelous	**mystérieux**, mysterious **paresseux**, lazy **précieux**, precious **sérieux**, serious
like ***neuf:***	**actif**, active **attentif**, attentive	**vif**, lively
like ***premier:***	**amer**, bitter **cher**, dear, expensive **dernier**, last **entier**, entire, whole	**fier**, proud **étranger**, foreign **léger**, light (in weight)
like ***gris:***	**anglais**, English **assis**, seated **exquis**, exquisite	**français**, French **mauvais**, bad
like ***égal:***	**général**, general **loyal**, loyal **national**, national	**principal**, principal **social**, social **spécial**, special

b. Certain adjectives double the final consonant before adding **e** to form the feminine.

SINGULAR		PLURAL		MEANING
MAS.	FEM.	MAS.	FEM.	
ancien	ancien*ne*	anciens	ancien*nes*	old, ancient, former
bas	bas*se*	bas	bas*ses*	low
bon	bon*ne*	bons	bon*nes*	good
cruel	cruel*le*	cruels	cruel*les*	cruel
épais	épais*se*	épais	épais*ses*	thick
européen	européen*ne*	européens	européen*nes*	European
gentil	gentil*le*	gentils	gentil*les*	nice, kind
gras	gras*se*	gras	gras*ses*	fat
gros	gros*se*	gros	gros*ses*	big, stout
italien	italien*ne*	italiens	italien*nes*	Italian
muet	muet*te*	muets	muet*tes*	silent, mute
pareil	pareil*le*	pareils	pareil*les*	like, similar
parisien	parisien*ne*	parisiens	parisien*nes*	Parisian
quel	quel*le*	quels	quel*les*	what? which? what a . . .!
sot	sot*te*	sots	sot*tes*	foolish, silly
tel	tel*le*	tels	tel*les*	such

c. Irregular adjectives:

SINGULAR		PLURAL		MEANING
MAS.	FEM.	MAS.	FEM.	
blanc	***blanche***	blancs	***blanches***	white
complet	***complète***	complets	***complètes***	complete
doux	***douce***	doux	***douces***	sweet, mild, gentle
faux	***fausse***	faux	***fausses***	false
favori	***favorite***	favoris	***favorites***	favorite
frais	***fraîche***	frais	***fraîches***	fresh, cool
franc	***franche***	francs	***franches***	frank
inquiet	***inquiète***	inquiets	***inquiètes***	uneasy, worried
long	***longue***	longs	***longues***	long
public	***publique***	publics	***publiques***	public
sec	***sèche***	secs	***sèches***	dry
secret	***secrète***	secrets	***secrètes***	secret
tout	toute	***tous***	toutes	all, whole, every
travailleur	travailleuse	travailleurs	travailleuses	industrious, hardworking
beau (***bel***)	***belle***	beaux	***belles***	beautiful, fine, handsome
fou (***fol***)	***folle***	fous	***folles***	mad, crazy
mou (***mol***)	***molle***	mous	***molles***	soft
nouveau (***nouvel***)	***nouvelle***	nouveaux	***nouvelles***	new
vieux (***vieil***)	***vieille***	vieux	***vieilles***	old

Note

The forms **bel, fol, mol, nouvel,** and **vieil** are used before a masculine singular noun beginning with a vowel or silent **h.**

un ***bel*** ouvrage	a fine work
un ***fol*** espoir	a mad hope
le ***vieil*** hôpital	the old hospital

AGREEMENT

French adjectives agree in gender and number with the nouns or pronouns they modify.

C'était **une nuit *fraîche*.** It was a cool night.

Ces cerises sont ***amères.***	These cherries are bitter.
Ils seront ***contents*** de partir.	They will be glad to leave.

An adjective modifying two or more nouns of *different* genders is in the masculine plural.

Son fils et **sa fille** sont ***intelligents.***	Her son and daughter are intelligent.

Participles used as adjectives agree with the nouns they modify.

Les livres sont-ils ***couverts?***	Are the books covered?
C'est **une enfant *obéissante.***	She is an obedient child.

POSITION

Unlike English adjectives, most descriptive adjectives in French *follow* the noun they modify.

une porte ***secrète***	a secret door
les vins ***blancs***	the white wines

Some short descriptive adjectives that usually precede the noun are:

beau	**gentil**	**jeune**	**mauvais**	**vieux**
bon	**grand**	**joli**	**nouveau**	**vilain**
court	**gros**	**long**	**petit**	

Other common adjectives that precede the noun are:

autre, other	**plusieurs,** several	**quelques** (*pl.*), some, a few
chaque, each	**premier,** first	**tel,** such
dernier, last	**quelque,** some	**tout,** all, whole, every

Note: The adjective **tout** precedes the definite article.

toute la maison	the whole house
tous les animaux	every animal

Certain French adjectives have two or more meanings. In their usual position, *after* the noun, they have their literal meaning. *Before* the noun, they have a different meaning.

une coutume ***ancienne*** une ***ancienne*** coutume	an old (ancient) custom a former custom
un garçon ***brave*** un ***brave*** garçon	a brave boy a fine (good, worthy) boy
une étoffe ***chère*** un ***cher*** ami	an expensive material a dear friend (= esteemed, cherished)
la semaine ***dernière*** la ***dernière*** semaine	last week (= just passed) the last week (of a series)
un auteur ***méchant*** un ***méchant*** auteur un ***méchant*** garçon	a spiteful (wicked, vicious, ill-natured) author a bad (pitiful, inept) author a bad (naughty) boy
la chose ***même*** la ***même*** chose	the very thing the same thing
mes gants ***propres*** mes ***propres*** gants	my clean gloves my own gloves
un homme ***seul*** le ***seul*** homme	a man alone, a single man (by himself) the only man

EXERCICES

A. Compléter l'expression de la première colonne en employant l'adjectif convenable de la seconde colonne:

1. des bijoux ______	chaque
2. une table ______	tous
3. ______ les Américains	étrangères
4. la ______ fois	chers
5. un ______ arbre	jolies
6. ______ jour	vieil
7. les ______ fleurs	beaux
8. un tapis ______	dernière
9. des langues ______	bleu
10. les ______ meubles	carrée

B. Mettre au féminin:

1. Les élèves ont été très attentifs.
2. Tu es toujours sérieux.
3. Le concierge était gentil.
4. C'est un touriste européen.
5. Sont-ils complets?
6. Les citoyens seront loyaux.
7. Quels Italiens charmants!
8. Les malades étaient inquiets.
9. Vous êtes trop fier.
10. Il est jeune et franc.

C. Compléter les phrases en anglais:

1. Il l'a écrit de sa propre main. He wrote it with ______.
2. On vient de construire un nouvel immeuble. They have just built ______.
3. Tu es un méchant garçon! You are ______!
4. Je l'ai vu le dernier jour du mois dernier. I saw him ______.
5. L'armée avance comme un seul homme. The army advances as ______.
6. Avez-vous jamais vu une telle plage? Have you ever seen ______?
7. Je peux lire vos pensées mêmes. I can read ______.
8. Quelle nuit affreuse! ______ night!
9. Deux corps ne peuvent occuper le même lieu en même temps. Two bodies cannot occupy ______.
10. Est-ce que le monde entier désire la paix? Does ______ want peace?

D. Donner les formes convenables des adjectifs entre parenthèses:

1. (sec) la gorge ______; des vins ______
2. (national) les musées ______; les fêtes ______
3. (gros) les ______ chiens; ses ______ lunettes
4. (fou) des chiens ______; elle est ______ de douleur
5. (long) une ______ vue; les ______ voyages
6. (délicieux) des parfums ______; une soupe ______
7. (beau) un ______ appartement; ses ______ dents
8. (pareil) une chose ______; des animaux ______
9. (gras) la peau ______; les veaux ______
10. (doux) la vie ______; des vents ______
11. (épais) des livres ______; l'herbe ______
12. (vif) des chevaux ______; une couleur ______
13. (frais) une douzaine d'œufs ______; les nuits ______
14. (exquis) Sa robe et son chapeau étaient ______.
15. (léger) Les plumes sont ______.

E. Compléter la phrase en français:

1. Marguerite est travailleuse, mais sa sœur est ______.
2. Un homme ______ n'a pas de cheveux.
3. Le géant n'était pas faible; il était ______.

4. Elle ne peut pas parler; c'est une enfant ______.
5. Cette histoire n'est pas vraie; elle est ______.
6. Est-ce que la tasse est pleine ou ______?
7. Quelle est la couleur des étoiles du drapeau américain? Elles sont ______.
8. En été les nuits sont courtes; en hiver, elles sont ______.
9. Les plafonds de la maison sont-ils hauts ou ______?
10. L'avenue était large, mais les rues, au contraire, étaient ______.

F. Compléter chaque phrase en donnant l'équivalent de l'adjectif entre parenthèses:

1. (several) Vous avez fait ______ fautes.
2. (boring) C'était une conversation ______.
3. (silly) Tu es très ______, Henriette.
4. (whole) Ils ont mangé ______ le fromage.
5. (favorite) Le football est mon sport ______.
6. (a few) Prêtez-moi ______ francs, s'il vous plaît.
7. (living) L'anglais est une langue ______.
8. (soft) Je dors sur un oreiller ______.
9. (secret) Nous avons assisté à une réunion ______.
10. (jealous) Sa femme est fort ______.

G. Choisir la réponse convenable entre parenthèses:

1. Une (brave femme, femme brave) est courageuse.
2. Mon (ancien professeur, professeur ancien) n'est plus mon professeur.
3. Un (méchant avocat, avocat méchant) manque de mérite.
4. Tous les deux avaient (les mêmes goûts, les goûts mêmes).
5. Décembre est le (dernier mois, mois dernier) de l'année.
6. Elle a peur d'y entrer à cause du (méchant chien, chien méchant).
7. Un (homme seul, seul homme) n'a pas de compagnie.
8. Mon (chapeau propre, propre chapeau) est celui qui n'est pas sale.
9. Une (maison ancienne, ancienne maison) est très vieille.
10. Un (brave garçon, garçon brave) est honnête et bon.

H. Donner l'équivalent en français:

1. the very day
2. my dear mother
3. every store
4. the closed window
5. a Parisian dress
6. his only suit
7. the dead leaves
8. the other travelers
9. the cruel sea
10. the principal bridges

4. NUMERALS

CARDINAL NUMBERS

0 **zéro**	19 **dix-neuf**	77 **soixante-dix-sept**
1 **un, une**	20 **vingt**	80 **quatre-vingts**
2 **deux**	21 **vingt et un**	81 **quatre-vingt-un**
3 **trois**	23 **vingt-trois**	88 **quatre-vingt-huit**
4 **quatre**	30 **trente**	90 **quatre-vingt-dix**
5 **cinq**	31 **trente et un**	91 **quatre-vingt-onze**
6 **six**	34 **trente-quatre**	99 **quatre-vingt-dix-neuf**
7 **sept**	40 **quarante**	100 **cent**
8 **huit**	41 **quarante et un**	101 **cent un**
9 **neuf**	47 **quarante-sept**	200 **deux cents**
10 **dix**	50 **cinquante**	316 **trois cent seize**
11 **onze**	51 **cinquante et un**	500 **cinq cents**
12 **douze**	52 **cinquante-deux**	580 **cinq cent quatre-vingts**
13 **treize**	60 **soixante**	1.000 **mille**
14 **quatorze**	61 **soixante et un**	1.001 **mille un**
15 **quinze**	70 **soixante-dix**	1.100 **mille cent**
16 **seize**	71 **soixante et onze**	3.000 **trois mille**
17 **dix-sept**	75 **soixante-quinze**	100.000 **cent mille**
18 **dix-huit**		

Note

1. The word **et** replaces the hyphen in 21, 31, 41, 51, 61, and 71. In all other compound numbers through 99, the hyphen is used.

2. **Quatre-vingts** and the plural of **cent** drop the s before another number.

   quatre-***vingts*** bateaux — eighty boats
   quatre-***vingt***-**deux** bateaux — eighty-two boats

   quatre ***cents*** mots — four hundred words
   quatre ***cent*** **cinquante** mots — four hundred fifty words

3. **Cent** and **mille** are not preceded by the indefinite article.

   cent mouchoirs — a (one) hundred handkerchiefs
   mille fois — a thousand times

4. **Mille** does not change in the plural.

   six ***mille*** plantes — six thousand plants

5. In French numerals, periods are used where English uses commas: 4.000 (*Fr.*) = 4,000 (*Eng.*).

6. Arithmetic operations:

cinq et six font onze	5 + 6 = 11
trois fois quatre font douze	3 × 4 = 12
huit moins cinq font trois	8 − 5 = 3
dix divisé par deux font cinq	10 ÷ 2 = 5

NOUNS OF NUMBER

Certain numerals are used as collective nouns to express a round number. The most frequent are:

une dizaine, about ten	**une centaine**, about a hundred
une douzaine, a dozen	**un millier**, (about) a thousand
une quinzaine, about fifteen	**un million**, a million
une vingtaine, about twenty, a score	**un milliard**, a billion
une cinquantaine, about fifty	

These numerals are followed by **de** before another noun. When used in the plural, these numerals add **s**.

deux douzaines ***d'***œufs	two dozen eggs
une centaine ***de*** vaches	about a hundred cows
des milliers ***d'***oiseaux	thousands of birds
un million ***d'***habitants	a million inhabitants
trois milliards ***de*** dollars	three billion dollars

ORDINAL NUMBERS

1st **premier, première**	6th **sixième**	16th **seizième**
2nd { **deuxième** / **second, seconde** }	7th **septième**	17th **dix-septième**
	8th **huitième**	20th **vingtième**
3rd **troisième**	9th **neuvième**	21st **vingt et unième**
4th **quatrième**	10th **dixième**	34th **trente-quatrième**
5th **cinquième**	11th **onzième**	100th **centième**

Note

1. Except for **premier** and **second**, the ordinal numbers are formed by adding **-ième** to the cardinal numbers. Silent **e** is dropped before **-ième.**

2. Originally, **second** referred to the second of a series of only two, while **deuxième** referred to the second of more than two. Today, however, this distinction is generally not observed.

3. Observe the **u** in **cinquième** and the **v** in **neuvième.**

4. The final **a** or **e** of the preceding word is not dropped before **huit, huitième, onze,** and **onzième.**

***la* huitième** maison	the eighth house
***le* onze** février	the eleventh of February

5. Cardinals precede ordinals in French.

les ***trois premières*** semaines	the first three weeks

FRACTIONS

1/2 { **la moitié** / **un demi**	1/5 **un cinquième**
1/3 **un tiers**	3/7 **trois septièmes**
1/4 **un quart**	7/8 **sept huitièmes**
3/4 **trois quarts**	1/100 **un centième**

Note

1. Fractions in French are formed, as in English, by combining cardinal and ordinal numbers. Only **moitié, tiers,** and **quart** are irregular.

2. **Moitié** is a noun and must have an article. **Demi,** generally used as an adjective, is invariable when used with a hyphen before the noun; otherwise, it agrees with its noun.

la moitié de la classe	half the class
une ***demi***-bouteille	a half bottle
une bouteille et ***demie***	a bottle and a half

TITLES OF RULERS

Charles ***Premier*** (Charles Ier)	Charles the First
But:	
Henri ***Deux*** (Henri II)	Henry the Second
Louis ***Quatorze*** (Louis XIV)	Louis the Fourteenth

Note

Premier is the only ordinal used in numerical titles of rulers; in all other cases, cardinal numbers are used. The definite article is omitted in French.

EXERCICES

A. Écrire en français en toutes lettres:

1. 199
2. 19 - 3 = 16
3. 861
4. 3/100
5. 41 × 2 = 82
6. 12.014
7. 1/4 + 1/3 = 7/12
8. 7.981
9. 51 + 20 = 71
10. 1.001.101

B. Donner l'équivalent en anglais:

1. la seconde moitié du seizième siècle
2. une quinzaine de cravates
3. Philippe Deux
4. la onzième ligne
5. des millions de lecteurs
6. trois quarts d'heure
7. les deux premiers paragraphes
8. une vingtaine d'années
9. deux fois quarante-huit font quatre-vingt-seize
10. plusieurs centaines d'étoiles

C. Compléter en français:

1. Six moins six font ______.
2. Richelieu fut le premier ministre de Louis ______.
3. Il y a ______ secondes dans une minute.
4. Ma sœur a vingt ans. L'année prochaine elle aura ______ ans.
5. Si soixante minutes font une heure, trente minutes font une ______.
6. Septembre est le ______ mois de l'année.
7. Voltaire (1694–1778) fut le plus grand philosophe du ______ siècle.
8. Alain avait soixante-dix francs. Son ami, Yves, lui a donné dix francs. Maintenant Alain a ______ francs.
9. Il y a ______ jours en janvier.
10. Après la chute de la Quatrième République, Charles de Gaulle a été élu le premier président de la ______ République française.

D. Compléter la phrase en donnant l'équivalent des mots en italique:

1. *five thousand* — Le pilote descend à ______ pieds.
2. *half* — J'ai mangé ______ du pain.
3. *ninety-one* — Ce palais compte ______ pièces.
4. *Thousands* — ______ de personnes visitaient l'exposition chaque jour.
5. *twenty-first* — C'était le ______ anniversaire de la victoire.
6. *two dozen* — Elle avait acheté ______ serviettes.
7. *Francis the First* — ______ encouragea les lettres et les arts.

8. *a half bottle* Qui a bu ______ de ce vin?
9. *a cup and a half* L'Anglaise a bu ______ de thé.
10. *a hundred ten* On faisait ______ kilomètres à l'heure.
11. *about ten* Donnez-moi ______ pêches, s'il vous plaît.
12. *the eighth* Ils étaient arrivés à ______ leçon.
13. *a billion* On dit que ce commerce vaut ______ francs.
14. *of eleven* C'est un immeuble ______ étages.
15. *the first ten days* Nous avons passé ______ de nos vacances à la campagne.

E. Répondre à chaque question par une phrase complète en français:

1. Combien font cent et mille?
2. Combien font cent fois mille?
3. Combien de minutes y a-t-il dans quatre heures?
4. Combien d'ans y a-t-il dans cinq siècles?
5. Quel roi de France donna aux protestants la liberté religieuse par l'Édit de Nantes?
6. Combien d'états forment les États-Unis?
7. Combien font cent moins un?
8. Combien de millions y a-t-il dans un milliard?
9. Combien font trois fois vingt-cinq?
10. Combien de mètres y a-t-il dans deux kilomètres?

5. TIME OF DAY; DATES

TIME OF DAY

Quelle heure est-il?	What time is it?
Il est une heure.	It is one o'clock.
Il est neuf heures vingt.	It is twenty after nine.
Il est huit heures et quart.	It is a quarter after eight.
Il est onze heures et demie.	It is half past eleven.
Il est trois heures moins dix.	It is ten (minutes) to three.
Il est deux heures moins un quart.	It is a quarter to two.
Il est midi.	It is twelve o'clock (noon).
Il est minuit.	It is twelve o'clock (midnight).
Il est midi (minuit) et demi.	It is half past twelve.

Note

1. To express time *after* the hour, the number of minutes is added. The word **et** is used only with **quart** and **demi(e)**. To express time *before* the hour, **moins** is used.
2. **Midi** and **minuit** are masculine.

OTHER TIME EXPRESSIONS

à quelle heure?	at what time?
à midi précis	at exactly noon
à cinq heures précises	at five o'clock sharp
trois heures du matin	three o'clock in the morning, 3:00 A.M.
quatre heures de l'après-midi	four o'clock in the afternoon, 4:00 P.M.
sept heures du soir	seven o'clock in the evening, 7:00 P.M.
midi vingt-cinq; minuit et quart	12:25 P.M.; 12:15 A.M.
vers neuf heures	about nine o'clock
un quart d'heure; une demi-heure	a quarter hour; a half hour
Quelle heure est-il à votre montre?	What time is it on your watch?
Ma montre avance (retarde) de dix minutes.	My watch is ten minutes fast (slow).

Note

In public announcements, such as timetables, the twenty-four-hour system is commonly used, with midnight as the zero hour.

00.20 = 12:20 A.M.
14 heures = 2:00 P.M.
20 h. 45 = 8:45 P.M.

DATES

LES JOURS DE LA SEMAINE

lundi, Monday	**vendredi,** Friday
mardi, Tuesday	**samedi,** Saturday
mercredi, Wednesday	**dimanche,** Sunday
jeudi, Thursday	

LES MOIS DE L'ANNÉE

janvier, January	**mai,** May	**septembre,** September
février, February	**juin,** June	**octobre,** October
mars, March	**juillet,** July	**novembre,** November
avril, April	**août,** August	**décembre,** December

LES SAISONS DE L'ANNÉE

le printemps, spring	**l'automne,** autumn
l'été, summer	**l'hiver,** winter

Note

1. Days, months, and seasons are all masculine and written with small letters in French.

2. To express *in* with months and seasons, **en** is used, except with **printemps.**

en janvier, in January	***en*** été, in (the) summer
en juillet, in July	***en*** automne, in (the) autumn
en décembre, in December	***en*** hiver, in (the) winter

But:

au printemps, in (the) spring

OTHER EXPRESSIONS USING DATES

Quel jour de la semaine est-ce aujourd'hui?
What day of the week is it today?

C'est aujourd'hui vendredi.
Today is Friday.

Ce sera demain samedi.
Tomorrow will be Saturday.

Quel jour (du mois) est-ce aujourd'hui?
Or:
Quel jour (du mois) sommes-nous aujourd'hui?
What is today's date?

C'est aujourd'hui le premier août.
Or:
Nous sommes aujourd'hui le premier août.
Today is August 1st (the first of August).

Nous reviendrons le onze septembre.
We will return on September 11th.

La bataille eut lieu en mil soixante-six.
The battle took place in 1066.

en dix-neuf cent soixante-dix
in 1970

le quatre juillet, dix-sept cent soixante-seize (le 4 juillet 1776)
July 4, 1776

Elle est née au mois de février.
She was born in the month of February.

il y a huit jours
a week ago

d'aujourd'hui en huit
a week from today

de demain en quinze
two weeks from tomorrow

Note

1. In dates, **le premier** is used for the first day of the month. For all other days, cardinal numbers are used.
2. The English words *on* and *of* are not expressed in French dates.
3. Years are commonly expressed in hundreds, as in English. The word for *one thousand* in dates, if used, is generally written **mil.**

EXERCICES

A. Donner l'heure indiquée en français:

B. Écrire en français en toutes lettres:

1. 4:30 P.M.
2. about 2:00 A.M.
3. 12:25 A.M.
4. at 1:00 sharp
5. in February
6. on the twelfth of October
7. in the summer
8. April 1, 1923
9. in 1831
10. November 30, 1670

C. Identifier en français:

1. la saison qui commence en septembre
2. le mois qui suit juillet
3. la date de la fête de Noël
4. le milieu de la nuit
5. le mois le plus court

6. le jour après jeudi
7. la plus froide des quatre saisons
8. le jour qui suit le trente et un mai
9. le dixième mois de l'année
10. les deux jours de congé des étudiants français

D. Compléter la phrase en français:

1. J'ai commencé mon travail à onze heures du matin et j'ai travaillé pendant une heure. J'ai fini le travail à ______ précis.
2. Le ______, c'est le Nouvel An.
3. George Washington naquit le ______ 1732.
4. Nous aimons à faire du ski ______ hiver.
5. C'est aujourd'hui mardi. Je vous verrai mardi prochain, c'est-à-dire, d'aujourd'hui ______.
6. Le ______ est le dernier jour de l'année.
7. Le jour qui suit vendredi est ______.
8. ______ est la saison où il fait le plus chaud.
9. Il est vraiment six heures et quart, mais à ma montre il est six heures précises. Ma montre ______ de quinze minutes.
10. Généralement il pleut beaucoup ______ printemps.

E. Répondre à chaque question par une phrase complète en français:

1. A quelle heure vous couchez-vous d'ordinaire?
2. Quels mois ont trente jours?
3. Vers quelle heure dîne-t-on chez vous le dimanche?
4. En quelle année Christophe Colomb arriva-t-il au Nouveau Monde?
5. Quel jour du mois est-ce aujourd'hui?
6. A quelle heure le soleil se lèvera-t-il demain matin?
7. Quelle est la date de la fête nationale de la France?
8. En quel mois commence le printemps?
9. Jusqu'à quelle heure la soirée de votre ami a-t-elle duré?
10. Nicole a quitté l'école à trois heures dix. Elle est arrivée à la maison vingt minutes plus tard. A quelle heure est-elle arrivée chez elle?

F. Compléter la phrase en donnant l'équivalent des mots en italique:

1. *two weeks from tomorrow* — Marcel espère revenir ______.
2. *a half hour* — Il a neigé pendant ______.
3. *in the month of* — Je suis née ______ février.
4. *Today is Monday.* — Quel jour de la semaine est-ce aujourd'hui? ______.
5. *in the evening* — Les invités sont arrivés à huit heures ______.
6. *the eleventh of March* — Ce sera demain ______.

7. *a quarter hour* — Les deux voisines ont passé ______ à causer.
8. *on Thursday* — J'ai assisté à l'opéra ______.
9. *is five minutes fast* — Votre montre ______.
10. *a week ago* — Nous aurions dû venir ______.

6. THE PARTITIVE; OTHER USES OF *DE*

PARTITIVE

The idea of *some* or *any* with a noun is expressed in French by:

de + *the definite article* of the noun	
du beurre frais	some (any) fresh butter
de la soie	some (any) silk
de l'herbe verte	some (any) green grass
des camions	some (any) trucks
de, *without the article*, after a negative	
Je **n'**ai **pas** fait *de* fautes.	I didn't make any mistakes. (I made no mistakes.)
Il **n'**a **guère** *d'*amis.	He has hardly any friends.
de, *without the article*, when an adjective precedes a plural noun	
de **vieux** souliers	some old shoes
de **longues** rues	long streets

Note

1. The words for *some* and *any* must be expressed in French, and must be repeated before each noun even though they are often omitted in English.

Voulez-vous ***du*** poisson? Non, je préfère ***de la*** viande et ***des*** légumes.	Do you want some fish? No, I prefer meat and vegetables.

2. Special cases of the partitive are:

   a. The definite article is retained before an adjective in the plural when the adjective is considered part of the noun.

des jeunes filles	girls
des petits pains	rolls
des petits pois	green peas

   b. After **ne . . . que** (*only*), **de** is used *with the article*, provided there is no adjective preceding the noun.

Nous **ne** lisons **que** ***des*** romans.	We read only novels.

c. After **sans** (*without*), **ne . . . ni . . . ni** (*neither . . . nor*), and expressions taking **de**, the partitive is omitted.

C'est un livre **sans** images.	It is a book without any pictures.
Nanette **ne** boit **ni** thé **ni** café.	Nancy drinks neither tea nor coffee. (Nancy doesn't drink any tea or coffee.)
As-tu besoin **de** billets?	Do you need (any) tickets?

The idea of *some* or *any* is translated by **en** if the noun is omitted. **En,** like personal pronoun objects, precedes the verb, except in affirmative commands.

A-t-il écrit des lettres?	Has he written any letters?
Oui, il ***en*** a écrit.	Yes, he has written some.
Écrivez-***en***.	Write some.

ADVERBS OF QUANTITY

Certain adverbs expressing quantity are followed by **de,** *without the article*, before a noun.

assez de, enough	**peu de,** little, few
autant de, as much, as many	**plus de,** more
beaucoup de, much, many	**que de,** how much, how many (used only in exclamations)
combien de, how much, how many	**tant de,** so much, so many
moins de, less, fewer	**trop de,** too much, too many

Avez-vous ***assez de*** temps et ***d'***énergie?	Have you enough time and energy?
Que de fois je l'ai grondé!	How many times I've scolded him!

NOUNS OF QUANTITY

Nouns that show quantity or measure are followed by **de,** *without the article*, before another noun. Some frequent nouns of quantity are:

une boîte, a box	**un morceau**, a piece
une bouteille, a bottle	**un nombre**, a number
une douzaine, a dozen	**une paire**, a pair
une foule, a crowd	**un panier**, a basket
un kilogramme } a kilogram	**un paquet**, a package
un kilo } a kilogram	**un sac**, a bag
un litre, a liter	**une tasse**, a cup
une livre, a pound	**un verre**, a glass
un mètre, a meter	

(See also Nouns of Number, page 113.)

Je dois acheter ***une livre de*** beurre et ***une bouteille de*** crème. — I have to buy a pound of butter and a bottle of cream.

Elle m'a envoyè ***une*** belle ***paire de*** gants. — She sent me a beautiful pair of gloves.

Note

1. The adverb **bien** (*much, many*) and the noun **la plupart** (*most*) are exceptional. They are followed by **de** *and the definite article.*

   Ils ont ***bien des*** devoirs (= **beaucoup de** devoirs) à faire. — They have much homework to do.

   La plupart des élèves réussissent. — Most students succeed.

2. **Plusieurs** (*several*) and **quelques** (*some, a few*) are adjectives and modify the noun directly.

   plusieurs affiches — several posters
   quelques minutes — a few minutes

3. If the noun is omitted after a word of quantity, the noun must be replaced by the pronoun **en**.

   Combien **de magasins** y a-t-il? Combien y ***en*** a-t-il? — How many stores are there? How many are there?

   A-t-elle bu **du lait**? Oui, elle ***en*** a bu un verre. — Did she drink any milk? Yes, she drank a glass.

4. Note the distinction between the use of **de**, in the sense of *containing*, and **à**, in the sense of *designed for.*

   une tasse ***de*** thé — a cup of tea
   une tasse ***à*** thé — a teacup

NOUNS OF MATERIAL

Nouns describing the material of which an object is made are preceded by **de** or **en**, *without the article.*

> une pièce ***d'or***, a gold coin
> un vase ***de porcelaine***, a china vase
> une porte ***de bois***, a wooden door
> des bas ***de nylon***, nylon stockings
> un couteau ***en acier inoxydable***, a stainless steel knife
> un portefeuille ***en cuir***, a leather wallet
> des vêtements ***en laine***, woolen clothing

Some frequently used nouns of material are:

l'acier (*m.*), steel
l'aluminium (*m.*), aluminum
l'argent (*m.*), silver
le bois, wood
la brique, brick
le bronze, bronze
le caoutchouc, rubber
le chocolat, chocolate
la cire, wax
le coton, cotton
le cristal, crystal
le cuir, leather
le cuivre, copper
la dentelle, lace
l'étoffe (*f.*), material, fabric
le fer, iron
la fourrure, fur
la laine, wool
le lin, linen
le marbre, marble
le métal, metal
le nylon, nylon
l'or (*m.*), gold
la paille, straw
le papier, paper
la pierre, stone
le plastique, plastic
le plomb, lead
la porcelaine, porcelain, china
la soie, silk
le verre, glass

POSSESSION AND RELATIONSHIP WITH *DE*

In French, possession and relationship are expressed by the preposition **de** where English generally uses *'s* or *s'*.

les patins ***de*** Michel	Michael's skates
le bureau ***du*** directeur	the principal's office
le mari ***de*** l'actrice	the actress' husband
la grand-mère ***des*** enfants	the children's grandmother

EXERCICES

A. Compléter les phrases en donnant les formes convenables du partitif:

1. Je vais chercher ______ papier et ______ encre.
2. Il y a toujours ______ bonnes places pour ceux qui désirent travailler.
3. Les abricots et les raisins sont ______ fruits.
4. Ces fromages sont préparés avec ______ bon lait et ______ crème fraîche.
5. Nous n'avons pas encore lu ______ journaux ce matin.
6. Garçon, apportez-nous ______ veau et ______ petits pois.
7. Le père de Théodore possède ______ vieilles maisons de bois dans cette rue.
8. M. Leroux ne portait que ______ complets bleus.
9. ______ belles nappes de lin couvraient les tables.
10. A-t-elle reçu de beaux cadeaux? Oui, elle ______ a reçu.

B. Compléter les phrases ou les expressions en anglais:

1. L'espagnol et l'italien sont des langues romanes. Spanish and Italian ______.
2. Nous avons traversé plusieurs ponts de pierre. We crossed ______.
3. Le toit est couvert de neige. The roof ______.
4. Qu'est-ce qui cause le plus grand nombre d'accidents? What causes ______.
5. Elle m'a donné des renseignements utiles. She gave me ______.
6. Ce moteur brûle des huiles lourdes sans trace de fumée. That motor burns ______.
7. Que de feuilles étaient tombées pendant la nuit! ______ during the night!
8. Le peintre était entouré d'une foule de gens. The painter was ______.
9. Ils l'ont fait pour de très bonnes raisons. They did it ______.
10. La plupart des oiseaux volent. ______ fly.
11. Chaque matin je bois un grand verre de jus d'orange. Each morning ______.
12. un chapeau de paille; une montre en acier inoxydable ______ hat; a stainless ______ watch
13. deux kilos de pommes de terre; des centaines de sacs de farine two ______; ______ four
14. son panier de fruits; des œufs en chocolat her ______; ______ eggs
15. le parapluie de M. Duval; bien des auteurs ______ umbrella; ______ authors

C. Compléter la phrase en français:

1. Il n'y a plus ______ fleurs dans le jardin. 
2. Un orphelin n'a ______ mère ______ père.
3. Ils passent la plupart ______ temps à jouer.
4. Ce marchand a peu ______ clients.
5. Le cuivre et le plomb sont ______ métaux.
6. Marianne a dix francs. Son frère a quinze francs. Marianne a ______ francs que son frère.
7. Combien de soie comptez-vous acheter? Je compte ______ acheter trois mètres.
8. Le chat a tué bien ______ souris.
9. L'oiseau a-t-il déjà des plumes? Non, c'est un petit oiseau sans ______.
10. Yvonne et Julie sont ______ jeunes filles.

D. Donner l'équivalent en français:

1. Dogs are animals.
2. Do you need any nylon stockings? No, I have enough.
3. Robert's uncle brought a box of candy.
4. I take my tea without sugar.
5. He has few enemies but many friends.
6. Has he only friends?
7. She eats neither meat nor fish.
8. a cotton dress; lace handkerchiefs; as much leather
9. some rolls; a few rolls; several rolls
10. too much soap; little wheat; a bottle of cider

E. Répondre à chaque question par une phrase complète en français:

1. Avez-vous jamais mangé des escargots?
2. Peut-on se passer d'argent?
3. Combien de morceaux de sucre votre père met-il dans son café?
4. Pourquoi a-t-on envoyé cet élève au bureau du directeur?
5. Les femmes préfèrent-elles généralement un manteau de laine ou un manteau de fourrure?
6. Pourquoi la France produit-elle tant de vin?
7. Quel animal domestique nous donne du lait?
8. Aimeriez-vous mieux gagner la médaille d'or ou la médaille d'argent?
9. Combien de livres de beurre votre mère achète-t-elle chaque semaine?
10. Est-ce que la plupart des professeurs de votre école sont des femmes ou des hommes?

7. COMPARISON OF ADJECTIVES

a. The comparative of inequality is formed by placing **plus** (*more*) or **moins** (*less*, *not so*) before the adjective. The comparative of equality is formed with **aussi** (*as*). The superlative is expressed by placing the proper form of the definite article before the comparative of inequality.

POSITIVE	COMPARATIVE	SUPERLATIVE
doux, mild	***plus*** doux (***que***), milder (than) ***moins*** doux (***que***), less mild (than), not so mild (as) ***aussi*** doux (***que***), as mild (as)	***le plus*** doux, (the) mildest ***le moins*** doux, (the) least mild
fatiguée, tired	***plus*** fatiguée (***que***), more tired (than) ***moins*** fatiguée (***que***), less tired (than), not so tired (as) ***aussi*** fatiguée (***que***), as tired (as)	***la plus*** fatiguée, (the) most tired ***la moins*** fatiguée, (the) least tired

Nous sommes ***plus*** fatigués ***que*** vous.	We are more tired than you.
Nous sommes ***moins*** fatigués ***que*** vous. Nous ne sommes pas ***si*** fatigués ***que*** vous.	We are not so tired as you.
Nous sommes ***aussi*** fatigués ***que*** vous.	We are as tired as you.
Nous sommes ***les plus*** fatigués ***de*** tous.	We are the most tired of all.

b. Comparative and superlative adjectives agree with the noun modified in gender and number. The position of these adjectives, before or after the noun, is generally the same as in the positive.

POSITIVE	une **longue** conversation	les lacs **profonds**
COMPARATIVE	une **plus longue** conversation	les lacs **plus profonds**
SUPERLATIVE	**la plus longue** conversation	les lacs **les plus profonds**

c. A few adjectives have irregular comparisons. **Bon** is always compared irregularly; **mauvais** and **petit** are compared both regularly and irregularly.

POSITIVE	COMPARATIVE	SUPERLATIVE
bon, good	***meilleur***, better	***le meilleur***, (the) best
mauvais, bad	plus mauvais / ***pire*** } worse	le plus mauvais / ***le pire*** } (the) worst
petit, small	plus petit, smaller (in size)	le plus petit, (the) smallest
	moindre, less (in importance)	***le moindre***, (the) least

d. When a superlative adjective *precedes* its noun, a possessive adjective may be used in place of the article.

sa plus jolie robe — her prettiest dress
nos meilleurs clients — our best customers

But:

leur voyage ***le*** plus intéressant — their most interesting trip

e. After a superlative, *in* is translated by **de**.

C'est l'avenue **la plus large *de*** la ville. — That's the widest avenue in the city.

La Seine est le fleuve **le plus navigable *de*** la France. — The Seine is the most navigable river in France.

EXERCICES

A. Compléter la phrase en français:

1. Le mont Blanc est ______ haute montagne de France.

2. C'était le quartier le plus pauvre ______ la ville.
3. Cette eau-ci est plus pure ______ cette eau-là.
4. Le bois est ______ dur que l'acier.
5. Les diamants sont ______ précieux que les perles.
6. Louis et Louise n'ont point d'argent. Louis est ______ pauvre que Louise.
7. Les rhumes sont mauvais mais la pneumonie est encore ______.
8. Est-ce que ce livre est intéressant? En effet, c'est le livre ______ que j'aie jamais lu.
9. Les jeunes filles ne sont pas (*so*) ______ fortes que les garçons.
10. La richesse est bonne mais le bonheur est même ______.

B. Compléter chaque phrase en donnant l'équivalent des mots entre parenthèses:

1. (as small as) Il est à peu près ______ moi.
2. (the youngest in) Frédéric est ______ la famille.
3. (lower than) Sa voix est ______ la tienne.
4. (the best) Les vins français sont ______.
5. (least) Je n'ai pas la ______ crainte des abeilles.
6. (the most beautiful city) Paris est ______ de l'Europe.
7. (worse than) Le remède est ______ la maladie.
8. (not so long as) Cette leçon-ci est ______ celle-là.
9. (happier than) Mme Dupont semble toujours ______ son mari.
10. (as attentive as) Les étudiants sont-ils ______ possible?
11. (the least difficult) Est-ce que l'anglais est la langue ______?
12. (better than) Vos notes sont ______ que les miennes.
13. (sincerest) C'est mon ami ______.
14. (more worried than) Son père sera ______ lui.
15. (less useful) Quel cadeau peut être ______ que celui-ci?

C. Compléter la phrase en anglais:

1. Les montres les plus jolies ne sont pas nécessairement les meilleures. The ______ watches are not necessarily ______.
2. Ces fraises-ci ne sont pas si délicieuses que les autres. These strawberries ______ the others.
3. On peut voir sur le visage de la Joconde le plus célèbre sourire du monde. You can see on the face of the Mona Lisa ______.
4. Je n'en ai pas la moindre idée. I haven't ______.
5. Si vous vous servez de cette pâte dentifrice, vos dents seront plus blanches. If you use this toothpaste, your teeth ______.
6. Le président porte les plus lourdes responsabilités de la nation. The President bears ______.
7. C'est le pire des voleurs. He is ______ thieves.

8. La machine la moins chère est-elle celle qui dure le plus longtemps? Is the ______ the one that lasts the longest?
9. Est-ce que le palais de Versailles est aussi grand que le Louvre? Is the Palace of Versailles ______ the Louvre?
10. Sirius est l'étoile la plus brillante du ciel. Sirius is the ______ sky.

D. Répondre à chaque question par une phrase complète en français:

1. Les citrons sont-ils plus doux ou moins doux que les pêches?
2. Quel est le moyen de transport le plus rapide pour voyager des États-Unis en France?
3. Quand portez-vous vos meilleurs vêtements?
4. Fait-il aussi chaud en hiver qu'en été?
5. Votre salle de classe est-elle plus grande, aussi grande, ou moins grande que la salle de séjour de votre maison?
6. Quel est le mois le plus court de l'année?
7. Êtes-vous aussi diligent(e) que les autres membres de votre classe?
8. Quelle province française est la plus riche en monuments romains?
9. Trouvez-vous les pièces de théâtre plus intéressantes ou moins intéressantes que les films?
10. Quelle est la planète la plus proche de la Terre?

Le lac d'Annecy

Quoiqu'il y ait peu de lacs en France, le lac d'Annecy peut rivaliser avec les plus beaux des lacs suisses et italiens. De très jolis villages se trouvent le long des rives de ce lac, situé dans les pittoresques Alpes de la Savoie.

8. ADVERBS: FORMATION; COMPARISON; POSITION

FORMATION OF ADVERBS FROM ADJECTIVES

a. To form the adverb, **-ment** is added to the masculine singular of an adjective that ends in a vowel.

autre: autre***ment***, otherwise
poli: poli***ment***, politely
utile: utile***ment***, usefully
vrai: vrai***ment***, truly

b. If the masculine singular of the adjective ends in a consonant, **-ment** is added to the feminine singular.

affreux: ***affreusement***, frightfully
amer: ***amèrement***, bitterly
doux: ***doucement***, gently
fou: ***follement***, madly
franc: ***franchement***, frankly
secret: ***secrètement***, secretly
seul: ***seulement***, only
tel: ***tellement***, in such a manner, so

c. A few adjectives change mute **e** to **é** before adding **-ment.**

aveugle: aveugl*é*ment, blindly
énorme: énorm*é*ment, enormously
précis: précis*é*ment, exactly
profond: profond*é*ment, deeply

d. Adjectives ending in **-ant** and **-ent** have adverbs ending in **-amment** and **-emment.**

constant: const***amment***, constantly
évident: évid***emment***, evidently
fréquent: fréqu***emment***, frequently
récent: réc***emment***, recently

Exception–lent: **lentement**, slowly

e. A few adjectives are used in the masculine singular in certain fixed expressions.

bas: parler ***bas***, to speak low
haut: parler ***haut***, to speak loud
bon: sentir ***bon***, to smell good
cher: payer ***cher***, to pay (for) dearly
droit: aller ***droit***, to go straight
dur: travailler ***dur***, to work hard

Ne parlez pas si ***haut.*** — Don't speak so loud.
Ces roses sentent ***bon.*** — These roses smell good.

f. As a substitute for an adverb, or where no adverb exists, French often uses the expressions **d'une façon** or **d'une manière** with a modifying adjective.

Elle a parlé ***d'une façon*** charmante.	She spoke charmingly.
Il agit ***d'une manière*** intelligente.	He acts intelligently.

OTHER COMMON ADVERBS

ailleurs, elsewhere
ainsi, thus, so
alors, then
après, afterwards
assez, enough, quite
aujourd'hui, today
auparavant, before
aussi, also, too
aussitôt, immediately
autant, as much
autrefois, formerly
beaucoup, much
bien, well, very
bientôt, soon
cependant, meanwhile
comme, as
davantage, more
dedans, inside
dehors, outside
déjà, already
demain, tomorrow
encore, still, yet, again
enfin, at last
ensemble, together
ensuite, then, afterwards
environ, about
exprès, on purpose
fort, very
hier, yesterday
ici, here
là, there
loin, far
longtemps, a long time
maintenant, now
mal, badly
même, even
moins, less
parfois, sometimes
partout, everywhere
peu, little
peut-être, perhaps, maybe
plus, more
plutôt, rather
près, near
presque, almost
puis, then
quelquefois, sometimes
si, so
souvent, often
surtout, especially
tant, so much
tard, late
tôt, soon
toujours, always, still
tout, quite, entirely
très, very
trop, too, too much
vite, quickly
volontiers, willingly

COMPARISON OF ADVERBS

Adverbs are compared like adjectives, except that the article in the superlative is always **le**.

POSITIVE	fièrement, proudly
COMPARATIVE	***plus*** fièrement (***que***), more proudly (than) ***moins*** fièrement (***que***), less proudly (than), not so proudly (as) ***aussi*** fièrement (***que***), as proudly (as)
SUPERLATIVE	***le plus*** fièrement, (the) most proudly ***le moins*** fièrement, (the) least proudly

A few adverbs have irregular comparisons.

POSITIVE	COMPARATIVE	SUPERLATIVE
bien, well	***mieux***, better	***le mieux***, (the) best
mal, badly	plus mal } worse ***pis*** } worse	le plus mal } (the) worst ***le pis*** } (the) worst
beaucoup, much	***plus***, more	***le plus***, (the) most
peu, little	***moins***, less	***le moins***, (the) least

Note

1. Some English adverbs have the same form as the corresponding adjectives: *better*, *best*, *worse*, *worst*, *little.* In translating into French, it is important to distinguish between the adjective and the adverb.

   Mon cahier n'est pas ***meilleur*** que le vôtre. — My notebook is not better than yours.
   Vous lisez ***mieux*** que moi. — You read better than I.

2. Before numerals, *than* is expressed by **de**.

   Nous avons dépensé plus ***de*** **cent** francs. — We spent more than a hundred francs.

3. *Most*, in the sense of *very*, *extremely*, is often translated by the adverbial expression **on ne peut plus**.

   Cette historie est ***on ne peut plus*** intéressante. — This story is most interesting.

POSITION OF ADVERBS

An adverb modifying a verb in a simple tense is usually placed directly after that verb.

Il prononce ***distinctement*** ses paroles.	He pronounces his words distinctly.

In compound tenses, the position of the adverb varies. Most adverbs, especially long ones and adverbs of time and place, generally follow the past participle. A few common ones, such as **bien, mal, souvent, toujours, déjà,** and **encore,** as well as the adverbs of quantity, usually precede the past participle.

Le médecin est venu ***immédiatement*** hier.	The doctor came immediately yesterday.
Nous avions ***beaucoup*** dormi ce jour-là.	We had slept a great deal that day.

EXERCICES

A. Ajouter à chaque phrase l'adverbe qui correspond à l'adjectif entre parenthèses:

Exemple: (probable) La lune est pleine ce soir.
La lune est probablement pleine ce soir.

1. (franc) Ce navigateur écrit ses impressions de voyage.
2. (récent) Je ne l'ai pas vue.
3. (tel) Les muscles de ses bras sont gros!
4. (profond) On avait examiné toutes les possibilités avant la décision.
5. (fou) Est-ce que toutes les jeunes filles aiment ce chanteur?
6. (mauvais) L'étudiant a compris les explications du professeur.
7. (affreux) Qu'as-tu? Tu es pâle!
8. (complet) Les vignes avaient été ruinées par la tempête.
9. (précis) N'a-t-on pas mesuré la distance de la terre au soleil?
10. (doux) Le soir, la paix descendait sur les champs.
11. (facile) Ce savant comprend nos problèmes les plus compliqués.
12. (constant) Sur les routes, un cycliste doit être alerte.
13. (amer) Les habitants du quartier se plaignaient du bruit des avions.
14. (vrai) C'est dommage que la neige se soit arrêtée.
15. (sec) Le candidat a répondu aux questions du journaliste.

B. Donner le contraire de:

1. beaucoup
2. dedans
3. rarement
4. pis
5. rapidement
6. le moins
7. tristement

Donner un synonyme de:

8. puis
9. aussitôt
10. davantage
11. rapidement
12. très
13. souvent
14. parfois
15. d'une manière cruelle

C. Donner l'équivalent en anglais:

1. Allez tout droit. L'hôtel est plus loin, près de la poste.
2. Quand je travaillais dur, je mangeais énormément.
3. Il me semble que bientôt tous les paysans porteront des souliers de cuir plutôt que des sabots.
4. Cette nuit-là il a beaucoup toussé.
5. Il a fallu à l'artiste moins de six mois pour achever le portrait.

6. Tu as perdu ma montre d'or! Elle valait très cher.
7. L'acteur avait joué son rôle d'une façon magnifique.
8. Elle croit que la Touraine est une région on ne peut plus charmante.
9. Ils avaient longtemps suivi le fleuve.
10. Quoique mon père soit toujours assez fort, il ne joue plus au tennis comme auparavant.

D. Donner le mot qui manque:

1. Nous sommes arrivés trop ______ à la gare. Le train était déjà parti!
2. Personne n'a regretté l'incident plus ______ lui.
3. —L'a-t-il embrassée avec timidité? —Bien sûr, il l'a embrassée ______.
4. Ne parlez pas si ______; nous ne sommes pas sourds.
5. Cet inventeur est on ne ______ plus illustre.
6. —Va-t-on interroger séparément les accusés? —Non, on les interrogera ______.
7. Une personne qui agit d'une façon polie agit ______.
8. —Vous avez cherché vos clefs dans tous les coins de la salle? —Oui, je les ai cherchées ______, mais sans succès.
9. Il y a moins ______ onze ascenseurs dans ce gratte-ciel.
10. —L'odeur de ces fleurs est si bonne! —Oui, elles sentent très ______, n'est-ce pas?

E. Répondre à chaque question par une phrase complète en français:

1. Où faites-vous généralement vos devoirs?
2. Comment le malade a-t-il dormi hier soir?
3. Quelle langue écrivez-vous mieux, le français ou l'anglais?
4. M'as-tu toujours dit la vérité?
5. Pourquoi cet homme parle-t-il si bas?
6. Vous êtes-vous levé(e) volontiers ce matin?
7. Est-ce que les invités sont déjà arrivés?
8. Quel membre de votre famille chante le mieux?
9. Pourquoi n'êtes-vous pas encore partis?
10. Avez-vous entendu distinctement tout ce que le professeur a dit?

F. Compléter la phrase en donnant l'équivalent des mots en italique:

1. *a little*	Après cette promenade, nous sommes ______ fatigués.
2. *especially*	On boit du cidre ______ en Normandie et en Bretagne.
3. *almost always walk*	Ils ______ sur les quais.
4. *accepted proudly*	La danseuse ______ le bouquet de roses.
5. *as attentively as*	Ils écoutaient ______ possible.
6. *more than eight*	Vous y trouverez un choix de ______ modèles.
7. *elsewhere*	Les oiseaux ont quitté la région froide pour habiter ______.
8. *evidently*	Tu as ______ de bonnes intentions.
9. *does not run so fast as*	Henri ______ son frère.
10. *obey blindly*	Tous ces gens ______ à leur chef.

9. POSSESSIVE ADJECTIVES AND PRONOUNS

POSSESSIVE ADJECTIVES

SINGULAR		PLURAL	MEANING
MAS.	FEM.	MAS. & FEM.	
mon	**ma**	**mes**	my
ton	**ta**	**tes**	your (*fam.*)
son	**sa**	**ses**	his, her, its
notre	**notre**	**nos**	our
votre	**votre**	**vos**	your
leur	**leur**	**leurs**	their

Note

1. Possessive adjectives, like other adjectives, agree in gender and number with the nouns they modify. They must be repeated before each noun.

nos rideaux et ***notre*** tapis	our curtains and rug
sa tante et ***son*** oncle	his aunt and uncle

2. The forms **mon, ton,** and **son** are used instead of **ma, ta,** and **sa** before a feminine singular noun beginning with a vowel or silent **h.**

mon idée, my idea
ton adresse, your address
son habitude, his habit

3. If it is necessary to distinguish between *his* and *her* for the sake of clarity, **à lui** or **à elle** are added.

C'est **sa** clef ***à lui.***	It is *his* key.
Avez-vous pris **ses** gants ***à elle?***	Have you taken *her* gloves?

4. With parts of the body, the possessive adjective is frequently replaced by the definite article if the possessor is clear.

Je me suis coupé *le* doigt.	I cut my finger.
Il avait un livre sous *le* bras.	He had a book under his arm.

POSSESSIVE PRONOUNS

SINGULAR		PLURAL		MEANING
MAS.	FEM.	MAS.	FEM.	
le mien	**la mienne**	**les miens**	**les miennes**	mine
le tien	**la tienne**	**les tiens**	**les tiennes**	yours (*fam.*)
le sien	**la sienne**	**les siens**	**les siennes**	his, hers, its
le nôtre	**la nôtre**	**les nôtres**	**les nôtres**	ours
le vôtre	**la vôtre**	**les vôtres**	**les vôtres**	yours
le leur	**la leur**	**les leurs**	**les leurs**	theirs

Note

1. The possessive pronoun replaces a possessive adjective and a noun. The pronoun agrees in gender and number with the noun it replaces.

Ma **voiture** est dans le garage. Où est ***la vôtre?***	My car is in the garage. Where is yours?
Vos **yeux** sont plus foncés que ***les siens.***	Your eyes are darker than his.

2. The definite article, a regular part of the possessive pronoun, contracts with the prepositions **à** and **de** in the usual way.

à nos fils et ***aux*** leurs	to our sons and theirs
de son voyage et ***du*** mien	of his trip and mine

3. To express simple possession after **être, à** is used with a disjunctive pronoun. The possessive pronoun is used after **être** to indicate distinction.

Cette montre est ***à moi.***	That watch is mine (belongs to me).
Cette montre est ***la mienne***, pas ***la vôtre.***	That watch is mine, not yours.

4. Note the French equivalents for "a . . . of mine," "a . . . of his."

une de mes amis, a friend of mine ***un de ses cousins***, a cousin of his

une de leurs voisines, a neighbor of theirs

EXERCICES

A. Mettre au singulier:

1. mes chaussettes
2. vos colis
3. tes amies
4. leurs bicyclettes
5. mes études
6. ses tasses
7. nos chevaux
8. tes valises
9. ses histoires
10. mes billets

B. Compléter chaque phrase avec la forme convenable de l'adjectif possessif:

Exemple: *Nous* avons fermé la porte de *notre* maison.

1. Le tailleur a pris les mesures de ______ client.

2. Les femmes n'ont pas encore fini ______ thé.
3. Avez-vous amené ______ enfants à la plage?
4. Je voudrais vivre ______ propre vie.
5. Nous avons joui d'un beau temps pendant ______ vacances.
6. Fais-tu ______ dernière année d'études?
7. J'ai dit bonjour en enlevant ______ chapeau.
8. Les paysans ont coupé la laine de ______ moutons.
9. Ne jouez pas avec ______ santé.
10. Mme Leroux va repasser ______ robes.

C. Remplacer les mots en italique par un pronom possessif:

1. Où sont *tes gants*, Pauline?
2. Pierre a oublié *sa brosse à dents.*
3. Donnez-moi *mes clefs.*
4. *Leur tristesse* est émouvante.
5. Suivez *mon exemple*.
6. Parliez-vous *de nos parents?*
7. *Son rhume* est affreux.
8. J'admire *ta confiance.*
9. Ont-ils retrouvé *leurs bijoux?*
10. *Ses habits* sont devenus trop petits.

D. Compléter la phrase en donnant l'équivalent des mots en italique:

1. *Her son and daughter* — ______ sont très intelligents.
2. *his head* — Tout à coup, il a levé ______.
3. *your apartment and ours* — Ils ont visité ______.
4. *mine* — A qui sont ces fleurs? Elles sont ______.
5. *ours* — Ces cravates sont ______, pas les leurs.
6. *my hands* — Je vais me laver ______.
7. *his* — C'est son tour ______, pas à elle.
8. *of yours* — Nous parlons souvent de nos voyages et ______.
9. *a neighbor of ours* — Marianne est ______.
10. *yours* — Pensez-vous à leur avenir ou ______?

E. Répondre à chaque question par une phrase complète en français:

1. Quand ferme-t-on d'ordinaire les yeux?
2. Est-ce que Gérard est un de tes amis?
3. Qu'avez-vous à la main?

Dans chacune des réponses suivantes, employer un pronom possessif:

4. Se rend-il compte de ses propres erreurs?
5. Ont-ils déjà pris leur dîner?
6. Si je réponds à tes lettres, répondras-tu aux miennes?
7. Se souviendront-ils de mon adresse?
8. Ont-ils assisté aux classes du nouveau professeur?
9. Avez-vous vu mes lunettes de soleil?
10. Puis-je me servir de votre stylo à bille?

10. GEOGRAPHICAL EXPRESSIONS

The definite article is used with names of countries, continents, provinces, mountains, and bodies of water, but *not* with names of cities.

Les Pyrénées séparent ***la France*** de ***l'Espagne***.	The Pyrenees separate France from Spain.
Parlez-vous de ***l'Asie*** ou de ***l'Afrique?***	Are you speaking of Asia or Africa?
La Seine passe par ***la Normandie***.	The Seine passes through Normandy.
Londres est la capitale de ***l'Angleterre***.	London is the capital of England.
La Loire se jette dans ***l'Atlantique***.	The Loire empties into the Atlantic.
Cherbourg se trouve sur ***la Manche***.	Cherbourg is on the English Channel.

PREPOSITIONS WITH PLACE NAMES

To express *to* or *in* with place names:

en	*feminine* { countries, continents, provinces	***en*** Suisse, to (in) Switzerland ***en*** Amérique, to (in) America ***en*** Bourgogne, to (in) Burgundy
au, aux	*masculine* countries	***au*** Mexique, to (in) Mexico ***aux*** États-Unis, to (in) the United States
dans + def. art.	*modified* place-names	***dans la*** belle France, in beautiful France ***dans l'***Europe occidentale, in western Europe
à	cities	***à*** Bruxelles, to (in) Brussels

Avez-vous jamais été ***en*** Suisse?	Have you evern been in Switzerland?
Nous allons ***au*** Mexique.	We are going to Mexico.
Ils demeurent ***dans l'***Europe occidentale.	They live in western Europe.
J'ai passé huit jours ***à*** Bruxelles.	I spent a week in Brussels.

To express *from* with place names:

de	*feminine* { countries, continents, provinces	***de*** Suisse, from Switzerland ***d'***Amérique, from America ***de*** Bourgogne, from Burgundy
de + def. art.	*masculine* countries *modified* place-names	***du*** Mexique, from Mexico ***de la*** belle France, from beautiful France ***de l'***Europe occidentale, from western Europe
de	cities	***de*** Bruxelles, from Brussels

Ces produits viennent ***de*** Suisse et ***du*** Mexique.	These products come from Switzerland and Mexico.
Elle était arrivée ***de l'***Europe occidentale.	She had arrived from western Europe.
Le train part ***de*** Bruxelles.	The train leaves from Brussels.

Note

1. With *masculine* countries, the definite article is always used.
2. Before modified place-names in which the modifier is an integral part of the name, *in* or *to* is expressed by ***en*** without the article, and *from* by ***de*** without the article.

   en Afrique du Nord, in North Africa
   d'Amérique du Sud, from South America

3. A few cities always have a definite article in French, since the article is part of the name.

	***le* Havre**, Havre	***la* Nouvelle-Orléans,** New Orleans
to, in:	***au*** Havre	***à la*** Nouvelle-Orléans
from:	***du*** Havre	***de la*** Nouvelle-Orléans

4. A few countries are used without the article. For example:

   Israël, en Israël, d'Israël

FEMININE COUNTRIES, CONTINENTS, PROVINCES

l'Algérie, Algeria
l'Allemagne, Germany
l'Angleterre, England
l'Argentine, Argentina
l'Autriche, Austria
la Belgique, Belgium
la Chine, China
l'Écosse, Scotland
l'Égypte, Egypt
l'Espagne, Spain
la France, France
la Grande-Bretagne, Great Britain

la Grèce, Greece
la Hongrie, Hungary
l'Inde, India
l'Irlande, Ireland
l'Italie, Italy
la Norvège, Norway
la Pologne, Poland
la Roumanie, Rumania
la Russie, Russia
la Suède, Sweden
la Suisse, Switzerland
la Turquie, Turkey
l'U.R.S.S., the Soviet Union, the U.S.S.R.

l'Afrique, Africa
l'Amérique du Nord, North America
l'Amérique du Sud, South America
l'Asie, Asia
l'Australie, Australia
l'Europe, Europe

l'Alsace, Alsace
la Bourgogne, Burgundy
la Bretagne, Brittany
la Champagne, Champagne
la Corse, Corsica
la Flandre, Flanders
la Lorraine, Lorraine
la Normandie, Normandy
la Provence, Provence

MASCULINE COUNTRIES

le Brésil, Brazil
le Canada, Canada
le Chili, Chile
le Danemark, Denmark
les États-Unis, the United States
Israël, Israel
le Japon, Japan
le Maroc, Morocco
le Mexique, Mexico
le Pakistan, Pakistan
les Pays-Bas, the Netherlands
le Pérou, Peru
le Portugal, Portugal

MOUNTAINS AND WATERWAYS

les Alpes (*f.*), the Alps
le Jura, the Jura Mountains
les Pyrénées (*f.*), the Pyrenees
les Vosges (*f.*), the Vosges Mountains
la Garonne, the Garonne River
la Loire, the Loire
la Manche, the English Channel
le Rhin, the Rhine
le Rhône, the Rhone
la Seine, the Seine
la mer Méditerranée, the Mediterranean Sea

EXERCICES

A. Compléter la phrase en français:

1. Un de mes amis, qui voyage ______ Europe, m'a envoyé un cadeau ______ Normandie.
2. Athènes est la capitale de ______.
3. Les Polonais demeurent ______ Pologne; les Danois, ______ Danemark.

4. Philadelphie est ______ l'Amérique du Nord.
5. ______ Rhône se jette dans la ______ près de Marseille.
6. L'avion a volé ______ Turquie en Israël.
7. Nous autres Américains, nous demeurons ______ Amérique.
8. Quand vos parents sont-ils revenus ______ Pérou?
9. Né ______ Genève, il a quitté ______ Suisse à l'âge de seize ans pour faire ses études ______ Grenoble, ______ France.
10. Ce paquebot vient ______ Havre.
11. La reine de (d') ______ demeure à Londres.
12. On produit des vins excellents ______ Champagne et ______ Bourgogne.
13. Nous voyageons souvent ______ l'Europe méridionale.
14. ______ Hongrie et ______ Roumanie se trouvent derrière le "rideau de fer."
15. Le Jura forme une frontière naturelle entre ______ et ______.

B. Donner l'équivalent en français:

1. Mexico, in Mexico, from Mexico
2. Brittany, in Brittany, from Brittany
3. to Spain, in beautiful Spain
4. from Italy, from the United States
5. in Bordeaux, from New Orleans
6. in Havre, from Strasbourg
7. from Australia, from modern Africa
8. the Garonne River, the Pyrenees
9. to Belgium, in the Netherlands
10. in Canada, from Japan

C. Construire des phrases selon le modèle en employant le vocabulaire donné:

Modèle: Christophe Colomb/ retourner/ Espagne/ 1493
Christophe Colomb retourna en Espagne en 1493.

1. capitale/ U.R.S.S./ être/ Moscou
2. depuis quand/ être/ ils/ Italie
3. Manche/ se trouver/ entre/ France/ Angleterre
4. je/ s'amuser/ flâner/ sur/ quais/ Seine
5. Maroc/ Algérie/ être/ pays/ Afrique du Nord
6. est-ce que/ famille Lamont/ demeurer/ maintenant/ Rouen/ ou/ Nice
7. plusieurs/ nos amis/ venir/ Irlande
8. nous/ compter/ traverser/ Norvège/ pour/ aller/ Suède
9. Jacqueline/ être/ partir/ pour/ Corse
10. Ottawa/ être/ capitale/ Canada

D. Compléter chaque phrase en donnant l'équivalent des mots entre parenthèses:

1. (in Asia)	L'Inde et le Pakistan se trouvent ______.
2. (The Loire)	______ est le plus long fleuve de France.
3. (from Lorraine)	Ces ouvriers viennent-ils ______?
4. (of Spain)	J'ai admiré la beauté ______.
5. (in the United States)	Le diplomate étranger va passer du temps ______.
6. (of Great Britain)	L'Écosse est la partie nord ______.
7. (from Portugal)	Nous arrivons ______.
8. (in New Orleans)	Il y a beaucoup de bons restaurants ______.
9. (of South America)	Je viens de lire un livre sur l'histoire ______.
10. (in Egypt)	Le canal de Suez, ______, relie la Méditerranée et la mer Rouge.
11. (of Japan)	On attendait l'arrivée de l'empereur ______.
12. (to Brazil)	Le voyage l'a amené ______.
13. (In China and Japan)	______, le riz est un aliment important.
14. (from The Netherlands)	Cette porcelaine est importée directement ______.
15. (Flanders)	______ est la principale région industrielle de la France.

E. Répondre à chaque question par une phrase complète en français:

1. Quelles montagnes se trouvent en Alsace?
2. Quelle est la capitale de la Belgique?
3. Nommez deux produits que nous importons d'Europe.
4. Dans quelle province française trouve-t-on beaucoup de monuments romains?
5. Quelles deux langues parle-t-on au Canada?
6. Dans quel continent faut-il aller pour visiter l'Argentine et le Chili?
7. Avez-vous jamais été en Autriche?
8. Quel fleuve forme une frontière entre la France et l'Allemagne?
9. Dans quelle ville a-t-on signé la Charte de l'O.N.U. (l'Organisation des Nations Unies)?
10. Quel est le sommet le plus élevé des Alpes?

11. PERSONAL OBJECT PRONOUNS

DIRECT OBJECT PRONOUNS	
me (m'), me	**nous**, us
te (t'), you (*fam.*)	**vous**, you
le (l'), him, it **la (l')**, her, it	**les**, them
se (s'),* himself, herself	**se (s')**, themselves

*For the complete set of reflexive pronouns, see Verb Lesson 8.

INDIRECT OBJECT PRONOUNS	
me (m'), (to) me	**nous**, (to) us
te (t'), (to) you (*fam.*)	**vous**, (to) you
lui, (to) him **lui**, (to) her	**leur**, (to) them
se (s'), (to) himself, (to) herself	**se (s')**, (to) themselves

a. Personal object pronouns, direct and indirect, are placed immediately before the verbs of which they are the object (except in affirmative commands).

Je ***vous*** comprends.	I understand you.
Lui a-t-il téléphoné?	Did he telephone her?
Elle ne ***se*** lève pas tard.	She does not get up late.
Vous devez ***le*** lire.	You must read it.

Note: **Voici** and **voilà** take a direct object pronoun.

Nous voici. ***La*** voilà.	Here we are. There she is.

b. In the *affirmative imperative* only, the object pronoun is placed *directly after* the verb and linked to it by a hyphen. The pronouns **me** and **te** change to **moi** and **toi** after the verb.

AFFIRMATIVE IMPERATIVE	
Aidez-***moi***.	Help me.
Dépêche-***toi***.	Hurry.
Buvez-***la***.	Drink it.
Répondons-***leur***.	Let us answer them.

NEGATIVE IMPERATIVE	
Ne ***m'***aidez pas.	Do not help me.
Ne ***te*** dépêche pas.	Don't hurry.
Ne ***la*** buvez pas.	Do not drink it.
Ne ***leur*** répondons pas.	Let's not answer them.

Note

1. The verbs **écouter** (*listen to*), **regarder** (*look at*), **chercher** (*look for*), **attendre** (*wait for*), **demander** (*ask for*), and **payer** (*pay for*) take a direct object in French.

L'écoutez-vous?	Are you listening to him?
Attendons-***les.***	Let us wait for them.

2. The verbs **répondre** (*answer*), **obéir** (*obey*), and **désobéir** (*disobey*) take an indirect object in French.

Nous ***lui*** avons répondu.	We answered her.
Ne ***leur*** désobéissez pas.	Do not disobey them.

Reminder: Past participles of verbs conjugated with **avoir** and of *reflexive* verbs agree in gender and number with the *preceding direct object* (if there is one). (See Verb Lesson 9.)

Il **les** a regardé***s.***	He looked at them.
Elles **se** sont fâché***es.***	They got angry.

THE ADVERBIAL PRONOUN *Y*

Y, used as both pronoun and adverb, always refers to things or places. It generally replaces **à** + noun, but may also replace other prepositions of position, such as **chez, dans, en, sous,** or **sur** + noun.

In English, **y** most commonly means *to it* (*them*), *in it* (*them*), *on it* (*them*), and *there* (when the place has already been mentioned). Sometimes the equivalent is not expressed in English.

Allez-vous **à la blanchisserie?** Oui, j'***y*** vais.
Are you going to the laundry? Yes, I am (going there).

Répondez **à sa carte.** Répondez-***y.***
Answer his card. Answer it.

Les allumettes sont-elles **dans la boîte?** Oui, elles ***y*** sont.
Are the matches in the box? Yes, they are (in it).

Quel temps fait-il **en France?** Il ***y*** fait doux.
How is the weather in France? It is mild there.

THE ADVERBIAL PRONOUN *EN*

En, used as both pronoun and adverb, replaces **de** + noun, and generally refers to things. It is usually translated into English by *some, any, of it* (*them*), *from there*.

En is always expressed in French, even though its equivalent may not be expressed in English. **En** must be used when the noun is omitted after a number, an adverb or noun of quantity, or an idiom requiring **de**.

Voici **des framboises.** ***En*** voulez-vous?
Here are some raspberries. Do you want some?

Elle n'***en*** a pas acheté.
She didn't buy any. (She bought none.)

N'***en*** parlons plus.
Let's not speak of it any more.

Vient-il **de la ville**? Oui, il ***en*** vient.
Does he come from the city? Yes, he does (come from there).

Je cherche un taxi. ***En*** voilà un.
I'm looking for a taxi. There's one.

Avez-vous **de la monnaie**? Oui, j'***en*** ai assez.
Have you any change? Yes, I have enough (of it).

Qui se sert **de cette cuiller**? Moi, je m'***en*** sers.
Who is using this spoon? I am.

Note

1. Like personal pronoun objects, **y** and **en** regularly precede the verb, except in the affirmative imperative, where they follow.

Ils ***y*** seront. Allons-***y***.	They will be there. Let's go there.
N'***en*** avez-vous pas? Prenez-***en***.	Don't you have any? Take some.

2. There is no agreement of the past participle with a preceding **en**.

A-t-elle reçu des lettres? Non, elle n'**en** a pas ***reçu***.	Has she received any letters? No, she hasn't.

EXERCICES

A. Copier chaque phrase en remplaçant les mots en italique par un pronom:

Exemple: Nous parlions *au médecin*. Nous lui parlions.

1. Avez-vous arrêté *la radio?*
2. Mettez *les fleurs* sur la table.

3. Voici *votre brosse à dents.*
4. Qui a donné le jouet *au bébé?*
5. Ne voulez-vous pas prendre *des raisins?*
6. Cherchez *la femme.*
7. Vont-ils souvent *au cirque?*
8. L'enfant ne voulait pas boire *le lait.*
9. J'ai mangé la moitié *de l'orange.*
10. N'écoutez-vous jamais *ce programme?*
11. Répondons *à leurs lettres.*
12. Ne montre pas la photo *à Berthe.*
13. A-t-on payé *les billets?*
14. Ont-ils attrapé plusieurs *lapins?*
15. Dis *à nos amis* que nous arriverons en retard.

B. Donner le pronom qui manque:

1. Qui étudie le russe? Les meilleurs élèves ______ étudient.
2. Étant fatiguée, elle ______ est assise sur le canapé.
3. Est-il content de ces chaussures? Oui, il ______ est très content.
4. Où sont les fourchettes? ______ voilà.
5. Je ne vais pas à la campagne aujourd'hui. Il ______ fait trop froid.
6. Ce thé vient-il de Chine? Oui, il ______ vient.
7. Dépêche-______, Maurice; nous devons partir tout de suite.
8. Où vous êtes-vous promené? Je ______ suis promené autour du lac.
9. Vous servez-vous du Guide Michelin? Oui, nous nous ______ servons.
10. Nous avez-vous reconnus? Non, je ne ______ ai pas reconnus.
11. Donnez-moi du bœuf. Combien ______ voulez-vous?
12. Si vous retrouvez mon crayon, gardez-______.
13. Seront-ils chez eux ce soir? Oui, ils ______ seront.
14. Est-ce que tu m'appelles, maman? Non, je ne ______ appelle pas.
15. Obéit-il à ses parents? Bien entendu, il ______ obéit.

DOUBLE OBJECT PRONOUNS

Double object pronouns, like single object pronouns, are placed directly before the verb, except in the affirmative imperative.

ORDER OF OBJECT PRONOUNS BEFORE THE VERB

me **te** **se** **nous** **vous**	**le (l')** **la (l')** **les**	**lui** **leur**	**y**	**en**	VERB

Ils ***me la*** vendent.	They sell it to me.
Je vais ***le lui*** montrer.	I'm going to show it to him.
Leur en avez-vous prêté?	Have you lent them any?
Nous ***les y*** avons rencontrés.	We met them there.
Il ***y en*** a plusieurs.	There are several.

Suggestion to the student: Memorize the following frequent combinations:

me le, me la, me les	*But:*
te le, te la, te les	le lui, la lui, les lui
nous le, nous la, nous les	le leur, la leur, les leur
vous le, vous la, vous les	

In the *affirmative imperative*, the object pronouns *follow* the verb and are connected to it, and to each other, by hyphens. The direct object precedes the indirect.

ORDER OF OBJECT PRONOUNS AFTER THE VERB (AFFIRMATIVE IMPERATIVE)

	DIRECT	INDIRECT		
VERB	**-le** **-la** **-les**	**-moi** **-toi** **-lui** **-nous** **-vous** **-leur**	**-y**	**-en**

Envoyez-***le-moi.***	Send it to me.
Montrons-***les-lui.***	Let's show them to him.
Attendez-***nous-y.***	Wait for us there.

Note

The combinations **moi + en** and **toi + en** become **m'en** and **t'en.**

Prêtez-***m'en.***	Lend me some.
Va-***t'en.***	Go away.

EXERCICES

C. Mettre à la forme affirmative:

1. Ne la lui vendez pas.
2. Ne nous les envoyez pas.
3. Ne t'en va pas.
4. Ne me la dites pas.
5. Ne les leur rendons pas.

D. Copier les phrases en remplaçant les mots en italique par des pronoms:

Exemple: Passez *le sucre à Henri.* Passez-le-lui.

1. L'agent a arrêté *le voleur dans la rue.*
2. Lisez *ce conte aux enfants.*
3. Je te félicite *de tes notes excellentes.*
4. La domestique nous a apporté *les haricots verts.*
5. Envoyons-lui *son cadeau.*
6. Le journaliste se souvient-il *de la question?*
7. Porte *ces livres à la bibliothèque.*
8. Voulez-vous bien me réciter *le poème?*
9. La Garonne se jette *dans l'océan Atlantique.*
10. Donnez-nous un demi-kilo *de beurre.*

E. Donner l'équivalent en français:

1. Lend it to me.
2. Do not lend them to her.
3. I will lend them to you.
4. Do not lend them any.
5. Aren't there any?
6. Lend him some.
7. I cannot lend you any.
8. Lend them to us.
9. Do not lend it to us.
10. I lent them to you (*fam.*).

F. Répondre aux questions suivantes par des phrases complètes en français. Dans les réponses, remplacer les mots en italique par des pronoms:

1. Avez-vous offert *du pain au mendiant?*
2. Le professeur enseignera-t-il *la biologie à ces étudiants?*
3. Qui a accompagné *vos amis en France?*
4. Combien *de timbres* vous a-t-il empruntés?
5. Quand allez-vous m'expliquer *le problème?*
6. Y a-t-il assez *d'argent* pour réaliser le projet?
7. Messieurs, voulez-vous que je vous écrive *ma réponse?*
8. Qui a donné *le pourboire au garçon?*
9. Depuis quand m'attendais-tu *dans la salle d'attente?*
10. Quand vous enverra-t-on *les chapeaux*, madame?

12. RELATIVE PRONOUNS

The most frequent relative pronouns are:

qui, *who, which, that:* subject of a verb; used for both persons and things

Où est l'enfant ***qui*** s'est fait mal?	Where is the child who hurt himself?
Le français est une langue ***qui*** nous plaît.	French is a language that pleases us.

que (qu'), *whom, which, that:* direct object of a verb; used for both persons and things

C'est l'actrice ***que*** nous avons vue hier soir.	She is the actress (whom) we saw last night.
Voici les phrases ***qu'***il a traduites.	Here are the sentences (that) he translated.

qui, *whom:* object of a preposition; used only for persons

Philippe est l'ami avec ***qui*** j'étudie.	Philip is the friend with whom I study.
L'homme à ***qui*** vous parliez est millionnaire.	The man to whom you were speaking is a millionaire.

lequel (*mas. sing.*)
laquelle (*fem. sing.*)
lesquels (*mas. plur.*)
lesquelles (*fem. plur.*)
} *which:* object of a preposition; used principally for things

C'est la porte par ***laquelle*** il est sorti.	That's the door through which he left.
Voici le bureau sur ***lequel*** j'ai laissé mes lunettes.	Here is the desk on which I left my glasses.

dont, *of whom, of which, whose:* used for both persons and things

Connaissez-vous le sculpteur ***dont*** tout le monde parle?	Do you know the sculptor everyone is talking about?
Donnez-lui les choses ***dont*** elle a besoin.	Give her the things she needs (of which she has need).
C'est le garçon ***dont*** la mère est malade.	He is the boy whose mother is sick.
C'est le garçon ***dont*** je connais la mère.	He is the boy whose mother I know.

où, *where, in which, on which:* may be used to replace **dans, à, sur** + a form of **lequel;** used in expressions of location

C'est la ville ***où*** (dans laquelle) je suis né.	It is the city in which I was born.

ce qui, *what* (= *that which*): subject of a verb
ce que (ce qu'), *what* (= *that which*): direct object of a verb
ce dont, *what* (= *that of which*): used with expressions taking **de**

Savez-vous ***ce qui*** s'est passé?	Do you know what happened?
Ce qu'il dit est vrai.	What he says is true.
Voici ***ce dont*** j'aurai besoin.	Here is what I will need.

Note: These forms are used after the pronoun **tout** to express *everything that, all that.*

tout ce qui est tombé	everything that fell
tout ce que vous avez dit	all you have said
tout ce dont je me sers	everything that I use

Note

1. The relative pronoun must always be expressed in French although it is frequently omitted in English.
2. Since **que** is a direct object pronoun and precedes the verb, the past participle of a compound verb agrees with **que**. (See Verb Lesson 9.)

les pays **que** j'ai ***visités***	the countries (that) I visited
la vache **qu'**il avait ***vendue***	the cow (that) he had sold

SUMMARY OF RELATIVE PRONOUNS

PRONOUN	MEANING	USE
qui	who, which, that whom	subject, for persons and things object of preposition, for persons
que (qu')	whom, which, that	object of verb, for persons and things
lequel, etc.	which	object of preposition, for things
dont	of whom, of which, whose	for persons and things
où	where, in which, on which	expressions of location
ce qui **ce que (ce qu')** **ce dont**	what (= that which) what (= that which) what (= that of which)	subject object of verb with expressions taking **de**

EXERCICES

A. Choisir la réponse convenable entre parenthèses:

1. Quelle est la chanson (qui, qu', ce qu') elle chante?
2. A qui sont les meubles anciens (dont, duquel, ce dont) vous m'avez parlé?
3. Je ne sais pas (que, ce qui, ce que) tu veux dire.
4. C'est l'architecte à (qui, lequel, que) nous avons téléphoné.
5. Voici la rue (dont, dans lequel, où) se trouve l'hôtel de ville.
6. Est-ce vous (qui, lequel, que) m'avez trompé?
7. Il fait tout (ce qui, qu', ce qu') il peut.
8. Elle a tué la mouche (laquelle, que, qui) la dérangeait.
9. Est-ce M. Legrand (à qui, de laquelle, dont) vous connaissez la femme?
10. Où est le stylo à bille avec (que, lequel, ce que) j'écrivais tout à l'heure?
11. Nous n'avons pas remarqué (ce qui, qu', ce qu') était dans la salle.
12. As-tu retrouvé la gomme (ce que, laquelle, que) tu cherchais?
13. C'est tout (dont, ce dont, ce que) je me souviens.
14. Le plombier (qui, que, dont) vous avez fait venir est arrivé.
15. Avez-vous décidé (ce que, dont, ce dont) vous aurez besoin?

B. Donner le pronom convenable pour compléter la phrase:

1. C'est le meilleur roman policier ______ j'aie jamais lu.
2. Ne croyez pas tout ______ Fernand vous dit.
3. Ils aiment le professeur ______ leur enseigne les mathématiques.
4. Le bâtiment ______ on voit le toit est le musée d'art.
5. Ils ont acheté la maison derrière ______ il y a un beau jardin.
6. Faites donc attention à ______ se passe autour de vous.
7. Voilà l'artiste ______ j'ai fait la connaissance.
8. Nous avons reçu les timbres ______ il nous a envoyés.
9. C'est moi ______ ai toussé.
10. L'élève a effacé ______ il avait écrit.
11. Seul votre médecin est qualifié pour vous prescrire les antibiotiques ______ vous avez besoin.
12. La jeune fille avec ______ tu dansais est charmante.
13. Voici l'usine ______ je travaille.
14. C'est un savant ______ le nom de famille est déjà célèbre.
15. Dis-moi ______ tu as fait!

C. Relier les deux phrases en employant un pronom relatif:

Exemples: *a.* Aimez-vous les gants? Geneviève a acheté les gants.
Aimez-vous les gants que Geneviève a achetés?

b. Voilà la maison. J'y suis née.
Voilà la maison où je suis née.

1. C'est un court-circuit. Il a causé l'accident.
2. Qu'est-ce qu'il a à cacher? Le savez-vous?
3. Montrez-nous le chef-d'œuvre. Tous les sculpteurs en parlent.
4. Voici la chambre. Nous y faison nos devoirs.
5. Armand montre un courage extraordinaire. Tout le monde admire son courage.
6. Ils ne l'ont pas vu. Qu'est-ce qui est tombé?
7. Donnez-moi un bon couteau. Je peux couper le rôti avec le couteau.
8. De quoi s'agit-il? Voulez-vous nous le dire?
9. Connais-tu cet homme? Il désire établir un motel sur la lune.
10. Mme Dubois ne peut pas ouvrir l'armoire. Elle y a laissé son manteau.
11. Je ne le comprends pas. Que cherchent-ils à accomplir?
12. Quelle est cette personne? Jules lui parlait.
13. Voilà les ouvriers. On va les féliciter.
14. Ont-ils de mauvaises notes? Ils en ont honte.
15. Je voudrais voir la plume. On a signé la Déclaration de l'Indépendance avec la plume.

D. Donner l'équivalent en français:

1. the plane that just left
2. the son of whom they are proud
3. everything that happened
4. the peasants whom we saw
5. what is possible
6. the park toward which we were walking
7. the apartment in which she lives
8. the meals she had prepared
9. the dog you're afraid of
10. the wood that is burning
11. the writer whose books I have read
12. the bridge on which people used to dance
13. all that he wanted
14. the friend with whom I dined
15. the tree under which we were seated
16. what he complains about
17. the lady who is singing
18. the vacation of which I am dreaming
19. what we ate
20. everything he uses

13. DEMONSTRATIVE ADJECTIVES AND PRONOUNS

DEMONSTRATIVE ADJECTIVES

The demonstrative adjectives are **ce, cet, cette** (*this*, *that*), and **ces** (*these*, *those*).

ce	before a masculine singular noun beginning with a consonant	***ce*** moulin	this (that) mill
cet	before a masculine singular noun beginning with a vowel or silent **h**	***cet*** appareil ***cet*** hiver	this (that) instrument this (that) winter
cette	before a feminine singular noun	***cette*** revue	this (that) magazine
ces	before all plural nouns	***ces*** moulins ***ces*** revues	this (those) mills these (those) magazines

Note

1. The demonstrative adjective must be repeated before each noun.

ce lac et ***cette*** plage	that lake and beach
ces aiguilles et ***ces*** épingles	these needles and pins

2. If it is necessary to distinguish between *this* and *that*, or between *these* and *those*, **ci** and **là** with hyphens are added to the nouns contrasted. To mean *this* or *these*, **-ci** is added; to mean *that* or *those*, **-là** is added.

cette écriture-***ci*** ou cette écriture-***là***	this handwriting or that handwriting
ces poèmes-***là*** et ces poèmes-***ci***	those poems and these poems

DEMONSTRATIVE PRONOUNS

The forms of the demonstrative pronoun **celui** are:

	MASCULINE	FEMININE
SINGULAR	**celui**	**celle**
PLURAL	**ceux**	**celles**

Celui and its forms are not used alone. They are generally used with one of the following: **de, -ci, -là, qui, que, dont.**

celui de, celle de, the one of	**ceux de, celles de,** the ones (those) of

Donnez-moi mon **billet** et ***celui de*** Gautier.	Give me my ticket and Walter's.
Il portait ses propres **livres** et ***ceux de*** sa sœur.	He was carrying his own books and his sister's (those of his sister).

celui-ci, celle-ci, this (one), the latter	**ceux-ci, celles-ci,** these, the latter
celui-là, celle-là, that (one), the former	**ceux-là, celles-là,** those, the former

Cette **dentelle**-ci est meilleure que ***celle-là.***	This lace is better than that.
Quels **bijoux** préférez-vous, ***ceux-ci*** ou ***ceux-là?***	Which jewels do you prefer, these or those?
Lamartine et **Balzac** étaient écrivains; ***celui-ci*** était romancier et ***celui-là*** poète.	Lamartine and Balzac were writers; the latter was a novelist and the former a poet.

celui qui, celle qui, the one that (subject)	**ceux qui, celles qui,** the ones (those) that
celui que, celle que, the one that (object)	**ceux que, celles que,** the ones (those) that
celui dont, celle dont, the one of which	**ceux dont, celles dont,** the ones of which

Ceux qui travaillent dur réussissent.	Those who work hard succeed.
La **maison** blanche est ***celle qu'***ils vont acheter.	The white house is the one they are going to buy.
C'est ***celui dont*** je vous ai parlé.	This is the one I spoke to you about.

EXERCICES

A. Remplacer les mots en italique par un pronom démonstratif:

1. Est-ce votre clef? Non, c'est *la clef* de mon frère.
2. Donnez-moi une douzaine de *ces œufs-là.*
3. J'admirais *l'horloge* que vous veniez d'acheter.
4. Gardez vous valises; nous aimons *les valises* que nous avons.
5. *Ce vêtement-ci* porte une étiquette spéciale.
6. *Les vins* de Bourgogne sont célèbres.
7. *L'encre* dont vous vous servez est bleue.
8. Je doute que *ces élèves-ci* étudient beaucoup.

9. *Les robes* de Caroline ne lui vont pas bien.
10. Nous ne lisons pas *ce journal-là.*

B. Traduire en français les mots en italique:

1. *These* ______ hors-d'œuvre sont délicieux.
2. Elle avait repassé mes mouchoirs et *John's* ______.
3. C'est un tigre semblable à *the one that* ______ nous avons vu dans le jardin zoologique.
4. *That man* ______ est aveugle tandis que *this one* ______ est sourd.
5. *Those who* ______ le connaissent ont une bonne opinion de lui.
6. Est-ce que la circulation de Paris est pire que *that of* ______ New York?
7. Denise et Martine sont mes cousines; *the latter* ______ est plus diligente que *the former* ______.
8. Voyez-vous cette cathédrale? C'est *the one of which* ______ nous vous avons parlé.
9. Quels patins achèteriez-vous, *these* ______ ou *those* ______?
10. Voilà deux voitures: *the baker's* ______ et la mienne.

C. Donner la forme convenable de l'adjectif ou du pronom démonstratif:

1. Cet ingénieur-ci travaille mieux que ______ -là.
2. ______ que vous avez rencontrée est notre voisine.
3. Voici vos lunettes et ______ de votre sœur.

4. ______ auteur est ______ dont vous avez entendu parler.
5. ______ croissants sont ______ que nous préférons.
6. De toutes nos plages, ______-ci est la plus belle.
7. Prenez votre chapeau et ______ de Béatrice.
8. ______ femme est ma grand-mère; ______ qui vous parlait est ma tante.
9. Est-ce que le sien écrit aussi bien que ______-ci?
10. ______ trottoir-ci est moins large que ______ des Champs-Élysées.

D. Donner l'équivalent en français:

1. this hotel or that one
2. this trip and the one we took last year
3. those mountains and these
4. that cup and the one you broke
5. your letter and the ones that are on the table
6. our address and our friends'
7. these presents or the ones I received
8. my notebooks and Michael's
9. Send me that book; it is the one I need.
10. The former are Frenchmen; the latter are Spaniards.

E. Répondre aux questions suivantes. Dans chaque réponse, employer un pronom démonstratif:

1. Est-ce que les chaussures de Mme Rochefort ou de Mme Moreau sont importées de France?
2. Je sais que ces fruits-là sont des fraises. Mais comment s'appellent ces fruits-ci?
3. Cette photo-ci n'est pas bonne. Où est la photo que Jean a prise?
4. Aimez-vous mieux le bruit du tonnerre ou le bruit de la pluie?
5. As-tu retrouvé les clefs dont tu as besoin?
6. Georges a quinze ans, et Henri a seize ans. Lequel est plus âgé, celui-ci ou celui-là?
7. Est-ce que les poèmes que vous écrivez sont meilleurs que les poèmes de Victor Hugo?
8. Savez-vous si cet ascenseur-là marche bien?
9. Quelle lumière est plus forte: la lumière qui vient du soleil ou la lumière qui vient de la lune?
10. Vous pouvez avoir une de ces deux chambres: l'une donne sur la rue, l'autre sur le lac. Laquelle préférez-vous?

14. INTERROGATIVES

Interrogatives are used to begin a question.

		who? whom? (persons)	what? (things)
a.	subject of a verb	**qui** **qui est-ce qui**	**qu'est-ce qui**
	direct object of a verb	**qui** **qui est-ce que (qu')**	**que (qu')** **qu'est-ce que (qu')**
	after a preposition	**qui**	**quoi**

Qui le fera? ***Qui est-ce qui*** le fera?	Who will do it?
Qu'est-ce qui est tombé?	What fell?
Qui cherchez-vous? ***Qui est-ce que*** vous cherchez?	Whom are you looking for?
Que cherchez-vous? ***Qu'est-ce que*** vous cherchez?	What are you looking for?
A ***qui*** pensez-vous?	Of whom are you thinking?
A ***quoi*** pensez-vous?	Of what are you thinking?

Note

1. As an interrogative pronoun, **qui** may be used for persons in all three cases: as subject of a verb, as direct object of a verb, and after a preposition.
2. The **e** of **que** is dropped before a word beginning with a vowel; the **i** of **qui** is never dropped.
3. After the direct object forms **qui** and **que**, the word order is inverted; after the long forms, the word order is regular.

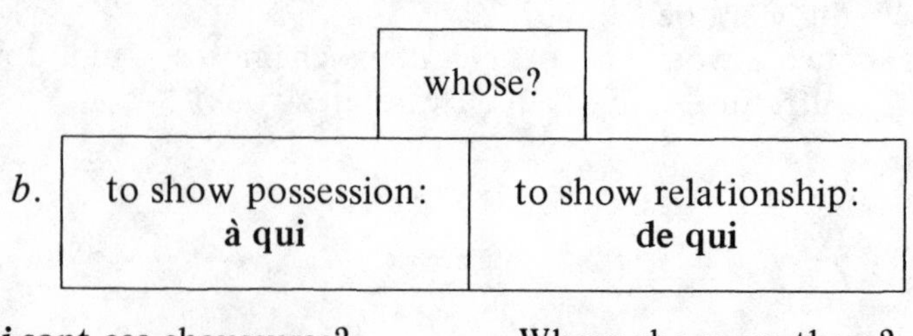

	whose?	
b.	to show possession: **à qui**	to show relationship: **de qui**

A qui sont ces chaussures?	Whose shoes are these?
De qui êtes-vous la nièce?	Whose niece are you?

c.

	which? what? (adjective)		which? which one(s)? (pronoun)	
	MAS.	FEM.	MAS.	FEM.
SINGULAR	**quel**	**quelle**	**lequel**	**laquelle**
PLURAL	**quels**	**quelles**	**lesquels**	**lesquelles**

Dans ***quelle*** **maison** demeurez-vous? — In which house do you live?
Quel est le **nom** de ce village? — What is the name of this village?
Lequel de ces **chapeaux** est le plus cher? — Which (one) of these hats is the most expensive?

Note

1. The adjective **quel** agrees with the noun it modifies. The pronoun **lequel** agrees in gender and number with the noun it replaces.
2. The only verb that may separate **quel** from its noun is **être**.

   Quelle ***était*** la question? — What was the question?

3. In exclamations, **quel** means *what a!* or *what!*

   Quelle machine! — What a machine!
   Quelles figues délicieuses! — What delicious figs!

4. When **à** and **de** are used before forms of **lequel**, the usual contractions take place.

	MAS.	FEM.	MAS.	FEM.
SINGULAR	**auquel**	**à laquelle**	**duquel**	**de laquelle**
PLURAL	**auxquels**	**auxquelles**	**desquels**	**desquelles**

Auquel de tes amis as-tu écrit? — To which of your friends did you write?

De quels enfants est-il fier? — Of which children is he proud?
Desquels est-il fier? — Of which ones is he proud?

d. Other interrogative expressions:

Qu'est-ce que c'est?	What is it?
Qu'est-ce que c'est que cela?	What is that?
Qu'est-ce que c'est qu'une roue?	What is a wheel?

EXERCICES

A. Choisir les mots entre parenthèses qui complètent correctement les phrases:

1. (Qui, Qui est-ce que) tu as rencontré à la soirée?
2. (Quoi, Quelle) est la température du corps humain?
3. (Qu'est-ce qui, Qu'est-ce qu') est tombé tout à l'heure?
4. (A qui, De qui) est ce marteau que vous tenez à la main?
5. (A quelles, Auxquelles) de vos amies avez-vous écrit?
6. Contre (qui, qui est-ce que) s'est-elle fâchée?
7. (Qui est-ce qui, Qui est-ce que) nous aidera à éteindre le feu?
8. Par (quoi, que) peut-on remplacer le verre cassé?
9. (A qui, De qui) M. Gilles est-il l'oncle?
10. Avec (laquelle, quelle) des trois sœurs va-t-il se marier?
11. (Que, Qu'est-ce que) fabrique-t-on dans cette usine?
12. (Quelles, Lesquelles) mines y a-t-il dans le nord de la France?
13. (Qu'est-ce qui, Qu'est-ce qu') on va servir avec le café?
14. A (qui, qui est-ce qui) posez-vous ces questions difficiles?
15. (Qu'est-ce que, Qu'est-ce qui) c'est qu'un orage?

B. Compléter les phrases en donnant l'équivalent des mots en italique:

1. *which one*	Derrière ______ des soldats marchiez-vous?
2. *What*	______ cette terre pauvre produit?
3. *What a*	______ beau champ de blé!
4. *Whose*	______ sont-ils les enfants?
5. *what*	De ______ vous occupez-vous?
6. *What*	______ a-t-elle oublié?
7. *Which ones*	______ sont les meilleures?
8. *What*	______ vous amuse?
9. *whom*	Chez ______ vont-ils se réunir?
10. *What*	______ sont ses raisons pour être revenue?

C. Donner l'adjectif ou le pronom interrogatif convenable:

1. ______ est-ce qui a servi le repas? Leur domestique l'a servi.
2. ______ provinces ont-ils visitées?
3. ______ cachiez-vous? Je cachais une lettre personnelle.
4. ______ c'est? C'est un haut-parleur.
5. Avec ______ l'avez-vous fait? Nous l'avons fait avec une brosse.

6. ______ est cette belle soie? Elle est à moi.
7. ______ de ces deux couteaux as-tu besoin?
8. ______ est arrivé? Rien.
9. ______ est son métier? Il est coiffeur.
10. ______ il a allumé? Il a allumé la lampe.

D. Donner la question pour chacune des réponses suivantes en remplaçant l'expression en italique par un pronom ou un adjectif interrogatif:

Exemple: *Le mécanicien* répare la voiture.
Qui répare la voiture?

1. *Le bruit de l'hélicoptère* a réveillé les enfants.
2. Cet idéaliste rêve du *bonheur de l'humanité.*
3. Le professeur de musique accompagnait *son élève* au piano.
4. Le musée *du Louvre*, à Paris, est un des plus beaux du monde.
5. Le petit Denis a déchiré *son pantalon.*
6. Ils s'approchaient *du plus haut* des sommets des Alpes.
7. *Robinson* a vécu longtemps dans une île déserte.
8. C'est *une machine électronique*.
9. Cette belle motocyclette est à *mon ami Gilbert*.
10. *La deuxième* de ces histoires est la plus amusante.
11. Le matin, je bois *un jus de fruit.*
12. Les acrobates causaient avec *le clown.*
13. *Le fer* est un bon conducteur de l'électricité.
14. Le gouverneur désirait obtenir un niveau de vie décent pour *les pauvres.*
15. Les touristes ont donné *un bon pourboire* au chauffeur de l'autocar.

E. Donner l'équivalent en français:

1. Whom did he blame?
2. What is burning?
3. Which birds were singing?
4. Whose brother are you?
5. To which of the men did you speak?
6. Of which ones did you speak?
7. What is that?
8. Who is going to accompany me?
9. Of what is she afraid?
10. Which one of the ties did he choose?
11. What are they looking at?
12. Whose curtains are these?
13. Which is the page?
14. With whom were you chatting?
15. What is war?

15. STRESS PRONOUNS

moi, I, me	**nous,** we, us
toi, you (*fam.*)	**vous,** you
lui, he, him	**eux,** they, them (*m.*)
elle, she, her	**elles,** they, them (*f.*)

The stress pronouns are used:

a. After a preposition:

vers ***moi***, toward me
chez ***elle***, at her house
après ***vous***, after you
sans ***eux***, without them

b. When the pronoun has no verb expressed:

Qui parle portugais? ***Moi.***	Who speaks Portuguese? I (do).
Qui a-t-on blâmé? ***Nous.***	Whom did they blame? Us.
Je gagne plus d'argent que ***toi.***	I earn more money than you.

c. In a compound subject or object:

Vous* et *moi, nous partirons ensemble.	You and I will leave together.
Je vous ai vus, ***toi* et *elle.***	I saw you and her.
***Eux* et leurs enfants** sont heureux.	They and their children are happy.

Note: Stress pronouns of different persons are usually summarized by the pronouns **nous** and **vous**.

d. For emphasis:

Moi, je gagne; ***toi***, tu perds.	I win; you lose.
Cela leur fera plaisir, à ***elles.***	That will please them.
Lui seul peut le faire.	He alone can do it.

e. After **ce + être**:

Qui est-ce? **C'est *elle.***	Who is it? It is she.
Ce n'**est** pas ***moi*** qui l'ait fait.	I'm not the one who did it.
Ce sont *eux* (***elles***).	They are the ones. (It is they.)
Est-ce *vous?* **Est-ce *eux?***	Are you the one? Are they the ones?

Note: The plural form **ce sont** is used only with **eux** and **elles.** However, the interrogative form is always **est-ce.**

f. With **-même (-mêmes)** to express the English *-self* (*-selves*):

Jean l'a vu ***lui-même.***	John saw it himself.
Nous le ferons ***nous-mêmes.***	We shall do it ourselves.

Note

Some French verbs take **à** with a stress pronoun rather than an indirect object. Among them are **penser à** (*to think of*), **songer à** (*to think of*), and **être à** (*to belong to*), and reflexive expressions taking **à**, such as **se fier à** (*to trust*).

Je ***pensais à*** **elle.**	I was thinking of her.
Ce colis ***est à*** **moi.**	That package is mine.
Ils ***se fient à*** **nous.**	They trust us.

EXERCICES

A. Traduire en français les mots en italique:

1. *She* aussi aime les fleurs.
2. *He* reste ici; *I*, je m'en vais.
3. Je ne connais que *him*.
4. Qui a-t-on choisi? Pas *me*.
5. Tant mieux pour *her!*
6. Je l'ai goûté *myself.*
7. Votre frère parle comme *you.*
8. Nous ne voulons pas leur faire peur, à *them.*
9. Que pense-t-elle de *us?*
10. *You*, tu parles trop!

B. Donner le pronom convenable:

1. Te moques-tu de moi? Mais non, je ne me moque pas de ______.
2. C'est ______ qui avons téléphoné à la police.
3. Ils l'ont fait ______-mêmes.
4. ______, je le sais; et toi?
5. Est-ce que Catherine vous a aidé? Oui, grâce à ______, j'ai beaucoup accompli.
6. S'est-elle présentée à l'ambassadeur? Je crois qu'elle s'est présentée à ______.
7. Ce sont ______ que j'ai vues.
8. Virginie et ______, nous sommes parties ensemble.
9. Est-ce ______ qui aimez à dessiner?
10. Si André décide de ne pas y assister, tu peux y aller au lieu de ______.

C. Donner l'équivalent en français:

1. The umbrella belongs to her.
2. They play but he works.
3. Were you thinking of us?
4. He will finish it himself.

5. They are not so pleasant as you.
6. She and I have already eaten.
7. Have you heard of him?
8. *I* do not lie.
9. Is she the one?
10. As for me, I enjoyed myself.

D. Répondre à chaque question par une phrase complète en français. Employer un pronom emphatique dans chaque réponse:

1. As-tu envie de chanter avec moi?
2. Est-ce Anne qui est entrée?
3. Sont-ils allés en Europe sans leur fils?
4. Vous fiez-vous à moi, monsieur?
5. Êtes-vous aussi jeunes que ces petites filles?
6. Chez qui vont-ils passer la semaine?
7. Est-ce vous, Gilbert?
8. Demeurent-ils près de leurs parents?
9. Est-ce que la concierge vous a salués, toi et ton père?
10. Pouviez-vous le soigner vous-mêmes?
11. Vous vous souvenez de moi, monsieur?
12. Est-ce que Mme Renaud est partie avant ou après son mari?
13. Qu'est-ce que tu vas faire, toi, pendant que je serai en ville?
14. Tout le monde est d'accord avec ces femmes?
15. Est-ce que le nouveau directeur nous aurait reconnus, Alain et moi?

La cueillette des fleurs

A cause du soleil et de la douceur de climat, des fleurs de toutes sortes poussent sur la Côte d'Azur. Des quantités de ces fleurs sont envoyées aux usines de Grasse, où l'on extrait l'essence de parfum contenue dans les pétales.

16. PRONOUNS *CECI, CELA, CE*

CECI, CELA

The demonstrative pronouns **ceci** and **cela** refer to things indicated but not named.

ceci, this

Donnez-lui ***ceci*** de ma part.	Give him this for me.
Qui a fait ***ceci?***	Who did this?

cela (ça), that

Cela **(*Ça*)** me fera plaisir.	That will please me.
Qu'est-ce que c'est que ***cela*** **(*ça*)**?	What is that?

Note: The form **ça** often replaces **cela** in conversation.

CE

The pronoun **ce (c')**, *it, he, she, this, that, they, these, those,* is used only with the verb **être**. **Ce** replaces **il, elle, ils,** and **elles** in the following cases:

a. Before a *modified noun:*

C'est un mouton.	It is a sheep.
C'est une affaire grave.	That's a serious matter.
Ce sont de vrais amis.	They are real friends.

But *unmodified:*

Il est pompier.	He is a fireman.

b. Before a *proper noun:*

Qui m'appelle? ***C'est Jeanne.***	Who is calling me? It is Joan.
Quelle est la capitale de l'Angleterre? ***C'est Londres.***	What is the capital of England? It is London.

c. Before a *pronoun:*

Je doute que ***ce soit lui.***	I doubt that it is he.
Est-ce vous qui avez ri?	Are you the one who laughed?
Ce sont les nôtres.	They (These, Those) are ours.
C'était celle de sa mère.	It was his mother's.

d. Before a *superlative:*

C'est la plus jeune de la famille.	She is the youngest in the family.
C'est le moindre de mes soucis.	That's the least of my worries.

e. In *dates:*

C'est aujourd'hui jeudi.	Today is Thursday.
Ce sera demain le deux mai.	Tomorrow will be May 2nd.

Note: In expressions denoting the hour of the day, **il** is used.

Il est trois heures.	It is three o'clock.

f. Before a masculine singular *adjective* to refer to an *idea* or *action* previously mentioned. In this case, the English equivalent of **ce** is *it* or *that.* However, in referring to a preceding noun, **il** and **elle** are used.

Roger comprend bien le français. ***C'est évident.***	Roger understands French well. That's obvious.
Puis-je vous aider? ***C'est inutile.***	May I help you? It's useless.

But:

Regardez cette fleur. **Elle** est parfaite.	Look at that flower. It is perfect.

g. Before an *adjective + à + passive infinitive.* (See Verb Lesson 13.)

C'est bon à savoir.	That's good to know.
C'est impossible à faire.	That's impossible to do.

Note: Impersonal **il** (= *it*) is used with **être** and an adjective before **de** + infinitive (see Verb Lesson 13) and before a clause beginning with **que**.

Il est impossible de faire cela.	It is impossible to do that.
Il est impossible que je le fasse.	It is impossible for me to do it.

EXERCICES

A. Donner le pronom convenable **(ce, c', il, elle, ils, elles):**

1. ______ est le musée d'histoire naturelle.
2. ______ sont revenues tard.
3. ______ est lui qui le fera.
4. ______ est écrivain.
5. ______ sont des climats froids.
6. ______ est Henri.
7. ______ n'était pas sa faute.
8. ______ est probable qu'elle m'a reconnu.
9. ______ est du sable blanc.
10. Est-______ une machine à laver?
11. Connaissez-vous Albert? ______ est très timide.
12. ______ est celui de l'avocat.
13. ______ sont les meilleurs du monde.
14. ______ est utile de savoir nager.
15. ______ était la marine française.
16. ______ sont toujours heureuses.

17. L'État, ______ est moi.
18. ______ est cela.
19. La paix est précieuse. Oui, ______ est précieuse.
20. ______ est le Rhône.
21. ______ sera demain vendredi.
22. Tout le monde aime le beau temps. ______ est vrai.
23. ______ était M. Sorel.
24. De quelle couleur sont les arbres? ______ sont verts.
25. ______ est le dos du livre.
26. ______ est neuf heures et demie.
27. ______ est le plus intelligent de la classe.
28. Quel est ce oiseau? ______ est un aigle.
29. Où sont vos fils à présent? ______ sont en Europe.
30. ______ est un projecteur de cinéma sonore.

B. Compléter les phrases en français:

1. (that) Partira-t-il malgré ______?
2. (It) ______ n'est pas une méthode nouvelle.
3. (They) ______ sont en guerre.
4. (They) ______ sont des bateaux à moteur.
5. (it) Est-______ un aliment qui donne des forces?
6. (This) ______ vous donnera la même impression.
7. (These) ______ sont les miens.
8. (She) ______ est actrice.
9. (She) ______ est la seule qui reçoive tant de lettres.
10. (It) ______ est mon tour.
11. (that) Qu'est-ce que ______ prouve?
12. (He) ______ est un savant illustre.
13. (they) Achetez ces roses; ______ sont très jolies.
14. (That) ______ n'est pas de la science-fiction.
15. (this) Regardez ______.

16. (It) ______ est Chamonix.
17. (They) A qui sont ces gants? ______ ne sont pas à moi.
18. (This) ______ est la plus difficile des questions.
19. (It) ______ est la fête de maman.
20. (Those) ______ sont les résultats de plusieurs années de recherches.

C. Donner l'équivalent en français:

1. She is my grandmother.
2. Who gave you this?
3. He is a sculptor.
4. He is a well-known sculptor.
5. Today is June 10th.
6. Those are beautiful leaves.
7. He came back? That's interesting!
8. Do you prefer this or that?
9. It is easy to read that.
10. That is easy to read.

D. Répondre aux questions suivantes en employant le vocabulaire indiqué. Commencer chaque réponse par une des expressions suivantes: *il est*, *ils sont*, *elle est*, *elles sont*, *c'est*, *ce sont:*

Exemple: M. Lefort est mal habillé? (bien)
Non, il est bien habillé.

1. Quelle est cette fleur? (violette)
2. Est-ce que l'air de "La Marseillaise" est beau? (très)
3. Qu'est-ce qu'elle bat? (des œufs)
4. Où sont les autres œufs? (dans le réfrigérateur)
5. Va-t-il pleuvoir cet après-midi? (possible)
6. Est-ce que Mme Duval entend bien? (un peu sourde)
7. Qu'est-ce qui tourne autour de la terre? (lune)
8. Ces étudiantes sont faibles en mathématiques? (fortes)
9. Quel est le métier de cet homme? (coiffeur)
10. Qu'est-ce que tu manges? (une glace à la vanille)
11. Ces patins appartiennent à Pierre? (les nôtres)
12. Tu peux l'accomplir? (impossible que)
13. Ce gratte-ciel est très haut, n'est-ce pas? (le plus haut de la ville)
14. Ces langues sont faciles à comprendre? (très)
15. Qui frappe à la porte, Léon? (nos voisins)
16. Qu'est-ce qu'on joue ce soir au théâtre? (pièce de Molière)
17. Sommes-nous en retard? (midi précis)
18. Quelles sont ces montagnes? (Pyrénées)
19. Cette voiture est bien construite? (construite pour durer)
20. Est-ce que Paulette est la sœur de Jacques? (de Bernard)

17. NEGATIVES

ne . . . pas, not	**ne . . . rien**, nothing
ne . . . pas du tout, not at all	**ne . . . personne**, no one, nobody
ne . . . point, not, not at all	**ne . . . ni . . . ni**, neither . . . nor
ne . . . jamais, never	**ne . . . que**, only
ne . . . plus, no more, no longer	**ne . . . aucun (aucune)**, no, none
ne . . . guère, hardly, scarcely	**ne . . . nul (nulle)**, no, none

a. In simple tenses, **ne** precedes the verb and pronoun objects; the second part of the negative follows the verb (or the subject pronoun in interrogative word order).

Son cœur ***ne*** battait ***plus.***	His heart was no longer beating.
Nous ***ne*** les admirons ***pas du tout.***	We don't admire them at all.
Ne vous faut-il ***qu'***une heure?	Do you need only an hour?

b. In compound tenses, the second part of most negatives precedes the past participle.

Je ***n'***aurais ***point*** passé mon temps à dormir.	I would not have spent my time sleeping.
Pourquoi Charles ***n'***a-t-il ***guère*** étudié?	Why has Charles scarcely studied?
Malgré sa joie, elle ***n'***avait ***rien*** dit.	In spite of her joy, she had said nothing.

c. However:

(1) **Personne** follows the past participle.

Elle ***n'***a jamais trompé ***personne.***	She has never deceived anyone.
Ils ***n'***en ont parlé à ***personne.***	They spoke to no one about it.

(2) **Que** precedes the word or words stressed, as does the word *only* in English.

Il ***n'***a acheté ***que*** des petits pains.	He bought only rolls.
Elle ***ne*** m'avait téléphoné ***que*** deux fois.	She had telephoned me only twice.

(3) Each part of **ni . . . ni** precedes the word or words stressed.

L'eau ***n'***était ***ni*** chaude ***ni*** froide.	The water was neither hot nor cold.
Je ***n'***ai ***ni*** vu le film ***ni*** lu le roman.	I've neither seen the film nor read the novel.

(4) **Aucun** and **nul** precede the nouns they modify.

Cela ***ne*** posera ***aucun*** problème.	That will pose no problem.
Nul homme ***ne*** sait le faire.	No man can do it.
Il ***ne*** pouvait le trouver ***nulle*** part.	He couldn't find it anywhere.

(5) Both parts of the negative generally precede the infinitive.

Il s'était arrêté pour ***ne pas*** tomber.	He had stopped in order not to fall.
Il vaut mieux ***ne rien*** dire.	It is better to say nothing.

d. **Rien** and **personne** may be used as subjects of the verb. **Ne** remains in its usual place, before the verb.

Rien n'est arrivé.	Nothing happened.
Personne ne savait prononcer le mot.	No one knew how to pronounce the word.

e. **Ne** is used only with a verb, but the second part of a negative may be used alone, without a verb.

Ils ***n'***y sont ***pas*** restés. Pourquoi ***pas?***	They didn't stay. Why not?
Qu'a-t-elle répondu? ***Rien du tout.***	What did she answer? Nothing at all.
Plus d'argent.	No more money.
Qui mérite le prix? ***Ni*** lui ***ni*** elle.	Who deserves the prize? Neither he nor she.

f. **Jamais** with a verb but without **ne** means *ever.*

Avez-vous ***jamais*** traversé la Manche?	Have you ever crossed the English Channel?

Jamais with a verb and **ne** means *never.* **Jamais** used without a verb also means *never.*

Non, je ***ne*** l'ai ***jamais*** traversée. ***Jamais?***	No, I have never crossed it. Never?

g. **Ne** is sometimes used without **pas** with the verbs **cesser, oser, pouvoir,** and **savoir.** In this case, the verb is generally followed by an infinitive.

Elles ***ne cessent*** de bavarder.	They don't stop chattering.
Nous ***n'osons*** le lui dire.	We don't dare tell him.
Je ***ne puis*** vous comprendre.	I cannot understand you.
Il ***ne sait*** que faire.	He doesn't know what to do.

Note

1. The negative **ne . . . point,** although stronger than **ne . . . pas,** is comparatively infrequent.
2. **Ne . . . nul** is generally restricted to literary writing.
3. **Si** (*yes*) is used to contradict a negative statement or question.

Vous n'avez pas fini le travail.	You haven't finished the work.
Si, je l'ai fini.	Yes, I have.
Ne joue-t-elle pas du piano?	Doesn't she play the piano?
Mais ***si!***	Why, yes!

4. The pronoun **personne** is masculine; the noun **personne** is feminine.

Personne n'est ***venu.***	No one came.
Une seule personne est ***venue.***	Only one person came.

5. The negative expression **ni . . . non plus** (*nor . . . either, neither*) may be used with a noun or stressed pronoun.

Jacques ne fume pas. ***Ni Raoul non plus.***	James doesn't smoke. Neither does Ralph.
Elle n'a pas faim. ***Ni moi non plus.***	She isn't hungry. Neither am I.

EXERCICES

A. Mettre la phrase à la forme négative en employant les mots entre parenthèses:

1.	(ne . . . pas)	Seriez-vous revenus?
2.	(ne . . . rien)	J'ai oublié.
3.	(ne . . . plus)	Pensez-y.
4.	(ne . . . jamais)	Avait-elle dansé?
5.	(ne . . . personne)	Il a attendu.
6.	(ne . . . aucun)	Elle en a vu.
7.	(ne . . . que)	Ils nous ont fait visite une fois.
8.	(ne . . . ni . . . ni)	Il peut entendre et voir.
9.	(ne . . . guère)	Nous l'avons reconnu.
10.	(ne . . . point)	La jeune fille a rougi.

B. Donner l'équivalent en anglais:

1. Il n'en aurait jamais rien dit.
2. Moi, je ne nage pas du tout.

3. Personne ne s'en doute. Personne?
4. Nous avons décidé de ne plus les attendre.
5. Aucune de ces choses ne m'appartient.
6. Il ne réussit à rien, même pas à écrire lisiblement.
7. Il n'y avait plus rien sur la table.
8. Elle ne les a guère remarqués. Ni moi non plus.
9. Avez-vous jamais mangé des escargots? Jamais.
10. Nul homme n'est prophète chez lui.
11. On ne peut rien refuser à une jolie femme.
12. Le ciel ne tombera sur la tête de personne.
13. Ils n'osent vous dire la vérité.
14. J'ai fait semblant de ne point comprendre.
15. Elle n'avait jamais dérangé personne, ni sa mère, ni son père, ni aucun autre membre de sa famille.

C. Remplacer chaque tiret en employant une fois un des mots indiqués à droit:

1. Mme Lagrange ne va ______ part sans ses enfants.
2. Le détective n'a ______ découvert d'important dans la salle.
3. ______ n'aime l'injustice.
4. Ce savant ne s'intéresse pas aux choses matérielles. Ni sa femme non ______.
5. Eugène nous a promis de ______ aller trop vite sur sa moto.
6. Dans cet hôtel, ______ détail de confort n'a été oublié.
7. Si le poète décidait de nous réciter ses vers, je ne (n') ______ l'interrompre.
8. —Vous n'avez pas changé votre façon de vivre? —Mais ______, j'ai dû la changer.
9. Est-ce que la machine remplacera ______ les hommes?
10. Pendant le dîner, il n'a ouvert la bouche ______ pour manger.

aucun
aucune
devrais
guère
jamais
ne pas
ne rien
non
nulle
oserais
pas
personne
plus
que
rien
si
voudrais

D. Répondre négativement à chaque question par une phrase complète en français:

1. Qui a-t-elle invité à dîner?
2. Quand neige-t-il en Algérie?
3. Savez-vous que faire?
4. Y a-t-il du sel dans ce potage?
5. Quel livre a-t-il perdu?
6. Qu'est-ce qui a changé ici?
7. Vous êtes-vous jamais promené(e) dans le Bois de Vincennes?

8. Qui préfère le fromage à la viande?
9. Laquelle de ces robes lui va bien?
10. Qu'a-t-il caché?

E. Compléter les phrases en donnant l'équivalent des mots en italique:

1. *Not at all.*	Fumez-vous? ______
2. *No one fell*	______ sur la glace.
3. *not to run*	Je préfère ______.
4. *lasted only*	La scène ______ dix minutes.
5. *have no*	Je ______ intention d'y aller.
6. *doesn't stop*	Il semble qu'il ______ de se plaindre.
7. *Yes*	—N'obéit-elle pas à sa mère? —______, elle lui obéit.
8. *Neither he nor she*	______ est très sage.
9. *No more*	______ café, madame. Voulez-vous de thé?
10. *Nor Helen either.*	Yvette n'a pas peur des souris. ______

Le Corbusier

Le Corbusier, dont le vrai nom est Édouard Jeanneret, est Suisse d'origine mais Français d'adoption. Le plus illustre des architectes français d'aujourd'hui, il a connu un grand succès en France et au-delà des frontières.

18. INDEFINITES

Indefinites may be adjectives, pronouns, or both. A number of them have already been studied in previous grammar lessons. Some, however, need additional clarification. They are:

a. **aucun, aucune** / **aucuns, aucunes** } any, no, none

Aucun may be used without **ne**. It is sometimes used with a noun for stress.

Avez-vous de l'argent? ***Aucun.***	Have you any money? None.
Il réussira, sans ***aucun*** doute.	He will succeed, without any doubt.

b. **autre**, other

un autre, une autre, another (= a different)
encore un, encore une, another (= an additional)

Donnez-moi ***un autre*** verre; celui-ci est sale.	Give me another glass; this one is dirty.
Donnez-nous ***encore un*** verre; nous sommes trois.	Give us another glass; there are three of us.

l'un(e) l'autre, each other (of two)
les un(e)s les autres, one another (of more than two)

These expressions are used to show reciprocal action, especially with reflexive verbs.

Elles ne se parlent pas ***l'une*** à ***l'autre.***	They don't speak to each other.
Ils s'aidaient ***les uns les autres***.	They used to help one another.

Autres may be added to **nous** and **vous** as emphasis to distinguish one group from another.

Nous autres Américains . . . , We Americans . . .
Vous autres avocats . . . , You lawyers . . .

c. **chaque,** each, every (adjective)
chacun, chacune, each, each one, everyone (pronoun)

These indefinites, used only in the singular, stress the individual.

Chaque ouvrier a sa spécialité.	Each (Every) worker has his specialty.
Chacun des ouvriers a sa spécialité.	Each one (Every one) of the workers has his specialty.

d. **on,** we, you, they, people, one

The subject pronoun **on** refers to an indefinite person or persons and always takes a third person singular verb. It has several possible equivalents in English. The active construction with **on** is often used in French where the English uses the passive. (See Verb Lesson 15.)

On prépare les repas dans la cuisine.	We prepare meals / You prepare meals / They prepare meals / People prepare meals / One prepares meals / Meals are prepared } in the kitchen.

After certain monosyllables ending in a pronounced vowel sound, such as **et, ou, où,** and **si,** the form **l'on** may be used for the sake of pronunciation.

la salle où ***l'on*** danse	the room in which we dance
si ***l'on*** tire la corde	if you pull the cord

e. **quelque,** some
quelques (*pl.*), some, a few } adjective

quelqu'un, quelqu'une, someone, somebody, anyone
quelques-uns, quelques-unes, some, any, a few } pronoun

Il y est resté pendant ***quelque*** temps.	He stayed there for some time.
Je vais prendre ***quelques*** billets.	I'm going to buy a few tickets.
Quelqu'un le lui a dit.	Someone told her so.
Ils m'ont prêté ***quelques-uns*** de leurs livres.	They lent me a few of their books.

f. **quelque chose** (*m.*), something, anything
rien (*m.*), nothing

These pronouns are followed by **de** before an adjective.

Avez-vous remarqué ***quelque chose de*** mystérieux?	Did you notice anything mysterious?
Il n'a ***rien*** dit ***d'***intéressant.	He said nothing interesting.

g. **soi,** oneself

This is the disjunctive pronoun for indefinite subjects such as **chacun, on,** and **personne.**

Chacun pour ***soi.***	Everyone for himself.
On ne doit pas penser toujours à ***soi.***	One should not always think of oneself.

h. **tout**, all, everything
tous (*pl.*), all, everyone

In addition to being adjectives, **tout** and **tous** are used as pronouns.

Tout est bien qui finit bien.	All's well that ends well.
Ils partageront ***tout***.	They will share everything.
Tous étaient présents.	Everyone was present. (They were all present.)

EXERCICES

A. Employer le pronom **on** pour compléter la phrase en français:

1. Comment *do you say* cela en russe?
2. A l'école *we used to work* dur.
3. *They eat* bien dans ce restaurant.
4. Savez-vous où *one can buy* de tels tricots?
5. *Is Spanish spoken* au Chili?
6. *They would have broken* la glace.
7. *People are never* satisfait.
8. *The door will be closed* avant la cérémonie.
9. *If you avoid* le danger, on y arrivera sain et sauf.
10. *The thief was caught* devant la banque.

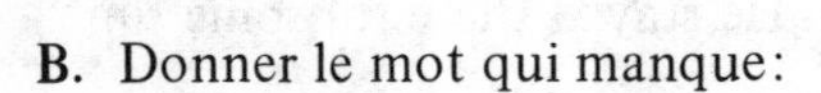

B. Donner le mot qui manque:

1. Vous m'avez donné quatre timbres, mais j'en ai besoin de cinq. Donnez-m'en ______ un.
2. Nous nous écrivions l'un à ______.
3. Pendant que vous étudierez, nous ______ garçons, nous irons à la pêche.
4. Il se tient au courant de ______ ce qui se passe dans le monde.
5. Si cela ne vous plaît pas, prenez ______ chose d'autre.
6. Dans une boulangerie, ______ vend le pain.
7. Ces souliers ne me vont pas. Montrez-m'en une ______ paire.
8. Qu'est-ce qu'il y a? Rien ______ grave.
9. Tout le monde a une bonne opinion de lui. Certainement, il jouit de l'estime de ______.
10. Quand on est modeste, on parle rarement de ______.

C. Compléter chaque phrase en donnant l'équivalent des mots entre parenthèses:

1. (a few)	Nous comptons passer ______ semaines à Grenoble.
2. (any)	Elle a pleuré sans ______ raison.
3. (one another)	Les trois soldats blessés se soignaient ______.
4. (Each)	______ province a ses coutumes.

5. (You) ______ médecins, vous avez beaucoup à contribuer à l'humanité.
6. (all) La pollution de l'air est un problème pour ______.
7. (some) Je vais corriger ______ de mes fautes.
8. (Each one) ______ travaille selon ses capacités.
9. (None) Combien de frères avez-vous? ______.
10. (You) ______ peut tromper quelqu'un tout le temps; ______ peut tromper tout le monde un certain temps; mais ______ ne peut tromper tout le monde tout le temps.

STRUCTURE REVIEW QUIZZES

A

Donner le mot qui manque:

1. ______ musée voudriez-vous visiter cet après-midi?
2. Il a demeuré deux ans ______ Bruxelles.
3. J'ai lu le roman ______ vous avez parlé.
4. Ils ______ ont choisi cinq.
5. Regardez toutes ces lettres ______ je dois répondre.
6. ______ qui êtes-vous le fils?
7. ______ sera demain mercredi.
8. ______ de ces cahiers ne lui appartient.
9. Nous prendrons l'avion d'aujourd'hui ______ huit.
10. Ce n'est pas ______ qui ai frappé à la porte.

B

Compléter chaque phrase en donnant l'équivalent des mots entre parenthèses:

1. (her best) Elle aurait mis ______ robe s'il avait fait beau.
2. (two hundred) Il y a ______ pages dans le livre.
3. (What a beautiful) ______ animal!
4. (Snow) ______ est blanche.
5. (ask him for it) Comptez-vous ______?
6. (woolen gloves) Quand je fais du ski, je porte toujours ______.
7. (everything that) Il fait ______ il peut.
8. (them) On ne peut rien faire pour ______.
9. (those) Ces rideaux-ci sont moins longs que ______.
10. (a few) Donnez-moi ______ de ces poires.

C

Choisir la réponse correcte:

1. Avez-vous jamais écrit (des, de) poèmes?
2. (Il, C') est étudiant.

3. Elle va partir pour Madrid (samedi, le samedi).
4. De (que, quoi) s'agit-il?
5. J'en ai fini moins (que, de) quinze.
6. Ces légumes coûtent deux francs (le, par) kilo.
7. (Qui, Qui est-ce qu') elle a rencontré?
8. Ils viennent (de, du) Danemark.
9. (Quelle, Laquelle) de ces cravates suggérez-vous que je porte aujourd'hui?
10. Ces roses sentent (bon, bonnes).

D

Choisir la réponse qu'on *ne peut pas* substituer pour l'expression en italique:

1. Qui connaît bien ces montagnes? *Notre guide.*

   (*a*) Pas nous. (*b*) Aucun. (*c*) C'est moi. (*d*) Lui.

2. Je ne sais pas pourquoi ils *nous* l'ont offert.

   (*a*) lui (*b*) me (*c*) vous (*d*) te

3. Ma famille vient de passer du temps au *Canada.*

   (*a*) Mexique (*b*) Japon (*c*) Havre (*d*) Suisse

4. Tout à coup, nous avons vu *beaucoup* d'aviateurs qui descendaient en parachute.

   (*a*) une dizaine (*b*) une paire (*c*) bien (*d*) un grand nombre

5. *Quel chemin* a-t-il suivi?

   (*a*) Qu' (*b*) Qui (*c*) Qu'est-ce qu' (*d*) Lequel

6. C'était *le bruit de la mer.*

   (*a*) facile de faire cela
   (*b*) celle de Germaine
   (*c*) le moindre de mes soucis
   (*d*) impossible à lever

7. N'avez-vous pas *déjà* exprimé votre opinion?

   (*a*) souvent (*b*) encore (*c*) toujours (*d*) hier

8. Antoine *ne cesse de* profiter de sa situation.

   (*a*) n'ose (*b*) ne voulait (*c*) ne saurait (*d*) ne pouvait

9. Tous les touristes tenaient à voir l'*église* célèbre.

   (*a*) horloge (*b*) hôtel (*c*) héros (*d*) hôpital

10. Samedi dernier, nous avons eu l'occasion de féliciter *Mlle Lambert.*

    (*a*) docteur Léger
    (*b*) ses deux grands-pères
    (*c*) notre amie
    (*d*) le petit René

E

Compléter chaque phrase en donnant l'équivalent des mots entre parenthèses:

1.	(No one)	______ le reconnaîtrait.
2.	(milder than)	Le printemps est ______ l'hiver.
3.	(President Wilson)	Quel président a précédé ______?
4.	(him)	Je suis tout à fait d'accord avec ______.
5.	(on the 11th of August)	Nous sommes arrivés ______.
6.	(Most)	______ soldats sont revenus.
7.	(Mary's)	Mon manteau est plus chaud que ______.
8.	(It is said)	______ c'est un peintre de talent.
9.	(What is)	______ cela?
10.	(the first two)	Comment as-tu passé ______ jours?

F

Compléter la phrase en français:

1. Les enfants ont bu deux bouteilles ______ lait.
2. Il y a des personnes qui doivent la considération ______ elles jouissent à leur fortune et non à leur mérite.
3. L'herbe et les champs sont verts ______ printemps.
4. Ont-ils parlé de l'affaire? Oui, ils ______ ont parlé.
5. Dès qu'il vendra sa maison, il ira ______ Angleterre.
6. Est-ce qu'elle lui sert la soupe? Non, elle ne ______ sert pas.
7. Qui demeure avec lui dans cet appartement? Son frère ______ demeure.
8. Ne voyez-vous pas ce ______ est sur la table?
9. L'arbre sous ______ vous vous reposez est un chêne.
10. La jeune fille ______ yeux bleus est Françoise.

G

Choisir la réponse correcte:

1. J'ai reçu (de, des) bonnes nouvelles ce matin.
2. (Que, Qu'est-ce que) cherchez-vous dans l'armoire?
3. Les écoles françaises sont fermées (mercredi, le mercredi).
4. (C', Il) est essentiel de savoir lire.
5. Ces chaussettes sont (à, de) Joseph.
6. Il était six heures (du, au) soir.
7. Elle a acheté une livre et (demi, demie) de beurre.
8. Ici on ne vend que (de, des) chapeaux.
9. (Qu'est-ce qui, Qui est-ce que) est arrivé hier?
10. Les êtres humains ont bien (de, des) défauts.

H

Compléter chaque phrase en donnant l'équivalent des mots entre parenthèses:

1. (fewer) Montrez-nous plus d'action et ______ paroles.
2. (The one who) ______ fait le pain s'appelle le boulanger.
3. (the heaviest) C'est la valise ______ que j'aie jamais portée.
4. (he) Sa mère et ______ vont en ville.
5. (Fish) ______ sont des animaux qui vivent dans l'eau.
6. (ate nothing) La malade ______.
7. (General Washington) ______ fut un de ses amis.
8. (1796) Jean-Baptiste Corot est né en ______.
9. (it to them) Voici la montre. Envoyez ______.
10. (How many) ______ voyages ils ont faits!

I

Compléter la phrase en français:

1. Beaucoup ______ touristes vont ______ Nouvelle-Orléans pour célébrer le Mardi Gras.
2. Écoutez attentivement ______ je vous dis.
3. Allez-vous me montrer vos cadeaux? Oui, je vais ______ montrer.
4. Deux fois cinq cents font ______.
5. Avez-vous assez ______ papier? Oui, nous ______ avons trop.
6. Avant d'aller ______ Mexique, il a visité ______ Canada.
7. C'est un jour ______ je me souviendrai à jamais.
8. Pourquoi as-tu mal ______ yeux?
9. Voici un magasin dans ______ on peut acheter du thé et du café.
10. Y a-t-il beaucoup de gens ______ parlent provençal?

J

Choisir la réponse qu'on *ne peut pas* substituer pour l'expression en italique:

1. Pourquoi a-t-on refusé de parler à ce *monsieur?*

   (*a*) malade (*b*) concierge (*c*) touriste (*d*) personne

2. Que faisaient-ils en *Suède?*

   (*a*) Russie (*b*) Israël (*c*) Pays-Bas (*d*) Grande-Bretagne

3. J'ai cherché partout, mais je n'ai vu *aucun colis.*

   (*a*) personne (*b*) que trois assiettes (*c*) rien (*d*) ni lui ni elle

4. La cérémonie a eu lieu *en avril.*

(*a*) le dimanche
(*b*) au printemps
(*c*) en 1976
(*d*) vers sept heures du soir

5. Les visiteurs ont admiré les *châteaux magnifiques*.

(*a*) bijoux merveilleux
(*b*) chef-d'œuvre
(*c*) étoffes chères
(*d*) gratte-ciel

6. Je ne comprends pas *votre réponse.*

(*a*) ce qu'elle veut dire
(*b*) italien
(*c*) pourquoi tu manques de courage
(*d*) les Russes

7. Après être rentré, Vincent a bu *du jus de tomate*.

(*a*) un peu de vin
(*b*) une demi-bouteille de lait
(*c*) une tasse à thé
(*d*) de l'eau minérale

8. *L'agent* a essayé d'attraper le voleur.

(*a*) On (*b*) Personne (*c*) Chacun (*d*) Quelqu'un

9. Adèle préfère que tu lui *téléphones* de temps en temps.

(*a*) écrives (*b*) envoies une lettre (*c*) répondes (*d*) penses

10. Cette fois, on avait commandé *assez* de crayons.

(*a*) deux mille
(*b*) plusieurs boîtes
(*c*) trop
(*d*) trois douzaines

K

Donner le mot qui manque:

1. Chez ______ vont-ils se réunir?
2. Il a été amené ______ États-Unis par ses parents.
3. Voici la maison ______ ils sont entrés.
4. Pense-t-elle à son avenir? Oui, elle ______ pense.
5. J'étais assise près d'une table ______ bois.
6. J'admire la bague ______ vous portez.
7. C'était le moment le plus dramatique ______ la pièce.
8. Sortez-vous d'ici? Oui, nous ______ sortons.
9. Je n'ai rien ______ autre à vous montrer.
10. ______ puis-je vous offrir?

L

Compléter chaque phrase en donnant l'équivalent des mots entre parenthèses:

1. (fresh) Elle nous a envoyé des fleurs ______.
2. (than they) Vous êtes plus forts ______.

3. (better than) Vous chantez ______ moi.
4. (Gold and iron) ______ sont des métaux utiles.
5. (that) La vie de l'homme est plus longue que ______ du chien.
6. (Neither he nor she) ______ a rompu le silence.
7. (a friend of ours) Antoine est ______.
8. (last month) Ils avaient l'intention de partir ______.
9. (not to see) Il a tourné la tête pour ______ l'accident.
10. (what) Dites-moi ______ ils auront besoin.

M

Dans chaque série, changer la première phrase en remplaçant les mots en italique par les mots indiqués. Faire tout autre changement nécessaire:

1. *Le chocolat* n'était pas délicieux; il était sec et amer. La pêche ______.
2. Avez-vous reçu ce que vous *avez demandé?* ______ aviez besoin?
3. Ce n'est pas difficile à *prouver.* ______ prouver cette théorie.
4. De qui a-t-il peur? Il n'a peur de *personne.* ______ rien.
5. La chatte est la femelle du *chat; le chat* est le mâle de la chatte. ______ coq; le taureau ______.
6. Carole aime bien *la dentelle* qu'elle a achetée en *Belgique*. ______ tout ______ Londres.
7. De qui *êtes-vous la sœur?* ______ sont ces disques de danse?
8. Généralement *les voyageurs* sont heureux de rentrer chez eux. ______ on ______.
9. Qui est-ce qui vous *aide?* ______ aidez?
10. *Le* vieillard est allé chez l'épicier pour acheter *un* ananas, *un* chou, et deux *livres* de pommes de terre. La ______ deux ______, deux ______, _______ livre ______.

MASTERY STRUCTURE DRILLS

Rewrite the two sentences in each question as a single sentence in accordance with the instructions, making changes and omissions as necessary. Do *not* begin the sentence with the word or words in italics unless you are specifically told to do so.

SAMPLE QUESTION: Join by using *que:* Nous le ferons. C'est important.
ANSWER: Il est important que nous le fassions.

A

1. Join by using *que:* Il va au cinéma. Je le défends.
2. Join by using *à:* Elle m'aidera. Je choisirai des vêtements.
3. Begin with *En:* J'ai reçu le télégramme. J'ai sauté de joie.
4. Join by using *quoique:* Il parle rarement espagnol. Il le sait bien.

5. Join by using *dont:* J'ait fait une grosse faute. J'en ai honte.
6. Join by using *que:* Ce restaurant est climatisé. Je ne le crois pas.
7. Begin with *Si:* Vous verrez Jean. Donnez-lui mes amitiés.
8. Begin with *Quand:* Hélène revient. Nous sortirons.
9. Join by using *ni . . . ni:* Elle n'a pas de stylo. Elle n'a pas de crayon.
10. Join the two sentences: Que voulez-vous? Je ne sais pas.

B

1. Begin with *Si:* Il n'aurait pas plu. Nous serions partis.
2. Join by using *que:* Il a pu le prouver. J'en doute.
3. Join by using *que:* Elle n'a pas reçu les lettres. Je lui avais écrit.
4. Begin with *Au lieu de:* Tu te taisais. Tu bavardais.
5. Join by using *pourvu que:* J'achèterai la robe. On me l'enverra.
6. Begin with *Après:* Elles rentrent. Elles n'ont plus envie de sortir.
7. Begin with *Dès que:* Ils ont fini le travail. Ils se reposeront.
8. Join by using *de:* Cesserez-vous jamais? Vous dites des mensonges.
9. Join by using *qui:* Je cherche une maison. Elle est bien construite.
10. Join by using *ce dont:* De quoi s'occupe-t-il? Le savez-vous?

C

1. Join by using *qui:* Y a-t-il un bon étudiant ici? Il peut expliquer cet exemple.
2. Begin with *Lorsque:* Nous avons soif. Nous buvons de l'eau.
3. Join by using *que:* L'élève ne sait pas la leçon. Le maître le regrette.
4. Join the two sentences: Je n'en suis pas sûr. Qu'a-t-il dit?
5. Join by using *par:* Ils ont fini. Ils ont corrigé l'injustice.
6. Join by using *sans que:* Ne partez pas. Je vous reverrai.
7. Begin with *Si:* Je courrais. J'y arriverais à l'heure.
8. Join the two sentences: Avez-vous retrouvé le portefeuille? Vous le cherchiez.
9. Begin with *En:* Elle annonce la nouvelle. Elle pleure.
10. Join by using *dont:* C'est la jeune fille. Je connais son père.

D

1. Begin with *Après:* Nous nous amusons. Nous avons quitté le bal.
2. Join by using *que:* Il n'arrivera pas à temps. Elle le craint.

3. Join by using *sans:* — Elle ne veut pas partir. Elle fera ses adieux.
4. Join the two sentences: — Je vais vous montrer la rue. J'y suis né.
5. Begin with *Si:* — Il fera beau. Nous irons à la campagne.
6. Join by using *à moins que:* — Je ne vous parlerai pas. Vous le ferez.
7. Join by using *dont:* — C'est l'actrice. J'ai fait sa connaissance.
8. Begin with *Aussitôt que:* — Elle voit sa mère. Elle l'embrassera.
9. Join the two sentences: — Quelles sont les provinces? Tu vas les visiter.
10. Join by using *que:* — Je lui dois de l'argent. Cela se peut.

E

1. Join by using *laquelle:* — Voilà la porte. Il est sorti par là.
2. Join by using *que:* — C'est l'histoire la plus drôle. Vous l'avez racontée.
3. Begin with *Après que:* — Vous êtes partis. Je pourrai étudier.
4. Join by using *que:* — Ils se sont fait mal. J'en ai peur.
5. Join the two sentences: — De quoi a-t-il besoin? Le voici.
6. Join by using *jusqu'à ce que:* — Je compte étudier. Je l'apprendrai par cœur.
7. Begin with *Si:* — Ils seraient allés au concert. Ils se seraient amusés.
8. Join by using *ni . . . ni:* — Je ne suis pas pauvre. Je ne suis pas riche.
9. Join the two sentences: — Ils ne pouvaient pas. Ils la finissaient.
10. Join by using *à:* — N'hésitez pas. Vendez les bijoux.

F

1. Join by using *de:* — Je le regrette beaucoup. Je vous ai dérangé.
2. Join by using *si:* — Il ne sait pas. Vous pourrez le faire.
3. Join by using *que:* — Ils sont très heureux. Le chien n'est pas mort.
4. Begin with *En:* — Elle a prononcé les mots. Elle a fait des erreurs.
5. Join by using *dont:* — Voici la brosse. Ils s'en servaient.
6. Begin with *Si:* — Le bébé dormira. Nous ne le réveillerons pas.
7. Join by using *que:* — Ce meuble vaut cher. Est-ce possible?
8. Join by using *avant que:* — Offrez-leur quelque chose. Ils s'en vont.
9. Begin with *Quand:* — Vous voulez partir. Faites-le-moi savoir.
10. Join by using *ce qui:* — Qu'est-ce qui est arrivé? Nous ne savons pas.

G

1. Join by using *que:*	Tu boiras le lait. C'est nécessaire.
2. Begin with *Dès que:*	Je dois vous parler. Je vous donnerai un coup de téléphone.
3. Join by using *sans:*	Peut-on parler? On ouvre la bouche.
4. Begin with *En:*	Il a bâti la maison. Il s'est blessé.
5. Join the two sentences:	Qu'a-t-elle acheté? Voici les gants.
6. Join by using *de peur que:*	Nous conduisons lentement. Il y aura un accident.
7. Begin with *Si:*	Vous étudieriez tous les jours. Vous seriez le premier de la classe.
8. Join by using *que:*	Il ne mentira pas. Je le préfère.
9. Join by using *avant de:*	Racontez-moi l'histoire. Allez-vous-en.
10. Join by using *qui:*	C'est moi. J'ai fermé la fenêtre.

H

1. Join by using *pour que:*	Fait-il assez chaud aujourd'hui? Ils vont à la plage.
2. Join by using *dont:*	Montrez-moi le portrait. Vous en êtes fier.
3. Join by using *que:*	C'est le meilleur roman. Je l'ai lu récemment.
4. Begin with *Si:*	Elle aurait chanté. J'aurais éclaté de rire.
5. Join by using *que:*	Louis ne m'a pas rendu visite. Je m'en étonne.
6. Begin with *Lorsque:*	Il a fini ses devoirs. Il se couchera.
7. Join by using *à:*	Nous sommes prêts. Mettons-nous en route.
8. Begin with *Après:*	Elle boit le thé chaud. Elle se sentira mieux.
9. Join by using *que:*	Attendez ici. Je reviendrai.
10. Join by using *où:*	Voilà l'immeuble. Ils y demeuraient.

I

1. Join by using *qui:*	Georges est l'ami. J'étudie avec lui.
2. Join by using *que:*	Ils sont déjà revenus. C'est possible.
3. Join by using *par:*	Nous commencerons. Nous jouerons au tennis.
4. Begin with *Si:*	Elle fera un voyage. Je l'accompagnerai.
5. Join by using *que:*	Le médecin ne veut pas. Le malade mourra.
6. Join by using *dont:*	Quel est le bruit? Elle s'en plaignait.

7. Join by using *ni . . . ni:* Jacques ne parle pas anglais. Sa sœur ne parle pas anglais.
8. Begin with *Aussitôt que:* Je reçois le colis. Je l'ouvrirai.
9. Begin with *En:* Nous voyagions en Angleterre. Nous admirions le paysage.
10. Join the two sentences: Qu'avez-vous écrit? Effacez-le.

J

1. Join by using *afin que:* Ils m'aideront. Je réussirai.
2. Begin with *Si:* Vous vous lèveriez de bonne heure. Vous verriez le lever du soleil.
3. Join by using *avant de:* Nous nous lavons. Nous nous habillons.
4. Join by using *que:* La domestique va au marché. Il le faut.
5. Join by using *bien que:* Nous irons à la pêche. Il pleut.
6. Join the two sentences: Qu'est-ce qui est dans la salle? Je ne l'ai pas remarqué.
7. Join by using *que:* Il vivra une longue vie. Nous le souhaitons.
8. Join by using *dont:* Nous connaissons l'architecte. Tout le monde parle de lui.
9. Join by using *de:* Dépêchez-vous. Je le lui ai conseillé.
10. Begin with *Après:* Remplissez-la. Donnez la tasse à Renée.

K

1. Join by using *où:* C'est le moulin. Daudet y écrivit ses lettres.
2. Join by using *à:* Elle l'a invité. Il peint son portrait.
3. Begin with *Après:* Ils se promenaient. Ils se reposaient.
4. Join by using *que:* Qui avez-vous rencontré? Est-ce Annette?
5. Join the two sentences: Je vais en Europe l'été prochain. Je le désire.
6. Join by using *que:* Pierre s'est fait mal. C'est dommage.
7. Begin with *Si:* Ils réfléchiraient plus. Ils se tromperaient moins.
8. Join by using *qui:* Où est l'actrice? Vous lui parliez.
9. Begin with *En:* Il jette la balle. Il perd son équilibre.
10. Join the two sentences: Je le lui avais demandé. Il m'attendait.

Part III—*Idioms*

I. IDIOMS WITH *AVOIR*

1. **avoir . . . ans,** to be . . . years old

   Quel âge a-t-elle? Elle ***a*** quatorze ***ans.***
   How old is she? She is fourteen years old.

2. **avoir beau** + infinitive, to do (something) in vain (The reason that the action is *in vain* must be added.)

   Il ***a beau*** essayer; il ne réussira pas.
   He tries in vain; he will not succeed.
   Or:
   No matter how much he tries, he will not succeed.

3. **avoir besoin de,** to need

   De quoi ***avez***-vous ***besoin?*** J'***ai besoin de*** bas.
   What do you need? I need stockings.

4. **avoir envie de,** to feel like

   Nous ***avons envie de*** voyager.
   We feel like traveling.

5. **avoir honte (de),** to be ashamed (of)

   N'***as***-tu pas ***honte de*** ce que tu as fait?
   Aren't you ashamed of what you've done?

6. **avoir lieu,** to take place

   Le concert ***aura lieu*** samedi soir.
   The concert will take place Saturday evening.

7. **avoir mal à** (+ part of body), to have a pain in, have a (an) . . . -ache

   J'***ai mal aux*** dents.
   I have a toothache.

8. **avoir peur (de),** to be afraid (of)

   Avez-vous ***peur des*** éclairs?
   Are you afraid of the lightning?

9. **avoir quelque chose,** to have something wrong

   Qu'a-t-il? Il ***n'a rien.***
   What's wrong with him? Nothing is wrong with him.

Qu'est-ce qu'il y a? (Qu'y a-t-il?)
What's the matter?

Il n'y a rien.
Nothing is the matter.

10. **avoir de la chance,** to be lucky

J'espère qu'elle ***aura de la chance.***
I hope she will be lucky.

11. **avoir de quoi** (+ infinitive), to have the means (material, enough) to

Avez-vous ***de quoi*** écrire?
Have you something to write with?

Il n'***a*** pas ***de quoi*** vivre.
He hasn't enough to live on.

12. **avoir l'air** (+ adjective), to seem, look

Mon cousin ***avait l'air*** content.
My cousin looked pleased.

13. **avoir l'air de** (+ infinitive), to seem to, look as if

Le bébé ***a l'air de*** dormir.
The baby seems to be sleeping.

14. **avoir l'habitude de,** to be accustomed to

Le fermier ***a l'habitude de*** se lever de bonne heure.
The farmer is accustomed to getting up early.

15. **avoir l'idée de,** to have a notion to

J'***ai eu l'idée de*** lui dire la vérité.
I had a notion to tell him the truth.

16. **avoir l'intention de,** to intend to

Ont-ils ***l'intention de*** partir bientôt?
Do they intend to leave soon?

17. **avoir l'occasion de,** to have the opportunity to

Quand ***aurez-***vous ***l'occasion de*** la voir?
When will you have the opportunity to see her?

18. **avoir le temps de,** to have (the) time to

Nous n'***avons*** pas ***le temps de*** vous parler.
We haven't time to speak to you.

19. **avoir la parole,** to have the floor (as a speaker)

Le sénateur ***a la parole*** ce matin.
The senator has the floor this morning.

20. Other idioms:

avoir chaud, to be warm (of persons)
avoir faim, to be hungry
avoir raison, to be right
avoir froid, to be cold (of persons)
avoir soif, to be thirsty
avoir tort, to be wrong
avoir sommeil, to be sleepy

Elle n'***a*** ni ***faim*** ni ***soif***.
She is neither hungry nor thirsty.

Est-ce que j'***ai raison*** ou ***tort?***
Am I right or wrong?

EXERCICES

A. Compléter les phrases en français:

1. Puisque j'avais ______, j'ai bu un verre d'eau fraîche.
2. Pour nous montrer ses films d'Europe, il aura ______ d'un projecteur.
3. Vous avez l'______ malade. Qu' ______-vous? J'ai ______ à la tête.
4. Le professeur avait ______ expliquer le problème; les élèves étaient trop jeunes pour le comprendre.
5. Je n'ai pas de ______ écrire. Pouvez-vous me prêter un stylo et du papier?
6. Si le député veut parler à l'assemblée, il peut avoir la ______.
7. La cérémonie a eu ______ dans l'hôtel de ville.
8. Elle n'a pas toujours tort; quelquefois elle a ______.
9. Que désirez-vous faire ce soir, Jérôme? J'ai ______ d'aller au théâtre.
10. Il n'aime pas les expéditions de chasse parce qu'il a ______ des animaux sauvages.

B. Remplacer les mots en italique par une expression équivalente contenant le mot entre parenthèses:

1. (peur) David *ne craignait pas le* géant Goliath.
2. (envie) Nous *désirons* prendre notre dîner dans un restaurant excellent.
3. (air) L'ambassadeur *semble* très fatigué ce matin.
4. (besoin) *Combien de temps lui faudra-t-il* pour achever l'ouvrage?
5. (intention) *On compte* téléviser ce programme par satellite.

6. (lieu) L'expérience scientifique *s'accomplira* dans le laboratoire de l'université.
7. (sommeil) La mère a couché le petit de bonne heure parce qu'il *avait besoin de dormir.*
8. (parole) Soyez patient; vous n'avez pas encore *le droit de parler.*
9. (habitude) *D'ordinaire je fais* une longue promenade chaque matin dans le parc.
10. (beau) Elle *attend en vain;* le train n'arrivera pas avant minuit.

C. Compléter la seconde partie de chaque série:

1. Qu'a-t-elle? Elle n'a rien. What ______.
2. En voyant le lac, il a eu l'idée de faire du ski nautique. On seeing the lake, ______ go water skiing.
3. S'il dépense tout son argent, il n'aura pas de quoi vivre. If he spends all his money, ______.
4. Ce mendiant a l'air d'avoir faim et soif. That beggar ______.
5. Le mathématicien a beau expliquer sa formule; personne ne le comprend. ______; no one understands him.
6. Aura-t-on l'occasion de poser des questions? ______ to ask questions?
7. How old is Michael? He will be fifteen tomorrow. ______ demain.
8. I feel like going swimming. ______ aller à la nage.
9. We were neither warm nor cold in the old castle. ______ dans le vieux château.
10. You will be lucky if you win the prize. ______ si vous gagnez le prix.

D. Répondre à chaque question par une phrase complète en français:

1. De quoi aurai-je besoin pour éclairer ma chambre?
2. Avez-vous souvent ou rarement mal à la gorge en hiver?
3. Où est-ce que l'accident a eu lieu?
4. Qu'est-ce qu'on doit faire quand on a sommeil?
5. As-tu l'habitude de lire beaucoup ou peu?
6. Quand est-ce que cette famille pauvre aura de quoi manger?
7. Guillaume est-il fier de ses mauvaises notes ou en a-t-il honte?
8. Quelle autre langue avez-vous l'intention d'étudier?
9. Y a-t-il quelque chose, Alfred?
10. A quelle heure est-ce que le docteur aura le temps de visiter mon frère malade?

2. IDIOMS WITH *FAIRE*

1. **faire** (with **il**)—used in expressions of weather

Quel temps fait-il?	How is the weather?
Il fait beau aujourd'hui.	The weather is fine (fair, good) today.
Il a fait mauvais hier.	The weather was bad yesterday.
Fait-il chaud ou ***froid?***	Is it warm or cold?
Fera-t-il frais ou ***doux*** demain?	Will it be cool or mild tomorrow?
Il fait du soleil; il fait du vent.	It is sunny; it is windy.
Il fait jour.	It is light (daylight, daytime).
Il fait nuit.	It is dark (nighttime).
Il fait des éclairs.	It is lightning.
Il fait du tonnerre.	It is thundering.

2. **faire** + infinitive, to have something done

J'***ai fait écrire*** deux lettres.
I had two letters written.

Je les ***ai fait écrire.***
I had them written.

Note: In this construction, the pronoun object is used with the verb **faire** rather than with the following infinitive. The past participle **fait** does not follow the rule of agreement; it is invariable.

3. **faire à sa tête,** to do as one pleases

Elle ***fait*** toujours ***à sa tête.***
She always does as she pleases.

4. **faire attention à,** to pay attention to

Il n'***a*** pas ***fait attention à*** son père.
He didn't pay attention to his father.

5. **faire de la peine à,** to grieve, distress, trouble

Sa maladie ***me fait de la peine.***
His illness distresses me.

6. **faire de son mieux** / **faire son possible** } to do one's best

Nous ***faisons*** rarement ***de notre mieux.*** / Nous ***faisons*** rarement ***notre possible.*** } We rarely do our best.

7. **faire des achats** / **faire des emplettes** } to go shopping

Je dois ***faire des achats*** (***emplettes***) en ville.
I have to go shopping in town.

8. **faire des progrès,** to make progress

   Font-ils ***des progrès*** en mathématiques?
   Are they making progress in mathematics?

9. **faire exprès,** to do on purpose

   Il sait que tu ne l'***as*** pas ***fait exprès.***
   He knows you didn't do it on purpose.

10. **faire la connaissance de,** to become acquainted with, meet

    Nous ***avons fait la connaissance de*** ce monsieur.
    We have met that gentleman.

11. **faire la queue,** to stand on line

    Ils ***faisaient la queue*** devant la gare.
    They were standing on line in front of the station.

12. **faire la sourde oreille,** to turn a deaf ear, pretend not to hear

    Quand on le gronde, il ***fait la sourde oreille.***
    When you scold him, he turns a deaf ear.

13. **faire mal à,** to hurt

    Ne ***faites*** pas ***mal à*** cet oiseau.
    Do not hurt that bird.

14. **faire peur à,** to frighten

    Les avions à réaction ne ***lui font*** pas ***peur.***
    Jet planes do not frighten him.

15. **faire plaisir à,** to please, give pleasure to

    La musique ***leur fait plaisir.***
    Music pleases them.

16. **faire savoir (à quelqu'un),** to let (someone) know

    Faites-moi savoir sa réponse.
    Let me know his answer.

17. **faire semblant de,** to pretend to, make believe

    Ne ***faites*** pas ***semblant d'***étudier
    Don't make believe you're studying.

18. **faire ses adieux,** to say good-bye

    Avant le voyage il ***fera ses adieux.***
    Before the trip he will say good-bye.

19. **faire une partie de,** to play a game of

Voulez-vous ***faire une partie de*** cartes?
Do you want to play a game of cards?

20. **faire une promenade,** to take a walk, a ride

Nous ***faisions une promenade*** dans le parc.
We were taking a walk in the park.

Ils vont ***faire une promenade*** en voiture.
They are going to take an automobile ride.

21. **poser une question (à),** to ask a question

Lui a-t-on ***posé une question*** difficile?
Did they ask her a difficult question?

22. **faire un voyage,** to take a trip

Je compte ***faire un voyage*** en bateau.
I intend to take a boat trip.

23. **faire venir,** to send for

Faites venir un plombier. ***Faites***-le ***venir.***
Send for a plumber. Send for him.

EXERCICES

A. Remplacer chaque tiret en employant une fois un des mots indiqués à droite:

1. Nous avons l'habitude d'aller à la plage quand il fait ______.
2. Si cette étudiante faisait ______ au professeur, elle ne lui ferait pas tant de ______.
3. Bien entendu, on ne peut toujours faire à sa ______.
4. Quand vont-ils faire ______ leur appartement?
5. Nous espérons que vous ne partirez pas sans faire vos ______.
6. Les souris ne font pas ______ à Hélène; elle fait ______ de ne pas les voir.
7. On ne pourra pas vous blâmer si vous faites votre ______.
8. Puisque Nicole est très travailleuse, elle continue à faire des ______ en mathématiques.
9. Est-ce que tes nouvelles chaussures te font ______?
10. Ayez la bonté de répondre à la question que je viens de vous ______.

adieux
attention
chaud
exprès
poser
mal
mieux
partie
peindre
peine
peur
possible
progrès
savoir
semblant
tête

B. Compléter en français:

1. Est-ce que le lac a gelé? Non, il ne fait pas assez ______.

2. C'est un enfant gâté qui veut toujours faire à sa ______.
3. Savez-vous s'il fera beau ou ______ demain?
4. Si vous faites de votre ______, vous réussirez.
5. La foule a fait la ______ pour attendre l'autobus.
6. Quel ______ fait-il? Il fait ______ soleil.
7. Est-ce qu'on a fermé les fenêtres? Oui, je les ai ______ fermer.
8. Écoute-moi, Antoine; ne fais pas la ______ oreille!
9. Connaissez-vous mon oncle? Mais oui, j'ai déjà fait la ______ de votre oncle.
10. Quelle nuit! Il fait du tonnerre et des ______.

C. Compléter la seconde phrase de chaque série:

1. Vous a-t-il fait savoir ce dont il a besoin? ______ what he needs?
2. Généralement, Mme Deschamps fait ses emplettes de Noël au milieu de décembre. Generally, ______ in the middle of December.
3. S'il fait plus frais demain, j'ai l'intention de me faire couper les cheveux. ______ tomorrow, I intend ______.
4. Personne ne vous fera mal si vous vous taisez. ______ if you keep quiet.
5. Je ne lui poserai plus de questions parce qu'il fait toujours la sourde oreille. ______ because ______.
6. Is it daytime or nighttime in Paris now? ______ à Paris maintenant?
7. Let them know the date of your arrival. ______ la date de votre arrivée.
8. Why does he pretend to be rich? Pourquoi ______ riche?
9. I doubt that they did it on purpose. Je doute ______.
10. The patient will be able to go out when the weather is milder. Le malade pourra sortir ______.

D. Répondre à chaque question par une phrase complète en français:

1. Pourquoi fait-on la queue devant ce guichet?
2. Est-ce que le travail vous fait peur?
3. Vont-ils faire une promenade en voiture ou à bicyclette?
4. Pourquoi voudriez-vous faire un voyage autour du monde?
5. Qui fait-on venir quand on est malade?
6. Préférez-vous faire une partie de golf ou de tennis avec moi?
7. Où comptent-ils faire bâtir leur maison?
8. Lequel des cours que tu suis te fait plaisir?
9. En quel mois fait-il d'ordinaire du vent?
10. Quand avez-vous fait la connaissance de votre meilleur(e) ami(e)?

La Seine à Paris

La Seine divise la "Ville Lumière" en deux parties. Grâce à ce fleuve navigable, Paris est le premier port fluvial de France. C'est aux bords de la Seine qu'on trouve de nombreux pêcheurs et flâneurs.

3. REFLEXIVE EXPRESSIONS

1. **s'agir de** (used impersonally with **il**), to be a question of, to be about

   De quoi ***s'agit-il?***
   What is it about?

   Il s'agit de sa santé.
   It is a question of his health.

2. **s'approcher de,** to approach

   Tous **s'approchent de** la cheminée.
   They all approach the fireplace.

3. **s'attendre à,** to expect

   Je ne ***m'attends*** pas ***à*** les voir.
   I do not expect to see them.

4. **se casser le bras (la jambe),** to break one's arm (leg)

   Elle ***s'est cassé le bras*** en tombant.
   She broke her arm falling.

5. **se charger de,** to take charge of, undertake

   Le guide ***se chargera de*** tout.
   The guide will take care of everything.

6. **se demander,** to wonder

   Je ***me demande*** s'il pleuvra ce soir.
   I wonder whether it will rain tonight.

7. **se douter de,** to suspect

   Le paysan ne ***se doutait de*** rien.
   The peasant suspected nothing.

8. **s'en aller,** to go away

   Elle ***s'en va. Allez-vous-en.***
   She is going away. Go away.

9. ***s'étonner de,*** to be astonished (surprised) at

   Je ***m'étonne de*** ses manières.
   I'm astonished at his manners.

10. **se fâcher contre,** to get angry with

    Ne ***vous fâchez*** pas ***contre*** eux.
    Do not get angry with them.

11. **se faire mal,** to hurt oneself, get hurt

    La petite ***s'est fait mal*** au pied.
    The child hurt her foot.

12. **se fier à**, to trust

    Nous ne ***nous fions*** pas ***à*** lui.
    We don't trust him.

13. **se marier avec**, to marry

    Elle ***s'est mariée avec*** un millionnaire.
    She married a millionaire.

14. **se mettre à**, to begin to

    Pourquoi ***s'est-*** elle ***mise à*** pleurer?
    Why did she begin to cry?

15. **se mettre en colère**, to get angry, lose one's temper

    Mon professeur ne ***se met*** jamais ***en colère.***
    My teacher never gets angry.

16. **se mettre en route**, to start out

    A quelle heure ***se sont-***ils ***mis en route?***
    At what time did they start out?

17. **se moquer de**, to make fun of, laugh at

    Ne ***te moque*** pas ***de*** moi.
    Don't make fun of me.

18. **s'occuper de**, to attend to, look after

    Je ***m'occuperai de*** l'affaire.
    I shall attend to the matter.

19. **se passer de**, to do without

    Elle peut ***se passer de*** gâteau.
    She can do without cake.

20. **se rendre à**, to go to

    Le facteur ***s'est rendu à*** la poste.
    The postman went to the post office.

21. **se rendre compte de** (or **que**), to realize, understand

    Vous rendez-vous ***compte de*** votre erreur?
    Do you realize your mistake?

    Je ***me rends compte que*** c'était un accident.
    I realize it was an accident.

22. **se servir de**, to use

    Le docteur voulait ***s'en servir.***
    The doctor wanted to use it.

23. **se souvenir de** } to remember
se rappeler

Elle ***s'est souvenue de*** la rue. } She remembered the street.
Elle ***s'est rappelé*** la rue.

24. **se tirer d'affaire,** to get along, manage

Je sais ***me tirer d'affaire.***
I know how to get along.

EXERCICES

A. Compléter la phrase en donnant le mot qui manque:

1. Nous devrons nous ______ en route de bonne heure demain matin.
2. Je me chargerai ______ son bonheur pendant qu'il sera sous notre toit.
3. ______ qui va-t-elle se marier?
4. —Vous ne fumez plus? —Non, j'ai décidé de me ______ de cigarettes.
5. Le candidat ne s'attendait pas ______ recevoir tant de courrier.
6. Peut-on se ______ d'affaire à l'étranger si l'on ne parle pas la langue du pays?
7. Au lever du soleil, les coqs se sont mis ______ chanter.
8. On se rendait ______ que l'étude des atomes avait fait de grands progrès.
9. J'espère que vous ne vous fâcherez pas ______ moi, madame.
10. —Tu as oublié sa date de naissance? —Oui, je ne ______ souviens plus.

B. Remplacer les mots en italique par une expression équivalente:

1. *J'ai commencé à* étudier la lecture.
2. *Vous rappelez-vous* l'été où j'ai fait votre connaissance?
3. *Elle s'est blessée* en travaillant dans la cuisine.
4. Allez-vous *épouser* cette belle dame?
5. *Il est question de* leur avenir.
6. *Je suis surpris de* ce qu'il a dit.
7. Pourquoi *vous fâchez-vous?*
8. *Il a employé* sa clef pour ouvrir la porte.
9. Comptent-ils *aller* à Reims la semaine prochaine?
10. *On rit de* sa casquette bizarre.
11. Qui *prendra la responsabilité de* préparer la réunion?
12. Pour nous chauffer, *nous sommes allés près de* la cheminée.
13. Est-ce qu'on peut *avoir confiance en* ce dentiste?
14. Quoique je préfère rester ici plus longtemps, il faut que *je parte.*
15. *Comprenez-vous le rôle* que la France a joué dans l'histoire de notre pays?

C. Compléter la seconde partie de chaque série:

1. M. Ledoux se rappelle tant de détails de son enfance! Je m'étonne de sa mémoire.
   Mr. Ledoux ______ so many details of his childhood! ______ his memory.
2. Nous n'avons pas de temps libre. Il y a toujours de quoi nous occuper.
   We have no free time. ______.
3. Si tu ne te fies pas à moi, va-t'en!
   If you don't ______!
4. Pendant que les voyageurs se rendaient à la banque, le porteur se chargeait des bagages.
   While the travelers ______ bank, the porter ______ the luggage.
5. On ne doit jamais se moquer d'un accent étranger.
   We should never ______.
6. What is it about? It's a question of money, isn't it?
   ______ d'argent, n'est-ce pas?
7. She expects to arrive in Italy before them.
   ______ en Italie avant eux.
8. How did Richard break his leg?
   Comment Richard ______?
9. Do you suspect their sincerity? No, I don't.
   ______ leur sincérité? Non, je ne ______ pas.
10. I wonder if I'll be able to get along without you.
    ______ si je pourrai ______ sans vous.

D. Répondre à chaque question par une phrase complète en français:

1. Quand est-ce que la neige s'est mise à tomber?
2. Pouvez-vous vous passer de chocolat?
3. De quoi se sert-on pour écrire au tableau noir?
4. Aimes-tu qu'on se moque de toi?
5. Contre qui la dame s'est-elle fâchée?
6. Vous rendez-vous compte de ce que vous avez fait?
7. Quel temps faisait-il quand les voyageurs se sont mis en route?
8. Quand vous attendez-vous à remplacer vos vieux meubles par des neufs?
9. A quelle heure est-ce que je dois me rendre à l'école?
10. Vous souvenez-vous du nom de votre premier professeur de français?

4. OTHER VERBAL IDIOMS–I

1. **adresser la parole à,** to address, speak to

   La reine ***adressa la parole à*** son ministre.
   The queen addressed her minister.

2. **aller,** to feel, be (of health)

   Comment ***vas-***tu? Je ne ***vais*** pas très bien.
   How are you? I'm not feeling very well.

3. **aller à,** to fit, suit

   Ce pardessus gris ***lui va*** bien.
   That gray overcoat fits him well.

4. **aller à la pêche,** to go fishing

   J'ai envie d'***aller à la pêche.***
   I feel like going fishing.

5. **aller à la rencontre de** } to go to meet
   aller au-devant de }

   Il ***est allé à la rencontre de*** sa femme. } He went to meet his wife.
   Il ***est allé au-devant de*** sa femme. }

6. **apprendre par cœur,** to memorize

   Elle ***a appris par cœur*** tous leurs noms.
   She memorized all their names.

7. **assister à,** to attend, be present at

   Nous ***assisterons à*** la conférence.
   We shall attend the lecture.

8. **changer de,** to change (one thing for another of its kind)

   André ne ***change*** jamais ***d'***avis.
   Andrew never changes his mind.

   Je dois ***changer de*** vêtements.
   I must change my clothes.

9. **demander quelque chose à quelqu'un,** to ask someone for something

   Demandez un pain frais ***au boulanger.***
   Ask the baker for a fresh (loaf of) bread.

10. **donner sur,** to face, look out on

    Ces fenêtres ***donnent sur*** la place.
    These windows face the square.

11. **éclater de rire,** to burst out laughing

    En l'entendant, ils ***ont éclaté de rire.***
    On hearing it, they burst out laughing.

12. **entendre dire que,** to hear that

    Avez-vous ***entendu dire qu'***elle est malade?
    Have you heard that she is ill?

13. **entendre parler de,** to hear of

    Il n'***a*** jamais ***entendu parler de*** ce pays.
    He has never heard of that country.

14. **en vouloir à,** to have a grudge against, be angry with

    En voulez-vous ***à*** Jean? Oui, je ***lui en veux.***
    Have you a grudge against John? Yes, I have.

15. **envoyer chercher,** to send for

    Je vais ***envoyer chercher*** ton père.
    I'm going to send for your father.

16. **être à,** to belong to

    A qui ***sont*** ces mouchoirs? Ils ***sont à*** moi.
    Whose handkerchiefs are these? They belong to me. (They are mine.)

17. **être bien aise de,** to be very glad to

    J'***étais bien aise de*** retrouver mes diamants.
    I was very glad to find my diamonds.

18. **être d'accord (avec),** to agree (with), be in agreement (with)

    Nous ne ***sommes*** pas ***d'accord avec*** lui.
    We do not agree with him.

19. **être de retour,** to be back

    Quand le tailleur ***sera***-t-il ***de retour?***
    When will the tailor be back?

20. **être en train de,** to be busy (doing something), be in the act of

    Les élèves ***sont en train d'***étudier.
    The pupils are (busy) studying.

21. **être enrhumé,** to have a cold

    Cette jeune fille ***est*** toujours ***enrhumée.***
    That girl always has a cold.

22. **être sur le point de,** to be about to

    Nous ***étions sur le point de*** le faire.
    We were about to do it.

23. **féliciter de,** to congratulate on

    Le général les ***a félicités de*** leur courage.
    The general congratulated them on their courage.

24. **finir par** (+ infinitive), to end by, finally do (something)

    Ils ***ont fini par*** remarquer l'araignée.
    They finally noticed the spider.

25. **jouer à,** to play (a game)

    Aimez-vous ***jouer aux*** cartes?
    Do you like to play cards?

26. **jouer de,** to play (a musical instrument)

    Son frère ***joue*** bien ***du*** violon.
    His brother plays the violin well.

27. **jouir de,** to enjoy (what one possesses)

    Cet avocat ***jouit d'***une bonne réputation.
    That lawyer enjoys a good reputation.

EXERCICES

A. Compléter la phrase en français:

1. Au revoir, messieurs. Je suis sur le ______ de partir.
2. L'aventure était si comique que j'ai éclaté de ______.
3. Ce balcon donne ______ la rue.
4. Les deux amis jouaient ______ tennis.
5. Le chauffeur adressait la ______ à l'agent de police.
6. Roger tousse et éternue; il est probablement ______.
7. Notre professeur jouit ______ un grand respect.
8. Nous avons changé ______ train à Lyon.
9. Il faut apprendre l'alphabet par ______.
10. Avez-vous jamais entendu ______ de cet auteur?

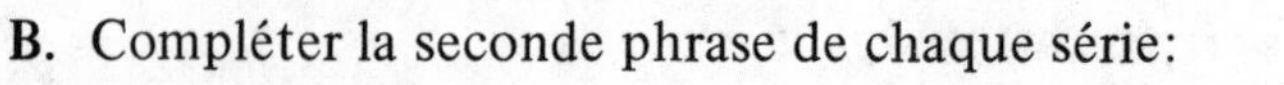

B. Compléter la seconde phrase de chaque série:

1. D'abord Étienne m'en voulait, mais nous avons fini par devenir amis.
   At first Stephen ______ friends.
2. Si vous avez envie de manger du poisson, nous irons à la pêche.
   If you ______ , we'll ______.

3. Pourquoi a-t-il éclaté de rire quand elle s'est mise à jouer de la harpe?
Why did he ______ when she ______ the harp?
4. Les garçons sont sur le point de jouer au baseball.
The boys ______ baseball.
5. Ces belles perles, dont tu as tant entendu parler, sont à ma mère.
These beautiful pearls, ______.
6. We congratulated him on his success.
Nous ______ son succès.
7. The red dress suits you better than the blue.
La robe rouge ______ la bleue.
8. I have heard that they are now in agreement.
______ qu'ils sont maintenant ______.
9. The woman wants to change her room.
La femme désire ______.
10. When you see Santa Claus, what will you ask him for?
Lorsque tu verras le Père Noël, ______?

C. Remplacer les mots en italique par une expression équivalente:

1. Eugénie était *près de* descendre quand le téléphone a sonné.
2. L'accusé a hésité un moment, puis *il a parlé directement* au juge.
3. Cette collection de timbres *vous appartient?* Non, *c'est celle de Jacques.*
4. Quand *j'ai un rhume*, je prends généralement de l'aspirine.
5. Nous étions *très contents* d'*être présents à* la cérémonie.
6. En la voyant de loin, Jean-Marc est allé *à la rencontre de* sa cousine.
7. Les fenêtres de ma chambre *offrent une vue des montagnes.*
8. Si Christine *ne se porte pas* mieux ce soir, nous *ferons venir* le médecin.
9. Après avoir beaucoup réfléchi, *il donne enfin* la réponse correcte.
10. La classe était *occupée à travailler* quand la porte s'est ouverte.

D. Répondre à chaque question par une phrase complète en français:

1. Jouissez-vous d'une bonne santé?
2. Si nous allons à la pêche, quand serons-nous de retour?
3. Qu'est-ce que le facteur est en train de faire?
4. M'en voulez-vous?
5. En quelle saison les feuilles des arbres changent-elles de couleur?
6. Est-il facile ou difficile de jouer du piano?
7. Combien de chansons françaises avez-vous apprises par cœur?
8. Croyez-vous que ce manteau de laine m'aille bien?
9. Êtes-vous d'accord avec ce que j'ai dit?
10. A qui est le stylo que vous avez à la main?

5. OTHER VERBAL IDIOMS–II

1. **manquer de** (+ noun), to lack

   Vous ***manquez de*** savoir-faire, monsieur!
   You lack tact, sir!

2. **manquer de** (+ infinitive) } almost (do something)
   faillir (+ infinitive)

   Elle ***a manqué de*** mourir. } She almost died.
   Elle ***a failli*** mourir.

3. **monter à cheval,** to go horseback riding

   En été nous ***montons à cheval.***
   In the summer we go horseback riding.

4. **n'en pouvoir plus,** to be exhausted

   A la fin du jour je ***n'en peux plus.***
   At the end of the day I'm exhausted.

5. **penser à** } to think of
   songer à

   Pensez-vous (***Songez***-vous) jamais ***à*** elle?
   Do you ever think of her?

6. **penser de,** to think of (= to have an opinion of)

   Que ***pensez***-vous ***de*** moi?
   What do you think of me?

   Vous savez ce que je ***pense de*** vous.
   You know what I think of you.

7. **pleuvoir à verse,** to rain hard, pour

   S'il ***pleut à verse***, je ne sors pas.
   If it pours, I don't go out.

8. **prendre garde de,** to be careful not to

   Prenez garde de casser le verre.
   Be careful not to break the glass.

9. **prendre le parti de,** to decide to, make up one's mind to

   Il ***a pris le parti de*** réussir.
   He made up his mind to succeed.

10. **prendre un billet,** to buy a ticket

    J'***ai pris un billet*** pour voir le film.
    I bought a ticket to see the film.

11. **profiter de**, to profit by, take advantage of

    Ils ***ont profité de*** mon absence.
    They took advantage of my absence.

12. **remercier de**, to thank for

    J'***ai remercié*** le juge ***de*** sa bonté.
    I thanked the judge for his kindness.

13. **rendre visite à (quelqu'un)**, to pay (someone) a visit, visit (someone)

    Nous allons ***rendre visite à*** nos cousins.
    We are going to visit our cousins.

14. **ressembler à**, to resemble, look like

    Tu ***ressembles*** beaucoup ***à*** ton père.
    You look a great deal like your father.

15. **rire de**, to laugh at

    On ***a ri de*** lui, pas de son histoire.
    They laughed at him, not at his story.

16. **sauter aux yeux**, to be evident

    Son intelligence ***saute aux yeux***.
    Her intelligence is evident.

17. **savoir bon gré à quelqu'un de quelque chose**, to be grateful to someone for something

    Je ***leur en sais bon gré***.
    I'm grateful to them for it.

18. **tarder à**, to be long (late) in

    Ne ***tardez*** pas ***à*** le faire.
    Don't be long in doing it.

19. **tenir à**, to insist upon, be anxious to, value

    Ils ***tiennent à*** payer la note.
    They insist upon paying the bill.

    Je ***tiens*** beaucoup ***à*** ce portrait.
    I value this portrait highly.

20. **valoir la peine de**, to be worth while

    Il ne ***vaut*** pas ***la peine de*** lui répondre.
    It isn't worth while answering her.

21. **valoir mieux**, to be better

    Il ***vaudrait mieux*** dire la vérité.
    It would be better to tell the truth.

22. **venir à,** to happen to

    Si je ***viens à*** le voir, je le lui donnerai.
    If I happen to see him, I will give it to him.

23. **venir à bout de,** to succeed in, manage to

    Ils ***sont venus à bout de*** gagner la bataille.
    They succeeded in winning the battle.

24. **venir de,** to have just (used in present and imperfect tenses)

    Ils ***viennent de*** recevoir les nouvelles.
    They have just received the news.

    Ils ***venaient de*** recevoir les nouvelles.
    They had just received the news.

25. **vouloir bien,** to be willing, to do (something) kindly

    Il ***veut bien*** me l'envoyer.
    He is willing to send it to me.

    Voulez-vous ***bien*** fermer la porte?
    Will you kindly close the door?

26. **vouloir dire,** to mean

    Que ***voulez***-vous ***dire?***
    What do you mean?

27. **y être,** to understand, see the point

    Vous ***y êtes?*** Oui, j'***y suis.***
    You understand? Yes, I see the point.

EXERCICES

A. Compléter la phrase en français:

1. Pleut-il beaucoup? Mais oui, il pleut à ______.
2. Je pense ______ ce que vous venez de dire.
3. Pourquoi rient-ils ______ moi?

4. Demain nous allons monter ______ cheval.
5. Vaut-il la ______ d'assister à ce bal?
6. Voulez-vous vous reposer un peu? Oui, je n'en ______ plus.
7. Merci de tout ce que vous avez fait. Je vous en sais bon ______.
8. Qu'est-ce que les critiques pensaient ______ son premier roman?
9. Je doute qu'il manque ______ courage.
10. Avez-vous remarqué combien Colette ressemble ______ sa sœur?

B. Remplacer les mots en italique par une expression équivalente:

1. La différence *est évidente.*
2. A quoi *pensait-il?*
3. La vieille *a manqué de* tomber.
4. Que *signifie* ce mot?
5. Mme Lebrun *est très fatiguée.*
6. Est-ce clair? Oui, *je comprends.*
7. *Il avait décidé de* s'en aller.
8. *Nous n'avons pas d'*argent.
9. L'agent *réussit à* attraper le voleur.
10. Elle *a un grand désir de* rentrer.
11. Prends un parapluie, Martine. *Il pleut très fort.*
12. Je voudrais ajouter un mot à ce que *j'ai dit tout à l'heure.*
13. *Quelle est votre opinion de* la libération féminine?
14. Il ne faut pas *se moquer de* son embarras.
15. Le pays développé *consent à* aider le pays en développement.

C. Donner l'équivalent en anglais:

1. Prenez garde de boire trop d'eau froide.
2. Elle tarde toujours à finir son travail.
3. Nous venons à rencontrer nos voisins chaque matin.
4. Vous sauront-ils bon gré de vos efforts?
5. Profitons du beau temps; allons à la plage.
6. Cela saute aux yeux, n'est-ce pas? Oui, j'y suis.
7. Il vaut la peine de dîner dans ce restaurant.
8. Viendra-t-elle à bout de battre le record?
9. Je venais de prendre les billets.
10. Voulez-vous bien envelopper ce cadeau?

D. Répondre à chaque question par une phrase complète en français:

1. A quel membre de votre famille ressemblez-vous?
2. Pourquoi n'en pouvez-vous plus?
3. Où pouvons-nous prendre des billets pour voir *Faust*?
4. Qu'est-ce que tu viens de faire?
5. Quand puis-je vous rendre visite?

E. Donner l'équivalent en français:

1. We almost lost the money.
2. I made up my mind to work hard.
3. Francis has just visited his friends.
4. We are exhausted.
5. It is better to go horseback riding.
6. I took advantage of it.
7. They are anxious to see him.
8. What does that mean?
9. I am willing to help you.
10. They thanked me for having come.

Cigognes

La cigogne est le symbole de l'Alsace. Ces oiseaux migrateurs font souvent leur nid sur des cheminées ou des toits de maisons.

6. IDIOMS INTRODUCED BY *À*–I

1. à (with characteristic), with

   La dame ***aux*** cheveux blonds est ma tante.
   The lady with the blond hair is my aunt.

2. à (when one is *on* the means of transportation), on, by

   à bicyclette, on a bicycle, by bicycle
   à cheval, on horseback
   à pied, on foot

   Le mousquetaire quitta Paris ***à cheval.***
   The musketeer left Paris on horseback.

3. ***à*** (with time expressions), good-bye until

   à bientôt, see you soon, so long
   à demain, see you tomorrow
   à samedi, good-bye until Saturday
   à ce soir, see you tonight
   au revoir, good-bye, see you again
   à tout à l'heure, see you in a little while

   Nous allons chez nous maintenant. ***A lundi.***
   We're going home now. See you Monday.

4. **à cause de,** because of, on account of

   J'ai mal à la tête ***à cause du*** bruit.
   My head hurts because of the noise.

5. **à côté de,** next to, beside

   Il y avait une lampe ***à côté de*** moi.
   There was a lamp next to me.

6. **à force de,** by, by means of, by dint of (= by repeated efforts)

   A force de travailler, il a réussi.
   By (dint of) working, he succeeded.

7. **à partir de,** from . . . on, beginning (with)

   A partir de ce moment, nous étions amis.
   From that moment on, we were friends.

8. **à propos de** / **au sujet de** } about, concerning

   J'ai beaucoup lu ***à propos*** (***au sujet***) ***de*** l'art.
   I have read much about art.

9. **à droite,** on (to) the right

   A droite on voit la Seine.
   On the right you see the Seine.

10. **à gauche,** on (to) the left

    Tournez ***à gauche*** devant l'église.
    Turn to the left in front of the church.

11. **à demi** / **à moitié** } half, halfway

    Elle a rempli le verre ***à demi.***
    She filled the glass halfway.

    La pomme est ***à moitié*** mangée.
    The apple is half eaten.

12. **à jamais,** forever

    Je garderai ***à jamais*** votre lettre.
    I shall keep your letter forever.

13. **à merveille,** wonderfully well, marvelously

    Lucie chante ***à merveille***, n'est-ce pas?
    Lucy sings wonderfully well, doesn't she?

14. **à part,** aside

    Il m'a pris ***à part*** pour me dire le secret.
    He took me aside to tell me the secret.

15. **à peine,** hardly, scarcely

    Le paysan savait ***à peine*** lire.
    The peasant could scarcely read.

16. **à présent,** now, at present

    Que font-ils ***à présent?***
    What are they doing now?

17. **à travers,** through, across

    Ce chemin mène ***à travers*** le parc.
    This road leads across the park.

18. **à haute voix,** aloud, out loud

    L'étudiant a récité le poème ***à haute voix.***
    The student recited the poem aloud.

19. **à voix basse,** in a low voice

    Dans la bibliothèque on parle ***à voix basse.***
    In the library we speak in a low voice.

20. **à peu près,** nearly, about, approximately

    Le préfet avait ***à peu près*** quarante ans.
    The prefect was about forty years old.

21. **à quoi bon** (+ infinitive)? what's the use of?

    A quoi bon se plaindre tout le temps?
    What's the use of complaining all the time?

22. **à son gré,** as one pleases, to one's liking

    J'agis toujours ***à mon gré.***
    I always act as I please.

23. **à tout prix,** at any cost

    L'artiste compte l'achever ***à tout prix.***
    The artist intends to complete it at any cost.

24. **à vrai dire,** to tell the truth

    A vrai dire, je m'en doutais.
    To tell the truth, I suspected it.

EXERCICES

A. Remplacer les mots en italique par une expression équivalente:

1. Ils demeurent *maintenant* au Danemark.
2. *Vraiment*, je ne l'ai pas reconnu.
3. Vous dansez *d'une façon merveilleuse.*
4. L'armée a marché *par le milieu de* la forêt.
5. Il y avait *environ* dix livres sur le bureau.
6. Nous *ne* voyageons *guère*.
7. *En étudiant* sérieusement, il devint le premier de la classe.
8. Elle avait promis à son mari de l'aimer *pour toujours.*
9. J'ai beaucoup appris *au sujet de* la civilisation française.
10. Le fermier était *à demi* endormi.

B. Remplacer chaque tiret en employant une fois un des mots indiqués à droite:

1. A ______ d'aujourd'hui, je vais mettre de l'argent à ______ chaque mois.
2. Parlons à voix ______; les enfants dorment.
3. On met la fourchette à ______ de l'assiette; le couteau et la cuiller à ______.
4. Il n'est pas nécessaire de te dépêcher. Tu peux faire le travail à ton ______.
5. La route passait à ______ une région tropicale.
6. —Vous vous sentez bien? —Certainement, je me porte à ______.
7. Quel est ce garçon ______ yeux bleus et ______ la figure ronde?
8. A ______ dire, j'ai oublié de mettre votre lettre à la poste.
9. Le docteur a un téléphone à ______ de son lit.

à
aux
basse
cause
côté
droite
gauche
gré
l'heure
jamais
merveille
moitié
part
partir
peine

10. Cette tasse est à ______ pleine.
11. Il y avait beaucoup de mines flottantes à ______ de la guerre.
12. —Vous tenez à les protéger? —Bien sûr, nous les protégerons à ______ prix.
13. Le monsieur m'a souri quoique je le connaisse à ______.
14. Comptent-ils demeurer à ______ dans cette ville?
15. A ______ bon attendre ici plus longtemps? Nous partons. A tout à ______.

quoi
tout
travers
vrai

C. Traduire en français les mots en italique:

1. Connaissez-vous cet homme *with the black beard?*
2. *From tomorrow on* nous étudierons ensemble.
3. *What's the use of* lui en parler?
4. Dans une voiture américaine, la place du chauffeur est *on the left.*
5. Mon père lisait le journal *aloud.*

6. Je l'ai fait *because of* vous.
7. Je dois vous quitter maintenant. *See you tomorrow night.*
8. Ils y sont allés *on foot*, pas *by bicycle.*
9. Elle arrange ses affaires *as she pleases.*
10. *By dint of* forger, on devient forgeron.

D. Répondre à chaque question par une phrase complète en français:

1. Qui est assis à côté de toi en classe?
2. Combien de temps nous faudra-t-il à peu près pour finir nos devoirs?
3. Avez-vous l'habitude de compléter les choses ou de les faire à demi?
4. Quelle histoire leur mère a-t-elle lue à haute voix aux petits enfants?
5. A propos de quoi vous a-t-on interrogé?

Malmaison—la chambre de l'impératrice Joséphine

Le château de la Malmaison, à l'ouest de Paris, fut le séjour de l'impératrice Joséphine, première femme de Napoléon Bonaparte. Actuellement c'est un musée napoléonien.

7. IDIOMS INTRODUCED BY *À*–II

1. **à la bonne heure!** Good! Fine!

   Je vous donnerai ma réponse demain. ***A la bonne heure!***
   I'll give you my answer tomorrow. Fine!

2. **à la campagne,** in (to) the country

   Nous avons passé quinze jours ***à la campagne.***
   We spent two weeks in the country.

3. **à l'école,** in (to) school

   Ceux qui étudient aiment à aller ***à l'école.***
   Those who study like to go to school.

4. **à l'étranger,** abroad

   Ma sœur et son mari demeurent ***à l'étranger.***
   My sister and her husband are living abroad.

5. **à la fin,** finally

   A la fin il s'est mis à pleuvoir.
   Finally it began to rain.

6. **à l'heure,** on time

   Est-ce que l'autobus est parti ***à l'heure?***
   Did the bus leave on time?

7. **à cette heure,** at this (that) time

   Où allez-vous ***à cette heure?***
   Where are you going at this time?

8. **à la fois,** at the same time

   Peut-on jouer et travailler ***à la fois?***
   Can we play and work at the same time?

9. **à temps,** in time

   Il arrive ***à temps*** pour dîner.
   He arrives in time for dinner.

10. **à la main,** in one's hand

    Qu'est-ce que le bébé tient ***à la main?***
    What is the baby holding in his hand?

11. **à la maison,** at home, home

    Serez-vous ***à la maison*** ce soir?
    Will you be home tonight?

12. **à la mode,** in style

    Ses robes sont toujours ***à la mode.***
    Her dresses are always in style.

13. **à l'occasion de,** at the time of, on the occasion of

    A l'occasion de son mariage, il a porté un complet bleu marin.
    On the occasion of his marriage, he wore a navy blue suit.

14. **à la page . . . ,** on page . . .

    La leçon commence ***à la page*** onze.
    The lesson begins on page eleven.

15. **au contraire,** on the contrary

    Ne sait-elle pas nager? ***Au contraire***, elle nage très bien.
    Can't she swim? On the contrary, she swims very well.

16. **au loin,** in the distance

    On pouvait voir ***au loin*** le navire.
    They could see the ship in the distance.

17. **au moins,** at least

    Cela coûte mille dollars ***au moins.***
    That costs at least a thousand dollars.

18. **au bas de,** at the bottom of

    Nous l'avons rencontré ***au bas de*** l'escalier.
    We met him at the bottom of the staircase.

19. **au bout de,** at the end of, after

    Au bout d'un mois, elle est rentrée.
    At the end of a month, she came home.

20. **au courant de,** informed of

    Le président est ***au courant des*** affaires étrangères.
    The President is informed about foreign affairs.

    Il m'a mis ***au courant des*** faits.
    He acquainted me with the facts.

21. **au-dessous de,** below, beneath

    Vous verrez mon nom ***au-dessous du*** vôtre.
    You will see my name below yours.

22. **au-dessus de,** above, over

    Un de mes amis demeure ***au-dessus de*** nous.
    One of my friends lives above us.

23. **au fond de,** in the bottom of

    Il y a de l'eau ***au fond du*** puits.
    There is water in the bottom of the well.

24. **au haut de,** at the top of

    Écrivez votre adresse ***au haut de*** la lettre.
    Write your address at the top of the letter.

25. **au lieu de,** instead of

    Réfléchissez un peu ***au lieu de*** parler.
    Think a little instead of speaking.

26. **au milieu de,** in the middle of

    Il s'est réveillé ***au milieu de*** la nuit.
    He woke up in the middle of the night.

27. **au pied de,** at the foot of

    Le concierge se tenait ***au pied de*** l'échelle.
    The concierge was standing at the foot of the ladder.

EXERCICES

A. Donner l'équivalent en anglais:

1. au fond de la mer
2. au lieu de se battre
3. au haut du gratte-ciel
4. au moins une douzaine
5. habillé à la dernière mode
6. au pied de la colline
7. au bout de huit jours
8. au bas de l'arbre
9. au milieu du 18e siècle
10. à l'occasion de mon seizième anniversaire

B. Remplacer chaque tiret en employant une fois un des mots indiqués à droite:

1. Le président se tient au ______ de l'état de l'économie.
2. Je me brosse les dents au ______ deux fois par jour.
3. –Jeanne voudrait attendre ici au ______ de faire la queue. –A la bonne ______!
4. A six heures du matin, le soleil se levait ______ de l'horizon.
5. Il me semble que les avions partent rarement à ______.
6. Armand ne s'occupe pas du passé. Au ______, il ne s'occupe que de l'avenir.
7. Puisqu'il faisait trop chaud pour porter des gants, Mme Duclos les tenait à la ______.
8. Le dentiste ne pouvait pas sauver la dent parce qu'elle n'avait pas été traitée à ______.
9. Le secrétaire était à la ______ souriant et grave.
10. Il faisait de plus en plus froid. A la ______, la température descendit jusqu'à dix degrés ______ de zéro.

au-dessous
au-dessus
bout
contraire
courant
étranger
fin
fois
fond
heure
l'heure
lieu
loin
main
mode
moins
temps

C. Compléter chaque phrase en donnant l'équivalent des mots entre parenthèses:

1. (Finally) ______ ils ont atteint le sommet du mont Blanc.
2. (in time) Est-ce que le médecin y est arrivé ______?
3. (below) Nous pouvions voir les maisons couvertes de neige ______ nous.
4. (in the distance) Tout à coup, ils ont remarqué ______ un pont de bois.
5. (at this time) Peut-on lui téléphoner ______?

6. (abroad) Quand comptez-vous aller ______?
7. (above the) L'aviateur voulait monter ______ nuages.
8. (on the contrary) Lisette n'est pas paresseuse; ______ elle est très diligente.
9. (Fine!) Les deux adversaires se sont mis d'accord? ______
10. (on time) Nous ne savons pas pourquoi Jacques n'arrive jamais ______.

D. Répondre à chaque question par une phrase complète en français:

1. Qui est-ce que je vois au bout de la rue?
2. Pourquoi tiens-tu à aller à l'école?
3. Quel village se trouve au pied du mont Blanc?
4. A quelle page se trouve cet exercice?
5. Y a-t-il un chiffre au bas ou au haut de cette page?
6. Pouvez-vous chanter et manger à la fois?
7. Qu'est-ce qu'on avait mis au milieu de la table?
8. Garçon qu'est-ce que je peux avoir au lieu de poisson?
9. Garde-t-elle ses chapeaux au-dessus ou au-dessous de ses robes dans l'armoire?
10. Qu'y a-t-il au fond de ce vase?
11. Êtes-vous au courant de ce qui se passe en France?
12. Quel est ce bruit que j'entends au loin?
13. As-tu un crayon ou un stylo à la main?
14. Si vous aviez l'occasion d'aller à l'étranger, où iriez-vous?
15. Que préférez-vous faire demain, aller à la campagne ou rester à la maison?

8. IDIOMS INTRODUCED BY *DE*

1. **d'abord,** first, at first

   D'abord essuyez vos larmes; puis nous parlerons.
   First dry your tears; then we will talk.

2. **D'accord.** Agreed. O.K.

   –Je vous prêterai l'argent à cinq pour cent. ***–D'accord.***
   "I'll lend you the money at five percent." "O.K."

3. **d'ailleurs,** besides, moreover

   D'ailleurs, je ne peux pas mentir.
   Besides, I cannot lie.

4. **d'avance,** in advance, beforehand

   Nous les avons payés ***d'avance.***
   We paid for them in advance.

5. **de bon appétit,** heartily, with a good appetite

   Je suis trop triste pour manger ***de bon appétit.***
   I'm too sad to eat heartily.

6. **de bon cœur,** willingly, gladly

   Ses voisins l'ont aidé ***de bon cœur.***
   His neighbors helped him willingly.

7. **de bonne heure,** early

   Le malade s'est couché ***de bonne heure.***
   The patient went to bed early.

8. **de l'autre côté (de),** on the other side (of)

   Le château se trouve ***de l'autre côté du*** parc.
   The castle is on the other side of the park.

9. **du côté de,** in the direction of, toward

   Nous voyageons ***du côté de*** Bordeaux.
   We are traveling in the direction of Bordeaux.

10. **de mon côté,** for my part, as for me

    De mon côté, je préfère dîner en ville.
    For my part, I prefer to dine out.

11. **de jour en jour,** from day to day

    Vous écrivez mieux ***de jour en jour.***
    You write better from day to day.

12. **de plus en plus,** more and more, -er and -er

    Elle devient ***de plus en plus*** belle (***de plus en plus*** faible).
    She is becoming more and more beautiful (weaker and weaker).

13. **de temps en temps** / **de temps à autre** } from time to time, occasionally

    De temps en temps / ***De temps à autre*** } on pouvait voir la bannière étoilée.
    From time to time, we could see the star-spangled banner.

14. **de nouveau** / **encore une fois** } again

    Il a examiné ***de nouveau*** (***encore une fois***) la voiture.
    He examined the car again.

15. **d'ordinaire,** usually

    D'ordinaire ce magasin ferme à six heures.
    Usually this store closes at six o'clock.

16. **de parti pris,** deliberately

    Lui ont-ils désobéi ***de parti pris?***
    Did they disobey her deliberately?

17. **de la part de,** on behalf of, from

    Il est venu ***de la part de*** son maître.
    He came on behalf of his master.

18. **de quelle couleur . . . ?** what color . . . ?

    De quelle couleur est le sable?
    What color is the sand?

19. **De rien.** / **Il n'y a pas de quoi.** / **Je vous en prie.** } You're welcome. Don't mention it.

    Merci de tout ce que vous avez fait. ***De rien.***
    Thanks for all you've done. Don't mention it.

20. **de rigueur,** (socially) obligatory, required

    A ce bal, le smoking sera ***de rigueur.***
    At that dance, a tuxedo will be obligatory.

21. **du matin au soir,** from morning till night

    Mon cousin chante ***du matin au soir.***
    My cousin sings from morning till night.

22. **du moins,** at least

Elle est, ***du moins***, très fière.
She is, at least, very proud.

EXERCICES

A. Donner le mot qui manque:

1. Que j'ai faim! Je vais manger de ______ appétit.
2. Quand mon frère est enrhumé, il tousse du matin au ______.
3. ______ quelle couleur est la pierre précieuse de votre nouvelle bague?
4. Je voudrais vous féliciter des progrès remarquables que vous faites de jour ______ jour.
5. De temps à ______, on entendait le murmure de la rivière.
6. –Merci mille fois de vos conseils. –Je vous en ______.
7. Tu ne nous tromperais pas de parti ______, n'est-ce pas?
8. De ______ côté, je suis heureux comme un poisson dans l'eau.
9. Vous arrivez de ______ heure. Le taxi n'est pas encore ici.
10. –Voulez-vous m'expliquer le problème? –Certainement, je vous l'expliquerai de bon ______.

B. Remplacer les mots en italique par une expression équivalente:

1. Le visiteur a frappé *de nouveau* à la porte.
2. Il habiterait *volontiers* le Quartier latin.
3. Le chapeau n'est pas *obligatoire* ce soir.
4. *Généralement* nous y allons à bicyclette.
5. L'avion volait *vers* l'Espagne.
6. Je vous en remercie. *De rien.*
7. *Pour moi*, j'ai décidé de me spécialiser en musique.
8. *Quelquefois* notre téléphone ne marche pas.
9. Nous doutons qu'il l'ait fait *exprès.*
10. Je sais qu'il n'a pas beaucoup d'argent, mais a-t-il, *au moins*, de quoi vivre?

C. Compléter la seconde phrase de chaque série:

1. Ce fut un appartement assez confortable, du moins au commencement.
   It was quite a comfortable apartment, ______.
2. De quel côté voulez-vous marcher? Du côté de la Madeleine.
   ______ do you want to walk? ______ the Madeleine.
3. De temps en temps, il refuse de se lever de bonne heure.
   ______, he refuses ______.

4. Les idées d'Einstein intéressaient de plus en plus les savants du monde.
   Einstein's ideas ______.
5. D'ailleurs, nous l'invitons à dîner chez nous parce qu'il mange de si bon appétit.
   ______, we invite him to dine with us because ______.
6. We sent the concierge a gift on behalf of our family.
   Nous avons envoyé un cadeau à la concierge ______.
7. They say it will be colder and colder.
   On dit qu'il fera ______.
8. "First, tell us your story." "O.K."
   —______, racontez-nous votre histoire. —______.
9. Usually the cook prepares the meals in advance.
   ______ la cuisinière prépare les repas ______.
10. We could see a narrow street on the other side of the Seine.
    On pouvait voir une rue étroite ______.

D. Répondre à chaque question par une phrase complète en français:

1. Est-ce que la cravate est de rigueur dans ce restaurant?
2. De quelle couleur sont les petits pois?
3. Si nous sommes en France, quel pays se trouve de l'autre côté de la Manche?
4. Où allez-vous d'ordinaire le samedi matin?
5. Si je désire voir cette pièce de théâtre, qu'est-ce que je dois prendre d'abord?

Palais de l'Élysée

Le palais de l'Élysée à Paris, construit en 1718, sert de résidence au Président de la République.

9. IDIOMS INTRODUCED BY OTHER PREPOSITIONS

1. **autour de,** around

   On va lancer une fusée ***autour de*** la lune.
   They are going to launch a rocket around the moon.

2. **chez** (+ person), to (at) the house (place) of (the person)

   Il ne va pas ***chez*** lui; il va ***chez*** le coiffeur.
   He is not going home; he is going to the barber's.

3. **en** (when one is *inside* the means of transportation), by

   en automobile (***auto***), by automobile
   en avion, by plane
   en bateau, by boat
   en train, by train
   en voiture, by car

   Préférez-vous y aller ***en voiture*** ou ***en avion?***
   Do you prefer to go by car or plane?

4. **en arrière,** backward(s), behind

   Le soldat a fait un pas ***en arrière.***
   The soldier took a step backward.

5. **en bas,** downstairs

   J'ai perdu mes clefs ***en bas.***
   I lost my keys downstairs.

6. **en haut,** upstairs

   Connaissez-vous la famille qui demeure ***en haut?***
   Do you know the family that lives upstairs?

7. **en effet,** (yes) indeed, as a matter of fact

   Attendez-vous depuis longtemps? ***En effet***, j'attends depuis une heure.
   Have you been waiting long? Yes, indeed, I've been waiting for an hour.

8. **en face de,** opposite

   Elle s'est assise ***en face de*** nous.
   She sat down opposite us.

9. **en famille,** as a family, within (in the privacy of) the family

   Nous avons dîné ***en famille.***
   We dined as a family.

10. **en même temps,** at the same time

    Les deux enfants pleuraient ***en même temps.***
    The two children were crying at the same time.

11. **en plein air**, in the open air, outdoors

    Les enfants aiment jouer ***en plein air.***
    Children like to play outdoors.

12. **en retard**, late (= not on time)

    Je suis ***en retard*** de cinq minutes.
    I'm five minutes late.

13. **en tout cas**, in any case, at any rate

    En tout cas, vous n'avez rien à craindre.
    In any case, you have nothing to fear.

14. **en ville**, downtown, in (to, into) town

    Le samedi nous allons ***en ville*** avec nos camarades.
    On Saturdays we go downtown with our friends.

15. **par conséquent**, therefore, consequently

    Elle est partie pour l'Italie. ***Par conséquent***, je ne la vois plus.
    She has left for Italy. Consequently, I no longer see her.

16. **par exemple**, for example

    Les fromages français sont excellents–***par exemple***, le camembert.
    French cheeses are excellent–for example, Camembert.

17. **par hasard**, by chance

    Si, ***par hasard,*** vous le retrouvez, faites-le-moi savoir.
    If, by chance, you find it (if you happen to find it), let me know.

18. **par ici**, this way, in this direction

    Passez ***par ici,*** s'il vous plaît.
    Step this way, please.

19. **par là**, that way, in that direction

    Par là on peut voir la mairie.
    In that direction you can see the city hall.

20. **par jour (semaine, mois**, etc.), a (per) day (week, month, etc.)

    Ces ouvriers gagnent cent francs ***par jour.***
    Those workers earn a hundred francs a day.

21. **sans doute**, without doubt, undoubtedly

    Ce tapis-ci est ***sans doute*** le plus joli.
    This rug is undoubtedly the prettiest.

EXERCICES

A. Donner le mot qui manque:

1. Ils vont célébrer l'anniversaire ______ famille.
2. Le travail dans les mines est ______ doute très dur.
3. –Garçon, une table pour quatre. –______ ici, messieurs, s'il vous plaît.
4. Non, Roger n'est pas en haut. Il doit être en ______.
5. –Avez-vous vu récemment votre oncle? –Oui, je l'ai rencontré hier ______ hasard.
6. Ce nouvel appareil est très pratique. ______ même temps, il coûte assez cher.
7. Regarde devant vous, Yvonne, pas en ______.
8. Je ne veux pas rentrer tout de suite. Restons encore quelques minutes en ______ air.
9. Anne-Marie est très forte en histoire. Par ______, elle a toujours de bonnes notes.
10. Peut-on aller au pôle nord ______ auto?
11. Connaissez-vous M. Rolland? En ______, j'ai fait sa connaissance la semaine dernière.
12. Puisque nous sommes assez fatigués, nous allons directement ______ nous.
13. Elle fait des emplettes deux fois ______ semaine.
14. On n'est pas toujours d'accord. En ______ cas, les gens de la ville sont divisés sur cette question.
15. Quand nous serons en France, nous comptons voyager de Paris à Marseille ______ train.

B. Compléter chaque phrase en donnant l'équivalent des mots entre parenthèses:

1. (opposite) — Quel est ce bâtiment ______ la banque?
2. (around us) — Les feuilles continuent à tomber ______.
3. (downtown) — Voulez-vous m'accompagner? Je vais ______.
4. (In any case) — ______, nous partirons de bonne heure.
5. (behind) — Attendez-moi. Je ne veux pas rester ______.
6. (for example) — De mon côté, je préfère les sports, ______, l'alpinisme.
7. (within the family) — Cela s'était passé ______.
8. (an hour) — La cloche sonnait une fois ______.
9. (Yes, indeed) — –S'est-elle blessée gravement? –______, elle s'est cassé le bras.
10. (At the same time) — Le soleil brûlait les champs. ______, les feuilles mouraient sur les vignes.
11. (That way) — –Où les athlètes ont-ils couru? –______.
12. (by car) — Ils voyageaient au Canada ______.

13. (Therefore) Edmond ne se sentait pas bien. ______, il ne pouvait pas assister au concert.
14. (outdoors) Les campeurs ont passé le mois de juillet ______.
15. (without doubt) Le trésor est protégé, ______, par un chien de garde.

C. Répondre à chaque question par une phrase complète en français:

1. Combien d'heures par jour dormez-vous?
2. Qu'est-ce qui tourne autour de la Terre?
3. Qui demeure en face de vous?
4. Chez qui va-t-on pour se faire arracher une dent?
5. Aimeriez-vous mieux traverser l'océan Atlantique en bateau ou en avion?
6. Est-il possible que deux corps occupent le même lieu en même temps?
7. As-tu l'habitude d'arriver à l'heure ou en retard?
8. Quand aurons-nous l'occasion de déjeuner en plein air?
9. Allez-vous rester en haut ou voulez-vous m'attendre en bas?
10. Est-ce que les Duval sont encore au bord de la mer ou sont-ils de retour en ville?

La basilique de Lourdes

Lourdes, dans les Pyrénées, est un lieu de pèlerinage célèbre. La basilique majestueuse attire chaque année des milliers de dévots et de malades en quête d'une guérison miraculeuse.

10. MISCELLANEOUS IDIOMS AND EXPRESSIONS

1. **bien entendu,** of course

   Aimez-vous les sciences? ***Bien entendu,*** je suis un cours de chimie à présent.
   Do you like the sciences? Of course; I'm taking a course in chemistry now.

2. **bon gré mal gré,** whether one wants to or not

   Tu le feras ***bon gré mal gré.***
   You will do it whether you want to or not.

3. **bon marché,** cheap
   meilleur marché, cheaper

   Cette crème dentifrice est ***bon marché,*** mais l'autre est ***meilleur marché.***
   This toothpaste is cheap, but the other one is cheaper.

4. **bon pour,** good (kind) to

   Nos professeurs sont toujours ***bons pour*** nous.
   Our teachers are always good to us.

5. **Cela m'est égal.** That makes no difference to me. That's all the same to me.

   A quelle heure voulez-vous partir? ***Cela m'est égal.***
   At what time do you want to leave? That makes no difference to me.

6. **Cela ne fait rien.** That does not matter. That makes no difference.

   Je doute qu'il nous attende. ***Cela ne fait rien.***
   I doubt that he will wait for us. That does not matter.

7. **c'est-à-dire,** that is to say

   Nous avons visité la plus belle ville du monde, ***c'est-à-dire,*** Paris.
   We visited the most beautiful city in the world, that is to say, Paris.

8. **C'est entendu.** It's agreed. All right.

   Si tu as froid aux mains, mets tes gants de laine. ***C'est entendu.***
   If your hands are cold, put on your woolen gloves. All right.

9. **en huit jours,** in (= during) a week
   en quinze jours, in two weeks

   L'étudiant a appris toutes les règles ***en huit jours.***
   The student learned all the rules in a week.

10. **et ainsi de suite,** and so forth

    Étudiez le vocabulaire, les verbes, les idiotismes, ***et ainsi de suite.***
    Study the vocabulary, verbs, idioms, and so forth.

11. **faute de,** for lack of

    Faute d'attention, Jacques a eu un zéro en arithmétique.
    For lack of attention, James received a zero in arithmetic.

12. **grâce à,** thanks to

    Grâce à vous, nous n'avons payé que la moitié du prix.
    Thanks to you, we paid only half the price.

13. **Il y a . . . ,** . . . ago

    On me l'a envoyé ***il y a*** longtemps.
    They sent it to me a long time ago.

14. **Il y avait une fois . . . ,** Once (upon a time) there was (were) . . .

    Il y avait une fois un grand méchant loup.
    Once there was a big, bad wolf.

15. **Jamais de la vie!** Never! Out of the question!

    Voulez-vous vendre le chef-d'œuvre? ***Jamais de la vie!***
    Do you want to sell the masterpiece? Never!

16. **le long de,** along

    Nous admirions les beaux arbres ***le long du*** canal.
    We admired the beautiful trees along the canal.

17. **n'importe,** never mind, no matter

    J'ai oublié mon pull. ***N'importe***, je vous prêterai le mien.
    I forgot my sweater. Never mind, I'll lend you mine.

18. **peu à peu,** little by little, gradually

    Peu à peu il apprend à étudier.
    Little by little he is learning to study.

19. **Plaît-il?** What did you say? Would you mind repeating? I beg your pardon.

    –La cloche a déjà sonné, Pierre.
    "The bell has already rung, Peter."

    –***Plaît-il***, monsieur?
    "What did you say, sir?"

20. **quant à,** as for

    Quant à moi, je préfère flâner sur les quais.
    As for me, I prefer to stroll on the quays.

21. **que** } how (in exclamations)
comme }

Que vous êtes joli! *Comme* il fait froid!
How pretty you are! How cold the weather is!

22. **tant bien que mal,** rather badly, after a fashion, so-so

Savez-vous patiner? *Tant bien que mal.*
Can you skate? After a fashion.

23. **tant mieux,** so much the better

J'ai ma propre voiture. *Tant mieux!*
I have my own car. So much the better!

24. **tant pis,** so much the worse

Il ne fait que jouer. *Tant pis* pour lui.
All he does is play. So much the worse for him.

25. **tous (les) deux,** both

Nous avons vu notre oncle et notre tante. *Tous les deux* se portent bien.
We saw our uncle and aunt. Both are feeling fine.

26. **tout à coup,** suddenly

Tout à coup il commença à pleuvoir.
Suddenly it began to rain.

27. **tout à fait,** entirely, quite

Le toit est *tout à fait* couvert de neige.
The roof is entirely covered with snow.

28. **tout à l'heure** { just now, a little while ago (referring to immediate past)
in a little while, presently (referring to immediate future)

Elle a nettoyé la chambre *tout à l'heure.*
She cleaned the room just now.

Elle nettoiera la chambre *tout à l'heure.*
She will clean the room in a little while.

29. **tout de même** } just the same
quand même }

Il n'est pas très intelligent, mais elle va l'épouser *tout de même.*
He isn't very intelligent, but she is going to marry him just the same.

30. **tout de suite** / **à l'instant** } immediately, at once

Ils m'ont téléphoné ***tout de suite.***
They telephoned me immediately.

Ramassez ce papier ***à l'instant.***
Pick up that paper at once.

EXERCICES

A. Compléter la phrase en français:

1. Sa fortune avait disparu peu ______ peu.
2. Cette cravate n'est pas chère; elle est ______ marché.
3. ______ à coup, il a décidé de rompre avec les traditions.
4. Comment vous portez-vous ce matin? Tant bien ______ mal.
5. Soyez bon ______ cet enfant; il est malade.
6. Son visage exprime toutes les émotions: la joie, la tristesse, la honte, la peur, et ainsi de ______.
7. ______ les deux sont tombés dans l'eau.
8. Chaque soir nous étudions bon gré ______ gré.
9. Comment! Ils ont l'intention de vous rendre visite avec leurs enfants? ______ pis pour vous!
10. ______ d'argent, il ne pouvait pas payer la note.

B. Donner l'équivalent en anglais:

1. Quant à nous, nous devrons quand même partir.
2. Il y avait une fois trois souris aveugles.
3. Pourra-t-elle oublier son enfance malheureuse? Jamais de la vie!
4. Il faut que tout le monde dorme bon gré mal gré.
5. Votre santé n'est jamais tout à fait la même chaque jour.
6. On peut peindre le portrait en quinze jours.
7. Peu à peu, le palais tombait en ruine.
8. J'y suis arrivé à temps, grâce à ma bicyclette.

9. –Monsieur, apportez-moi un café noir. –Plaît-il, madame? –N'importe, j'ai changé d'avis.
10. Nous aimons les fruits d'été, c'est-à-dire, les fraises, les melons, les pêches, et ainsi de suite.

C. Remplacer les mots en italique par une expression équivalente:

1. Il va pleuvoir *dans un instant.*
2. *Naturellement*, nous avons commandé un bon repas dans le restaurant.
3. L'armée avait entouré *graduellement* les troupes ennemies.
4. Cette robe coûte beaucoup d'argent, mademoiselle. *Cela ne me fait rien.*
5. *De mon côté*, j'ai envie de prendre un bain de soleil.
6. On peut *quand même* se demander comment cette machine fonctionne.
7. *Que* votre fils est travailleur!
8. Nous ne sommes pas *entièrement* satisfaits de cette peinture.
9. *Je viens de déjeuner.*
10. On nous avait envoyé la nouvelle *à l'instant.*

D. Traduire en français les mots en italique:

1. Je vous verrai ce soir à l'Opéra. *It's agreed.*
2. Il n'y a pas de taxes à payer. *So much the better!*
3. Leur mère les a grondés *both.*
4. On a construit la maison *in a week.*
5. Sait-il danser? *After a fashion.*
6. Elle n'en est pas *quite* sûre.
7. *Thanks to* notre professeur, nous avons réussi à l'examen.
8. J'ai cassé un verre. *That does not matter.*
9. *For lack of* une bonne réponse, la femme s'est tuée.
10. Je me suis fait mal *a month ago.*

E. Répondre à chaque question par une phrase complète en français:

1. A qui parliez-vous tout à l'heure dans la rue?
2. Où le bon vin est-il meilleur marché, en France ou en Amérique?
3. Connaissez-vous quelqu'un qui soit tout à fait content?
4. Quels beaux édifices est-ce que les touristes visitent le long de la Loire?
5. Après une opération sérieuse, guérit-on tout de suite ou peu à peu?

IDIOM REVIEW QUIZZES

A

Choisir le mot ou l'expression qui complète le sens de la phrase:

1. Les voyageurs partiront (à la bonne heure, de bonne heure) dimanche matin.
2. Je sais ce que vous pensez (à, de) moi.
3. Puisqu'il est trop gros, il (se passe, se charge) de sucre.
4. Avez-vous (fait, eu) nettoyer la chambre?

5. Après une journée de travail, je (viens à bout, n'en peux plus).
6. Elle (s'agit, est en train) d'ouvrir le courrier.
7. Bien entendu, nous avons entendu (parler, dire) de Jean-Jacques Rousseau.
8. Je comprends (à peu près, à travers) tout ce que le professeur a dit.
9. Que vous jouez bien (de, à) la clarinette!
10. Après l'orage, elle est rentrée (à la fois, à moitié) morte.

B

Traduire en français l'expression entre parenthèses:

1. (She was pretending to) être princesse.
2. Est-ce que je peux (take advantage of) cette occasion pour vous remercier?
3. (What's the use of) faire des promesses qu'on ne peut pas tenir?
4. Est-ce que cet homme d'état (lacks) ambition personnelle?
5. La fenêtre de ma chambre (looks out on) la rue de Rivoli.
6. (They were accustomed to) dîner tard.
7. La qualité de la vie, c'est (first) la qualité de l'endroit où l'on vit.
8. Connaissez-vous ce garçon (with the black hair)?
9. La viande devient (more and more) chère chaque mois.
10. Je me demande si (she suspects) la vérité.

C

Choisir la réponse qu'on *ne peut pas* substituer pour l'expression en italique:

1. Cela m'a fait *plaisir.*

   (*a*) mal (*b*) pleurer (*c*) peur (*d*) colère

2. Nous *avons besoin de* lui.

   (*a*) nous fâchons contre
   (*b*) assistons à
   (*c*) avons entendu parler de
   (*d*) nous fions à

3. Espérons qu'il *l'a appris par cœur.*

   (*a*) en pensera
   (*b*) ne pleuvra pas à verse
   (*c*) les en a remerciés
   (*d*) ne tardera pas à venir

4. –Au revoir. Je vous reverrai plus tard chez Hélène. *–A bientôt.*

   (*a*) D'accord.
   (*b*) A part.
   (*c*) A tout à l'heure.
   (*d*) C'est entendu.

5. Nos amis ont décidé de faire bâtir leur nouvelle maison *au pied de la colline.*

   (*a*) en face du parc
   (*b*) à côté de la nôtre
   (*c*) au fond de la mer
   (*d*) de l'autre côté de la rivière

6. Je doute qu'il puisse *monter à cheval.*

   (*a*) faillir
   (*b*) se tirer d'affaire
   (*c*) y être à l'heure
   (*d*) se mettre en route demain

7. De quoi *parlaient-elles?*

   (*a*) s'agit-il (*b*) te sers-tu (*c*) riait-il (*d*) entendez-vous dire

8. —Comment Claudine danse-t-elle? —*Très bien.*

   (*a*) D'une façon formidable.
   (*b*) A merveille.
   (*c*) D'ordinaire.
   (*d*) Tant bien que mal.

9. Il se peut qu'on le fasse *vite.*

   (*a*) exprès (*b*) à demain (*c*) de bon cœur (*d*) tout de même

10. N'avez-vous pas *honte* de le faire?

    (*a*) le temps (*b*) envie (*c*) de quoi (*d*) l'habitude

D

Donner une expression équivalente à celle en italique:

1. On lui a demandé de se taire *immédiatement.*
2. Tout le monde *a commencé à* chanter.
3. *Quelquefois* nous le rencontrons dans le métro.
4. *Tu parles en vain;* nous refusons de suivre tes conseils.
5. *Après* une demi-heure, il s'était endormi.
6. Je vais *envoyer chercher* le père de cet enfant.
7. Juliette *a épousé* un poète bien connu.
8. Si vous marchez *vers* la banque, vous trouverez l'hôtel.
9. Le pêcheur *a failli* tomber dans la mer.
10. Nous allons *être présents à* la réunion demain soir.

E

Compléter les phrases en donnant l'équivalent des mots entre parenthèses:

1. (From today on)	______ ils vont être très sages.
2. (she does not feel like)	Le matin ______ se lever.
3. (I am grateful to him for)	______ tout ce qu'il a fait pour moi.
4. (is about to)	Une vague ne paraît jamais plus forte que lorsqu'elle ______ se briser.
5. (have you a grudge against)	Pourquoi ______ votre voisin?
6. (whether she wants to or not)	Elle aime les desserts, mais elle devra s'en passer ______.
7. (We had just discovered)	______ la cause de la maladie.

8. (Do you realize the) ______ possibilités de la science?
9. (she changes her mind) Chaque fois qu'on lui parle ______.
10. (In any case) ______, il faut penser à ce qui arrivera avant d'agir.

F

Choisir la réponse qu'on *ne peut pas* substituer pour l'expression en italique:

1. *Tout à coup*, nous entendîmes son cri.

   (*a*) Grâce au silence (*b*) En même temps (*c*) Tant mieux (*d*) Par hasard

2. Henri ne *s'occupe* de rien.

   (*a*) s'attend (*b*) se doute (*c*) se moque (*d*) s'étonne

3. Je crois qu'il a *dix-huit ans.*

   (*a*) de la chance (*b*) beau (*c*) mal aux dents (*d*) la parole

4. Ils préfèrent l'obtenir *tout de suite.*

   (*a*) quand même (*b*) tout à fait (*c*) peu à peu (*d*) d'avance

5. Les soldats *ont célébré* leur victoire.

   (*a*) songent à (*b*) ont joui de (*c*) profitaient de (*d*) se souviennent

6. L'acteur *continue à* rire.

   (*a*) a éclaté de (*b*) les a faits (*c*) avait l'air de (*d*) s'est mis à

7. René va *à la campagne.*

   (*a*) la bonne heure (*b*) la pêche (*c*) l'étranger (*d*) la rencontre de son ami

8. Nous sommes certains qu'elle fait *des progrès.*

   (*a*) la sourde oreille (*b*) son mieux (*c*) des emplettes (*d*) à sa tête

9. Je lui *pose une question.*

   (*a*) en veux (*b*) fais savoir mon adresse (*c*) demande une réponse (*d*) fais venir

10. Il paraît que M. Leblanc *ne parle* à personne.

   (*a*) ne rend visite (*b*) ne s'approche (*c*) ne ressemble (*d*) ne se fie

11. SOME COMMON PROVERBS

1. **A force de forger on devient forgeron.**
   Practice makes perfect.
2. **A l'œuvre on connaît l'ouvrier.**
   A workman is known by his work.
3. **L'appétit vient en mangeant.**
   The more you have, the more you want.
4. **Les bons comptes font les bons amis.**
   Short reckonings make long friends.
5. **Chose promise est chose due.**
   Promises should be kept.
6. **Contentement passe richesse.**
   Contentment is better than riches.
7. **Dis-moi qui tu hantes, je te dirai qui tu es.**
   A man is known by the company he keeps.
8. **Il faut battre le fer pendant qu'il est chaud.**
   Strike while the iron is hot.
   Make hay while the sun shines.
9. **Il n'est pire eau que l'eau qui dort.**
   Still waters run deep.
10. **Le mieux est l'ennemi du bien.**
    Leave well enough alone.
11. **Ne vendez pas la peau de l'ours avant de l'avoir tué.**
    Don't count your chickens before they're hatched.
12. **Ne remettez pas au lendemain ce que vous pouvez faire aujourd'hui.**
    Never put off till tomorrow what you can do today.
13. **Noblesse oblige.**
    Rank imposes obligation.
14. **On connaît ses amis au besoin.**
    A friend in need is a friend indeed.
15. **Quand le chat n'y est pas, les souris dansent.**
    When the cat is away, the mice will play.
16. **Qui ne risque rien, n'a rien.**
    Nothing ventured, nothing gained.
17. **Si jeunesse savait, si vieillesse pouvait.**
    If youth but knew and age could do.

18. **Tout vient à point à qui sait attendre.**
    Everything comes to him who waits.

19. **L'union fait la force.**
    In union there is strength.

20. **Un "tiens" vaut mieux que deux "tu l'auras."**
    A bird in the hand is worth two in the bush.

EXERCICES

A. Compléter le proverbe:

1. Contentement passe ______.
2. Tout vient à point ______.
3. Les bons comptes ______.
4. Si jeunesse savait, ______.
5. Le mieux est l'ennemi ______.
6. Quand le chat n'y est pas, ______.
7. A l'œuvre on connaît ______.
8. Ne remettez pas au lendemain ______.
9. Chose promise est ______.
10. Noblesse ______.

B. Donner le proverbe français qui exprime chacune des idées suivantes:

1. Le bonheur est plus précieux que l'argent.
2. Un succès ne peut s'obtenir sans quelque risque.
3. Plus on a, plus on veut avoir.
4. Posséder peu, mais sûrement, vaut mieux qu'espérer beaucoup, sans certitude.
5. Les jeunes manquent d'expérience; les vieillards, de force.
6. On juge une personne d'après la société qu'elle fréquente.
7. Avec du temps et de la patience, on obtient ce que l'on désire.

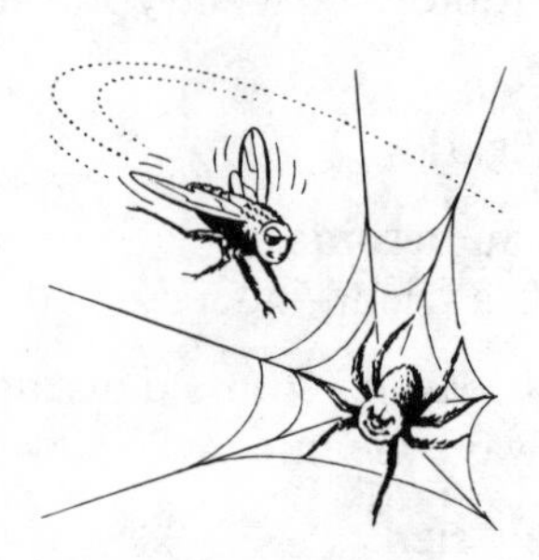

8. On risque de tout perdre en voulant trop gagner.
9. Quand le professeur est absent, les élèves profitent de leur liberté.
10. On est obligé de faire ce qu'on a promis.

C. Donner le proverbe équivalent en anglais:

1. Il n'est pire eau que l'eau qui dort.
2. A force de forger on devient forgeron.
3. Ne vendez pas la peau de l'ours avant de l'avoir tué.
4. On connaît ses amis au besoin.
5. Dis-moi qui tu hantes, je te dirai qui tu es.
6. Un "tiens" vaut mieux que deux "tu l'auras."
7. L'appétit vient en mangeant.
8. Qui ne risque rien, n'a rien.
9. L'union fait la force.
10. Il faut battre le fer pendant qu'il est chaud.

D. Donner le proverbe français qui s'applique à chaque situation:

1. Si je dois emprunter de l'argent, je le rends le plus tôt possible.
2. En regardant le tableau qu'il avait peint, on savait que Gauguin était un grand artiste.
3. Malgré les mauvaises manières de la foule, l'ambassadeur resta calme et poli.
4. Travaillons ensemble, messieurs, et nous réussirons!
5. Pierre joue au tennis tous les jours; c'est la raison qu'il est expert.
6. Son mari lui a donné un collier de perles; maintenant elle désire un collier de diamants.
7. Je doute qu'il soit diligent; ses amis n'étudient jamais.
8. Elle a voyagé trente kilomètres par la neige pour voir son amie à l'hôpital.
9. Cet homme est d'apparence inoffensive, mais on dit que c'est un criminel dangereux.
10. Ma mère est bien aise d'avoir fait ses achats jeudi; vendredi il a plu à verse.

Danses régionales

Malgré la pénétration des danses modernes dans toutes les régions de la France, les danses folkloriques sont encore très en vogue.

Part IV—*Composition*

SUGGESTIONS FOR WRITING COMPOSITIONS IN FRENCH:

1. Plan each composition before you write it. Draw up an outline of your ideas.
2. Organize the ideas by arranging them in a logical sequence.
3. Attempt to crystallize your thoughts in French. Use vocabulary that you have already acquired. To give the flavor of the foreign language, be sure to include idiomatic expressions.
4. Devise an effective topic sentence. The last sentence should be an appropriate conclusion. To make either of these sentences more dramatic, a question, an exclamation, or even a proverb may be used.
5. Show your command of the language by using varied vocabulary. Use synonyms, where possible, to avoid repetition. Variety is essential in good composition writing.
6. Vary the sentence structure to avoid monotony. Include constructions such as those connected with the present participle, **depuis, quand, après,** the subjunctive, and "**si**" clauses.
7. Use connectives such as **par conséquent, d'ailleurs, à vrai dire, néanmoins, bien entendu,** and relative pronouns to achieve coherence, make transitions smooth, and give the composition a mature tone.
8. Reread the composition after you have written it. Check particularly the spelling, accentuation, and agreement.

WRITING LETTERS IN FRENCH:

1. The date is written as follows:

   le 1er avril 1978
   le 9 février 1984

2. Some salutations used in writing to relatives and friends are:

Cher Louis,	**Mes (très) chers parents,**
Chère Louise,	**Mon cher cousin,**
Mon cher ami,	**Ma chère tante,**
Chère amie,	

3. Some endings used in such letters are:

Votre ami (dévoué),	**Salutations empressées,**
Ton fils reconnaissant,	**Amicalement vôtre,**
Votre nièce affectueuse,	**A bientôt,**
Bien cordialement,	**Dans l'espoir de (te) vous lire bientôt,**
Cordialement à vous,	**Je vous serre bien cordialement la main.**
Affectueusement,	**Recevez mes meilleurs souvenirs.**
Bien à vous,	**Je vous embrasse de tout mon cœur.**

EXAMPLE OF A GUIDED COMPOSITION:

The exercises in guided composition provide a variety of questions to prepare the student for writing a well-ordered and coherent composition. Following these exercises is a list of other topics suitable for free composition.

To assist the student in writing guided compositions, an example of a question and a suggested answer are given below.

Question:

Write a letter in French to a friend about the homework you do each night. Include the information called for in the following outline:

a. how much time the homework takes
b. how you feel about doing the assignment
c. where you work and why
d. what preparations you make before starting
e. what interruption sometimes occurs
f. how you cope with such a situation
g. what action you take if you cannot do part of the assignment
h. what you do to prevent boredom when the assignment is very long
i. you are hoping to hear from your friend soon

Suggested Answer:

Springfield, le 6 mai 19--

Cher Gérard,

Je n'ai guère le temps de vous écrire car je dois passer plus de deux heures et demie chaque soir à faire mes devoirs. Puisqu'il est nécessaire de travailler dur pour réussir, j'étudie diligemment.

Pour éviter le bruit de la télévision, c'est dans ma chambre que je travaille la plupart du temps. Avant de commencer, je m'assure que j'ai tout ce qu'il me faut, surtout des bonbons à manger. De temps à autre, un de mes amis paresseux, qui aime bavarder au lieu d'étudier, me donne un coup de téléphone. Mais comme je n'ai pas envie de mettre mon père en colère, je ne cause pas trop longtemps.

Si je trouve impossible de faire une partie des devoirs, je téléphone à Étienne qui, me semble-t-il, a appris tous les livres par cœur. Afin de ne pas m'ennuyer quand les devoirs sont très longs, j'interromps mon travail pendant quelques minutes pour me quereller avec mon frère cadet. Voilà la façon dont je fais mes devoirs, moi!

Espérant recevoir bientôt de vos nouvelles, je vous salue bien cordialement.

Votre dévoué,
Victor

EXERCISES IN GUIDED COMPOSITION

A. En vous laissant guider par les suggestions et le vocabulaire suivants, écrivez une composition de cent mots environ sur le sujet suivant:

PORTRAIT D'UNE GRANDE VILLE

a. Pourquoi on devrait visiter cette ville
b. Les quartiers divers qui s'y trouvent
c. Les curiosités et les monuments à voir
d. Les avantages et les désavantages qu'elle offre
e. Pourquoi je l'aime (je ne l'aime pas)

Vocabulaire utile

habiter une ville moderne
demeurer dans une ville cosmopolite, à Chicago
une rue tranquille, calme, silencieuse, à sens unique
une avenue large, fréquentée, animée, bruyante
un bâtiment = un édifice
se presser = se dépêcher
une église, la bibliothèque, la banque, la poste, le musée, la fabrique
le gratte-ciel (les gratte-ciel), une université, le théâtre, le cinéma
le parc, le jardin zoölogique, le restaurant, le grand magasin, la gare
le marché, le trottoir, le pont, la statue, une grande place
un habitant, un agent de police, un autobus, le taxi, le métro

le bac, ferry
la banlieue, suburb
le centre, downtown district
la circulation, traffic
écraser, to run over
la foule, crowd
le guichet, box office, ticket window
l'hôtel de ville, city hall
un immeuble, apartment house
le kiosque, newsstand
le quai, wharf
stationner une voiture, to park a car
toutes les commodités modernes, all modern conveniences
traverser la chaussée avec précaution, to cross the street carefully
la vitrine, shop window, showcase

Idiotismes utiles

au loin = à une grande distance
avoir lieu
donner sur = avoir vue sur
du matin au soir
en face de
faire des progrès
il s'agit de = il est question de
prendre un billet

B. You have to purchase a gift for someone for a special occasion. Write an account in ten sentences describing the circumstances. Include in your composition the answers to the following questions:

a. What is the occasion?
b. About how much money do you intend to spend?
c. Where will you shop?
d. What two gifts might be suitable?
e. What will you ask the salesperson about the merchandise?
f. Supposing the recipient already owns the item chosen, what will you do?
g. How will the gift be delivered?
h. What message will you enclose with the gift?
i. How would you like to receive a similar gift?
j. Why?

C. Vous venez de recevoir de votre correspondant(e) français(e) une lettre dans laquelle il (elle) vous pose les questions suivantes. Écrivez une lettre à votre correspondant(e) dans laquelle vous répondez à toutes ces questions:

a. Comment et à quelle heure arrivez-vous à l'école chaque jour?
b. Que faites-vous d'ordinaire en route?
c. Pourquoi cette école vous plaît-elle?
d. Quelle amélioration suggérez-vous qu'on y fasse?
e. Quels cours suivez-vous cette année?
f. Quelle classe aimez-vous le mieux? Pourquoi?
g. Quelles sont les qualités de votre professeur préféré?
h. A quelles activités scolaires après les classes prenez-vous part?
i. Que comptez-vous faire après avoir reçu votre diplôme?

D. You are going out with a friend next Saturday evening. In connected paragraph form, explain the situation with particular reference to the following points:

a. how the appointment was arranged
b. whom you are going with and where you will meet
c. the outfit you intend to wear
d. where you expect to go and for what reason
e. what expenses will be involved
f. what refreshments you will probably have

g. what change there will be in your plans if the weather is bad
h. what kind of time you expect to have
i. what makes you think so
j. at what time you have to be home

E. Écrivez en français, d'après le plan suivant, une composition de 100 mots environ sur un voyage réel ou imaginaire:

a. Où êtes-vous allé?
b. Quand avez-vous fait ce voyage?
c. Comment et pourquoi l'avez-vous fait?
d. Quels préparatifs avez-vous dû faire?
e. Décrivez un endroit ou une ville qui vous a plu.
f. Racontez une aventure intéressante qui vous est arrivée.
g. Dites ce que vous avez aimé le mieux et pourquoi.

F. En vous laissant guider par les suggestions et le vocabulaire suivants, écrivez une composition de 100 mots environ sur le sujet suivant:

POURQUOI J'AIME L'HIVER

a. Le temps qu'il fait
b. La façon dont vous vous habillez
c. Comment vous vous amusez
d. Pourquoi vous (ne) préférez (pas) l'hiver aux autres saisons

Vocabulaire utile

il fait froid, il fait du vent, il neige, il gèle

geler = transformer en glace
la neige couvre la terre
la chute de neige, snowfall
glisser, to slide
glissant, slippery
le flocon de neige, snowflake

mettre des vêtements chauds
le pardessus, le manteau, une paire de gants
porter des sous-vêtements de laine
le cache-nez, muffler

le sport d'hiver
jeter des boules de neige
patiner sur la glace
se promener en traîneau, to go sleighing
les vacances de Noël
faire un bonhomme de neige
faire du ski

Idiotismes utiles

avoir froid aux mains
en plein air
manger de bon appétit
tenir à = avoir un grand désir de
s'amuser à = prendre plaisir à
se faire mal = se blesser
s'enrhumer = contracter un rhume
se porter bien = aller bien

G. Write a letter to a friend relating what happened when someone was recently ill in your family. The letter is to consist of nine grammatically complete sentences in French, containing the information called for below. Be sure to include in your letter the date, the salutation, and the complimentary close.

a. what symptoms the patient had
b. when you sent for the doctor
c. what you did to help the patient before the doctor came
d. what the doctor did
e. the doctor's diagnosis and prescription
f. the patient's reaction to the visit
g. how long the illness lasted
h. how the illness changed the family routine
i. what finally happened to the patient

H. Après beaucoup de réflexion, vous avez choisi votre carrière (career) future. Expliquez votre décision en traitant les points suivants:

a. la carrière que vous avez choisie
b. la raison de votre choix
c. les cours dont vous aurez encore besoin
d. le temps qu'il vous faudra
e. les possibilités d'avancement
f. un avantage de cette carrière
g. un désavantage possible
h. l'argent que vous espérez gagner
i. ce qui vous fait croire que vous réussirez à cette carrière
j. ce que votre famille pense de votre choix

I. You often help at home with the family chores. Write in connected paragraph form an account of what you do, including the following information:

a. what chores you usually help with
b. why you do them
c. how you feel about doing them
d. what particular job you had to do last week
e. how long it took you to do it
f. what you will probably do next week
g. what benefits are derived from your work
h. what you sometimes wish you were doing instead
i. what would happen if you refused to help
j. what you generally do when the chores are finished

J. Écrivez à votre oncle une lettre dans laquelle vous décrivez un accident dont vous avez été témoin (witness). Expliquez chacun des points suivants:

a. ce qui est arrivé
b. ce qui l'a causé
c. où et quand l'accident a eu lieu
d. les autres témoins
e. les dommages
f. les secours dont on avait besoin et pourquoi
g. votre rôle dans l'accident
h. le résultat de l'accident
i. ce que l'accident vous a enseigné

K. En vous laissant guider par les suggestions et le vocabulaire suivants, écrivez une composition de 100 mots environ sur le sujet suivant:

UNE JOURNÉE AU BORD DE LA MER

a. Les moyens de transport dont vous vous servez
b. Description générale de la plage
c. Les personnes qu'on y trouve
d. Ce que vous faites pour vous amuser
e. Comment vous vous sentez après l'excursion

Vocabulaire utile

prendre le train, le métro
aller en voiture, en autobus

une plage longue, large, étendue
une mer calme, agitée
un océan profond
l'eau de mer
le sable blanc, propre, sale
le costume de bain
la vague haute, high wave
la coquille, shell
le parasol, beach umbrella
la promenade, boardwalk
la serviette de bain, bath towel
la foule

se baigner; le baigneur
nager; le nageur
aller à la pêche; le pêcheur
le vendeur de limonade
la vendeuse de glaces
plonger, to dive; **le plongeur**
un coup de soleil, sunburn
basané, sunburned
prendre une douche, to take a shower
faire un pique-nique

Idiotismes et proverbes

au soleil, in the sun
à l'ombre, in the shade
manquer de se noyer, to almost drown
A chacun son goût.
se mettre en route
n'en pouvoir plus = éprouver une grande fatigue
le long de
Tout est bien qui finit bien.

L. One of your friends has been talking to you about purchasing a car someday. Write him (her) a letter on the subject of what you would do if you had a car of your own. Discuss the following points:

a. what make and color car you would buy
b. how large a car you would choose and why
c. how you would learn to drive
d. under what circumstances you would use the car
e. when you would not drive it
f. what trips you might take
g. how you would take care of it
h. where you would park it at night
i. how you and your family would benefit from your having the car

M. Vous avez assisté récemment à une réunion sociale. Décrivez-la en expliquant les points suivants:

a. l'occasion de la réunion
b. le lieu et l'heure
c. les vêtements que vous avez portés
d. les invités
e. quelques-uns des divertissements
f. ce qu'on a servi
g. un incident intéressant
h. pourquoi un des invités est parti de bonne heure
i. le retour chez vous
j. votre impression de la soirée

N. You have been given the choice of a pet for your birthday. In connected paragraph form, write the ideas on this subject that you might enter in a diary. Include the following information:

a. why you want this pet
b. what kind of pet you will choose
c. where you will keep it
d. how you will take care of it
e. what you will teach it to do
f. what you will buy for it
g. what problem may arise from owning it
h. how this pet will change your daily routine
i. how your friends will share the pet with you
j. if you can no longer keep the pet, what you will do with it

O. Dans une lettre, invitez un ami à faire une excursion à bicyclette avec vous. Discutez tous les points suivants:

a. la date et la longueur de temps de l'excursion
b. le but de l'excursion

c. l'itinéraire
d. les curiosités que vous comptez visiter
e. les bagages et les vêtements qu'il vous faudra
f. les frais (expenses)
g. les logements
h. les repas
i. le retour

TOPICS FOR FREE COMPOSITION

1. Ce que je fais pour être en bonne santé
2. En voyageant on apprend beaucoup
3. Si je visitais la France
4. Rira bien qui rira le dernier
5. Ma vie de famille
6. C'est moi qu'on blâme toujours
7. Les premiers pas sont difficiles
8. C'était vendredi le treize
9. Mon meilleur ami (Ma meilleure amie)
10. Si on m'avait écouté
11. Un souvenir de mon enfance
12. Ma possession la plus précieuse
13. Une surprise agréable
14. Un incident dans notre classe
15. Vouloir, c'est pouvoir
16. Le moment le plus embarrassant de ma vie
17. Un rêve que j'ai fait
18. Les quatre saisons
19. Une lettre à une connaissance française mentionnant des incidents intéressants de votre vie quotidienne et vos plans pour l'avenir.
20. Vous êtes allé(e) visiter un musée (ou un marché). En rentrant, vous notez l'impression générale que vous avez eue.

Part V—*Civilization*

1. LA GÉOGRAPHIE DE LA FRANCE

Le pays qu'on appelle souvent "la douce France" ou "la belle France" occupe une position favorable dans le continent européen, entre deux des mers les plus importantes du monde: la Méditerranée et la Manche. La France est un pays extrêmement varié. Elle est remarquable par la diversité et l'harmonie de ses aspects: le climat, le relief, le paysage, le sol, les ressources naturelles, et les produits.

POSITION GÉOGRAPHIQUE, CLIMAT

Située en pleine zone tempérée, entre le 42e et le 51e degré de l'hémisphère nord, la France est presque à égale distance de l'équateur et du pôle nord. Paris est sous la même latitude que Montréal.

Grâce à cette latitude, à son relief de moyenne élévation, à l'influence modératrice du Gulf Stream qui réchauffe ses côtes, et à la proximité de quatre mers, la plus grande partie de la France jouit d'un climat doux. Cependant, le climat devient plus rigoureux, mais sans passage brusque, quand on s'éloigne de la mer. Puisque les mers qui entourent la France régularisent les températures et les pluies, la France est, en général, bien arrosée (watered); il n'y a presque pas de région tout à fait sèche.

SUPERFICIE, POPULATION, LIMITES

La France a une superficie (area) de 551.000 kilomètres carrés (= 213.000 milles carrés). Quoiqu'elle soit plus petite que l'état du Texas, la France est le pays le plus grand de l'Europe à l'ouest de l'Union Soviétique.

La France a une population d'environ 55.000.000 d'habitants, y compris la Corse.

Le pays a la forme d'un hexagone régulier, c'est-à-dire, d'une figure géométrique à six faces. Trois de ces faces sont des frontières maritimes, baignées par les plus importantes mers européennes. La France est bornée au nord par **la Manche** et **la mer du Nord**, à l'ouest par **l'océan Atlantique**, au sud par **la mer Méditerranée.** Les côtes de la France présentent les aspects les plus variés.

Les trois autres faces de l'hexagone ont des frontières continentales. La France est bornée par six pays: au nord-est par **la Belgique** et **le Luxembourg**; à l'est par **l'Allemagne, la Suisse,** et **l'Italie**; au sud par **l'Espagne.**

Cinq des faces de l'hexagone sont des frontières naturelles. La seule qui est artificielle se trouve au nord-est, s'étendant du Rhin à Dunkerque.

MONTAGNES

Il y a cinq massifs montagneux en France. Les Alpes, les Pyrénées, et le Jura sont des montagnes jeunes. Leur altitude est haute et leur relief très accidenté (jagged). Ces montagnes servent de frontières à la France. Les Vosges et le Massif Central sont des massifs anciens. Ce sont des montagnes peu élevées dont les sommets ont été arrondis par l'érosion.

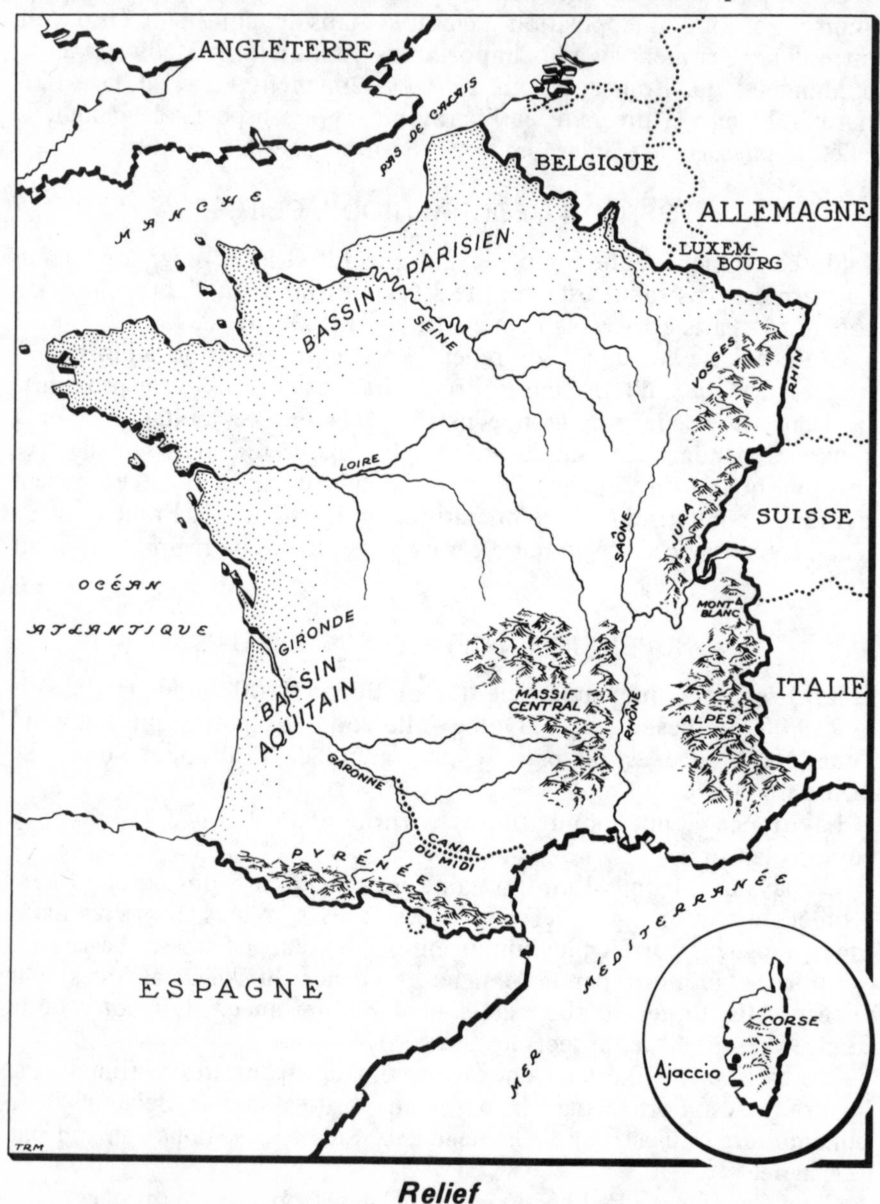

Relief

1. **Les Alpes**, les montagnes les plus élevées, s'étendent entre la France, l'Italie, et la Suisse. C'est dans les Alpes que se trouve

le plus haut sommet de l'Europe, **le mont Blanc** (4.807 mètres = 15.780 pieds).

2. **Les Pyrénées** forment une barrière naturelle entre la France et l'Espagne. Moins hautes que les Alpes, les Pyrénées ont de nombreux pics élevés et aigus.
3. **Le Jura**, une chaîne moins élevée, s'étend du Rhin aux Alpes. C'est la frontière principale entre la France et la Suisse.
4. **Les Vosges** se trouvent en Alsace, près de l'Allemagne.
5. **Le Massif Central**, ou **le Plateau Central**, est le vaste ensemble de hautes terres du centre de la France. C'est la chaîne de montagnes la plus ancienne où se trouvent de nombreux volcans éteints qu'on appelle "puys." **Les Cévennes** font partie du Massif Central.

La France a un relief assez varié et généralement modéré. La distribution des montagnes est favorable aux communications intérieures et extérieures. Les plaines occupent plus de la moitié de la superficie du pays. Des régions très fertiles et bien cultivées sont: au nord **le bassin parisien**, la plaine la plus vaste; au sud-ouest **le bassin aquitain**; et au sud **la vallée du Rhône.**

FLEUVES

1. **La Seine**, le fleuve de Paris, est le plus navigable et le plus utilisé des fleuves français. Elle naît dans le centre de la France, coule à travers la Normandie, et se jette dans la Manche près du Havre.
2. **La Loire** est le plus long fleuve de France mais le moins utile au point de vue économique. Elle prend sa source dans le Massif Central et se jette dans l'Atlantique. La vallée de la Loire est célèbre par ses châteaux magnifiques.
3. **La Garonne**, le plus court fleuve important, prend naissance dans les Pyrénées et après Bordeaux se jette dans l'Atlantique, où elle s'élargit dans **la Gironde**, un véritable bras de mer. C'est un fleuve médiocre pour la navigation mais qui produit beaucoup d'énergie hydro-électrique.
4. **Le Rhône** est un fleuve rapide et puissant. Descendant des Alpes suisses, il traverse le lac Léman (lac de Genève), reçoit **la Saône** à Lyon, et se jette dans la Méditerranée près de Marseille. Le vaste delta que forme ce fleuve à son embouchure s'appelle **la Camargue.** Les barrages (dams) énormes qu'on a construits sur le Rhône, tels que Génissiat et Donzère-Mondragon, fournissent de grandes quantités d'énergie hydro-électrique.
5. **Le Rhin**, un des plus longs fleuves d'Europe, sépare la France de l'Allemagne.

Les fleuves et les rivières navigables sont unis par de nombreux canaux, dont le plus célèbre est le vieux canal du Midi. Ce canal relie la Méditerranée avec la Garonne et, par conséquent, avec l'Atlantique.

Le réseau fluvial (river system) français sert de moyens de transport, d'irrigation, et de source d'énergie hydro-électrique.

EXERCICES

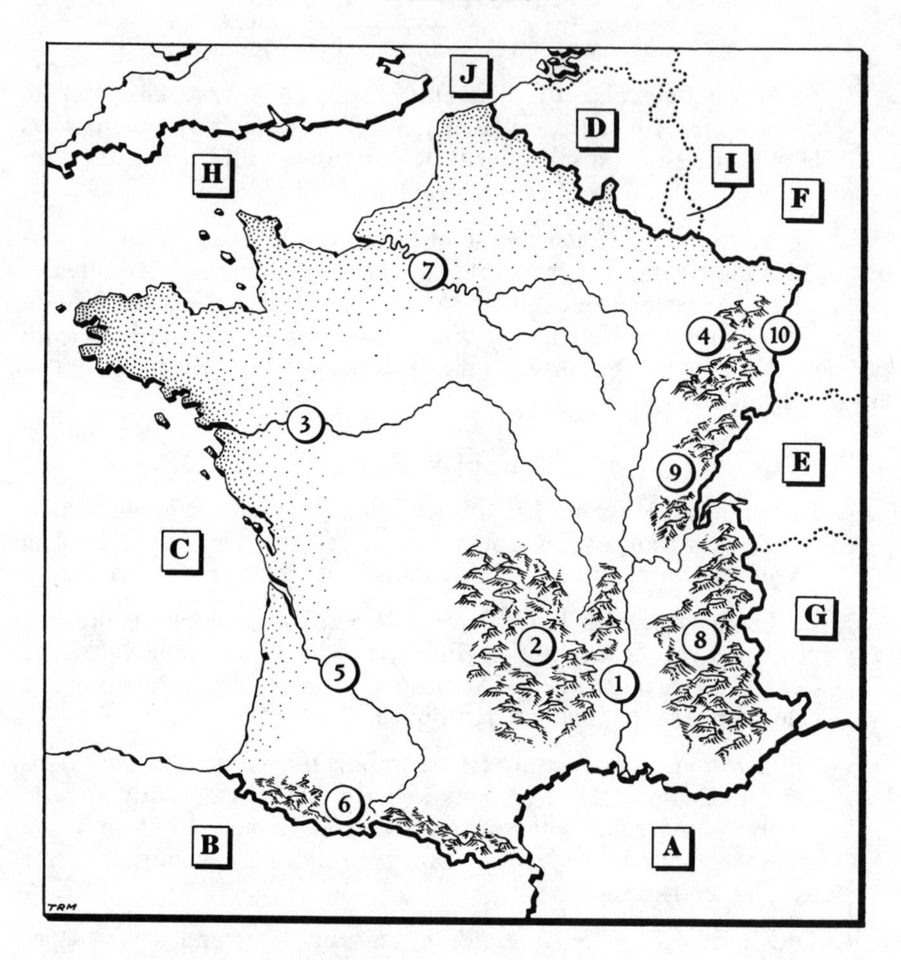

A. Identifier les montagnes et les fleuves en choisissant le numéro correspondant de la carte:

les Alpes	les Pyrénées
la Garonne	le Rhin
le Jura	le Rhône
la Loire	la Seine
le Massif Central	les Vosges

B. Mettre en relation les lettres sur la carte avec les frontières suivantes:

l'Atlantique	le Luxembourg
l'Allemagne	la Manche
la Belgique	la Méditerranée
l'Espagne	la mer du Nord
l'Italie	la Suisse

C. Pour chaque expression de la première colonne, donner la lettre du nom correspondant de la seconde colonne:

1. courant d'eau chaude	*a.* les puys
2. frontière principale entre la France et l'Italie	*b.* la Camargue
3. rivière qui se jette dans le Rhône	*c.* les Alpes
4. montagnes anciennes en Alsace	*d.* le bassin parisien
5. île française dans la Méditerranée	*e.* le Massif Central
6. plaine vaste	*f.* le Gulf Stream
7. delta du Rhône	*g.* la Seine
8. volcans éteints	*h.* la Corse
9. fleuve le plus navigable	*i.* les Vosges
10. chaîne de montagnes la plus ancienne	*j.* la Saône

D. Vrai ou faux?

1. Le climat français est le plus rigoureux près de la mer.
2. Généralement la France reçoit une quantité suffisante de pluie.
3. Le paysage et le sol de la France sont très variés.
4. Paris se trouve sous la même latitude que Boston.
5. Génissiat est le nom d'un grand canal.
6. L'étendue de la France est inférieure à celle de l'état du Texas.
7. Les hautes montagnes françaises se trouvent sur les frontières continentales.
8. La Seine se jette dans la Manche près du Havre.
9. Le canal du Midi relie la France et l'Espagne.
10. Les montagnes françaises empêchent la communication intérieure.

E. Compléter en français:

1. La France est presque à égale distance du pôle nord et de ______.
2. Les Cévennes font partie du ______.
3. On peut voir de nombreux ______ magnifiques dans la vallée de la Loire.
4. ______ des faces de l'hexagone français sont des frontières maritimes.
5. La France compte environ ______ millions d'habitants.

6. Les Alpes culminent au ______, le point le plus élevé de l'Europe.
7. ______ est la frontière principale entre la France et la Suisse.
8. La France est située tout entière dans la zone ______.
9. ______ est le fleuve le plus long mais le moins utile de France.
10. La seule frontière artificielle s'étend au nord-est, entre Dunkerque et le ______.
11. ______, qui prend naissance dans les Alpes suisses, est un fleuve qui fournit des quantités énormes d'énergie hydro-électrique.
12. Les Pyrénées séparent la France de ______.
13. Après Bordeaux, la Garonne s'élargit dans un estuaire, la ______.
14. Le bassin ______ se trouve au sud-ouest de la France.
15. ______, qui prend sa source dans le centre de la France, traverse la Normandie.

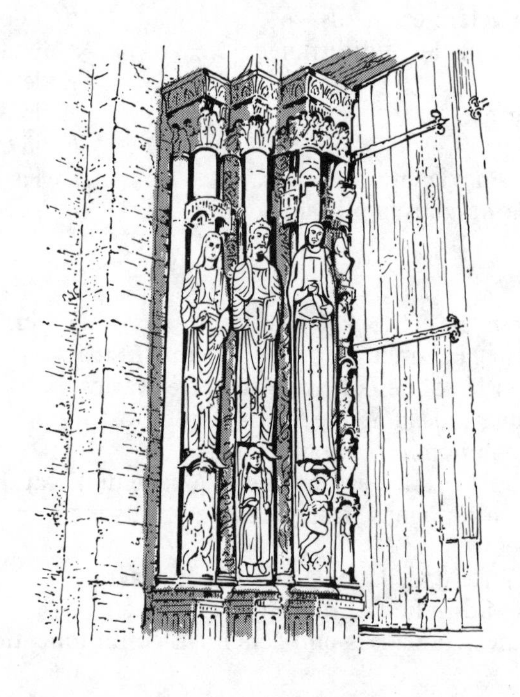

Portail royal—Cathédrale de Chartres

La cathédrale de Chartres, un mélange de style roman et gothique, est ornée de centaines de sculptures remarquables. Les statues, qui représentent des personnages de la Bible, sont vêtues à la mode du XIIe siècle.

2. L'AGRICULTURE, L'INDUSTRIE, LE COMMERCE

1. L'agriculture, l'industrie, et le commerce représentent des forces essentielles de l'économie française. La France, pays fortement industrialisé, est aussi le premier producteur agricole de l'Europe occidentale. L'agriculture française se caractérise par un mouvement d'expansion. On continue à substituer une agriculture intensive et commercialisée, basée sur des techniques modernes, à l'ancienne agriculture traditionnelle.

Agriculture

Voici quelques termes du vocabulaire de l'agriculture pour mieux comprendre la carte:

Bétail–Cattle
Betteraves à sucre–Sugar beets
Céréales–Grain
Volaille–Poultry

Le sol, qui est généralement fertile, suffit à rendre la France presque indépendante en matière d'alimentation. Les plaines et les bassins des fleuves sont les régions les plus fertiles. Grâce à la diversité des sols et des climats, les produits français sont très variés.

2. Le blé, dont on fait le pain—la nourriture fondamentale des Français —est un produit agricole important. Les Français sont de grands mangeurs de pain. On cultive aussi une abondance d'autres céréales et une variété de fruits et de légumes, y compris la betterave à sucre (sugar beet). Les bois et les forêts, qui couvrent environ un cinquième de la superficie totale du pays, fournissent une bonne quantité de bois pour l'industrie.

3. La viticulture (vine-growing) est une des grandes richesses agricoles de la France, et les vignes en font le premier pays du monde en ce qui concerne la production du vin. La France fournit une grande partie de la production mondiale de vins. Quelques-uns des vins plus renommés sont **le champagne, le bourgogne,** et **le bordeaux. Le cognac**, une eau-de-vie (brandy) distillée du vin; les nombreuses liqueurs—**la chartreuse, la bénédictine, le cointreau**—et les apéritifs qui stimulent l'appétit—**le dubonnet, le byrrh**—sont très estimés. D'autres boissons produites en France sont le cidre, surtout de Normandie et de Bretagne, la bière, et les eaux minérales, comme celles de Vichy et de Vittel.

4. La France, connue pour l'excellence de ses animaux—vaches, bœufs, moutons, chèvres, porcs, chevaux, volaille (poultry)—est un grand pays d'élevage, la production animale. Les provisions de viande d'excellente qualité et de produits laitiers augmentent chaque année. La Normandie, en particulier, est une région laitière très riche. Les Français sont experts dans la fabrication des fromages, dont les plus connus sont **le brie, le camembert, le gruyère, le port-salut,** et **le roquefort,** qui est fabriqué avec du lait de brebis.

5. Les Français se nourrissent aussi des produits de la mer. L'industrie de la pêche est active sur les côtes, spécialement en Bretagne.

Grâce à toutes ces richesses de la terre et de la mer, les industries alimentaires fleurissent en France.

6. De plus, le sol fertile de la Côte d'Azur fournit des quantités énormes de fleurs qu'on envoie à Grasse, où l'on extrait les essences parfumées. La fabrication des parfums est achevée à Paris, centre des cosmétiques. Quelques-uns des parfumeurs réputés dans le monde entier sont: **Caron, Chanel, Coty, Fragonard, Guerlain, Lanvin**, et **Patou.**

7. L'industrie française est très variée, depuis la production de machines lourdes jusqu'à la fabrication d'instruments de précision

délicate, depuis l'immense usine moderne jusqu'à l'atelier du petit artisan. En général, les ouvriers français sont des artistes qui, préférant la bonne qualité à la grande quantité, sont fiers de leur travail: une combinaison d'originalité et d'habileté artistique. Pour maintenir sa position dans la compétition internationale, la France intensifie ses efforts dans le domaine des recherches scientifiques et des applications industrielles.

8. Parmi les industries les plus importantes sont la métallurgie et les industries textiles. On produit des machines diverses, du matériel roulant (wagons, locomotives), des bicyclettes, et des armes. La France est le sixième pays du monde pour la production de l'acier. Elle possède beaucoup de bauxite, dont on fabrique l'aluminium.

9. En ce qui concerne l'énergie, la France doit importer le pétrole qui est essentiel à son économie. Elle développe de l'énergie atomique dans ses laboratoires et ses usines. Elle utilise l'énergie hydroélectrique de ses torrents pour produire de l'électricité. Le gaz naturel contribue aussi aux besoins de l'économie. De plus, dans la France d'aujourd'hui, le soleil, les vagues de la mer, et les marées sont devenus d'autres sources d'énergie.

10. Les industries textiles fleurissent surtout au Nord-Est, près de Lille. Rouen, en Normandie, est aussi un centre textile. La France fabrique des textiles de laine, de coton, et de lin (linen) aussi bien que des textiles synthétiques. Lyon est le centre de la production de la meilleure soie française, naturelle et artificielle.

11. Dans les industries mécaniques–la production de machines et d'appareils divers–ainsi que dans la construction électrique et électronique, l'activité française est remarquable. L'application de la haute technique de ces industries n'a pas été limitée au territoire français. Les Français ont réalisé dans divers pays à l'étranger des œuvres de grande importance.

12. L'industrie automobile joue un rôle important dans l'équilibre de la balance commerciale. On exporte des voitures françaises dans toutes les parties du monde. Les quatre marques principales sont: **Citroën, Peugeot, Renault,** et **Simca.**

13. Dans l'industrie aérospatiale, on construit des avions, des hélicoptères, et des engins spatiaux. Il faut mentionner les programmes de construction en coopération avec l'Angleterre pour le Concorde, et l'Allemagne et les Pays-Bas pour l'Airbus. La France participe à la réalisation d'un satellite européen de télécommunications. Elle fournit des accessoires de haute précision, servant notamment à l'équipement des satellites et des engins spatiaux américains. La plus grande ligne d'aviation européenne, Air France, met la France en communication avec les autres pays du monde.

14. Sa situation stratégique a fait de la France une puissance maritime. Les ports de mer sont nombreux. Il y a des constructions navales surtout dans les régions des ports de l'Atlantique et de la Manche.
15. L'industrie chimique prend une importance de plus en plus considérable. Par conséquent, la France est maintenant un pays exportateur de produits chimiques et pharmaceutiques. La production du verre, du caoutchouc, et des matières plastiques est toujours en augmentation.

Industries

Voici quelques termes du vocabulaire de l'industrie pour mieux comprendre la carte:

Industries alimentaires–Food processing
Minerai de fer–Iron ore
Potasse–Potash
Produits de caoutchouc–Rubber products

16. Paris est la capitale de la haute couture (fashions). C'est ici que la mode féminine est devenue un art. Quelques-uns des couturiers les plus connus sont: **Chanel, Dior, Fath, Cardin, Saint Laurent,** et **Patou.**

17. Dans un pays où l'art et l'industrie s'unissent, les ouvriers bien qualifiés peuvent se distinguer dans les métiers qui exigent de l'élégance et de la délicatesse–les industries de luxe. Les Français ont une renommée universelle pour la perfection de leurs produits. Paris fabrique une grande quantité d'articles de luxe: bijoux, argenterie, objets en cuir, tapisseries des Gobelins, objets d'art, produits photographiques, instruments de précision. D'autres villes aussi doivent leur réputation à des spécialités:

    Alençon–dentelles
    Aubusson et **Beauvais**–tapis
    Baccarat–cristallerie
    Besançon–montres et horloges
    Grenoble–gants
    Limoges et **Sèvres**–porcelaine de luxe

18. Le tourisme, surtout le tourisme étranger, mérite une mention spéciale puisqu'il contribue beaucoup à l'économie française.

19. La France importe des matières premières (raw materials) pour ses industries: pétrole, laine, coton, soie, caoutchouc; et des produits alimentaires: café, cacao, fruits tropicaux.

    Elle exporte: tissus (fabrics), vêtements, automobiles, avions, produits chimiques et pharmaceutiques, articles de luxe, parfums, et produits alimentaires–vins, fromages, conserves (canned foods).

20. Les activités économiques sont liées aux moyens de transport intérieurs et extérieurs: le réseau fluvial, le réseau routier, les chemins de fer, la navigation maritime, et la navigation aérienne.

21. La France possède un excellent réseau fluvial–l'ensemble des fleuves, des rivières, et des canaux. Les nombreux canaux qui relient les fleuves et les rivières permettent un transport économique de marchandises lourdes. Les principaux ports fluviaux sont Paris, Rouen, Strasbourg, et Lyon.

22. Le réseau routier est très dense. On modernise les voies et l'on crée un ensemble d'autoroutes (superhighways). Les principales routes nationales rayonnent de Paris vers les frontières. Sur les routes, généralement bordées d'arbres, on voit des milliers de bicyclettes et de motocyclettes.

23. **La S.N.C.F. (Société Nationale des Chemins de Fer),** agence du gouvernement, administre les chemins de fer français. Le réseau

forme une toile d'araignée (spider's web) autour de Paris, d'où partent toutes les grandes lignes. Ce réseau relie la capitale avec les ports de mer et les autres pays d'Europe. Les trains français sont les plus rapides du monde. Les voitures ont deux classes, et d'ordinaire elles sont divisées en compartiments.

24. Certains autres moyens de communication en France sont également la responsabilité du gouvernement central. Les postes, les télégraphes, et les téléphones, par exemple, sont administrés par l'État. On peut acheter les timbres dans les bureaux de tabac autant que dans les bureaux de poste. En France, le tabac est un monopole du gouvernement.

25. Les communications aériennes sont assurées par **la Compagnie Air France** et quelques compagnies privées. Le plus fort trafic est à destination de l'étranger. **Charles de Gaulle**, près de Paris, est le plus grand aéroport international de la France.

26. La France, qui fait partie du **Marché Commun**, joue un rôle important dans la vie économique de l'Europe.

EXERCICES

A. Pour chaque expression de la première colonne, donner la lettre du nom correspondant de la seconde colonne:

1. liqueur célèbre	*a.* Lyon
2. fromage français	*b.* cidre
3. produit de Vichy	*c.* Renault
4. montres et horloges	*d.* brie
5. maison de haute couture	*e.* articles de luxe
6. essences pour la parfumerie	*f.* Dior
7. voiture française	*g.* eau minérale
8. soie	*h.* Besançon
9. boisson de Normandie	*i.* Grasse
10. exportation française	*j.* bénédictine

B. Vrai ou faux?

1. Il y a en France un bon équilibre entre la vie agricole et la vie industrielle.
2. En général, le sol fournit aux Français les moyens suffisants de se nourrir.
3. La France est le troisième pays du monde pour la production des vins.
4. Les Français cultivent une variété de fruits et de légumes.
5. Pour la plupart des ouvriers français, la quantité compte plus que la qualité.
6. La France est un grand pays d'élevage.

7. Les principales industries françaises sont l'industrie automobile et le tourisme.
8. La France manque de bons ports.
9. La France est exportatrice de produits chimiques et de produits alimentaires.
10. La production française de machines et d'appareils électriques est presque négligeable.
11. La France doit importer de grandes quantités de bauxite.
12. La France joue un rôle actif dans le Marché Commun.
13. Une grande partie de la richesse française provient des métiers de luxe.
14. Il y a deux classes dans les trains français.
15. La France est indépendante en matière d'énergie.

C. Identifier:

1. centre de haute couture
2. région laitière très riche
3. ville connue pour sa cristallerie
4. région qui fournit des quantités énormes de fleurs
5. fromage fabriqué avec du lait de brebis
6. aéroport international de France
7. specialité de Grenoble
8. agence qui administre les chemins de fer
9. ville principale des industries textiles
10. grande ligne française d'aviation

D. Compléter en français:

1. Les plaines et les bassins des ______ sont les régions les plus fertiles.
2. La ______ est une industrie très active sur les côtes bretonnes.
3. Le champagne, le ______, et le bordeaux sont des vins renommés.
4. En France, c'est l'État qui administre les postes, les télégraphes, et ______.
5. La France importe surtout des matières ______ pour ses industries.
6. Les ______ qui relient les fleuves et les rivières permettent de transporter à bon marché des cargaisons lourdes.
7. Les routes françaises sont généralement bordées de (d') ______.
8. Deux grands ports fluviaux sont Paris et ______.
9. Le réseau des chemins de fer forme une toile d'araignée autour de ______.
10. Il y a des constructions navales surtout dans les ports de l'Atlantique et de la ______.
11. Les villes de Limoges et de Sèvres produisent de belles ______.
12. Les Français et les ______ ont coopéré pour produire le Concorde.

3. LES PROVINCES

Avant la Révolution de 1789, la France était composée de 32 **provinces.** Chacune avait ses propres mœurs (customs), ses propres traditions culturelles, et ses traits particuliers.

Quoique la France soit aujourd'hui divisée en **départements**, les Français ont encore l'habitude d'employer les noms des anciennes provinces, surtout en parlant de leur terre natale. Chaque province avait un costume régional qu'on porte même aujourd'hui à l'occasion d'une fête. La coiffe et les sabots se voient encore de nos jours dans certaines parties de la France.

Voici quelques-unes des provinces les mieux connues:

1. **La Bretagne** est la péninsule au nord-ouest de la France qui s'avance dans l'Atlantique. Une grande partie de sa population est d'origine celte, et aujourd'hui encore il y a ceux qui parlent **breton,** l'ancienne langue de cette province. Dans cette région de faible altitude, baignée de trois côtés de la mer et arrosée de pluies abondantes, les habitants vivent surtout de la mer. Les marins et les pêcheurs bretons ont toujours joué un grand rôle dans les traditions maritimes de la France. Dans la marine militaire et la marine marchande se trouve un grand nombre de Bretons.

   Les Bretons sont généralement conservateurs et superstitieux. A l'occasion des **pardons,** fêtes religieuses, on porte le costume traditionnel. La Bretonne se distingue surtout par sa **coiffe** blanche. Il y a en Bretagne de grandes pierres historiques, isolées ou alignées l'une derrière l'autre, dont la signification est demeurée mystérieuse.

2. **La Normandie** est située au nord-ouest de la France, sur les côtes de la Manche. Avec son climat humide, c'est une région de fermes fertiles et de pâturages (pastureland). La Seine coule à travers cette province. Le long des côtes, il y a plusieurs ports de commerce et de pêche ainsi que des plages bien connues. Les belles vaches de la Normandie produisent le lait qui sert à fabriquer le beurre et les fromages normands de renommée mondiale. Il y a aussi en Normandie de grands centres industriels. Deux événements importants sont liés à l'histoire de la Normandie: la conquête de l'Angleterre en 1066 par Guillaume le Conquérant, duc de Normandie, et le débarquement libérateur des forces alliées en 1944.

3. **L'Ile-de-France,** dans le bassin parisien, est une région fertile et industrialisée. Avec sa capitale, Paris, ce fut le véritable cœur administratif du pays et le berceau (cradle) de la monarchie française. La langue parlée en Ile-de-France est devenue la langue officielle de France.

4. **L'Alsace** et **la Lorraine** se trouvent au nord-est de la France. Pendant de nombreuses années, la France et l'Allemagne se disputèrent ces deux provinces. L'Alsace est principalement une région agricole. La Lorraine, avec ses mines de fer les plus riches d'Europe, est importante au point de vue industriel.

5. **La Provence,** la province ensoleillée, se trouve au sud-est. Elle est bornée par le Rhône, les Alpes, et la Méditerranée. Puisque le climat y est doux la plupart du temps, on y voit toute une végétation exotique. Les fleurs, qui poussent en toute saison, sont une des richesses de la terre. Entre Marseille et la frontière italienne se trouve le littoral célèbre qui s'appelle **la Côte d'Azur (la Riviera)** à cause du bleu intense du ciel et de la Méditerranée. En certaines saisons, un vent violent, froid, et sec–**le mistral**– souffle du nord et descend la vallée du Rhône. En Provence, on

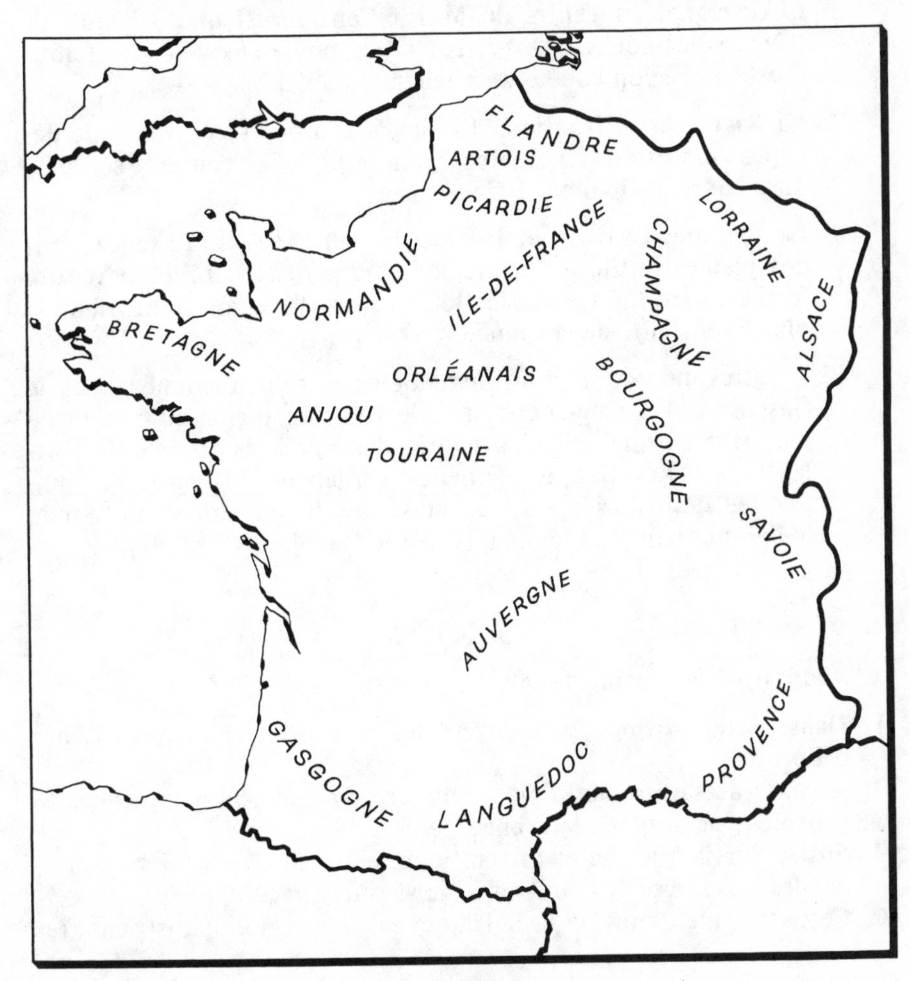

Provinces

trouve des monuments romains bien conservés. Même aujourd'hui beaucoup de Provençaux parlent **provençal**, la langue des anciens troubadours.

6. Dans la vallée de la Loire se trouvent trois anciennes provinces: **la Touraine, l'Orléanais,** et **l'Anjou.** Cette région s'appelle "le pays des châteaux" parce qu'aucune autre région ne possède tant de châteaux sur une étendue si limitée. **Azay-le-Rideau, Blois, Chambord,** et **Chenonceaux** sont les plus connus de ces beaux châteaux. En Touraine, "le jardin de la France," on produit une grande quantité de fruits et de légumes.

7. **La Bourgogne** et **la Champagne** sont deux provinces fertiles où l'on cultive la vigne. Les vins de ces provinces sont estimés dans le monde entier.

8. **L'Auvergne,** au centre du Massif Central, est une province de terres volcaniques. On y trouve les **puys,** des volcans éteints. C'est une région vouée essentiellement à l'élevage.

9. **La Savoie,** à la frontière d'Italie, est la province principale des Alpes françaises. En Savoie, connue pour la beauté de son paysage, se trouve le mont Blanc.

10. **La Flandre, l'Artois,** et **la Picardie,** au nord de la France, sont des plaines fertiles et des régions industrielles. La Flandre, qui forme la frontière avec la Belgique, est la région industrielle la plus importante de la France.

11. D'autres provinces dont les noms sont bien connus sont **la Gascogne** et **le Languedoc,** dans le Midi. La région qu'on appelle "le pays basque" se trouve près des Pyrénées et près de l'Atlantique. Les Basques parlent une langue différente et compliquée dont l'origine est un mystère. Ils ont donné au monde le **béret** et leur jeu régional, la **pelote** (jai alai).

EXERCICES

A. Identifier la province:

1. Dans cette province se trouvent les mines de fer les plus riches d'Europe.
2. A cause de sa production de fruits et de légumes, on appelle cette province "le jardin de la France."
3. Située sur la Manche et l'Atlantique, cette péninsule tire ses principales ressources de la mer et de la vie maritime.
4. Cette province, près de la Belgique, est une région industrielle très importante.

5. Une région de fermes riches et de pâturages, cette province a des plages célèbres sur la Manche.
6. On y trouve beaucoup de monuments romains bien conservés.
7. Cette province du Massif Central est une région d'origine volcanique.
8. C'est la province principale des Alpes françaises.
9. Cette province, dont Paris fut la capitale, est une région fertile et industrialisée.
10. Cette province est bornée par le Rhône, la Méditerranée, et les Alpes.

B. Vrai ou faux?

1. Chacune des trente-deux provinces avait ses propres traditions culturelles.
2. La Normandie est une région purement agricole.
3. L'Alsace est importante principalement au point de vue industriel.
4. Les Bretons sont généralement conservateurs.
5. La Touraine, l'Orléanais, et l'Anjou se trouvent dans la vallée du Rhône.
6. En Provence on peut voir un grand nombre de pierres historiques alignées l'une derrière l'autre.
7. L'élevage est l'industrie principale de l'Auvergne.
8. Blois et Chenonceaux sont en Bourgogne.
9. L'Artois et la Picardie sont des plaines fertiles et des régions industrielles.
10. Le pays basque se trouve près des Pyrénées.

C. Compléter en français:

1. La ______ coule à travers la Normandie.
2. Les ______, qui poussent toute l'année, sont une des richesses de la Provence.
3. La femme bretonne porte une ______ blanche sur la tête.
4. Les célèbres ______ d'Azay-le-Rideau et de Chambord attirent chaque année un grand nombre de touristes.
5. C'est la langue de ______ qui est devenue la langue officielle de la nation française.
6. Deux provinces dont les vins sont renommés dans le monde entier sont ______ et ______.
7. Le ______ est le nom de la fête religieuse des Bretons.
8. C'est en ______, connue pour la beauté de ses montagnes, que se trouve le mont Blanc.
9. En 1066, Guillaume le Conquérant, duc de ______, traversa la Manche et envahit l'Angleterre.
10. Deux provinces souvent disputées par la France et l'Allemagne sont ______ et ______.

D. Pour chaque expression de la première colonne, donner la lettre du nom correspondant de la seconde colonne:

1. berceau de la monarchie française	*a.* Bretons
2. puys	*b.* Provençaux
3. habitants d'origine celte	*c.* Côte d'Azur
4. béret et pelote	*d.* Ile-de-France
5. littoral méditerranéen	*e.* Normandie
6. débarquement des armées alliées en 1944	*f.* vallée de la Loire
7. langue des anciens troubadours	*g.* Auvergne
8. vent froid qui descend la vallée du Rhône	*h.* Basques
9. pays des châteaux	*i.* mistral
10. Marseillais	*j.* provençal

Tapisserie de Bayeux

Cette broderie, qu'on attribue souvent à la reine Mathilde, femme de Guillaume le Conquérant, est encore en bon état au musée de Bayeux, en Normandie. Elle représente la conquête de l'Angleterre par les Normands. L'immense tapisserie, mesurant plus de 70 mètres, est un document artistique et archéologique de premier ordre.

4. PARIS

A l'origine, Paris s'appelait **Lutèce**. C'était le village des Parisii, tribu gauloise, qui ont donné leur nom à la ville. Lutèce se trouvait sur une île qu'on appelle aujourd'hui **l'île de la Cité**, "le berceau de Paris."

Paris, la capitale politique, économique, et intellectuelle de la France, est situé au centre du bassin parisien. La "Ville Lumière" est le cerveau (brain) du pays. C'est le centre de la vie artistique et littéraire, le premier centre commercial et industriel de la France, le centre de la mode féminine, et le premier port français de navigation intérieure.

Comme toutes les villes, son visage change de jour en jour. Tandis que la ville proprement dite compte moins de 3 millions d'habitants, la région parisienne–Paris et ses environs–a une population de presque 11 millions d'habitants. Cette concentration humaine fait de Paris l'une des villes du monde dont la densité de population est la plus forte.

Pour son administration, Paris est divisé en 20 **arrondissements.** C'est une ville de beauté, célèbre pour ses monuments magnifiques, ses musées, ses églises, et ses jardins.

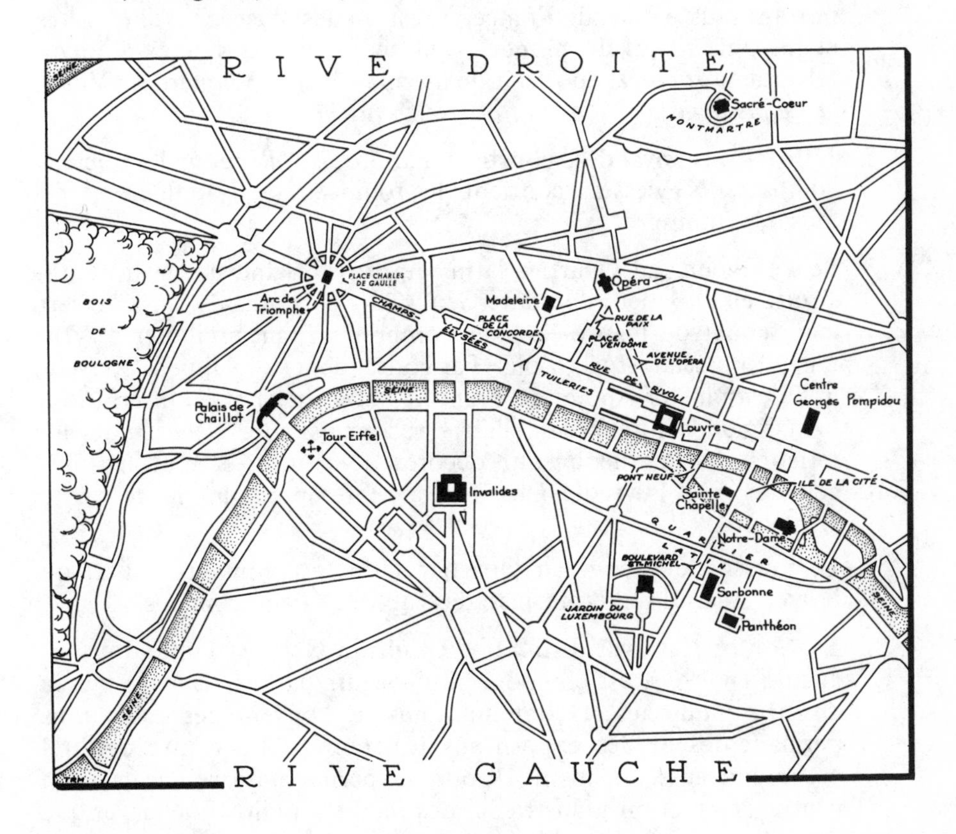

Paris

La Seine divise la ville en deux parties: la rive droite et la rive gauche. **La rive droite**, au nord, est plus grande et plus animée. C'est le centre des affaires–maisons de commerce, grands magasins–et de la vie mondaine–grands boulevards, théâtres, restaurants. C'est sur la rive droite que se trouve **Montmartre.**

Le Quartier latin, où les étudiants parlaient latin au Moyen Age, et **Montparnasse** sont sur **la rive gauche.** C'est au Quartier latin–le centre de l'enseignement–qu'on trouve la plupart des grandes écoles: la Sorbonne, le Collège de France, l'École Polytechnique, l'École de Médecine, et l'École Normale Supérieure. Montparnasse et Montmartre sont connus comme centres de la vie bohémienne. Quelques-uns des cafés bien connus de la rive gauche sont **le Dôme, les Deux Magots**, et **le Café de Flore.**

Le Pont-Neuf, construit au XVIe siècle, est le plus ancien et le plus renommé des nombreux ponts de Paris. Il traverse la Seine à l'île de la Cité.

MUSÉES

1. **Le musée du Louvre**, dans l'ancien palais royal, est le plus important musée d'art de France. C'est un des musées les plus vastes et les plus riches du monde. On peut y voir des chefs-d'œuvre tels que *la Joconde* (portrait de Monna Lisa) de Léonard de Vinci, *la Vénus de Milo*, et *la Victoire de Samothrace*.

2. **L'Hôtel des Invalides**, construit par Louis XIV pour les anciens combattants blessés, contient le tombeau de Napoléon et un musée militaire.

3. **Le Panthéon**, au Quartier latin, était à l'origine une église construite en l'honneur de sainte Geneviève, patronne de Paris. Il sert maintenant de mausolée à de nombreux Français illustres: Voltaire, Rousseau, Hugo, Zola. Par conséquent, on l'appelle souvent le "Westminster Abbey de France." L'édifice porte l'inscription: "Aux grands hommes la Patrie reconnaissante." Les murs intérieurs du Panthéon sont décorés de peintures dont les plus célèbres, par Puvis de Chavannes, représentent la vie de sainte Geneviève.

4. **Le musée de Cluny**, au Quartier latin, est consacré à l'art du Moyen Age. Il renferme aussi des ruines de bains romains.

5. **Le Centre National d'Art et de Culture Georges Pompidou**, inauguré en 1977, est composé de plusieurs parties. Dans le musée des arts modernes et contemporains se trouvent des collections permanentes et des expositions itinérantes. Ce centre culturel comprend aussi un institut pour l'expérimentation musicale, un centre de création industrielle, des facilités audio-visuelles, et une bibliothèque publique d'information.

ÉGLISES

1. La cathédrale de **Notre-Dame de Paris,** dans l'île de la Cité, est une merveille de l'architecture gothique. Commencé au XIIe siècle, c'est le plus bel édifice religieux de la ville.
2. L'élégante église de **la Madeleine,** avec sa majestueuse colonnade, a l'aspect d'un temple grec.
3. **Le Sacré-Cœur** est une église blanche qui ressemble à une mosquée. Bâtie au XIXe siècle sur la colline de Montmartre, l'église domine la ville. De là, la vue sur Paris est magnifique.
4. **La Sainte-Chapelle,** dans l'île de la Cité, est célèbre par ses beaux vitraux (stained-glass windows) en couleurs superbes. C'est saint Louis (Louis IX) qui l'a fait construire au XIIIe siècle pour servir de chapelle à la famille royale et pour abriter (protect) des reliques précieuses. On appelle l'église "le bijou de l'architecture gothique."
5. L'église romane (Romanesque) de **Saint-Germain-des-Prés,** au Quartier latin, est une des plus anciennes de Paris.

JARDINS ET BOIS

1. **Le bois de Boulogne,** ancienne forêt, est le vaste parc public du côté ouest de Paris. On y trouve des lacs, des jardins de fleurs, deux champs de courses (race tracks), et des restaurants.
2. **Le jardin des Tuileries** était autrefois un jardin particulier des rois de France. Ce parc, avec ses nombreuses statues, est situé près de la Seine, entre le Louvre et la place de la Concorde.
3. **Le jardin du Luxembourg,** sur la rive gauche, est un rendez-vous favori d'étudiants.
4. Dans **le bois de Vincennes,** au sud-est de Paris, il y a un jardin zoologique célèbre.

PLACES

1. **La place de la Concorde** est la plus grande et la plus belle de Paris. C'est ici qu'on a guillotiné des centaines de Français, y compris Louis XVI et Marie-Antoinette, pendant la Révolution. Au milieu de la place se trouvent l'obélisque égyptien de Louqsor, entre deux belles fontaines, et des statues qui représentent huit des grandes villes de France.
2. **La place Charles de Gaulle** avait le nom *place de l'Étoile* jusqu'à 1970; elle s'appelait ainsi parce que les douze avenues qui rayonnent autour de **l'Arc de Triomphe** dessinent une étoile. Napoléon avait ordonné de construire cet arc gigantesque pour commémorer

ses victoires. Sous l'arc, où brûle la flamme éternelle, se trouve **le tombeau du Soldat Inconnu**, mort pour la France pendant la première guerre mondiale. Le célèbre bas-relief, **la Marseillaise**, chef-d'œuvre de l'artiste Rude, décore une des faces de l'arc.

3. **La place de l'Opéra** est située au cœur de la ville. Le grandiose **Opéra**, qui date de 1875, domine l'animation de la place. L'édifice splendide, avec ses façades sculptées, son grand escalier en marbre, et son foyer somptueux, est l'œuvre de Charles Garnier. Au coin de la place se trouve **le Café de la Paix**, rendez-vous international, où l'on entend parler toutes les langues du monde.

4. **La place Vendôme** est le centre des magasins élégants. Au milieu de la place s'élève **la colonne Vendôme**, avec ses spirales de bronze où sont representées des scènes des campagnes militaires de Napoléon. Au sommet de la colonne se voit la statue de l'empereur.

5. C'est sur **la place de la Bastille** que se trouvait autrefois la vieille prison que les Français ont prise et détruite en 1789. Aujourd'hui au centre de la place se dresse **la colonne de Juillet**, élevée à la mémoire des Parisiens tués dans la révolution de juillet 1830.

AUTRES MONUMENTS ET CURIOSITÉS

1. **La Tour Eiffel** est le monument parisien le plus universellement connu. Construite en acier par l'ingénieur Alexandre Gustave Eiffel pour l'Exposition de 1889, elle a une hauteur de 336 mètres, y compris la cabine de télévision. On peut monter au sommet par les ascenseurs ou les escaliers. Les deux restaurants servent de bons repas. La tour est utilisée comme poste émetteur de T.S.F. et de télévision.

2. **La Sorbonne**, fondée en 1253 par Robert de Sorbon, chapelain de saint Louis, est la partie la plus ancienne de l'Université de Paris. C'est la Faculté des lettres et des sciences de l'université.

3. **Le palais de Chaillot**, qui date de 1937, est un des meilleurs exemples de l'architecture moderne. Le palais contient plusieurs musées et un théâtre. L'Assemblée des Nations-Unies s'y est réunie.

4. **La Cité Universitaire**, composée d'un grand nombre de bâtiments, est la section résidentielle de l'Université de Paris. Des étudiants français et étrangers y demeurent. La Cité encourage la compréhension mutuelle entre les jeunes gens de tous les pays du monde et facilite l'organisation de leur vie d'étudiant.

5. **La Conciergerie** est l'ancienne prison dans l'île de la Cité. C'est ici qu'un grand nombre de victimes de la Révolution, y compris Marie-Antoinette, ont passé leurs dernières heures.

6. **Les Halles,** le grand marché, reçoivent des provisions de toutes les régions pour alimenter la population de Paris. Ce marché se trouve à Rungis, pas loin de Paris.
7. Quelques-uns des grands magasins de Paris sont: **les Galeries Lafayette, le Bon Marché,** et **Au Printemps.**
8. Il y a deux palais célèbres près de Paris. Situé dans un immense parc est le magnifique palais de **Versailles,** construit au XVIIe siècle pour Louis XIV. Dans **la Galerie des Glaces,** on a signé le traité de Versailles en 1919. Le château de **Fontainebleau,** entouré d'une belle forêt, était la retraite préférée de Napoléon.

RUES

1. **L'avenue des Champs-Élysées** est la promenade large et splendide qui s'étend de la place de la Concorde à la place de l'Étoile. Le long de cette avenue—un centre de commerce et de divertissement—se trouvent des boutiques, des magasins d'automobiles, des maisons de couture, de grands hôtels, des théâtres, et des cinémas.
2. **L'avenue de l'Opéra, la rue de la Paix, la rue Royale,** et **la rue St-Honoré** sont connues pour leurs boutiques élégantes.
3. Sous les arcades de **la rue de Rivoli,** qui s'étend parallèlement à la Seine, il y a des magasins de luxe, qui attirent des milliers de touristes.
4. Les grands boulevards sont de larges avenues bordées d'arbres qui forment des artères de Paris. **Le boulevard St-Michel** est la rue principale du Quartier latin. D'autres boulevards également bien connus sont les boulevards **Montmartre, Montparnasse, Haussmann, des Capucines, de la Madeleine,** et **des Italiens.**
5. Les **quais** sont les rues qui bordent les deux rives de la Seine. C'est ici que **les bouquinistes,** dont les boîtes garnissent les parapets, vendent des livres d'occasion (secondhand).

TRANSPORTS

La situation commerciale de Paris est excellente. C'est le premier port fluvial de la France et le centre du réseau routier. Toutes les grandes lignes des chemins de fer passent par la ville, où il y a six gares. Deux aéroports desservent la ville: Charles de Gaulle, le vaste aéroport international à Roissy, et Orly. La ville est donc reliée au reste du pays et aux points les plus éloignés du monde.

Pour voyager dans la ville même, il y a deux moyens de transport public:

1. **Le métro (Métropolitain),** le chemin de fer souterrain, a des voitures de première et de seconde classe. Bien que les portières se ferment automatiquement, on doit les ouvrir avec la main.

2. Un réseau d'autobus dessert la ville entière et les banlieues (suburbs). A chaque arrêt, il y a une machine qui distribue des tickets numérotés. Par conséquent, il n'est pas nécessaire de faire la queue; les passagers montent dans l'autobus suivant l'ordre des numéros indiqués sur les tickets.

Si l'on prend un des **bateaux-mouches** qui descendent et remontent la Seine, on peut faire une belle excursion sur le fleuve et admirer plusieurs des monuments historiques de la ville.

EXERCICES

A. Pour chaque expression de la première colonne, donner la lettre du nom correspondant de la seconde colonne:

1. Aux grands hommes la Patrie reconnaissante
2. tribu gauloise
3. chapelain de saint Louis
4. jardin zoologique
5. église romane du Quartier latin
6. palais de Louis XIV
7. centre de magasins de luxe
8. auteur de peintures murales
9. colonne de Juillet
10. lacs, champs de courses, restaurants
11. sculpteur de bas-relief sur l'Arc de Triomphe
12. Café de la Paix
13. grand magasin
14. église blanche de Montmartre
15. ingénieur du XIXe siècle

a. bois de Vincennes
b. Sacré-Cœur
c. Versailles
d. Parisii
e. place de la Bastille
f. bois de Boulogne
g. Panthéon
h. Eiffel
i. Rude
j. Bon Marché
k. Puvis de Chavannes
l. St-Germain-des-Prés
m. place Vendôme
n. Sorbon
o. place de l'Opéra

B. Compléter en français:

1. Au temps des Romains, Paris s'appelait ______.
2. La région parisienne a une population d'environ ______ millions d'habitants.
3. On appelle la capitale de la France la "Ville ______."
4. Les grandes écoles, telles que l'École Polytechnique et l'École de Médecine, se trouvent sur la rive ______.
5. On peut voir *la Joconde*, *la Vénus de Milo*, et *la Victoire de Samothrace* si on visite le ______.
6. Le roi ______ fit bâtir la Sainte-Chapelle.
7. Les étalages des bouquinistes se trouvent le long des ______, les rues qui bordent la Seine.

8. ______ et ______ sont les deux grands aéroports de Paris.
9. Le Panthéon sert de mausolée aux Français illustres, tels que ______ et ______.
10. La flamme éternelle brûle sur le tombeau ______.
11. Le château de ______, dans une belle forêt près de Paris, était une résidence favorite de Napoléon.
12. Trois rues connues pour leurs boutiques élégantes sont ______, ______, et ______.
13. ______ s'étend de la place de la Concorde à la place Charles de Gaulle.
14. La ______, composée de nombreux bâtiments, est le domicile d'étudiants français et étrangers.
15. L'obélisque de Louqsor et les huit statues de villes françaises se trouvent sur la place ______.

C. Identifier le monument:

1. le musée d'art médiéval au Quartier latin
2. l'édifice qui contient le tombeau de Napoléon Ier
3. le grand marché qui alimente Paris
4. "le bijou de l'architecture gothique"
5. l'église en forme de temple grec
6. l'ancienne prison dans l'île de la Cité où Marie-Antoinette passa ses dernières heures
7. le monument qui se trouve au milieu de la place Charles de Gaulle
8. le palais moderne contenant plusieurs musées et un théâtre
9. la colonne, avec des spirales de bronze, dominée par la statue de Napoléon
10. le monument en acier, très élevé, utilisé comme poste émetteur de télévision

D. Vrai ou faux?

1. Paris est divisé en vingt arrondissements.
2. Douze avenues rayonnent de la place de la Bastille.
3. L'Opéra est l'œuvre de l'architecte Charles Garnier.
4. Paris est un grand port fluvial.
5. Pour prendre un autobus à Paris, on fait la queue.
6. Au Printemps est un beau jardin.
7. La Cité Universitaire encourage la compréhension mutuelle entre les étudiants de tous les pays.
8. On a signé le traité de 1919, qui a mis fin à la première guerre mondiale, dans les Galeries Lafayette.
9. Le Sacré-Cœur ressemble à une mosquée.
10. La rive gauche est le centre principal du commerce parisien.

E. Compléter les paragraphes suivants en français:

Le matin, après la visite du Louvre, nous avons traversé le plus ancien des ponts de Paris, le ______, pour voir le centre de l'enseignement, le Quartier ______, sur la rive ______. Le calme des petites rues contraste avec l'animation du boulevard ______, la rue principale du quartier. Nous avons visité la ______, la plus ancienne partie de l'Université de Paris. Ensuite, nous sommes entrés dans le ______ pour y admirer les peintures murales qui représentent la vie de ______, patronne de Paris. Plus tard, pour nous reposer un peu, nous nous sommes assis sur un banc au jardin ______, rendez-vous favori d'étudiants.

L'après-midi, nous avons pris un de ces bateaux-______ qui descendent et remontent la ______. Quelle promenade inoubliable! La place ______, la plus grande de Paris, offre au visiteur de belles perspectives. Puis nous avons vu près du fleuve le jardin ______, ancien jardin des rois de France. En nous approchant de l'île ______, le berceau de Paris, nous avons reconnu ce chef-d'œuvre de l'architecture gothique, la cathédrale ______. Enfin, n'en pouvant plus, nous avons pris le ______, le chemin de fer souterrain, pour retourner à l'hôtel.

Le Puy

Le Massif Central est une région géologique d'origine volcanique. Dans la ville pittoresque du Puy se dressent trois énormes rochers de basalte. Au sommet du rocher Saint-Michel se voit une chapelle de style roman. Cette ville est un centre important de la dentelle.

5. AUTRES VILLES FRANÇAISES

Parmi les villes principales de la France, au point de vue de la population, sont: Marseille, Lyon, Lille, Toulouse, Bordeaux, et Nice.

PORTS

1. **Marseille,** sur la Méditerranée, près de l'embouchure du Rhône, est la deuxième ville de France et son plus grand port de mer. Marseille, qui relie la France à l'Afrique du Nord et à l'Orient, est aussi un centre industriel très actif.

2. **Le Havre,** à l'embouchure de la Seine, est le plus grand port sur la Manche. Par ce port se fait la plus grande partie du trafic qui est tourné vers l'Amérique du Nord.

3. **Bordeaux,** à l'embouchure de la Garonne, est un port actif, surtout dans le commerce des vins renommés de la région.

4. **Nantes,** à l'embouchure de la Loire, est un centre de constructions navales.

5. D'autres ports maritimes sont:

   sur la Manche: **Cherbourg** (port militaire), **Boulogne, Calais, Dunkerque**
   sur l'Atlantique: **Brest** (port militaire), **Saint-Nazaire, La Rochelle**
   sur la Méditerranée: **Toulon** (port militaire), **Sète**

VILLES INDUSTRIELLES

1. **Lyon,** au confluent du Rhône et de la Saône, est la troisième ville de France. C'est une ville commerciale et le centre principal des industries de la soie et de la rayonne.

2. **Lille,** au nord-est de la France, est le grand centre de l'industrie textile. La ville est renommée aussi pour la fabrication de machines.

3. **Strasbourg,** sur le Rhin, est une ville industrielle et un port fluvial important. Cette ancienne capitale de l'Alsace est connue pour son pâté de foie gras. Dans la magnifique cathédrale gothique se trouve la célèbre horloge astronomique.

4. **Reims,** le centre de la préparation du champagne, possède une des plus belles cathédrales gothiques de France, un chef-d'œuvre d'architecture et de sculpture. Dans cette cathédrale, on couronnait les rois de France.

   D'autres villes connues pour leur cathédrale gothique sont **Chartres** et **Amiens.**

5. **Nancy,** ancienne capitale de la Lorraine, et **Metz,** également en Lorraine, se trouvent dans la région des industries du charbon et de la métallurgie.
6. **Rouen,** sur la Seine en Normandie, est une ville industrielle et un port fluvial. Jeanne d'Arc y fut brûlée en 1431.
7. **Grenoble,** au sud-est, est le centre principal de la fabrication des gants.
8. **Toulouse,** sur la Garonne, est le centre industriel et commercial de la région.
9. **Clermont-Ferrand,** dans le centre du pays, est la métropole française du caoutchouc. On y fabrique des pneus (*tires*).

Villes

STATIONS D'ÉTÉ ET D'HIVER

1. **Nice,** la plus grande ville de la Côte d'Azur, et la ville avoisinante de **Cannes** sont deux stations balnéaires (seaside resorts) qui attirent beaucoup de touristes, surtout en hiver et au printemps.
2. **Chamonix,** situé au pied du mont Blanc, est un centre important d'alpinisme (mountain climbing) et de sports d'hiver.
3. **Deauville** et **Trouville** sont des plages populaires sur la Manche.
4. **Vichy** est la grande station thermale (spa) dans le Massif Central. Ses eaux minérales sont exportées aux quatre coins du monde. La ville était le siège du gouvernement français pendant la deuxième guerre mondiale.

   D'autres stations thermales sont **Évian, Vittel,** et **Aix-les-Bains.**
5. **Biarritz,** dans le pays basque, est une station balnéaire sur l'Atlantique, près de l'Espagne.

VILLES HISTORIQUES

1. **Carcassonne** se trouve dans le Midi de la France. Célèbre par les remparts qui l'entourent, c'est le meilleur exemple d'une ville fortifiée du Moyen Age.
2. **Le Mont-Saint-Michel,** qu'on appelle "la Merveille de l'Occident," est situé sur un îlot rocheux de la Manche, entre les côtes de la Bretagne et de la Normandie. C'est une forteresse médiévale dominée par une abbaye bénédictine en style gothique.
3. **Avignon,** ville provençale sur le Rhône, est renommé pour son **palais des Papes.** Ce palais était la résidence papale au quatorzième siècle. **Le pont Saint-Bénézet** est bien connu, grâce à la vieille chanson fameuse.
4. **Nîmes** et **Arles,** deux villes méridionales, conservent quelques-uns des plus beaux monuments romains de France. A Nîmes se trouvent **la Maison Carrée,** temple romain, et les arènes. Pas loin de la ville, on peut voir **le pont du Gard,** aqueduc romain. A Arles aussi il y a un théâtre antique et les arènes.
5. **Lourdes,** dans les Pyrénées, est le lieu de pèlerinage (pilgrimage) le plus célèbre de France. Ce grand centre religieux attire chaque année des milliers de catholiques du monde entier. **Lisieux,** en Normandie, est un autre lieu de pèlerinage.

EXERCICES

A. Pour chaque description de la première colonne, donner la lettre de la ville correspondante de la seconde colonne:

1.	ancienne capitale de la Lorraine	*a.*	Marseille
2.	centre de l'industrie de la soie	*b.*	Reims
3.	ville normande où Jeanne d'Arc mourut	*c.*	Lyon
4.	premier port de mer, sur la Méditerranée	*d.*	Strasbourg
5.	ville industrielle sur le Rhin	*e.*	Bordeaux
6.	station balnéaire de la Côte d'Azur	*f.*	Nancy
7.	grand port au sud-ouest, actif dans le commerce des vins	*g.*	Le Havre
		h.	Rouen
8.	lieu de pèlerinage en Normandie	*i.*	Lisieux
9.	centre de la préparation du champagne	*j.*	Cannes
10.	port transatlantique à l'embouchure de la Seine		

B. Vrai ou faux?

1. A cause de la douceur de leur climat, Nice et Cannes attirent beaucoup de touristes en hiver.
2. On peut voir la célèbre horloge astronomique dans la cathédrale de Chartres.
3. On fabrique un grand nombre de machines à Lille.
4. Nancy et Metz sont des ports fluviaux.
5. La ville de Carcassonne est dominée par une abbaye bénédictine.
6. Biarritz est sur l'Atlantique, près de l'Espagne.
7. La Maison Carrée d'Arles fut un temple romain.
8. Toulouse, sur la Garonne, est une ville industrielle et commerciale.
9. Au point de vue de la population, Bordeaux est plus grand que le Havre.
10. Le pont du Gard, près de Nîmes, est un aqueduc du Moyen Age.

C. Compléter en français:

1. Les trois plus grandes villes de la France sont Paris, ______, et ______.
2. Lyon se trouve au confluent de la Saône et ______.
3. ______, dans le Massif Central, est le centre de l'industrie du caoutchouc.
4. Trois ports sur la Manche sont ______, ______, et ______.
5. Le palais des Papes se trouve à ______.
6. Le port de Marseille relie la France à l'Afrique du Nord et à ______.
7. Le Mont-Saint-Michel est situé sur un îlot de la ______, entre la ______ et la ______.
8. Deux ports militaires sont ______ et ______.
9. Reims et Amiens sont célèbres par leur ______ gothique.
10. ______ et ______ sont des plages populaires sur la Manche.

11. La ville de ______ était le siège du gouvernement français pendant la deuxième guerre mondiale.
12. ______, situé au pied du mont Blanc, est un centre de sports d'hiver.
13. Deux villes méridionales connues pour leurs beaux monuments romains sont ______ et ______.
14. Nantes, à l'embouchure de la ______, est un centre de constructions ______.
15. La Rochelle et Saint-Nazaire sont des ports sur ______.

D. Identifier la ville:

1. centre principal de la fabrication des gants
2. station balnéaire du pays basque
3. "la Merveille de l'Occident"
4. ancienne capitale de l'Alsace
5. grand centre de l'industrie textile
6. le plus grand port sur la Manche
7. lieu de pèlerinage le plus célèbre de France
8. ville principale de la Riviera
9. le meilleur exemple d'une ville fortifiée du Moyen Age
10. grande station thermale dans le Massif Central

La Madeleine

L'église parisienne de la Madeleine, construite de 1764 à 1842, présente l'aspect d'un temple grec. La majestueuse colonnade de 52 piliers autour de l'église supporte une frise richement sculptée. Les cérémonies religieuses de la Madeleine sont très élégantes.

6. LA CINQUIÈME RÉPUBLIQUE FRANÇAISE

1. En 1958, les Français ont approuvé une nouvelle constitution préparée par le gouvernement du général de Gaulle. Cette constitution marque la naissance de **la Cinquième République** française, fondée sur l'égalité et la solidarité des peuples qui la composent. Elle assure une stabilité et une continuité au gouvernement. Les pouvoirs du Président sont plus étendus que ceux donnés par la constitution précédente. Charles de Gaulle a été élu premier Président de la Cinquième République.

2. La France est une république indivisible, laïque (secular), démocratique, et sociale. Elle garantit l'égalité devant la loi de tous les citoyens sans distinction d'origine, de race, ou de religion. Elle respecte toutes les croyances. Le suffrage est universel, égal, et secret. Tous les citoyens français âgés de plus de 18 ans des deux sexes ont le droit de voter.

3. **L'Exécutif** se compose du Président de la République et du Gouvernement dirigé par le Premier Ministre.

4. **Le Président de la République** représente l'autorité suprême de la nation. C'est le véritable chef du gouvernement. Il assure le fonctionnement régulier des pouvoirs publics ainsi que la continuité de l'État. Il est élu pour sept ans directement par tous les électeurs. Le Président de la République nomme le Premier Ministre et, sur la proposition de celui-ci, les autres membres du Gouvernement (le Conseil des Ministres). Il promulgue les lois. Il est le chef des armées. Il peut soumettre au référendum des projets de loi. Il peut, après consultation du Premier Ministre et des présidents des deux Chambres du Parlement, prononcer la dissolution de l'Assemblée Nationale. En période de crise, il peut exercer des pouvoirs exceptionnels. Sa résidence officielle est **le palais de l'Élysée**, à Paris.

5. **Le Gouvernement**, composé du Premier Ministre et de ses ministres, assure l'exécution des lois. **Le Premier Ministre**, nommé par le Président, dirige l'action du Gouvernement. Avec **le Conseil des Ministres**, il détermine (formulates) et conduit la politique (policy) de la nation. Il est responsable de la défense nationale. Le Gouvernement est responsable devant l'Assemblée Nationale. Pourtant, la difficulté de renverser le Gouvernement en assure la stabilité. Il n'est pas permis aux ministres d'être membres du Parlement. Par conséquent, les ministres sont exempts de la pression politique.

6. **Le Parlement**, qui possède le pouvoir législatif, comprend **l'Assemblée Nationale** et **le Sénat**. Les députés à l'Assemblée Nationale sont élus au suffrage direct pour cinq ans. Les sénateurs, élus pour neuf ans au suffrage indirect, représentent les départements et les Français établis hors de France. Le Parlement vote la loi et autorise

la déclaration de guerre. L'Assemblée Nationale ne peut obliger le Gouvernement à démissionner (resign) que si une motion de censure est votée à la majorité absolue des députés.

7. **Le Conseil Constitutionnel** a pour rôle d'assurer le respect de la constitution. Ce Conseil veille à (watches over) la régularité de l'élection du Président de la République et des opérations de référendum. Il se prononce sur la conformité des lois à la constitution.

8. Le pouvoir judiciaire est indépendant des autres pouvoirs. L'autorité judiciaire, garantie par la constitution, est la gardienne de la liberté individuelle. **La Cour de Cassation,** qui siège à Paris, est le tribunal suprême.

9. Le territoire français est divisé en **95 départements** au point de vue administratif. **Le préfet,** qui est nommé par le Gouvernement, est à la tête du département. Il est assisté d'un **conseil général,** élu au suffrage universel. Chaque département est divisé en **arrondissements,** subdivisés à leur tour en **cantons** et **communes.**

10. L'emblème national est le drapeau tricolore: bleu, blanc, et rouge. L'hymne national, *la Marseillaise*, fut composé en 1792 par **Rouget de Lisle.** La devise de la République est *Liberté, Égalité, Fraternité* —la devise même de la Révolution française. Le quatorze juillet—l'anniversaire de la prise de la Bastille par le peuple de Paris en 1789—est la date de la fête nationale française. La Bastille, prison royale, était le symbole de la tyrannie de l'ancien régime. On peut voir la clef de la Bastille à Mount-Vernon; c'est La Fayette qui l'a donnée à George Washington. Pour célébrer la fête nationale, on danse dans les rues. Il y a aussi des revues militaires, des cérémonies au tombeau du Soldat Inconnu, et des représentations gratuites aux théâtres.

EXERCICES

A. Vrai ou faux?

1. La France est une république constitutionnelle.
2. Le Premier Ministre est le chef des armées.
3. Le Parlement vote les lois, le Président les promulgue, et le Gouvernement en assure l'exécution.
4. L'Assemblée Nationale est responsable devant le Gouvernement.
5. Les ministres du Gouvernement peuvent être membres du Parlement.
6. Les sénateurs sont élus au suffrage direct.
7. Le Premier Ministre est responsable de la défense nationale.
8. Le canton est plus grand que l'arrondissement.
9. La constitution française garantit l'indépendance de l'autorité judiciaire.
10. La clef de la Bastille se trouve dans la ville de Washington, D.C.

B. Choisir la réponse convenable entre parenthèses:

1. Le (Président de la République, Premier Ministre) peut prononcer la dissolution de l'Assemblée Nationale.
2. Les députés à l'Assemblée Nationale sont élus au suffrage (direct, indirect).
3. Le (Premier Ministre, Parlement) autorise la déclaration de guerre.
4. Quand la République est menacée d'une manière grave et immédiate, le (Premier Ministre, Président de la République) peut prendre des mesures exceptionnelles.
5. (La Cour de Cassation, Le Conseil Constitutionnel) veille à la régularité des opérations de référendum.
6. Le préfet est le chef d'un (arrondissement, département).
7. Le préfet est (élu au suffrage universel, nommé par le Gouvernement).
8. La France est composée de (95, 32) départements.
9. Il est relativement (facile, difficile) de renverser un Gouvernement français.
10. Tous les citoyens français âgés de plus de (18, 21) ans ont le droit de voter.

C. Compléter en français:

1. Aujourd'hui la France vit sous la ______ République. En 1958, ______ a été élu le premier Président de cette République.
2. L'Exécutif de la République Française se compose du ______ et du Gouvernement dirigé par le ______.
3. Le ______ est le véritable chef de la nation. Il est élu pour ______ ans au suffrage universel.
4. C'est lui qui nomme le ______ et, sur la proposition de celui-ci, les autres membres due ______.
5. Les deux Chambres du Parlement sont ______ et ______.
6. La résidence officielle du Président à Paris est le palais de ______.
7. Les députés sont élus pour ____ ans; les sénateurs, pour ____ ans.
8. La Cour de ______, qui est le tribunal suprême, siège à Paris.
9. Pour faire démissionner le Gouvernement, il faut qu'une motion de censure soit votée à la ______ absolue des députés de l'Assemblée Nationale.
10. Chaque département est divisé en ______.
11. L'emblème national français est le drapeau ______: bleu, blanc, et rouge.
12. En 1792, ______ a composé l'hymne national, *la* ______.
13. La devise de la République Française est ______, ______, ______.
14. Le ______ juillet marque l'anniversaire de la prise de la ______ par les Parisiens en ______. Pour célébrer cette fête, on danse dans les ______.
15. Le Président de la République aujourd'hui est M. ______.

7. LA VIE QUOTIDIENNE

1. RELIGION

La plupart des Français sont catholiques, mais il n'y a pas de religion officielle en France. La Cinquième République respecte toutes les croyances.

2. ENSEIGNEMENT

L'instruction en France est gratuite (free) et obligatoire pour tous les enfants de six à seize ans. L'enseignement est administré par le ministère (ministry) de l'Éducation, et à cet effet la France est divisée en régions, appelées **Académies.** A côté des écoles publiques, il y a des établissements privés, généralement catholiques. Les écoles françaises cherchent à donner à chaque élève un enseignement en rapport avec ses aptitudes.

L'enseignement préscolaire, donné dans des écoles maternelles aux enfants de deux à cinq ans, n'est pas obligatoire.

L'enseignement élémentaire, commun à tous les enfants français, dure cinq ans. Les jours de congé sont le mercredi et le dimanche. Le samedi, il y a des classes de huit heures du matin jusqu'à midi.

L'enseignement secondaire consiste en deux cycles. Le premier cycle, donné dans les collèges, est obligatoire. Il dure quatre ans. Le second cycle est facultatif (optional), et peut être **long** ou **court.** Le second cycle long, de trois ans, est donné dans les lycées. Il mène au **baccalauréat** et à l'enseignement supérieur. Le second cycle court, de deux ans, offre des cours techniques.

L'enseignement supérieur se donne dans les facultés des universités et dans les "grandes écoles," des écoles de spécialisation qui préparent aux carrières supérieures de l'administration, de l'enseignement, de l'industrie, du commerce, de l'armée, de la marine, etc. Parmi les grandes écoles, citons: **l'École Normale Supérieure** (où sont préparés les professeurs de l'enseignement secondaire et supérieur); **l'École Polytechnique** (qui forme des ingénieurs civils); **l'École des Beaux-Arts**; **l'École des Mines**; et les écoles militaires–**l'École Interarmes** (autrefois l'École militaire de Saint-Cyr), qui est le "West Point" de France; **l'École Navale**; et **l'École de l'Air.**

3. LOISIRS

a. Les sports ont conquis une place importante en France, où l'on trouve aujourd'hui des milliers de sociétés sportives. Parmi les sports favoris, il faut mentionner le football (qui ressemble au *soccer* américain), le cyclisme, l'alpinisme (les ascensions en montagne), le ski, la natation, la pêche, et le tennis. Chaque année les sports sous-marins deviennent de plus en plus à la mode. Les Français, qui aiment vivre en plein air, font beaucoup de camping. Il y a aussi des sports régionaux: du pays basque vient la **pelote**; le jeu de **boules** est populaire surtout dans le Midi.

La course de bicyclettes la plus célèbre est **le Tour de France**, qui se dispute tous les ans en juillet. Cette épreuve internationale, qui dure plus de trois semaines, est sans doute l'événement sportif auquel les Français s'intéressent le plus.

b. **Le café** joue un rôle social dans la vie quotidienne (de tous les jours) des Français. C'est un lieu social où l'on rencontre ses amis. Au café, les clients peuvent lire le journal, écrire des lettres, ou jouer aux cartes. La plupart des cafés ont aussi des terrasses en plein air sur le trottoir, où sont placées des tables et des chaises.

c. Le théâtre, le cinéma, l'opéra, le ballet, et les concerts attirent un grand nombre de Français. Paris est le centre de la vie théâtrale, mais il y a des centres dramatiques dans toutes les parties de la France. Les théâtres nationaux, subventionnés par l'État, sont: **l'Opéra** et **l'Opéra-Comique**, qui donnent des opéras de tous les pays; **la Comédie-Française** et **le Théâtre National de l'Odéon**, qui jouent des pièces françaises; et **le Théâtre National Populaire**, où l'on peut voir des expériences et des innovations.

Dans les théâtres français, on annonce le lever du rideau par trois coups frappés derrière la scène. En France, on donne un pourboire aux ouvreuses (celles qui placent les spectateurs dans les théâtres et les cinémas).

d. Les Français aiment aussi à lire et à visiter les musées et les expositions d'art. On publie des milliers de livres en France chaque année. Parmi les journaux de Paris, citons: *France-soir*, *Le Monde*, *Le Figaro*, *L'Aurore*, et *Le Parisien libéré*. Le nombre de postes récepteurs de télévision augmente sans cesse. Quant à la Loterie nationale, autorisée par le gouvernement, elle est très populaire.

e. A la longue liste d'attractions, ajoutons celle qui s'appelle "Son et Lumière." C'est un spectacle dramatique dont l'action a lieu à l'endroit même où sont situés des monuments historiques, tels que les châteaux de la Loire, le palais des Papes à Avignon, et la Cité de Carcassonne. Le *Son* est la narration du drame accompagnée d'une partie musicale appropriée; la *Lumière* est constituée par des effets de lumière ou de couleurs qui soulignent dramatiquement la présentation.

4. FÊTES

Les Français célèbrent beaucoup de fêtes, dont la plupart sont d'origine religieuse. Les principales fêtes publiques sont:

a. **le Jour de l'An**–le 1er janvier; on donne et reçoit des étrennes (cadeaux) et on souhaite à tout le monde "une bonne et heureuse année"

b. **Pâques** (Easter)–fête religieuse, en mars ou avril

c. **la fête du Travail**–le 1er mai; le muguet (lily of the valley), qui doit porter du bonheur, se vend partout dans les rues

d. **l'Ascension**–fête religieuse célébrée quarante jours après Pâques

e. **la fête de Jeanne d'Arc**–le deuxième dimanche du mois de mai

f. **la Pentecôte** (Pentecost, Whitsuntide)–fête religieuse qui a lieu le septième dimanche après Pâques

g. **la fête nationale**–le 14 juillet; l'anniversaire de la prise de la Bastille

h. **l'Assomption**–fête religieuse qui tombe le 15 août

i. **la Toussaint**–le 1er novembre; fête religieuse en l'honneur de tous les saints

j. **la fête de l'Armistice**–le 11 novembre; commémore la fin de la guerre de 1914-1918

k. **Noël**–le 25 décembre. En France, seulement les enfants reçoivent des cadeaux. Ils déposent leurs souliers devant la cheminée ou près de l'arbre de Noël pour la visite du Père Noël. Après la messe de minuit à l'église, la famille prend un grand repas, le réveillon.

5. CUISINE

Pour le Français, la cuisine est un art et une tradition. Puisque le Français est un **gourmet**, c'est-à-dire, quelqu'un qui aime la bonne chère (good living), les repas sont toujours préparés avec soin. Il faut beaucoup de temps pour prendre un repas en France parce que manger est un grand plaisir. Comme le climat et le sol du pays, la cuisine française est très variée. Chaque région a ses propres spécialités délicieuses. Le Français ne pouvant rien manger sans pain, le régime (diet) français en comprend une grande quantité.

Vers huit heures du matin, on prend le petit déjeuner: du café au lait ou du chocolat, et du pain beurré ou des croissants ou des brioches. Le déjeuner, qu'on prend vers midi, et le dîner, pris après sept heures du soir, consistent en plusieurs plats: hors-d'œuvre ou potage, poisson, viande ou volaille (poultry) accompagnée de légumes, salade, fromage, et fruits. Pendant le repas, on boit du vin, du cidre, ou de l'eau minérale. A la fin du repas, le Français préfère du café.

Quelques-uns des plats célèbres dont la France a enrichi l'art culinaire sont: la soupe à l'oignon, le pâté de foie gras, le coq au vin, le pot-au-feu, la bouillabaisse (spécialité culinaire de Marseille), et les crêpes Suzette.

Dans les restaurants français, les plats sont généralement servis sur commande. On peut commander un repas **à la carte** (le prix de chaque plat étant indiqué) ou **à prix fixe** (le prix du repas entier étant déterminé d'avance). La carte du jour se trouve bien en vue devant chaque restaurant pour faire savoir aux clients les plats du jour et les prix. **Le bistro,** ce petit restaurant simple, est très fréquenté par les Français.

6. UNITÉS DE MESURE

a. **Le système métrique** fut institué en France au début du 19e siècle. Ce système, dont le mètre est la base, est très simple parce qu'il n'a que des multiples et des subdivisions décimales. Il est en vigueur aujourd'hui dans presque tous les pays de l'Europe et de l'Amérique du Sud. Les savants du monde entier l'emploient.

Le mètre est l'unité de longueur.
1 mètre = 100 centimètres (= 39.37 inches)
1.000 mètres = 1 kilomètre (= $\frac{5}{8}$ mile)

Le gramme est l'unité de masse.
1.000 grammes = 1 kilogramme (= 2.2 pounds)

Le litre est l'unité de mesure de capacité pour les liquides et les matières sèches. Il vaut un peu plus que le "quart" américain.

b. L'unité monétaire en France est **le franc,** qui a une valeur approximative de 21 "cents" américains. Il y a 100 **centimes** dans un franc.

c. Le thermomètre **centigrade,** qu'on emploie en France, comprend 100 divisions. Le point 0 correspond à la température de la glace fondante, et le point 100 à celle de la vapeur d'eau bouillante.

EXERCICES

A. Pour chaque expression de la première colonne, donner la lettre du nom correspondant de la seconde colonne:

1. spectacle dramatique	*a.* école maternelle
2. fête des étrennes	*b.* réveillon
3. enseignement préscolaire	*c.* pâté de foie gras
4. spécialité culinaire	*d.* Jour de l'An
5. unité de capacité	*e.* gramme
6. croissants et brioches	*f.* bistro
7. repas fait dans la nuit de Noël	*g.* litre
8. petit restaurant populaire	*h.* Pâques
9. unité de masse	*i.* petit déjeuner
10. fête religieuse	*j.* Son et Lumière

B. Vrai ou faux?

1. L'enseignement public est gratuit en France.
2. La plupart des Français sont protestants.
3. Le premier cycle de l'enseignement secondaire, qui dure quatre ans, est obligatoire.
4. On cherche à donner à chaque élève français la forme d'enseignement qui répond le mieux à ses aptitudes.
5. Pour voir des pièces de théâtre en France, il faut aller à Paris.
6. Le gouvernement français autorise des loteries.
7. Le système métrique fut institué en France pendant le règne de Louis XV.
8. L'École Interarmes est l'équivalent français de notre Académie Navale d'Annapolis.
9. En France, on donne des pourboires aux ouvreuses de cinéma et de théâtre.
10. D'ordinaire, les Français donnent des cadeaux à leurs amis pour la fête de Noël.

C. Identifier:

1. la grande école qui forme des ingénieurs civils
2. un sport d'origine basque
3. la fleur qui se vend dans la rue le 1er mai
4. une spécialité culinaire de Marseille faite avec une variété de poissons
5. une personne qui aime la bonne chère
6. l'unité monétaire de France
7. l'événement sportif le plus suivi en France
8. mille mètres
9. la fête du 1er novembre en l'honneur des saints
10. le thermomètre qui s'emploie en France

D. Compléter en français:

1. Pour administrer l'enseignement, la France est divisée en régions, appelées ______.
2. La scolarité en France est obligatoire à partir de ______ ans et jusqu'à l'âge de ______ ans.
3. On donne l'enseignement supérieur dans les facultés des ______ et dans les "______ écoles."
4. A la fin des études de trois ans dans le lycée, on obtient le ______, appelé aussi le *bachot*.
5. L'École ______ Supérieure forme les professeurs de l'enseignement secondaire.
6. En France, il n'y a pas de classes le ______ et le dimanche.
7. Beaucoup de ______ français ont des terrasses sur le trottoir.
8. Le ______ vaut à peu près 2.2 livres américaines.
9. On joue aux boules, sport régional, surtout dans le ______ de la France.
10. La ______, célèbre théâtre national où l'on joue des pièces françaises, fut fondée en 1680 par ordre de Louis XIV.
11. Les enfants français déposent leurs ______ devant la cheminée pour la visite du ______ Noël.
12. Deux journaux quotidiens de Paris sont ______ et ______.
13. On annonce le ______ dans les théâtres par trois coups frappés derrière la scène.
14. On peut commander un repas à la ______ ou à prix ______.
15. Le franc a une valeur approximative de ______ "cents" américains.

Mardi Gras

Le Mardi Gras est le dernier jour du Carnaval. A cette occasion, un grand défilé de chars et de géants en papier mâché a lieu à Nice, où des milliers de personnes célèbrent cette fête.

8. PERSONNAGES ET ÉVÉNEMENTS DE L'HISTOIRE DE FRANCE

1. La France est riche en vestiges de civilisations préhistoriques. On a découvert dans plusieurs grottes françaises, comme celles des Eyzies et de Lascaux, des squelettes d'hommes et des dessins sur pierre. Les menhirs et les dolmens–des blocs de pierre préhistoriques–sont nombreux en Bretagne.

2. Au premier siècle avant Jésus-Christ, la France s'appelait **la Gaule**. C'était le territoire des **Celtes**, ou **Gaulois**, qui avaient une civilisation primitive. Les Gaulois étaient divisés en un grand nombre de tribus rivales qui se faisaient souvent la guerre. Leurs prêtres, appelés **druides**, occupaient une place importante dans leur société. Les druides, qui étaient aussi médecins et juges, exerçaient une influence sociale et politique en même temps que religieuse. Adorateurs de la nature, ils enseignaient que le gui (mistletoe), plante toujours verte, était sacré et que l'âme était immortelle.

3. **Jules César**, le général romain, profita de la désunion des Gaulois pour entreprendre la conquête du pays entier. Cette conquête se termina par la bataille d'Alésia en 52 av. J.-C.

   Vercingétorix, chef courageux et général habile, réussit à former une coalition des peuples gaulois contre César. Après la défaite des Gaulois à Alésia, Vercingétorix fut emmené à Rome, où il figura dans le triomphe de César. Au bout de six ans de prison, le chef gaulois fut exécuté. On considère Vercingétorix comme le premier héros national de la France.

4. Sous le gouvernement des Romains, qui dura plus de 400 ans, la Gaule prospéra. Les Gaulois adoptèrent les coutumes, la religion, et le code de justice des vainqueurs, et ils apprirent le latin, la langue de Rome. Les Romains développèrent l'agriculture et le commerce. Ils construisirent de belles routes, des aqueducs, des amphithéâtres, des temples, et d'autres bâtiments publics. La conquête romaine donna à la Gaule la paix et la sécurité.

5. L'empire romain était très vaste et, par conséquent, difficile à défendre. A partir du IIIe siècle, des peuplades barbares–Wisigoths, Vandales, Burgondes, Huns–commencèrent à envahir la Gaule. Au Ve siècle, une tribu germanique, **les Francs**, conquit le pays et s'y installa. Ce sont eux qui ont donné leur nom à la France.

6. **Clovis** (465–511), roi des Francs, battit les Romains et se fit maître de presque toute la Gaule. Il se convertit au christianisme, qui devint la religion officielle du pays.

7. **Sainte Geneviève** est la patronne de Paris. Au Ve siècle, quand les Huns étaient sur le point d'attaquer Paris (alors Lutèce), Geneviève, une bergère, donna aux habitants le courage de rester dans la ville. Elle avait raison, car l'armée d'Attila changea de direction, et Paris fut sauvé.

8. En 732, **Charles Martel** sauva la France de l'invasion musulmane en écrasant les Arabes à la bataille de Poitiers.

9. **Charlemagne**, ou Charles le Grand, petit-fils de Charles Martel, fut le souverain le plus puissant du Moyen Age. En 800, à Rome, le pape le couronna empereur d'Occident. Il gouverna un empire immense: la plus grande partie de l'Europe occidentale. Charlemagne était un administrateur sage qui essayait d'améliorer la condition de son peuple. Il promulgua des lois bonnes et justes. Protecteur des arts et des lettres, il encouragea l'enseignement en créant de nombreuses écoles. Ses exploits guerriers sont célébrés dans *la Chanson de Roland*, le premier chef-d'œuvre de la littérature française. Malheureusement, après la mort de Charlemagne, son vaste empire fut démembré.

10. A la fin du IXe siècle, quand la France ne pouvait plus se défendre, le pays fut ravagé par **les Normands**, les hommes du Nord. Ces pirates, qui venaient par mer, remontaient les fleuves et pillaient tout sur leur passage. Ils finirent par rester dans la région qu'on appelle aujourd'hui la Normandie.

11. En 1066, **Guillaume le Conquérant**, duc de Normandie, traversa la Manche, fit la conquête de l'Angleterre, et devint roi de ce pays.

12. **Louis IX**, ou **saint Louis**, est connu pour son amour de la justice et de la paix. Il s'intéressait à ses sujets, surtout aux pauvres. Très pieux, il prit une part active aux Croisades du XIIIe siècle. Louis IX fit beaucoup pour consolider le pouvoir royal.

13. Pendant la guerre de Cent Ans, de 1337 à 1453, les armées anglaises envahirent la France. Les rois d'Angleterre, qui prétendaient à la couronne de France, dévastèrent le pays. Grâce au courage d'une jeune paysanne française, la France fut sauvée.

    Jeanne d'Arc, appelée *la Pucelle* (Maid) *d'Orléans*, est l'héroïne nationale de la France. Elle naquit en 1412 à Domremy, en Lorraine. Jeanne crut entendre des voix surnaturelles qui lui commandaient de délivrer la France. A la tête d'une armée française, elle battit les Anglais à Orléans et fit sacrer Charles VII roi de France dans la cathédrale de Reims. Trahie, elle fut prise et vendue aux Anglais. Ceux-ci, l'ayant accusée d'hérésie, la brûlèrent vive à Rouen en 1431. Après la mort de Jeanne d'Arc, les Français, inspirés par son courage, chassèrent les Anglais de France.

14. **François Ier** fut roi de France pendant la première moitié du XVIe siècle, l'époque de la Renaissance. Administrateur brillant et patron des arts, il fit venir à sa cour de grands artistes italiens, des hommes de lettres, et des savants. Il fonda le Collège de France, fit construire de beaux châteaux le long de la Loire, et encouragea l'exploration. Sous son règne, Jacques Cartier prit possession du Canada.

15. **Henri IV**, le premier monarque de la famille des Bourbons, est le plus aimé des rois de France. On l'appelle souvent "le bon roi Henri" parce qu'il gouvernait avec intelligence et humanité. Né protestant, il se convertit au catholicisme pour mettre fin aux guerres de religion et pour restaurer la paix en France. Par le célèbre **Édit de Nantes** de 1598, il accorda aux protestants la liberté du culte (worship). Henri IV entreprit l'œuvre de restaurer l'autorité royale, de réorganiser l'administration, et de rétablir la prospérité du pays. Il encouragea l'industrie, le commerce, et l'agriculture. Il fit construire des routes et des ponts. Un de ses capitaines, Champlain, fonda Québec en 1608.

16. **Le cardinal Richelieu**, le premier ministre intelligent et énergique de Louis XIII, fut un grand homme d'état. En abaissant la puissance des grands seigneurs et en forçant les protestants à se soumettre au roi, il fonda l'absolutisme royal. Il améliora la vie économique de la France et réforma les finances et la législation. Protecteur des lettres, des arts, et des sciences, il fonda l'Académie française en 1635. Richelieu fit de la France une des plus grandes nations du monde.

17. **Louis XIV**, appelé *le Roi Soleil*, fut le maître absolu de la France et le monarque le plus puissant de l'Europe. Son despotisme se résume dans les fameuses paroles: "L'État, c'est moi." Son règne de soixante-douze ans fut une époque de gloire militaire et de grandeur littéraire et artistique. Le magnifique palais qu'il fit construire à Versailles devint le centre politique, social, et culturel de la France. Son ministre brillant et infatigable, Colbert, mit de l'ordre dans les finances, protégea le commerce et l'industrie, et encouragea les travaux publics.

    Mais l'égotisme et l'ambition du roi causèrent de longues guerres qui furent désastreuses pour la France. Ces guerres et la cour somptueuse du roi finirent par ruiner le pays. En 1685, Louis XIV révoqua l'Édit de Nantes et persécuta les protestants.

18. **Louis XV** régna de 1715 à 1774. Au lieu de s'intéresser aux affaires du royaume, il s'occupait de ses propres plaisirs, dépensant de grandes sommes d'argent pour s'amuser. A cette époque, la France perdit le Canada. On prête à Louis XV la phrase sinistre:

"Après moi, le déluge." En effet, le mécontentement créé sous son règne fut une des causes principales de la Révolution française.

19. **Louis XVI**, plein de bonnes intentions mais manquant de décision, ne savait pas gouverner. Il écoutait les mauvais conseils de sa femme frivole, **Marie-Antoinette.** Ennemie des réformes, la reine perdit tout de suite l'estime du peuple. Louis était incapable de résoudre la crise financière, politique, et sociale qui troublait le pays. Le 14 juillet 1789, le peuple de Paris attaqua la Bastille et prit la prison détestée. Cet événement historique marqua le commencement de **la Révolution française** et la chute de la royauté. En 1793, le roi et la reine furent condamnés à mort et guillotinés.

20. Trois nobles français qui aidèrent les colonies américaines à conquérir leur indépendance dans la lutte contre l'Angleterre se sont assuré la reconnaissance affectueuse du peuple américain:

    Le jeune **marquis de La Fayette** prit une part active à la guerre d'Indépendance en Amérique. Il devint un ami personnel du général Washington. Après la Révolution américaine, La Fayette retourna en France pour défendre les causes libérales dans son pays natal. En 1917, quand les troupes américaines débarquèrent en France, un des officiers du général Pershing exprima ces paroles célèbres: "La Fayette, nous voici."

    Le comte de Rochambeau commanda l'armée française envoyée au secours des Américains, et **l'amiral de Grasse** commanda la flotte française.

    Tous les trois contribuèrent à la défaite des Anglais à la bataille de Yorktown.

21. En 1789, on vota la *Déclaration des droits de l'homme et du citoyen*, qui proclamait les droits fondamentaux de l'individu que le gouvernement devait respecter. **La Première République** française fut établie en 1792 dans le but de substituer à un régime fondé sur le privilège une société basée sur l'égalité de tous. Mais les premières années de la république étaient une période de crises et de violences. Parmi les grandes personnalités de cette époque révolutionnaire, il faut mentionner **Mirabeau**, partisan d'une monarchie constitutionnelle; **Danton**, grand orateur; **Marat**, médecin journaliste; et **Robespierre**, chef de **la Terreur.**

22. **Napoléon Bonaparte**, né à Ajaccio, en Corse, en 1769, exerça sur son temps une grande influence. Dans l'armée Républicaine, il se distingua comme capitaine et plus tard comme général. Il devint Premier consul après un coup d'état; et en 1804, se fit couronner Empereur des Français sous le nom de Napoléon Ier. Génie militaire à ambition énorme, il essaya de conquérir l'Europe et d'en faire une espèce de fédération. En 1814, les ennemis de la France en-

vahirent le pays; et Napoléon, obligé d'abdiquer, se retira à l'île d'Elbe. Quelques mois plus tard, il retourna en France. Mais en 1815, il fut vaincu à Waterloo, en Belgique, par les armées réunies de ses ennemis. Les Anglais l'exilèrent à Sainte-Hélène, où il mourut en 1821.

Malgré ses guerres désastreuses et ses mesures despotiques qui épuisèrent la France, Napoléon fit des contributions permanentes à son pays. Il réforma l'organisation judiciaire: **le Code Napoléon** est encore aujourd'hui la base de la justice française. Il encouragea l'industrie et l'agriculture, établit l'administration préfectorale, et fit construire un réseau de routes modernes. En donnant à la France un système d'éducation centralisé, en fondant des lycées, et en réorganisant l'Université de Paris, il réforma l'enseignement. Napoléon institua un nouveau système financier au moyen de **la Banque de France** et créa **la Légion d'Honneur.** C'est lui qui vendit la Louisiane aux États-Unis.

23. La France proclama **la Seconde République** en 1848, et **Louis-Napoléon**, neveu de Napoléon Bonaparte, en fut élu le Président. En 1852, il se fit empereur sous le nom de Napoléon III et fonda **le Second Empire.** Il enleva beaucoup des libertés qu'avaient gagnées les Français, mais il donna au pays une période de prospérité économique. Son gouvernement entreprit de nombreux travaux publics et stimula l'agriculture, l'industrie, et le commerce. A cette époque Paris fut transformé et embelli. Pourtant la politique extérieure de l'empereur fut désastreuse. Après la défaite de la France dans la guerre franco-allemande de 1870–1871, les Français renversèrent l'empire et établirent **la Troisième République.**

24. La Grande Guerre entre la France et l'Allemagne éclata en 1914. Le maréchal **Foch** fut le généralissime à la tête de toutes les troupes alliées, y compris les américaines. En 1918, après une longue guerre, les armées alliées obligèrent l'Allemagne à se rendre. La France fut victorieuse, mais épuisée.

25. En 1940, la France fut encore une fois envahie par les armées de l'Allemagne. Cette année de la Seconde Guerre Mondiale marque la fin de la Troisième République et le commencement de l'occupation allemande. Le chef du gouvernement collaborationniste de Vichy fut le maréchal Pétain. Les Alliés débarquèrent en Normandie en 1944, et bientôt après la France fut libérée. **La Quatrième République** date de 1947.

26. Après la chute de la Troisième République en 1940, le général **Charles de Gaulle** s'échappa de France et prit la tête de la résistance française. Il encouragea le peuple par son appel à tous les Français: "La France a perdu une bataille! Mais la France n'a pas perdu la guerre!"

En 1959, il fut élu le premier Président de **la Cinquième République.** Il s'est retiré de la présidence en 1969.

27. Les explorateurs français ont joué un rôle important dans l'histoire de l'Amérique.

   a. **Jacques Cartier** découvrit le Saint-Laurent en 1535 et prit possession du Canada au nom du roi de France. Plus tard il remonta le fleuve jusqu'à la montagne qu'il appela Montréal.

   b. **Samuel de Champlain** fonda la ville de Québec en 1608 et découvrit le lac Champlain.

   c. **Le père Jacques Marquette** explora la région des Grands Lacs et découvrit le Mississippi. Lui et **Louis Joliet** descendirent le fleuve en 1673.

   d. **Robert Cavelier de La Salle** explora le Mississippi jusqu'au Golfe du Mexique en 1682. Il prit possession de l'immense vallée du fleuve, la nommant "Louisiane" en l'honneur de Louis XIV.

   On trouve aujourd'hui aux États-Unis beaucoup de noms géographiques d'origine française, tels que Bayonne, Champlain, Detroit, Joliet, Louisiana, New Orleans, New Rochelle, St. Louis, Terre Haute, et Vermont.

EXERCICES

A. Mettre dans l'ordre chronologique:

l'Édit de Nantes
l'invasion des Francs
la Troisième République
le couronnement de Charlemagne
la Renaissance
le gouvernement de Vichy
la conquête de la Gaule par les Romains
la Déclaration des droits de l'homme
la vente de la Louisiane aux États-Unis
la conquête de l'Angleterre par les Normands
la Cinquième République
la guerre de Cent Ans

B. Vrai ou faux?

1. Henri IV, né protestant, se convertit au catholicisme.
2. Rome gouverna la Gaule pendant plus de quatre cents ans.
3. Le palais de Versailles fut construit pour Louis XVI.

4. Le Code Napoléon est même aujourd'hui la base de la justice en France.
5. Louis XVI était un monarque indifférent, s'occupant surtout de ses propres plaisirs.
6. Jeanne d'Arc réussit à chasser les Anglais de France.
7. Jacques Cartier découvrit le Saint-Laurent.
8. Louis XIV révoqua l'Édit de Nantes.
9. Les Celtes avaient une civilisation bien avancée.
10. C'est Louis IX qu'on appelle saint Louis.

C. Pour chaque expression de la première colonne, donner la lettre du nom correspondant de la seconde colonne:

1. ministre de Louis XIII	*a.* Lascaux
2. "La Fayette, nous voici."	*b.* La Salle
3. dessins préhistoriques	*c.* Danton
4. "L'État, c'est moi."	*d.* Napoléon III
5. île d'Elbe	*e.* Richelieu
6. Second Empire	*f.* Louis XV
7. Mississippi	*g.* Louis XVI
8. grand orateur	*h.* officier américain
9. ministre de Louis XIV	*i.* Bretagne
10. "Après moi, le déluge."	*j.* Napoléon Bonaparte
11. menhirs et dolmens	*k.* Colbert
12. roi à l'époque de la Révolution française	*l.* Louis XIV

D. Compléter en français:

1. Autrefois la France s'appelait ------.
2. La plante verte que les Celtes considéraient sacrée est le ------.
3. Quand ------ se convertit, le christianisme devint la religion officielle de la France.
4. Charles ------ repoussa l'invasion arabe en 732.
5. Les exploits de Charlemagne sont célébrés dans ------, le premier chef-d'œuvre de la littérature française.
6. Jeanne d'Arc, née dans le village de ------, en Lorraine, fut brûlée à ------, ville de Normandie.
7. Sous le règne de ------, on bâtit de nombreux châteaux sur la Loire.
8. ------ fonda l'Académie française.
9. ------ commanda l'armée française, et ------ commanda la flotte française à la bataille de Yorktown.
10. Le génie militaire, Napoléon Bonaparte, naquit en Corse et mourut à ------, où les Anglais l'avaient emmené.

E. Identifier:

1. le plus aimé des rois de France
2. les prêtres des Gaulois
3. le souverain le plus puissant du Moyen Age
4. le Roi Soleil
5. la dernière bataille de Napoléon Ier
6. le roi de France pendant la Renaissance
7. le fondateur de la Légion d'Honneur
8. la Pucelle d'Orléans
9. le généralissime des troupes alliées en 1918
10. le premier héros national de la France
11. le fondateur de la ville de Québec
12. le général romain qui conquit les tribus gauloises
13. le chef de la résistance française en 1940
14. la sainte patronale de Paris
15. le chef de la Terreur

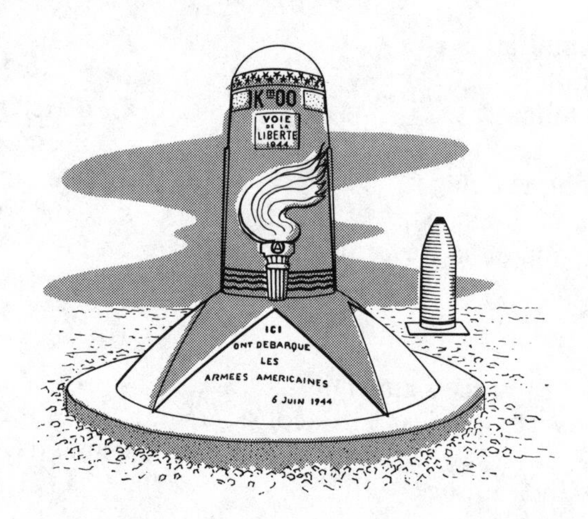

Monument en Normandie

Ce monument à Ste-Marie-du-Mont (Utah Beach) se trouve sur le circuit des "Plages du Débarquement." C'est sur cette côte de la Normandie que les Alliés ont débarqué en 1944 pour libérer la France de l'occupation allemande.

9. LA LANGUE ET LA LITTÉRATURE

LA LANGUE

1. Le français—comme l'italien, l'espagnol, le portugais, et le roumain—est une **langue romane,** c'est-à-dire, une langue dérivée du latin. C'est le latin populaire ou vulgaire, la langue parlée par le peuple, qui est devenu peu à peu le français.

2. Au Moyen Age, deux idiomes principaux florissaient en France: **la langue d'*oïl*** dans le Nord et **la langue d'*oc*** dans le Midi. La Loire formait la frontière entre ces deux régions linguistiques. Puisque le centre politique de la France était l'Ile-de-France, c'est le dialecte de cette province, un dialecte de la langue d'oïl, qui est devenu la langue officielle du pays.

   Néanmoins, la langue d'oc est toujours vivante. Elle a donné son nom à l'ancienne province méridionale du Languedoc. **Le provençal,** le dialecte le plus important de la langue d'oc, se parle encore dans le Midi de la France. En effet, elle a donné naissance à toute une littérature provençale, dont le représentant le plus illustre est le poète **Frédéric Mistral.**

   Il y a des restes d'autres dialectes en France: **le celtique,** la langue des Gaulois, en Bretagne; **le basque,** dans les Pyrénées; **le bas-allemand,** en Alsace. Dans la langue française d'aujourd'hui, on peut trouver des traces du celtique et de l'allemand.

3. Le français est connu pour la clarté de sa syntaxe, de son expression, et de sa pensée. Au 18e siècle, l'écrivain Rivarol exprima l'importance de cette clarté en ces termes: "Ce qui n'est pas clair n'est pas français."

   Pour étudier, conserver, et perfectionner le français le cardinal Richelieu fonda **l'Académie française** en 1635. L'Académie fut chargée de la rédaction (writing) du Dictionnaire de la langue française et d'une grammaire. Une nouvelle édition de ce dictionnaire paraît environ tous les cinquante ans. On appelle les membres de l'Académie "les quarante immortels."

4. Le français a exercé une influence profonde sur la langue anglaise. Quand le duc de Normandie traversa la Manche en 1066 et fit la conquête de l'Angleterre, le français devint la langue officielle de la cour royale, des nobles anglais, et de la justice. Par conséquent, un grand nombre de mots français sont entrés dans la langue anglaise.

LA LANGUE FRANÇAISE DANS LE MONDE

Il y a des francophones—des personnes qui parlent français—dans les deux hémisphères du monde.

En Europe, on parle français non seulement en France mais aussi en Belgique, en Suisse, et au Luxembourg.

On parle français dans les départements d'Outre-Mer (Overseas), tels que la Martinique et la Guadeloupe, et dans les territoires d'Outre-Mer, tels que la Polynésie et la Nouvelle-Calédonie.

Le français est langue officielle et langue d'enseignement dans plusieurs des nouvelles républiques d'Afrique, par examples, le Gabon, la République Centrafricaine, et la Côte d'Ivoire. Dans d'autres pays africains, comme le Maroc, la Tunisie, et l'Algérie, c'est la langue d'enseignement dans les écoles.

Au Canada, le français est devenu une des deux langues officielles, puisque c'est la langue maternelle de plusieurs millions de Canadiens qui demeurent dans l'Est du pays, surtout dans la province de Québec.

Aux États-Unis, on s'en sert encore en Louisiane, où il bénéficie d'un statut officiel.

Le français est aussi une langue officielle de l'O.N.U. (l'Organisation des Nations Unies). C'est une langue universelle.

LA LITTÉRATURE

1. On considère traditionnellement les *Serments de Strasbourg*—le traité d'alliance conclu par Louis le Germanique et Charles le Chauve en 842—comme le premier document en vieux français. Mais les premières œuvres littéraires, les **chansons de geste**, datent du Moyen Age. Ces poèmes épiques célèbrent avec un enthousiasme patriotique et religieux les exploits légendaires des chevaliers de la société féodale.

   La Chanson de Roland, composée au commencement du 12ᵉ siècle, est la plus ancienne et la plus belle des chansons de geste. Ce premier chef-d'œuvre de la littérature française, dont on ne connaît pas l'auteur, raconte l'histoire idéalisée de Charlemagne et de son neveu, Roland, dans les guerres contre les Sarrasins d'Espagne.

2. **François Villon**, poète éloquent du 15ᵉ siècle, mena une vie aventureuse, une vie de bohème. On le considère comme le premier des grands poètes lyriques français. Avec un accent personnel, plein de sincérité et de sentiment, il chante ses propres fautes, les misères du temps, et la mort. Dans une de ses ballades, on trouve le vers si souvent cité: "Mais où sont les neiges d'antan?" ("But where are the snows of yesteryear?")

Au 16ᵉ siècle, la littérature française perd son caractère populaire. On découvre l'antiquité gréco-latine, et on écrit pour une élite de lettres. C'est l'époque de **la Renaissance**.

3. **François Rabelais** (vers 1494–1553) exprime l'enthousiasme de la Renaissance et l'amour de la vie sous toutes les formes. Dans ses

romans amusants et satiriques, *Gargantua* et *Pantagruel*, où il raconte les aventures de deux géants imaginaires, il nous peint avec une verve (zest) extraordinaire la société et les mœurs de son temps. Esprit érudit, il énonce des idées modernes sur l'éducation et sur le développement complet de l'individu.

4. **Pierre de Ronsard** (1524–1585), le plus grand poète du 16ᵉ siècle, fut le chef de **la Pléiade**, un groupe de sept jeunes poètes. S'inspirant de l'antiquité, il essaya de renouveler la forme de la poésie française à l'imitation des anciens et des Italiens.

5. **Michel de Montaigne** (1533–1592), philosophe, humaniste, et moraliste, inventa un nouveau genre de littérature. Ses observations personnelles et morales se trouvent dans ses *Essais*, où il étudie l'homme en général et lui-même en particulier. Affirmant que l'homme ne peut trouver la vérité et la justice, Montaigne recommande la modération, du bon sens, et un esprit de tolérance. Son scepticisme se résume dans la question: "Que sais-je?"

Le 17ᵉ siècle, surtout le règne de Louis XIV, est vraiment l'âge d'or de la littérature française. C'est la période du **classicisme**, doctrine littéraire fondée sur le respect de la tradition antique. Le classicisme est un mouvement d'ordre et de discipline dans tous les genres. Les auteurs, en analysant les sentiments humains, cherchent une perfection de forme, d'expression, et de style. Dans le théâtre, on établit la règle des trois unités: action, temps, et lieu. D'après cette règle dramatique, la pièce entière doit se développer en une seule action principale, dans tout l'espace d'une journée, et dans le même lieu.

Les deux grands poètes dramatiques du 17ᵉ siècle sont Corneille et Racine.

6. **Pierre Corneille** (1606–1684) est le créateur de l'art classique au théâtre. Ses héros intellectuels, attirés par les sentiments les plus nobles, doivent choisir entre leur devoir et leur passion dans des situations compliquées. C'est la volonté (will), plutôt que l'amour, qui influence leurs actions. Les tragédies remarquables de Corneille comprennent *Le Cid*, *Cinna*, *Horace*, et *Polyeucte*.

7. **Jean Racine** (1639–1699), le plus grand des poètes tragiques, analysa les passions humaines en état de crise. Son théâtre est l'expression la plus pure du génie classique. Parmi ses œuvres principales, citons *Andromaque*, *Athalie*, et *Phèdre*.

8. **Molière**, pseudonyme de Jean-Baptiste Poquelin (1622–1673), est le plus grand écrivain français de comédies classiques. Appelé souvent le Shakespeare français, il peint des types éternels plutôt que des individus. Il s'attaque d'une façon comique aux vices humains dans ses chefs-d'œuvre: *Les Précieuses ridicules, Le Médecin malgré lui, Le Bourgeois Gentilhomme, Tartuffe, L'Avare.*

La langue française

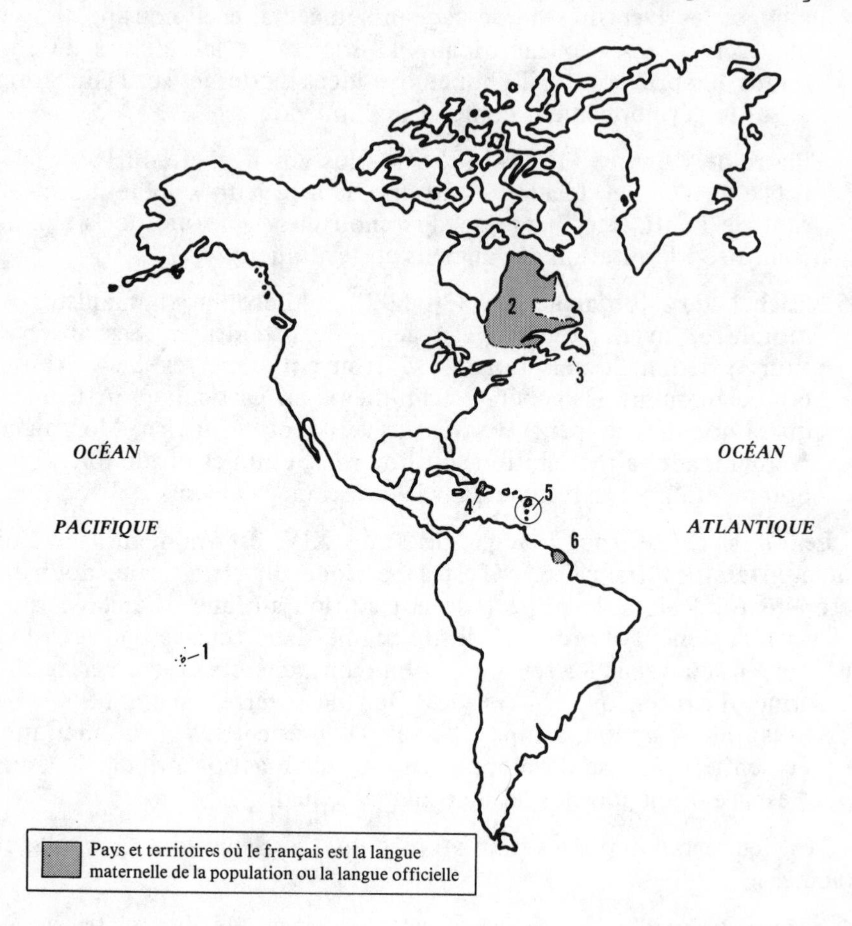

1. Tahiti
2. le Canada (le Québec)
3. Saint-Pierre et Miquelon
4. Haïti
5. les Antilles (la Guadeloupe, la Martinique, Saint-Martin)
6. la Guyane
7. la Belgique
8. le Luxembourg
9. la Suisse
10. la France
11. la Corse

9. **Jean de la Fontaine** (1621–1695), l'admirable fabuliste français, peint, sous le couvert du règne animal, un tableau de la vie humaine et de la société de son époque. Ses *Fables* en vers sont des chefs-d'œuvre de morale et de style.

D'autres écrivains illustres du 17e siècle sont: les philosophes **Pascal** et **Descartes** ("Je pense, donc je suis."); le moraliste **La Bruyère**; le poète et critique **Boileau**; et **Mme de Sévigné**, auteur de *Lettres* adressées à sa fille, dans lesquelles elle fait un tableau intéressant de la vie du 17e siècle.

dans le monde

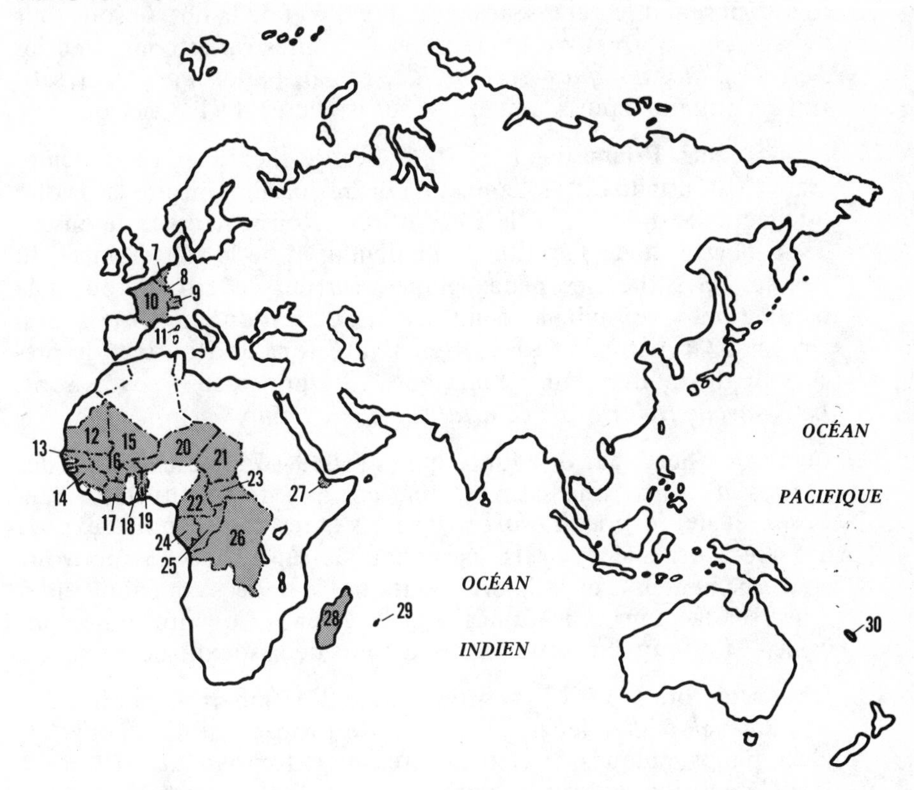

12. la Mauritanie
13. le Sénégal
14. la Guinée
15. le Mali
16. la Haute-Volta
17. la Côte-d'Ivoire
18. le Togo
19. le Benin
20. le Niger
21. le Tchad
22. le Cameroun
23. la République Centrafricaine
24. le Gabon
25. le Congo
26. le Zaïre
27. Djibouti
28. la République Malgache
29. la Réunion
30. la Nouvelle-Calédonie

La littérature du 18ᵉ siècle est une littérature militante, presque entièrement en prose, opposant à la tradition et à l'autorité la raison humaine et l'individualisme. C'est l'époque de l'esprit critique et scientifique, l'époque des nouvelles idées politiques et sociales, l'époque des grands philosophes. Les principaux précurseurs de la Révolution française sont Voltaire, Rousseau, Montesquieu, et Diderot. Les auteurs de la Constitution américaine adoptèrent plusieurs de leurs idées.

10. **Voltaire** (1694–1778), dont le vrai nom était François-Marie Arouet, domine le 18ᵉ siècle. Esprit satirique, il attaque l'absolu-

tisme, l'injustice sociale, et les autres abus des institutions françaises. Il se fait le défenseur de l'humanité et de la liberté sous tous les aspects. Son œuvre immense et de genres variés comprend les *Lettres philosophiques* et *Candide*, roman philosophique et satirique. Voltaire a puissamment agi sur la pensée du 18e siècle.

11. **Jean-Jacques Rousseau** (1712–1778) est le théoricien de la démocratie. En attaquant violemment l'ordre social, il inspire la révolte intellectuelle qui mène à la Révolution. Rousseau est le défenseur de la liberté et de l'égalité de l'individu, et de la souveraineté du peuple. Ses théories pédagogiques, surtout celle du retour à la nature, ont profondément influencé l'éducation moderne. Son amour de la nature et sa sentimentalité font de Rousseau le précurseur du mouvement romantique. Ses principales œuvres sont: *La Nouvelle Héloïse, Le Contrat social*, et *Émile.*

12. **Charles de Secondat de Montesquieu** (1689–1755) est l'auteur des *Lettres persanes*, une satire et une critique des institutions françaises, et de *l'Esprit des lois.* Dans ces livres, Montesquieu expose des idées originales sur la législation, la séparation des pouvoirs gouvernementaux, et la liberté politique. Ses idées contribuèrent à renverser la monarchie française et à créer la Constitution américaine. Montesquieu est un des fondateurs de la sociologie moderne.

13. **Denis Diderot** (1713–1784) dirigea, avec d'Alembert, la publication de *l'Encyclopédie*, le grand arsenal de propagande des nouvelles idées philosophiques. Cette gigantesque entreprise fut écrite avec la collaboration de tous les savants et de tous les hommes de lettres du siècle. Attaquant la tradition, Diderot exprime sa foi dans le progrès de l'humanité.

La première moitié du 19e siècle produit une réaction littéraire contre la tradition classique. C'est l'époque du **romantisme,** qui veut laisser à l'écrivain toute liberté. Ce mouvement, qui trouve son origine dans les œuvres de Rousseau, continue à se développer au début du 19e siècle dans les théories de **Mme de Staël** et dans les ouvrages de **Chateaubriand.** Dans la littérature romantique, qui essaie de produire de l'émotion, chaque écrivain exprime librement sa personnalité et son individualisme. C'est une littérature lyrique dont les éléments essentiels sont l'imagination, le sentiment, et l'amour de la nature.

14. **Victor Hugo** (1802–1885) fut le chef de l'école romantique et son plus grand poète. Il est renommé aussi pour ses pièces de théâtre et ses romans *Notre-Dame de Paris* et *Les Misérables.*

Les autres poètes romantiques de cette époque sont **Alphonse de Lamartine**, **Alfred de Musset**, et **Alfred de Vigny**. **George Sand** (nom de plume d'Aurore Dupin) est l'auteur d'un nombre de romans lyriques, et **Stendhal** (nom de plume de Henri Beyle) reflète dans ses romans psychologiques l'influence du romantisme.

15. **Honoré de Balzac** (1799–1850) peint un tableau des mœurs et des problèmes de son temps dans *La Comédie humaine*, une série de vingt-quatre romans admirables et de nombreuses nouvelles (novelettes). Deux des romans de ce chef-d'œuvre sont *Eugénie Grandet* et *Le Père Goriot*. Avec Balzac, le roman évolue du romantisme vers **le réalisme.** C'est un écrivain remarquable par la puissance de son observation, par sa peinture exacte de toutes les classes de la société, et par son imagination féconde.

16. **Alexandre Dumas père** (1802–1870) écrivit un grand nombre de romans historiques, qui sont populaires encore aujourd'hui dans le monde entier, comme *Les Trois Mousquetaires* et *Le Comte de Monte-Cristo.*

Au milieu du 19e siècle naissent des tendances nouvelles qui s'opposent au romantisme. La littérature se rapproche de la vie réelle, de la vérité, et du matérialisme. Ce **mouvement réaliste** évolue vers **le naturalisme,** qui cherche à analyser et à peindre la vie et la nature telles qu'elles sont. On devient impersonnel, intellectuel, et même scientifique.

17. **Gustave Flaubert** (1821–1880), quoique romancier réaliste, garde quelques traits de l'imagination romantique. Ses romans, tels que *Madame Bovary*, sont caractérisés par une observation et une documentation minutieuses.

18. **Alphonse Daudet** (1840–1897) est connu surtout pour ses romans d'une sensibilité (feeling) délicate qui représentent la vie du Midi de la France, comme *Tartarin de Tarascon*, *Lettres de mon moulin*, et *Le Petit Chose.*

19. **Émile Zola** (1840–1902), chef de l'école naturaliste, observa et analysa d'une façon scientifique les personnages de ses romans sociaux. Il est sans égal dans la peinture des masses. *L'Assommoir* et *Germinal* sont parmi ses ouvrages principaux.

20. **Guy de Maupassant** (1850–1893) est le type même du romancier naturaliste. C'est le plus grand maître français de contes, tels que *La Parure* (*The Necklace*) et *La Ficelle* (*The Piece of String*).

21. **Edmond de Goncourt** (1822–1896) et son frère **Jules de Goncourt** (1830–1870), écrivains de l'école naturaliste, substituent dans leurs romans la pathologie à la psychologie. Leur style impressionniste a une précision intense et originale.

22. **Jules Verne** (1828–1905) est l'auteur de romans d'aventures fantastiques et le créateur de la fiction scientifique: *Vingt mille lieues sous les mers, Le Tour du monde en 80 jours.*

23. **Alexandre Dumas fils** (1824–1895) essaie de défendre dans ses pièces de théâtre dramatiques et brillantes une thèse de morale sociale: *La Dame aux camélias.*

Les poètes de l'époque naturaliste veulent être impersonnels, intellectuels, et scientifiques. **Charles Leconte de Lisle** est le chef des **Parnassiens,** des poètes qui défendent l'art pour l'art. **Charles Baudelaire** et **Paul Verlaine** contribuent à la fondation du **mouvement symboliste.**

24. **Anatole France** (1844–1924) est un romancier, satiriste, et philosophe plein d'érudition. Ses ouvrages sont d'une ironie délicate et d'un style parfait. Citons: *Le Crime de Sylvestre Bonnard* et *Le Livre de mon ami.*

25. **Pierre Loti** (1850–1923), romancier impressionniste, est attiré par les paysages et les civilisations exotiques. Il est l'auteur de *Pêcheur d'Islande.*

26. **Edmond Rostand** (1868–1918) est un auteur dramatique de style brillant. Citons: *Cyrano de Bergerac.*

27. D'autres représentants de la littérature française du 20ᵉ siècle sont:

    Marcel Proust—romancier qui analyse ses sentiments personnels dans son vaste roman, *A la recherche du temps perdu*

    André Gide—auteur de romans psychologiques

    Paul Claudel—poète mystique et dramaturge puissant

    André Maurois—écrivain d'études sur l'Angleterre et de biographies

    François Mauriac—auteur de romans psychologiques

    Albert Camus—auteur d'essais, de romans, et de pièces de théâtre

    Jean-Paul Sartre—chef de **l'existentialisme**

28. Parmi les Français qui ont gagné le prix Nobel de littérature sont: **Frédéric Mistral, Romain Rolland, Anatole France,** le philosophe **Henri Bergson, André Gide, François Mauriac, Albert Camus,** et le poète **Saint-John Perse.**

29. Les prix littéraires les plus importants qu'on décerne chaque année en France sont les prix de l'Académie française, le prix Goncourt, et le prix Fémina.

EXERCICES

A. Vrai ou faux?

1. Le classicisme est fondé sur le respect de la tradition antique.
2. On parle français dans plusieurs pays d'Afrique.
3. Le plus grand poète tragique du 17ᵉ siècle est Rabelais.
4. Molière peint des types éternels plutôt que des individus.
5. Les auteurs de la Constitution américaine influencèrent les idées des grands philosophes français du 18ᵉ siècle.

6. Lamartine, Musset, et Vigny sont des poètes romantiques.
7. L'auteur des *Trois Mousquetaires* et du *Comte de Monte-Cristo* est Balzac.
8. Le chef de l'existentialisme est Jean-Paul Sartre.
9. Ronsard fut le chef de la Pléiade, un groupe de jeunes poètes du 16ᵉ siècle.
10. Gide, Mauriac, et Camus ont reçu le prix Nobel.

B. Choisir la réponse convenable entre parenthèses:

1. Le philosophe du 18ᵉ siècle qui a influencé l'enseignement moderne est (Voltaire, Rousseau).
2. Les chansons de geste datent (du Moyen Age, de la Renaissance).
3. Le premier des grands poètes lyriques est (Villon, Ronsard).
4. (Montesquieu, Diderot) dirigea la publication de *l'Encyclopédie*.
5. Le (seizième, dix-septième) siècle est l'époque de la Renaissance.
6. Le premier document en vieux français s'appelle (*les Serments de Strasbourg, la Chanson de Roland*).
7. "Je pense, donc je suis" est une phrase de (Boileau, Descartes).
8. L'auteur de biographies littéraires est (Camus, Maurois).
9. Les auteurs (classiques, romantiques) cherchaient une perfection de forme et d'expression.
10. Deux poètes du 19ᵉ siècle sont (Flaubert, Baudelaire) et (Verlaine, Loti).

C. Pour chaque œuvre de la première colonne, donner la lettre de l'auteur de la seconde colonne:

1. *Essais*	*a.* Loti
2. *Émile*	*b.* Voltaire
3. *Gargantua*	*c.* Corneille
4. *La Comédie humaine*	*d.* Balzac
5. *Pêcheur d'Islande*	*e.* Rousseau
6. *Madame Bovary*	*f.* Mme de Sévigné
7. *Le Cid*	*g.* Rabelais
8. *Candide*	*h.* Molière
9. *La Dame aux camélias*	*i.* Montaigne
10. *Lettres*	*j.* Dumas fils
11. *A la recherche du temps perdu*	*k.* Rostand
12. *Le Bourgeois Gentilhomme*	*l.* Proust
13. *Les Misérables*	*m.* Flaubert
14. *Cyrano de Bergerac*	*n.* France
15. *Le Crime de Sylvestre Bonnard*	*o.* Hugo

D. Compléter en français:

1. C'est le dialecte de la province de ______ qui est devenu la langue officielle de la France.
2. "Ce qui n'est pas ______ n'est pas français."
3. C'est le ______ siècle qu'on appelle l'âge d'or de la littérature française.
4. Deux œuvres d'Alphonse Daudet sont ______ et ______.
5. Le dialecte le plus important de la langue d'oc est le ______.
6. Les deux grands poètes dramatiques du 17e siècle sont ______ et ______.
7. Le mouvement littéraire dont les éléments essentiels sont l'imagination, le sentiment, et l'amour de la nature est le ______.
8. L'Académie française publie une ______ et un ______.
9. Le grand ouvrage de propagande du 18e siècle, écrit avec la collaboration de nombreux savants, est ______.
10. Le français a exercé une influence profonde sur la langue ______.
11. Les principaux précurseurs de la Révolution française sont ______, ______, ______, et Diderot.
12. Le grand romancier qui peint dans ses œuvres un tableau de toutes les classes de la société de la première moitié du 19e siècle est ______.

E. Identifier:

1. les quarante immortels
2. le chef de l'école naturaliste
3. le grand poète provençal
4. le chef du romantisme littéraire
5. le créateur de la fiction scientifique
6. le célèbre fabuliste français
7. la plus belle des chansons de geste
8. le plus grand maître de contes
9. les deux frères qui faisaient partie de l'école naturaliste
10. le plus grand écrivain de comédies classiques

10. LES BEAUX-ARTS

L'histoire des beaux-arts en France remonte aux temps préhistoriques. Dans les cavernes du Périgord on a trouvé les premières œuvres d'art—d'admirables peintures d'animaux dessinées sur les murs par l'homme primitif.

A l'époque gallo-romaine, des édifices remarquables furent construits: des temples, des arènes, des amphithéâtres. Les meilleurs exemples de ces monuments romains se trouvent aujourd'hui dans les régions de Nîmes et d'Arles, en Provence.

Au Moyen Age, les arts étaient associés à la religion. Les églises romanes (Romanesque) devaient être des édifices lourds à cause de l'épaisseur des murs. Puisque les ouvertures étaient rares et petites, l'intérieur était nécessairement obscur. C'est aussi à cette époque que la reine Mathilde, femme de Guillaume le Conquérant, aurait brodé la célèbre *tapisserie de Bayeux*, qui représente la conquête de l'Angleterre par les Normands.

Pour remplacer la sombre église romane, la France créa un nouveau style d'architecture qui montre le génie artistique français. **L'architecture gothique**, née au 12ᵉ siècle en Ile-de-France, permet la construction d'édifices de vastes dimensions. Cette architecture, avec l'arc de voûte (arch) pointu supporté par des piliers et des arcs-boutants (flying buttresses) à l'extérieur, permet d'amincir l'épaisseur des murs, de les percer de nombreuses ouvertures, et d'élever les édifices à de grandes hauteurs. Pour ne pas avoir un excès de lumière à l'intérieur des églises, on couvre les ouvertures de vitraux (stained-glass windows) dont les couleurs sont souvent magnifiques. L'architecture gothique est ornée de sculpture, de statues, et de gargouilles.

Quelques-uns des chefs-d'œuvre de cette architecture essentiellement religieuse sont: la Sainte-Chapelle, la cathédrale de Notre-Dame de Paris, et les cathédrales d'Amiens, de Chartres, et de Reims.

Les Français qui se sont distingués dans les arts sont nombreux.

PEINTRES

Poussin, Watteau, David, et Ingres sont les principaux représentants du **classicisme**.

1. **Nicolas Poussin** (1594–1665), qui composait avec le plus grand soin ses "paysages historiques," combinait l'antiquité et la nature. On trouve dans ses tableaux la perfection de la forme et de la couleur.
2. **Antoine Watteau** (1684–1721), le plus grand peintre du 18ᵉ siècle, créa des scènes pastorales pleines de charme. Ses tableaux des fêtes galantes (merry celebrations) sont des reflets de la société élégante de son époque. Watteau est un coloriste de premier ordre.

D'autres artistes classiques du 18e siècle sont **Fragonard, Chardin,** et **Greuze.**

3. **Louis David** (1748–1825), chef de l'école néo-classique, était le peintre de la Révolution française et plus tard de la cour de Napoléon. Il peignait avec précision des scènes de l'histoire grecque aussi bien que des portraits.

4. **Dominique Ingres** (1780–1867), élève de David, devint le champion de la peinture académique: l'exactitude de l'observation, la perfection du dessin, et la pureté de la ligne.

Au 19e siècle, la peinture française jouissait d'une célébrité universelle. Plusieurs écoles fleurissaient, et Paris devint un centre mondial de la peinture. Beaucoup d'artistes appartenaient à plus d'une école et essayaient plus d'un genre.

Le romantisme, voulant rompre avec la discipline et les règles du classicisme, réagit contre l'art antique de David. L'école romantique, qui s'intéressait au sentiment et à la couleur, fut dirigée par Géricault et Delacroix.

5. **Théodore Géricault** (1791–1824), le premier des peintres romantiques, peignait surtout des scènes historiques pleines de mouvement et de grandeur.

6. **Eugène Delacroix** (1798–1863), le chef de l'école romantique et son plus grand peintre, était un coloriste extraordinaire. Ses tableaux surnaturels, orientaux, et moyenâgeux débordent (overflow) de vitalité et de mouvement dramatique.

Le réalisme fut la réaction à la fois contre le romantisme et le classicisme. Les artistes réalistes voulaient peindre la vie quotidienne et la nature telles qu'ils les voyaient et sans les idéaliser.

7. **Gustave Courbet** (1819–1877), le champion du réalisme, préférait des scènes de la vie réelle et des paysages.

8. **Honoré Daumier** (1808–1879) est connu surtout pour ses caricatures politiques et sociales. C'était un peintre réaliste de talent.

Plusieurs paysagistes (landscape painters) qui s'établirent à Barbizon, un petit village près de Fontainebleau, formèrent un groupe connu sous le nom de **l'École de Barbizon.**

9. **Jean-François Millet** (1814–1875), chef de l'École de Barbizon, aimait peindre la vie des paysans: *l'Angélus, les Glaneuses.*

10. **Jean-Baptiste Corot** (1796–1875), le plus grand paysagiste de l'École de Barbizon, était un idéaliste qui savait peindre avec un charme poétique.

Dans la seconde moitié du 19e siècle, **l'impressionnisme** évolua du réalisme. Les impressionnistes essayaient de traduire leurs sensations visuelles. Ils choisissaient leurs sujets dans la vie moderne, rendaient l'impression sans tous les détails, et faisaient de la lumière l'objet essentiel de leur peinture.

11. **Édouard Manet** (1832–1883), un maître du naturalisme, fut un des fondateurs de l'école impressionniste. Il aimait travailler en plein air.

12. **Claude Monet** (1840–1926) était le plus grand paysagiste de l'impressionnisme. Il se plaisait à rendre les jeux de la lumière, à représenter le même sujet diversement éclairé à des moments différents du jour: *Cathédrale de Rouen.*

13. **Auguste Renoir** (1841–1919) était un des maîtres de l'impressionnisme. On lui doit un grand nombre de portraits de femmes et de jeunes filles.

14. **Edgar Degas** (1834–1917) savait bien exprimer les formes et le mouvement. Il est connu surtout pour ses tableaux des danseuses de l'Opéra.

15. **Georges Seurat** (1859–1891) fonda **le pointillisme,** une technique néo-impressionniste qui consiste à peindre en se servant d'une multitude de points de couleurs pures.

    D'autres peintres qui faisaient partie du groupe impressionniste sont **Pissarro** et **Sisley**.

Malgré les nouveaux mouvements artistiques du 19e siècle, il y avait des artistes qui préféraient le traditionalisme.

16. **Rosa Bonheur** (1822–1899) peignait les travaux de la ferme et la vie des champs: *le Marché aux Chevaux*.

17. **Pierre Puvis de Chavannes** (1824–1898) est l'auteur de peintures murales qui décorent le Panthéon—*la Vie de Sainte Geneviève*—et la Sorbonne. Ses œuvres, aux sobres couleurs, ont une douceur et une noblesse admirables.

Le post-impressionnisme, le mouvement moderne de la fin du 19e siècle, fut la réaction contre les excès de l'impressionnisme et du réalisme. Les modernistes, en évitant la représentation photographique, n'hésitent pas à déformer la nature et le corps humain. Chacun de ces artistes est un individualiste qui peint à sa manière particulière.

18. **Paul Cézanne** (1839–1906) est le père de l'art moderne et l'inspirateur de la nouvelle peinture. Ses paysages et ses natures mortes (still lifes), où il déforme souvent les objets, donnent l'impression d'une troisième dimension.

19. **Paul Gauguin** (1848–1903) voulait exprimer ses émotions dans ses peintures. Après avoir fait des paysages bretons, il partit pour Tahiti, où il composa des scènes tahitiennes d'un style décoratif en vives couleurs.

20. **Vincent van Gogh** (1853–1890), peintre expressionniste d'origine hollandaise, trouva son inspiration en Provence, dans la région d'Arles. Ses toiles–natures mortes, paysages, portraits–sont pleines de couleurs brillantes et de soleil.

21. **Henri de Toulouse-Lautrec** (1864–1901), peintre de scènes de music-hall et de cirque, fit du dessin des affiches (posters) un nouvel art.

22. **Henri Matisse** (1869–1954) était le chef du **fauvisme**, mouvement artistique de la première moitié du 20e siècle. On considère Matisse, qui aimait la simplicité et l'harmonie, comme le plus grand peintre de son époque. Son chef-d'œuvre d'art décoratif est la chapelle de Vence.

    Les artistes qui s'appelaient les **Fauves** (animaux sauvages) réagirent contre l'analyse impressionniste et décidèrent de peindre à leur gré. Dans ce groupe se trouvent aussi **Rouault** et **Dufy**.

23. **Georges Braque** (1882–1963), un grand peintre de natures mortes, était le fondateur du **cubisme**. Cette école d'art se proposait de représenter les objets sous des formes géométriques.

    Pablo Picasso, l'artiste le plus illustre de l'époque moderne, et **Fernand Léger** ont joué un rôle important dans le mouvement cubiste.

24. D'autres artistes renommés du 20e siècle sont: **Maurice Utrillo,** peintre des coins de Montmartre; **Henri Rousseau,** peintre primitif; et **Marc Chagall.**

SCULPTEURS

1. **Jean-Antoine Houdon** (1741–1828), sculpteur réaliste, exécuta les bustes de plusieurs personnages célèbres: Voltaire, Rousseau, Diderot, La Fayette, Washington, Franklin, et Jefferson.

2. **François Rude** (1784–1855), sculpteur de l'école romantique, est l'auteur de *la Marseillaise*, le merveilleux bas-relief qui décore une des faces de l'Arc de Triomphe de l'Étoile.

3. **Jean-Baptiste Carpeaux** (1827–1875) sculpta du mouvement et du rhythme dans ses œuvres. Son groupe de *la Danse* embellit la façade de l'Opéra.

4. **Frédéric-Auguste Bartholdi** (1834–1904) est le sculpteur de la statue colossale qui se trouve à l'entrée du port de New York, *la Liberté éclairant le monde.*

5. **Auguste Rodin** (1840–1917), le plus grand sculpteur des temps modernes, savait exprimer en marbre les émotions et la puissance de la vie. Ses œuvres principales sont: *le Penseur, les Bourgeois de Calais,* et *la Porte de l'Enfer.*

6. **Aristide Maillol** (1861–1944) allie la grâce et la simplicité à des formes solides. Il est connu surtout pour ses statues de femmes.

ARCHITECTES

1. **Jules Hardouin Mansard,** ou **Mansart** (1646–1708), premier architecte de Louis XIV, construisit la plus grande partie du palais de Versailles, le dôme des Invalides, et la place Vendôme.

2. **Eugène Viollet-le-Duc** (1814–1879) restaura de nombreux monuments historiques du Moyen Age, tels que Notre-Dame de Paris, la cathédrale d'Amiens, et la cité de Carcassonne.

3. **Le Corbusier** (1887–1965) est le chef de l'école moderne. Architecte créateur, il cherche des solutions nouvelles pour l'habitation, surtout pour les ensembles urbains.

EXERCICES

A. Vrai ou faux?

1. Les murs des églises romanes sont plus épais que ceux des églises gothiques.
2. Le plus grand paysagiste de l'École de Barbizon est Corot.
3. L'art du Moyen Age est surtout religieux.
4. Carpeaux est connu pour ses natures mortes.
5. L'architecture gothique remonte à l'époque gallo-romaine.
6. Mansard était le premier architecte de Louis XVI.
7. *Les Bourgeois de Calais* et *la Porte de l'Enfer* sont deux chefs-d'œuvre de Rodin.
8. Claude Monet était un des plus célèbres paysagistes de l'école impressionniste.
9. La cathédrale de Reims est un chef-d'œuvre de l'architecture romane.
10. Géricault et Ingres faisaient partie du même mouvement artistique.

B. Pour chaque œuvre de la première colonne, donner la lettre de l'artiste de la seconde colonne:

1. scènes de ballet	*a.* Rodin
2. *l'Angélus*	*b.* Degas
3. ensembles urbains	*c.* Matisse
4. *le Marché aux Chevaux*	*d.* Bartholdi
5. scènes de Tahiti	*e.* Le Corbusier
6. la chapelle de Vence	*f.* Rude
7. *le Penseur*	*g.* Millet
8. *la Marseillaise* (bas-relief)	*h.* Puvis de Chavannes
9. *la Vie de Sainte Geneviève*	*i.* Bonheur
10. *la Liberté éclairant le monde*	*j.* Gauguin

C. Choisir la réponse convenable entre parenthèses:

1. On trouve les meilleurs exemples de monuments romains en (Provence, Normandie, Bretagne).
2. L'architecture (romane, gallo-romaine, gothique) permet de percer un grand nombre d'ouvertures dans les murs.
3. Matisse était le chef du (pointillisme, fauvisme, cubisme).
4. *La tapisserie de Bayeux* représente la conquête de (la Gaule, l'Angleterre, l'Allemagne).
5. Les artistes de l'École de Barbizon peignaient surtout des (portraits, natures mortes, paysages).
6. L'objet essentiel de la peinture impressionniste est (la lumière, le détail, le sentiment).
7. L'architecture gothique a pris naissance en (Touraine, Provence, Ile-de-France).
8. Le "grand siècle" de la peinture française est le (dix-septième, dix-huitième, dix-neuvième).
9. Renoir et Seurat faisaient partie de l'école (impressionniste, romantique, classique).
10. L'architecte du 19ᵉ siècle qui a restauré Carcassonne et Notre-Dame est (Mansard, Le Corbusier, Viollet-le-Duc).

D. Identifier:

1. le plus grand peintre du 18ᵉ siècle
2. le peintre de la Révolution et de la cour de Napoléon
3. le chef de l'école romantique et son plus grand peintre
4. le créateur du pointillisme
5. le peintre réaliste de caricatures politiques et sociales
6. le chef de l'École de Barbizon
7. le père de la peinture moderne
8. le plus grand sculpteur des temps modernes
9. le chef de l'architecture moderne en France
10. le sculpteur de bustes de personnages célèbres (Voltaire, Washington)

E. Compléter en français:

1. Deux artistes de l'école classique sont ______ et ______.
2. Les peintures murales de ______ décorent le Panthéon et la Sorbonne.
3. L'arc de voûte pointu est une caractéristique de l'architecture ______.
4. Les peintres ______ tenaient à représenter la nature telle qu'elle est sans chercher à l'idéaliser.
5. Le palais de Versailles et la place Vendôme sont les œuvres de ______.
6. Maurice ______, qui peint des scènes de Montmartre, et Henri ______, le peintre primitif, sont deux artistes bien connus du 20e siècle.
7. Le ______, dont le premier peintre fut Géricault, réagit contre la discipline du classicisme.
8. Le sculpteur moderne, ______, est connu surtout pour ses statues de femmes.
9. Georges Braque a fondé le ______, une école d'art qui représente les objets sous des formes géométriques.
10. Le peintre expressionniste, ______, né en Hollande, trouva son inspiration en Provence.

Vendanges (Récolte du raisin) en Bourgogne

La Bourgogne, région gastronomique, est un des grands centres vinicoles de la France. On y produit des vins d'une distinction incomparable. Les vendanges ont lieu en Bourgogne de septembre à octobre.

11. LA MUSIQUE ET LES SCIENCES

COMPOSITEURS

1. **Jean-Baptiste Lully**, ou **Lulli** (1632–1687), Italien de naissance, fut le créateur de l'opéra français. Il était le compositeur de la cour de Louis XIV, qui le nomma directeur de l'Opéra de Paris. Pour amuser le roi, il écrivit la musique de plusieurs comédies de Molière.

   Les grands musiciens classiques sont Couperin et Rameau:

2. **François Couperin** (1668–1733), le plus grand maître français du clavecin (harpsichord), composa des morceaux charmants pour cet instrument.

3. **Jean-Philippe Rameau** (1683–1764), claveciniste et organiste, était le plus célèbre compositeur français de son temps. Il fit une contribution importante à la science de l'harmonie.

4. **Hector Berlioz** (1803–1869), le plus grand compositeur de l'époque romantique, était un maître de l'orchestration. Ses œuvres, comme *la Damnation de Faust*, sont remarquables par la force du sentiment dramatique.

   Dans la seconde moitié du 19ᵉ siècle, la musique française commença à briller d'un grand éclat.

5. **César Franck** (1822–1890), Belge de naissance, était un organiste de grand renom. Il fonda l'école de musique moderne en France.

6. **Camille Saint-Saëns** (1835–1921) était un virtuose du piano et de l'orgue. Il écrivit des poèmes symphoniques, tels que *la Danse Macabre*, et des opéras, dont le mieux connu est *Samson et Dalila.*

7. **Claude Debussy** (1862–1918), le plus illustre des compositeurs contemporains, fut influencé par les symbolistes et les impressionnistes. Sa musique est rêveuse et délicate. Parmi ses œuvres principales sont: *l'Après-midi d'un faune, la Mer, Clair de lune*, et l'opéra *Pelléas et Mélisande.*

8. **Maurice Ravel** (1875–1937), un des grands artistes de la musique moderne, écrivait avec précision et tendresse. Il composa des pièces pour le piano et pour l'orchestre: *Ma mère l'Oye, Boléro, Daphnis et Chloé.*

9. D'autres compositeurs d'opéras célèbres sont:

   a. **Georges Bizet**: *Carmen, Les Pêcheurs de perles*
   b. **Gustave Charpentier**: *Louise*
   c. **Léo Delibes**: *Lakmé*
   d. **Charles Gounod**: *Faust, Roméo et Juliette*
   e. **Jules Massenet**: *Manon, Thaïs*
   f. **Jacques Offenbach**: *Les Contes d'Hoffmann* (opérette)
   g. **Ambroise Thomas**: *Mignon*

10. Au 20e siècle, la musique française reste toujours vivante avec des compositeurs de talent comme **Georges Auric, Arthur Honegger, Darius Milhaud,** et **Francis Poulenc.**

SAVANTS; HOMMES ET FEMMES DE SCIENCE

1. **René Descartes** (1596–1650), philosophe, mathématicien, et physicien (physicist), fonda la méthode scientifique, basée sur le raisonnement. Il expliqua son point de vue dans le *Discours de la méthode.* Descartes est le créateur de la géométrie analytique.
2. **Blaise Pascal** (1623–1662), mathématicien, physicien, et philosophe, formula les lois de la pression atmosphérique et de l'équilibre des liquides. C'est l'inventeur de la presse hydraulique et de la première machine à calculer. Ses idées se trouvent réunies dans les *Pensées.*
3. **Antoine-Laurent de Lavoisier** (1743–1794) est un des fondateurs de la chimie moderne. Il établit la nomenclature chimique, découvrit les lois de la combustion, et détermina la composition de l'air. Il exprima la loi de la conservation de la matière en ces mots: "Rien ne se perd, rien ne se crée; dans la nature tout se transforme." Lavoisier fut guillotiné sous la Terreur.
4. **André Ampère** (1775–1836) créa l'électrodynamique. On lui doit l'invention de l'électro-aimant (electromagnet) et les principes de la télégraphie électrique. *L'ampère,* l'unité d'intensité des courants électriques, porte son nom.
5. **Jean-Baptiste de Lamarck** (1744–1829), le grand précurseur de Darwin, énonça une théorie sur les transformations des êtres vivants.
6. **Georges Cuvier** (1769–1832) est le créateur de l'anatomie comparée et de la paléontologie, la science qui traite des fossiles.
7. **Jean-François Champollion** (1790–1832) réussit à déchiffrer les hiéroglyphes égyptiens de la pierre de Rosette.
8. **Claude Bernard** (1813–1878) est le fondateur de la physiologie moderne et de la médecine expérimentale. Il définit les principes fondamentaux de toute recherche scientifique.
9. **Louis Pasteur** (1822–1895), chimiste et biologiste, fut un grand bienfaiteur de l'humanité. En établissant que les fermentations sont causées par des cellules vivantes, les microbes, il fonda la bactériologie moderne. Il prouva que les maladies contagieuses sont dues à la transmission de microbes et trouva des vaccins pour les combattre. Il trouva le moyen de guérir la rage (rabies) et le charbon (anthrax) des moutons. Il découvrit les procédés de la pasteurisation, l'élimination des fermentations dangereuses. Ses travaux remarquables ont révolutionné la médecine.

L'Institut Pasteur de Paris fut fondée en 1886 par souscription internationale dans le but d'étudier les maladies infectieuses et pour perfectionner la chimie biologique. Aujourd'hui il y a plusieurs de ces instituts qui continuent les travaux de Pasteur dans le monde entier.

10. **Pierre Curie** (1859–1906) et sa femme **Marie Curie** (1867–1934) découvrirent le radium en 1899. Leur découverte a complètement changé nos idées sur la constitution de la matière et les sources de l'énergie. Leur fille, **Irène Joliot-Curie,** et son mari, **Frédéric Joliot,** poursuivirent ces recherches scientifiques sur la structure de l'atome et découvrirent la radioactivité artificielle.

11. D'autres savants français et leurs contributions au domaine des sciences sont:

    a. **Charles-Augustin de Coulomb** (1736–1806)–les lois mathématiques de l'électricité et du magnétisme (*Le coulomb* est l'unité de quantité de l'électricité.)

    b. **Pierre-Simon Laplace** (1749–1827)–une théorie importante sur la formation du système planétaire

    c. **Joseph Gay-Lussac** (1778–1850)–les lois de la dilatation (expansion) et de la combinaison des gaz

    d. **Louis-Jacques Daguerre** (1789–1851)–le perfectionnement de la photographie

    e. **Louis Braille** (1809–1852)–l'écriture et la lecture en relief pour les aveugles

    f. **Ferdinand de Lesseps** (1805–1894)–la construction du canal de Suez

    g. **Marcelin Berthelot** (1827–1907)–des travaux sur la chimie organique

    h. **Henri Becquerel** (1852–1908)–la découverte de la radioactivité

    i. **Alphonse Bertillon** (1853–1914)–l'usage des empreintes digitales (fingerprints) pour établir l'identité des criminels

    j. **Émile Roux** (1853–1933)–la découverte d'un sérum pour guérir la diphtérie

    k. **Henri Poincaré** (1854–1912)–des contributions aux mathématiques, à la physique, et à l'astronomie (un des plus grands mathématiciens de tous les temps)

    l. **Alexis Carrel** (1873–1944)–des recherches sur la conservation, la culture, et la greffe (grafting) de tissus

    m. **Louis de Broglie** (1892–1976)–la théorie de la mécanique ondulatoire (wave mechanics)

EXERCICES

A. Pour chaque contribution de la première colonne, donner la lettre du Français correspondant de la seconde colonne:

1. *Damnation de Faust*	*a.* Bizet
2. paléontologie	*b.* Offenbach
3. *Lakmé*	*c.* Pasteur
4. *Contes d'Hoffmann*	*d.* Berlioz
5. culture de tissus	*e.* Delibes
6. *Carmen*	*f.* Joliot-Curie
7. vaccination contre la rage	*g.* Cuvier
8. recherches sur la structure de l'atome	*h.* Lavoisier
9. *Faust*	*i.* Carrel
10. "Rien ne se perd, rien ne se crée."	*j.* Gounod

B. Choisir la réponse convenable entre parenthèses:

1. Le plus grand compositeur de l'époque romantique est (Berlioz, Ravel).
2. Les deux grands clavecinistes de l'époque classique sont Couperin et (Franck, Rameau).
3. (Lully, Debussy) fut le créateur de l'opéra français.
4. Le compositeur de *Carmen* écrivit aussi l'opéra (*Les Pêcheurs de perles, Mignon*).
5. Le précurseur français de Darwin est (Lamarck, Cuvier).
6. (Gay-Lussac, Laplace) formula une théorie importante sur la formation du système planétaire.
7. (Coulomb, Roux) fit des contributions importantes dans le domaine de l'électricité.
8. Le compositeur de *Samson et Dalila* est (Thomas, Saint-Saëns).
9. (Becquerel, Berthelot) découvrit la radioactivité.
10. (Louis de Broglie, Alphonse Bertillon) imagina une méthode qui emploie les empreintes digitales pour identifier les criminels.

C. Identifier:

1. Compositeur et organiste, il fonda l'école de musique moderne en France.
2. Il fit percer le canal de Suez.
3. L'unité d'intensité des courants électriques porte son nom.
4. Musicien illustre de l'école impressionniste, il composa l'opéra *Pelléas et Mélisande.*
5. Ils découvrirent le radium en 1899.
6. Il inventa l'alphabet en relief à l'usage des aveugles.
7. Il fonda la méthode scientifique et la géométrie analytique.
8. Chimiste et biologiste, il créa la bactériologie moderne.
9. Il inventa la presse hydraulique et la première machine à calculer.
10. Il fonda la physiologie moderne et la médecine expérimentale.

D. Compléter en français:

1. Le savant Henri Poincaré était un des plus grands ______ de tous les temps.
2. Deux compositeurs français du 20ᵉ siècle sont ______ et ______.
3. Daguerre contribua au perfectionnement de la ______.
4. Le savant ______, un des fondateurs de la ______ moderne, fut guillotiné sous la Terreur.
5. *Manon* et *Thaïs* sont deux opéras de ______.
6. L'archéologue ______ déchiffra les hiéroglyphes égyptiens.
7. Pasteur prouva que les ______ sont la cause de maladies contagieuses et réussit à trouver des ______ pour les combattre.
8. *L'Après-midi d'un faune* et *Clair de lune* sont les œuvres de ______.
9. Les deux célèbres savants–philosophes, mathématiciens, et physiciens–du 17ᵉ siècle sont ______ et ______.
10. ______ découvrit un sérum pour guérir la diphtérie.

E. Identifier chaque personnage comme architecte, compositeur, couturier, écrivain, explorateur, homme d'état, peintre, savant, ou sculpteur:

1. Daumier
2. Mansard
3. Richelieu
4. Delibes
5. Proust
6. Watteau
7. Cardin
8. Rude
9. Champlain
10. Verlaine
11. Monet
12. Henri Poincaré
13. Rouault
14. Ingres
15. Colbert
16. Honegger
17. Poussin
18. Chanel
19. Puvis de Chavannes
20. Henri Rousseau
21. J.-J. Rousseau
22. Louis de Broglie
23. Greuze
24. Racine
25. Braille
26. Stendhal
27. La Salle
28. Berlioz
29. Sisley
30. Becquerel
31. Montesquieu
32. Ampère
33. Milhaud
34. Sartre
35. Bonheur
36. Mistral
37. De Gaulle
38. Patou
39. Toulouse-Lautrec
40. Rameau
41. Rodin
42. Viollet-le-Duc
43. Daudet
44. Van Gogh
45. Poulenc
46. Corneille
47. Géricault
48. Goncourt
49. Couperin
50. Cartier
51. Lavoisier
52. Camus

53. Lamartine
54. Saint Laurent
55. Pissarro
56. Houdon
57. Gay-Lussac
58. Degas
59. Duhamel
60. Coulomb
61. Massenet
62. Dufy
63. Villon
64. Flaubert
65. Laplace
66. Verne
67. Carpeaux
68. Gauguin
69. Ronsard
70. Utrillo
71. Offenbach
72. Marquette
73. Delacroix
74. Maillol
75. Dior
76. Corot
77. Rouget de Lisle
78. Léger
79. Franck
80. Musset
81. Roux
82. Chagall
83. La Fontaine
84. Le Corbusier
85. Seurat
86. Charpentier
87. Daguerre
88. Gide
89. Courbet
90. Picasso
91. Baudelaire
92. Ravel
93. Montaigne
94. David
95. Fath
96. Braque
97. Gounod
98. Bartholdi
99. Manet
100. Debussy

CIVILIZATION REVIEW QUIZZES

Choisir l'expression qui complète le sens de la phrase:

A

1. La chaîne de montagnes la plus ancienne de la France est (*a*) le Jura (*b*) le Massif Central (*c*) les Alpes (*d*) les Vosges.
2. La France est relativement pauvre en (*a*) charbon (*b*) fer (*c*) bauxite (*d*) potasse.
3. Les principaux ports fluviaux de France sont (*a*) Paris, Strasbourg, Brest, Bordeaux (*b*) Paris, Rouen, Nancy, Toulouse (*c*) Paris, Rouen, Strasbourg, Lyon (*d*) Paris, Lyon, Lille, Reims.
4. L'amiral des forces navales françaises dans la Révolution américaine fut (*a*) Rochambeau (*b*) La Fayette (*c*) Louis Napoléon (*d*) De Grasse.
5. Louis Braille a créé (*a*) la chimie moderne (*b*) un sérum pour guérir la diphtérie (*c*) l'alphabet en relief à l'usage des aveugles (*d*) les lois de la dilatation et de la combinaison des gaz.
6. Parmi les peintres suivants, celui qui n'est pas de l'école impressionniste est (*a*) Renoir (*b*) Delacroix (*c*) Manet (*d*) Monet.

7. Le mistral est (*a*) un apéritif (*b*) un vent froid (*c*) un gâteau (*d*) une chanson méridionale.
8. Ronsard et Villon se distinguèrent dans le domaine de (*a*) la poésie (*b*) la tragédie (*c*) la vie politique (*d*) la philosophie.
9. Orly est (*a*) un centre important de métallurgie (*b*) l'agence qui administre les chemins de fer (*c*) une maison de haute couture (*d*) un aéroport de Paris.
10. La ville de Paris doit son nom à (*a*) un héros légendaire (*b*) un général romain (*c*) une tribu gauloise (*d*) une célèbre bataille.

B

1. Le touriste qui visite Avignon ne devrait pas manquer d'y voir (*a*) le palais des Papes (*b*) la cathédrale gothique (*c*) l'aqueduc romain (*d*) le théâtre antique.
2. La résidence officielle du Président de la République est (*a*) le palais de Versailles (*b*) le palais de Chaillot (*c*) le château de Fontainebleau (*d*) le palais de l'Élysée.
3. L'adjectif qui caractérise le mieux le français est (*a*) doux (*b*) difficile (*c*) clair (*d*) riche.
4. La pelote et les boules sont des (*a*) fêtes régionales (*b*) sports (*c*) desserts (*d*) danses provinciales.
5. Le roi français qui a donné son nom à la Louisiane est (*a*) Louis XVI (*b*) Louis XIV (*c*) Louis IX (*d*) Louis XV.
6. Le peintre de scènes de music-hall qui éleva le dessin des affiches au niveau de l'art est (*a*) Toulouse-Lautrec (*b*) Gauguin (*c*) Puvis de Chavannes (*d*) Matisse.
7. Mirabeau et Danton ont joué des rôles importants pendant (*a*) la bataille de Yorktown (*b*) la défaite de Napoléon (*c*) les guerres de religion (*d*) la Révolution française.
8. L'explorateur qui découvrit le Saint-Laurent en 1535 et prit possession du Canada au nom du roi de France est (*a*) La Salle (*b*) Joliet (*c*) Cartier (*d*) Champlain.
9. "Les quarante immortels" sont (*a*) les plus grands poètes de France (*b*) les écrivains de *l'Encyclopédie* (*c*) les membres de l'Académie française (*d*) les impressionnistes.
10. Quand on entend parler de la Garonne et de la Gironde, on pense à la ville de (*a*) Lyon (*b*) Bordeaux (*c*) Nantes (*d*) Marseille.

C

1. Les deux grands poètes tragiques du 17e siècle, l'âge d'or de la littérature française, sont (*a*) Corneille et Racine (*b*) Rabelais et Montaigne (*c*) Molière et Descartes (*d*) Musset et Vigny.
2. Le code civil de la justice française d'aujourd'hui date du temps de (*a*) Charlemagne (*b*) Richelieu (*c*) Henri IV (*d*) Napoléon.

3. Parmi les Français qui ont contribué au domaine des sciences sont Claude Bernard et (*a*) Couperin (*b*) Lamarck (*c*) Ingres (*d*) Gide.
4. Le pointillisme et le fauvisme sont des mouvements (*a*) artistiques (*b*) littéraires (*c*) musicaux (*d*) scientifiques.
5. *L'Aurore* et *Le Monde* sont les noms de deux (*a*) théâtres (*b*) bistros célèbres (*c*) journaux (*d*) grands magasins.
6. Les druides étaient les prêtres des (*a*) Romains (*b*) Gaulois (*c*) Francs (*d*) Normands.
7. Le tribunal suprême de la France est (*a*) la Cour de Cassation (*b*) le Conseil Constitutionnel (*c*) la Cour Arbitrale (*d*) l'Assemblée Nationale.
8. Quelle ville, située entre la Normandie et la Bretagne, est dominée par une abbaye bénédictine? (*a*) Chartres (*b*) Lisieux (*c*) Le Mont-Saint-Michel (*d*) Avignon
9. A Paris, on peut voir les bouquinistes, marchands de livres d'occasion, si l'on passe par (*a*) les Halles (*b*) les quais (*c*) le Quartier latin (*d*) les grands boulevards.
10. La province qu'on appelle "le jardin de la France" est (*a*) la Touraine (*b*) la Normandie (*c*) la Bourgogne (*d*) l'Ile-de-France.

D

1. Massenet a composé la musique de (*a*) *Samson et Dalila* (*b*) *Louise* (*c*) *Mignon* (*d*) *Thaïs*.
2. Le Bon Marché et Au Printemps sont les noms (*a*) de musées (*b*) de salles de concert (*c*) de grands magasins (*d*) de journaux de Paris.
3. Calais, Boulogne, et Dunkerque sont (*a*) des centres de l'industrie textile (*b*) des stations de sports d'hiver (*c*) des ports sur la Manche (*d*) connus pour leurs cathédrales gothiques.
4. Le Rhône se jette dans (*a*) l'Atlantique (*b*) la Méditerranée (*c*) la Manche (*d*) la mer du Nord.
5. Ampère fit des découvertes importantes en (*a*) électricité (*b*) chimie (*c*) médecine (*d*) biologie.
6. Pour faire de l'alpinisme et du ski, on va à (*a*) Cannes (*b*) Lisieux (*c*) Chamonix (*d*) Deauville.
7. Daumier est renommé pour (*a*) ses paysages (*b*) ses animaux (*c*) ses natures mortes (*d*) ses caricatures.
8. Colbert est le ministre qui a bien servi (*a*) François Ier (*b*) Napoléon (*c*) Louis XV (*d*) Louis XIV.
9. Le tombeau du Soldat Inconnu se trouve sur la place (*a*) de la Bastille (*b*) Charles de Gaulle (*c*) Vendôme (*d*) de la Concorde.
10. Cardin et Dior se sont distingués dans le domaine de (*a*) la haute couture (*b*) l'industrie lourde (*c*) la peinture (*d*) la haute cuisine.

E

1. Limoges et Sèvres produisent (*a*) des tapis (*b*) des dentelles (*c*) des porcelaines (*d*) des montres.
2. Le fleuve puissant qui fournit des quantités d'énergie hydro-électrique est (*a*) le Rhin (*b*) la Seine (*c*) la Loire (*d*) le Rhône.
3. Le principal représentant de la littérature provençale est (*a*) Frédéric Mistral (*b*) Pierre Ronsard (*c*) Alphonse Daudet (*d*) Alphonse de Lamartine.
4. Une phrase célèbre de Descartes est (*a*) "Que sais-je?" (*b*) "Je pense, donc je suis." (*c*) "Mais où sont les neiges d'antan?" (*d*) "Ce qui n'est pas clair n'est pas français."
5. Des rois suivants, celui qui a contribué le moins à la grandeur de la France est (*a*) Henri IV (*b*) François Ier (*c*) Louis XIV (*d*) Louis XV.
6. Le peintre des danseuses de l'Opéra est (*a*) Monet (*b*) Corot (*c*) Degas (*d*) Renoir.
7. Les trois coups qu'on entend dans une salle de spectacle annoncent (*a*) le lever du rideau (*b*) la fin de la pièce (*c*) le commencement de l'entracte (*d*) une situation dangereuse.
8. Le meilleur exemple d'une ville fortifiée du Moyen Age est (*a*) Lourdes (*b*) Avignon (*c*) Arles (*d*) Carcassonne.
9. Vichy, Évian, et Vittel sont (*a*) des stations balnéaires (*b*) des stations thermales (*c*) des centres d'alpinisme (*d*) des villes industrielles.
10. L'église blanche de Montmartre qui domine la ville de Paris est (*a*) le Sacré-Cœur (*b*) la Madeleine (*c*) la Sainte-Chapelle (*d*) Saint-Germain-des-Prés.

F

1. Molière fut (*a*) le meilleur écrivain de la Renaissance (*b*) le père de la tragédie française (*c*) le premier écrivain du 18e siècle (*d*) le créateur de la comédie en France.
2. La ville de Lourdes attire beaucoup de touristes chaque année parce que c'est (*a*) un centre religieux (*b*) une station balnéaire (*c*) un bon exemple d'une ville fortifiée (*d*) un centre gastronomique.
3. L'édifice de Paris qui contient plusieurs musées et un théâtre est (*a*) la Conciergerie (*b*) la Cité Universitaire (*c*) le palais de Chaillot (*d*) l'Hôtel des Invalides.
4. En France, le Premier Ministre (*a*) est élu pour sept ans (*b*) peut soumettre au référendum des projets de loi (*c*) assure l'exécution des lois (*d*) est le chef des armées françaises.
5. Le premier des grands poètes lyriques de France est (*a*) Villon (*b*) Verlaine (*c*) Hugo (*d*) Ronsard.

6. Le fleuve français le plus navigable est (*a*) la Loire (*b*) le Rhône (*c*) la Seine (*d*) la Garonne.
7. Le savant qui découvrit un vaccin contre la rage fut (*a*) Claude Bernard (*b*) André Ampère (*c*) Louis Pasteur (*d*) Georges Cuvier.
8. Le plus grand centre industriel de la France se trouve (*a*) dans le Midi (*b*) au nord-est (*c*) dans la région de Lyon (*d*) au centre du pays.
9. La Banque de France et la Légion d'Honneur sont des créations de (*a*) Louis XIV (*b*) la Révolution française (*c*) la Troisième République (*d*) Napoléon Ier.
10. L'école impressionniste, qui doit son nom au tableau de Monet intitulé *Impression*, fleurissait au (*a*) XVIe siècle (*b*) XVIIe siècle (*c*) XVIIIe siècle (*d*) XIXe siècle.

G

1. L'édifice qui sert de mausolée à des Français éminents est (*a*) le Louvre (*b*) le Sacré-Cœur (*c*) la Sainte-Chapelle (*d*) le Panthéon.
2. La Bretonne se distingue surtout par (*a*) sa gaieté (*b*) son accent méridional (*c*) sa coiffe blanche (*d*) les belles couleurs de son costume.
3. Azay-le-Rideau et Chenonceaux sont des (*a*) châteaux (*b*) cathédrales (*c*) monuments romains (*d*) stations thermales.
4. Le chef de l'école existentialiste s'appelle (*a*) Gide (*b*) Zola (*c*) Sartre (*d*) Mauriac.
5. Quelles fleurs vend-on dans les rues en France le premier mai? (*a*) les pensées (*b*) les muguets (*c*) les violettes (*d*) les roses
6. Les volcans éteints qu'on appelle "puys" se trouvent dans (*a*) le Massif Central (*b*) les Alpes (*c*) les Pyrénées (*d*) les Vosges.
7. Corot est renommé pour (*a*) ses portraits (*b*) ses animaux (*c*) ses paysages (*d*) ses scènes de Montmartre.
8. Une île française près de l'Amérique du Sud est (*a*) Ste-Lucie (*b*) la Martinique (*c*) la Jamaïque (*d*) la Trinité.
9. L'ordre chronologique correct est
   (*a*) l'Édit de Nantes, la guerre de Cent Ans, la Révolution française, la vente de la Louisiane aux États-Unis
   (*b*) la guerre de Cent Ans, l'Édit de Nantes, la vente de la Louisiane aux États-Unis, la Révolution française
   (*c*) la guerre de Cent Ans, l'Édit de Nantes, la Révolution française, la vente de la Louisiane aux États-Unis
   (*d*) l'Édit de Nantes, la guerre de Cent Ans, la vente de la Louisiane aux États-Unis, la Révolution française.
10. Peugeot et Simca sont les noms de deux (*a*) voitures (*b*) parfums (*c*) porcelaines (*d*) apéritifs.

H

1. Le premier héros national de la France fut (*a*) Charlemagne (*b*) Clovis (*c*) Saint Louis (*d*) Vercingétorix.
2. La France a des frontières naturelles excepté (*a*) au nord-est (*b*) au sud-ouest (*c*) au nord-ouest (*d*) au sud-est.
3. Comment s'appelle le chef-d'œuvre de Balzac dans lequel il peint un tableau de la société du 19e siècle? (*a*) *Les Misérables* (*b*) *L'Encyclopédie* (*c*) *La Comédie humaine* (*d*) *Lettres philosophiques*
4. Becquerel et Lavoisier sont connus pour leur contributions au domaine (*a*) de la musique (*b*) des sciences (*c*) des beaux-arts (*d*) de la philosophie.
5. L'influence la plus profonde de la culture romaine en France est encore évidente (*a*) en Normandie (*b*) en Provence (*c*) en Bretagne (*d*) en Auvergne.
6. Les Français dansent dans les rues chaque année pour célébrer (*a*) la fête nationale (*b*) la fête du Travail (*c*) Pâques (*d*) la fête de l'Armistice.
7. On appelle (*a*) Maupassant (*b*) Voltaire (*c*) Verne (*d*) Dumas "le père de la fiction scientifique."
8. La Lutèce gauloise était limitée à (*a*) l'île de la Cité (*b*) la rive gauche (*c*) la rive droite (*d*) Montmartre.
9. Le fleuve le plus long mais le moins utile de France est (*a*) la Garonne (*b*) la Loire (*c*) la Seine (*d*) le Rhône.
10. L'aqueduc romain le mieux conservé en France s'appelle (*a*) le Pont-Neuf (*b*) le pont d'Avignon (*c*) le pont du Gard (*d*) le pont du Rhin.

I

1. Si l'on visite le Panthéon et la Sorbonne, on peut y voir des fresques de (*a*) Toulouse-Lautrec (*b*) Gauguin (*c*) Puvis de Chavannes (*d*) Renoir.
2. L'école romantique fut profondément influencée par (*a*) Molière (*b*) Rousseau (*c*) Voltaire (*d*) Montesquieu.
3. Le Corbusier est connu pour (*a*) sa musique symphonique (*b*) son architecture originale (*c*) ses romans psychologiques (d) ses théories scientifiques.
4. La France est un pays importateur de (*a*) matières premières (*b*) minerai de fer (*c*) textiles (*d*) produits laitiers.
5. Quand le pêcheur a raconté fièrement des anecdotes de sa province natale où l'on célèbre chaque année les "pardons," il était évident qu'il parlait de (*a*) la Flandre (*b*) l'Ile-de-France (*c*) la Normandie (*d*) la Bretagne.

6. Sous la constitution de la Cinquième République, (*a*) seulement les hommes ont le droit de voter (*b*) la division administrative est la province (*c*) le Président de la République nomme les membres de l'Assemblée Nationale (*d*) le Président a plus d'autorité que le Président de la Quatrième République.
7. Caron et Guerlain sont des (*a*) chanteurs (*b*) poètes (*c*) parfumeurs (*d*) musiciens.
8. "Après moi, le déluge" est une phrase attribuée à (*a*) Louis XIII (*b*) Napoléon (*c*) Louis XIV (*d*) Louis XV.
9. Le pays basque se trouve (*a*) dans les Vosges (*b*) entre la Bretagne et la Normandie (*c*) près de la frontière italienne (*d*) dans la région des Pyrénées.
10. Le Dôme et les Deux Magots sont les noms de deux (*a*) cinémas (*b*) cafés (*c*) revues parisiennes (*d*) grands magasins.

J

1. La région de fermes fertiles où les armées alliées ont débarqué en 1944 est (*a*) la Côte d'Azur (*b*) la Normandie (*c*) la Camargue (*d*) la Bretagne.
2. Si l'on part de l'Arc de Triomphe et si l'on se promène jusqu'au bout de l'avenue des Champs-Élysées, on arrive (*a*) à la place de la Concorde (*b*) à l'Opéra (*c*) à la Tour Eiffel (*d*) au jardin du Luxembourg.
3. Le grand port fluvial renommé pour sa magnifique cathédrale et pour sa production de pâté de foie gras est (*a*) Clermont-Ferrand (*b*) Amiens (*c*) Strasbourg (*d*) Toulouse.
4. Les chansons de geste datent (*a*) de l'âge classique (*b*) de la Renaissance (*c*) de la période gallo-romaine (*d*) du Moyen Age.
5. La Première République française fut établie en (*a*) 1598 (*b*) 1792 (*c*) 1848 (*d*) 1918.
6. Le nom de Daguerre fait penser (*a*) à l'anatomie comparée (*b*) à la radioactivité (*c*) aux mouvements des planètes (*d*) à la photographie.
7. Lille est une ville connue pour (*a*) son industrie textile (*b*) ses pneus (*c*) ses dentelles (*d*) son château.
8. Pour voir la Sorbonne, le musée de Cluny, et le Panthéon, il faut visiter (*a*) la rive droite (*b*) Montmartre (*c*) le Quartier latin (*d*) les Champs-Élysées.
9. La France doit son nom à (*a*) un général romain (*b*) une tribu germanique (*c*) François Ier (*d*) un chef gaulois.
10. Le Jura s'étend (*a*) du Rhin aux Alpes (*b*) entre la France et l'Italie (*c*) entre l'Alsace et la Lorraine (*d*) du Rhin à la Manche.

READING COMPREHENSION

Lire chaque passage. Puis choisir les réponses convenables dans les exercices.

A

Deux hommes étaient voisins. Chacun d'eux avait plusieurs petits enfants. L'un de ces hommes s'inquiétait, se disant: "Si je meurs, que deviendront mes enfants?" Il était triste et troublé à cause de sa crainte.

Un jour qu'il travaillait aux champs, il vit deux nids posés côte à côte, et, dans chacun, plusieurs petits oiseaux encore sans plumes. De temps en temps, il levait les yeux et regardait deux oiseaux qui allaient et venaient, portant la nourriture à leurs petits. Tout d'un coup, un vautour saisit un des oiseaux et l'enleva. Le pauvre oiseau jeta des cris perçants.

A cette vue, l'homme qui travaillait se sentit plus troublé qu'auparavant. Tout le jour il fut triste, et la nuit il ne dormit point.

Le lendemain, de retour aux champs, il se dit: "Plusieurs petits, sans doute, ont déjà péri." Il alla vers le buisson (thicket) et il vit les petits bien portants. Étonné, il se cacha pour observer ce qui se passait. L'homme aperçut le second oiseau rapportant en hâte de la nourriture qu'il donna à tous les petits indistinctement. Les orphelins ne furent pas abandonnés dans leur misère.

Le soir, le père raconta à son voisin ce qu'il avait vu et dit: "Si je meurs avant vous, vous serez le père de mes enfants. Si vous mourez avant moi, je serai le père des vôtres."

–D'après Lamennais

1. Qu'est-ce que les deux voisins avaient en commun?

   a. Tous les deux étaient inquiets.
   b. Ils aimaient regarder les oiseaux.
   c. Ils ne pouvaient pas dormir.
   d. Ils étaient pères de famille.

2. Qu'est-ce qui troublait surtout un des hommes?

   a. son travail dur
   b. l'avenir de ses enfants
   c. le bruit des oiseaux
   d. la peur de la mort

3. Quel malheur est arrivé à un des oiseaux?

   a. Il est tombé de son nid.
   b. Un oiseau de proie l'a emporté.
   c. Il a perdu ses plumes.
   d. Un chasseur l'a blessé.

4. Pourquoi le père a-t-il été étonné le jour suivant?

   a. Les orphelins étaient sains et saufs.
   b. Les petits oiseaux avaient disparu.
   c. Tous les oiseaux étaient dans le même nid.
   d. Les oiseaux n'avaient pas peur de lui.

5. Quel parti le père prend-il enfin?

   a. Il va s'occuper des oiseaux.
   b. Il compte gagner plus d'argent.
   c. Il décide de retourner aux champs.
   d. Il va suivre l'exemple des oiseaux.

B

Louis XIII était jaloux du cardinal de Richelieu tout en ne pouvant pas se tirer d'affaire sans ses services.

Dans un bal qu'on donnait à la cour, le roi, qui s'y ennuyait, voulut se retirer au moment même où le cardinal se retirait également.

Tout le monde se rangeait pour laisser passer le ministre, et le roi remarqua qu'on rendait beaucoup plus de respect à ce dernier qu'à lui-même. Richelieu ignorait que le roi le suivait, mais voyant s'avancer quelques pages, il le devina et se rangea de côté, pour le laisser passer. Le roi, de son côté, s'arrêta et lui dit:

–Pourquoi ne passez-vous pas, monsieur le Cardinal? N'êtes-vous pas le maître?

Le sens de cette réflexion n'échappa pas à Richelieu. Il prit un flambeau des mains d'un page, et marchant devant le roi, lui dit:

–Sire, je peux passer devant Votre Majesté seulement en faisant les fonctions du plus humble de ses serviteurs.

1. Pourquoi Louis XIII gardait-il le cardinal de Richelieu comme son ministre?

   a. Le roi avait besoin de lui.
   b. Le roi avait peur de lui.
   c. Le roi l'aimait bien.
   d. Le roi ne voulait pas lui faire du mal.

2. Pourquoi le roi voulait-il quitter le bal?

   a. Il était jaloux du cardinal.
   b. Il était furieux contre le cardinal.
   c. Il ne s'y amusait pas.
   d. Il voulait partir avant le cardinal.

3. Qu'est-ce que les invités faisaient pendant que le cardinal partait?

   a. Ils se taisaient.
   b. Ils se préparaient à partir.
   c. Ils regardaient le roi.
   d. Ils s'écartaient pour lui faire place.

4. Pourquoi Richelieu a-t-il précédé le roi?

   a. Richelieu ne savait pas que le roi était derrière lui.
   b. Richelieu voulait montrer à tout le monde lequel des deux était plus puissant.
   c. Richelieu désirait se moquer du roi.
   d. Richelieu feignait de ne pas voir le roi.

5. Quels services Richelieu met-il dans la catégorie la plus basse?

   a. ceux de ministre
   b. ceux de page
   c. ceux de roi
   d. ceux de courtisan

C

En 1347, les habitants de Calais, attaqués par les Anglais, avaient excité au plus haut point la colère d'Édouard III, roi d'Angleterre, par leur longue résistance. Édouard fit grâce à la ville, à la condition qu'on lui livrerait six des plus notables bourgeois.

La désolation fut grande à Calais. Alors Eustache de Saint-Pierre, se levant le premier dans l'assemblée, se dévoua avec cinq autres bourgeois; ils allèrent pieds nus, la corde au cou, présenter les clefs de la ville au roi anglais.

Le roi ordonna aussitôt de les tuer. La reine se jeta alors aux pieds d'Édouard, le suppliant d'avoir pitié de ces hommes. Le roi parut vivement contrarié, mais son cœur s'attendrit et il dit à la reine d'en disposer selon son plaisir.

La reine fit lever les six bourgeois, leur fit donner des vêtements et à manger, puis les renvoya chez eux.

1. Quelle était l'attitude d'Édouard III envers les habitants de Calais?

   a. Il les craignait.
   b. Il admirait leur courage.
   c. Il leur en voulait.
   d. Il éprouvait de la sympathie pour eux.

2. Quel prix le roi exigea-t-il des Calaisiens?

   a. une grosse somme d'argent
   b. la vie de plusieurs de leurs chefs illustres
   c. les clefs de la ville
   d. la dissolution de leur assemblée municipale

3. Comment les habitants de la ville réagirent-ils?

   a. Le prix les enchanta.
   b. Ils restèrent calmes.
   c. Ils protestèrent violemment.
   d. Ils furent accablés de douleur.

4. Le roi voulait

   a. rendre aux bourgeois leurs clefs
   b. exécuter tout de suite les bourgeois
   c. mettre à mort plus tard les bourgeois
   d. offrir aux bourgeois des habits

5. Qu'est-ce qu'on fit enfin des bourgeois?

   a. On les libéra.
   b. On les exila en Angleterre.
   c. On les tua.
   d. On les fit marcher pieds nus.

D

Un matin, en m'éveillant, je vis que l'hiver était venu; sa blanche lumière remplissait ma petite chambre; de gros flocons de neige descendaient du ciel. Dehors régnait le silence, pas une âme ne courait dans la rue, tout le monde avait fermé sa porte et les oiseaux se taisaient. Moi, couché sous la couverture, je revoyais les hivers passés. Je me représentais les glissades sur la rivière, les parties de traîneau, la bataille à pelotes de neige, les éclats de rire, la vitre cassée qui tombe et la vieille grand-mère qui crie, tandis que la bande se disperse. Tout cela, dans une seconde, me revint à l'esprit, et moitié triste, moitié content, je me dis: "C'est l'hiver!"

1. Comment l'auteur sait-il que l'hiver est arrivé?
   a. Ses amis l'appellent.
   b. Les vitres sont cassées.
   c. Des flocons de neige tombent.
   d. Des enfants crient.

2. Où est l'auteur?
   a. près de la cheminée
   b. au lit
   c. à l'école
   d. sur la rivière

3. Que font les oiseaux?
   a. Ils jettent des cris.
   b. Ils courent dans la rue.
   c. Ils glissent sur la rivière.
   d. Ils ne font pas de bruit.

4. Comment est la rue?
   a. déserte *b.* large *c.* bruyante *d.* cassée

5. Que faisait la grand-mère?
   a. Elle grondait les enfants.
   b. Elle pleurait.
   c. Elle éclatait de rire.
   d. Elle revoyait les heures passées.

E

M. Lepic arrive de Paris ce matin même. Il ouvre sa malle. Des cadeaux en sortent pour grand frère Félix et sœur Ernestine, de beaux cadeaux, dont (comme c'est drôle!) ils ont rêvé toute la nuit. Ensuite M. Lepic, les mains derrière son dos, regarde malicieusement Poil de Carotte et lui dit:

–Et toi, qu'est-ce que tu aimes le mieux: une trompette ou un pistolet?

En vérité, Poil de Carotte est plutôt prudent que courageux. Il a toujours entendu dire qu'un garçon de son âge ne peut jouer sérieusement qu'avec des armes, des sabres, des engins de guerre.

–J'aime mieux un pistolet, dit-il hardiment, sûr d'avoir deviné ce que son père avait choisi.

Il va même un peu plus loin et ajoute:

–Il est inutile de le couvrir; je le vois!

—Ah! dit M. Lepic embarrassé, tu aimes mieux un pistolet! tu as donc bien changé?

Tout de suite Poil de Carotte répond:

—Mais non, mon papa, c'était pour rire. Sois tranquille, je les déteste, les pistolets. Donne-moi vite ma trompette, que je te montre comme ça m'amuse de souffler dedans.

—D'après Jules Renard

1. A quoi Félix et Ernestine avaient-ils pensé pendant la nuit?
   - *a.* à des choses drôles
   - *b.* à ce qu'ils allaient recevoir
   - *c.* au cadeau de leur frère
   - *d.* au voyage de leur père
2. Qu'est-ce que M. Lepic a fait du cadeau de Poil de Carotte?
   - *a.* Il l'a remis dans la malle.
   - *b.* Il l'a caché derrière lui.
   - *c.* Il l'a donné aussitôt à son fils.
   - *d.* Il l'a laissé tomber par terre.
3. Pourquoi le garçon a-t-il dit qu'il préférait un pistolet?
   - *a.* Il voulait faire plaisir à son père.
   - *b.* Il aimait jouer à la guerre.
   - *c.* Il avait demandé un pistolet.
   - *d.* Il comptait le donner à son frère.
4. Pourquoi le garçon a-t-il l'air de changer d'avis?
   - *a.* Il doit accepter l'instrument malgré lui.
   - *b.* Il est allé trop loin.
   - *c.* Il veut faire un mauvais tour à son père.
   - *d.* Il se rend compte qu'il s'est trompé.

F

Il y a quarante ans environ, un Français dont on n'a pu me dire le nom, mais qui appartenait à une famille noble et riche, aborda en Amérique, après avoir été forcé de quitter son pays en révolution. Notre émigré était jeune et bien portant; il ne souffrait jamais de l'estomac. Il avait de plus une femme qu'il aimait de tout son cœur. Du reste, il manquait du premier sou pour vivre. Un ami auquel il s'adressa lui offrit de lui prêter quelque argent, au moyen duquel il pourrait se procurer les choses les plus nécessaires à la vie et s'établir dans quelque coin où la terre ne serait pas chère. Dans ce temps-là l'ouest de l'État de New-York était encore inculte; les bois qui le couvraient n'étaient encore habités que par les tribus indiennes de la confédération des Iroquois. Sa jeune femme eut le courage de vouloir le suivre dans ce désert. Ils arrivèrent sur les bords du lac Onéida. Pour un peu de poudre et de plomb, ils achetèrent des Indiens la terre qui se trouve au milieu de ses eaux. Jamais Européen ni peut-être humain n'avait imaginé d'en faire sa demeure. Il fallut couper des arbres, bâtir une cabane et lutter contre tous les besoins de la vie. Les premiers temps furent difficiles à passer mais, la seconde année, la tâche leur devint plus facile.

—D'après A. de Tocqueville

1. Pourquoi le Français quitta-t-il son pays?

   a. Il avait besoin d'argent.
   b. Il préférait demeurer en Amérique.
   c. Sa femme voulait partir.
   d. La situation politique était dangereuse.

2. A l'heure de son départ,

   a. il était sur le point de se marier
   b. il se sentait malade
   c. il était en bonne santé
   d. il possédait beaucoup d'argent

3. A cette époque, la partie occidentale de l'État de New-York

   a. ressemblait à un jardin royal
   b. était couverte d'eau
   c. était sauvage
   d. produisait de beaux fruits

4. Sa femme tenait à

   a. accompagner son mari
   b. attendre son mari en France
   c. offrir de l'argent à son mari
   d. rejoindre plus tard son mari

5. Où le Français s'établit-il enfin?

   a. sur la rive d'un lac
   b. dans un désert aride
   c. sur une montagne boisée
   d. dans une île

G

François Rabelais, raconte-t-on, se trouva un jour à Lyon sans argent pour payer son hôtel. En même temps, il se voyait dans l'impossibilité de continuer son voyage jusqu'à Paris où il devait se rendre auprès du roi. Rabelais, toujours ingénieux, employa alors le stratagème suivant: il fit écrire, par un jeune garçon, des étiquettes qu'il lui fit placer sur de petites enveloppes. Ces étiquettes portaient les mots: poison pour le roi, poison pour la reine, poison pour le jeune prince. L'enfant effrayé courut prévenir l'aubergiste. Celui-ci s'empressa d'appeler la police. On vint aussitôt arrêter notre homme.

Rabelais fut conduit à Paris sous bonne escorte, et aux frais de l'État. Arrivé dans la capitale, il demanda qu'on le menât immédiatement devant le roi. François Ier reconnut immédiatement le prétendu criminel qu'on lui présentait. Il devina qu'il s'agissait de quelque nouvelle aventure de Rabelais. Il se fit conter l'histoire et en rit beaucoup avec le héros de l'aventure. C'est dans cette anecdote qu'il faudrait, selon certains auteurs, voir l'origine d'une expression bien connue: le quart d'heure de Rabelais. On appelle ainsi le moment embarrassant où l'on doit tirer de l'argent de sa poche pour payer ses dettes, et, par extension, tout moment fâcheux.

—D'après Claude Augé

1. Pourquoi Rabelais allait-il à Paris?

   a. Il voulait empoisonner le roi et sa famille.
   b. Le roi l'y avait invité.
   c. Il cherchait de l'argent.
   d. Il n'avait jamais vu la capitale.

2. Que fit le jeune garçon?

   a. Il avertit l'hôtelier.
   b. Il détruisit les étiquettes.
   c. Il courut chez le roi.
   d. Il appela la police.

3. Comment Rabelais trouva-t-il le moyen de voyager à Paris?

   a. Il vendit ses services.
   b. On l'y amena de force.
   c. Rabelais tira de l'argent de sa poche.
   d. L'aubergiste lui prêta de l'argent.

4. Quelle fut la réaction du roi?

   a. Il se fâcha.
   b. Il s'amusa.
   c. Il fut frappé de stupeur.
   d. Il se tut.

5. "Le quart d'heure de Rabelais" veut dire

   a. quinze minutes d'attente
   b. un moment favorable
   c. du temps pour se reposer
   d. une occasion désagréable

H

Pendant les beaux soirs d'automne, on voit souvent le ciel traversé d'une belle étoile filante (shooting star). Une superstition nous dit que voir l'étoile filante porte bonheur; une autre nous dit que tout souhait fait sur une étoile filante est réalisé. Mais laissons de côté la superstition et parlons de la science.

Les étoiles filantes ne sont pas des étoiles! Elles sont des morceaux de pierre que la terre rencontre dans les espaces interplanétaires. On appelle ces morceaux, en termes techniques, des aérolithes.

Ces aérolithes tombent sur notre globe à une telle vitesse qu'ils entrent en combustion et deviennent lumineux en traversant l'atmosphère. Ils se consument avant d'arriver à la terre.

Parfois, cependant, les morceaux sont si grands qu'ils tombent jusqu'à la terre. Le plus gros dont la chute a été observée est tombé dans l'état d'Arkansas en 1930. Il pesait à peu près 68 kilogrammes.

Heureusement il est tombé dans un endroit peu habité. S'il était tombé en ville, il y aurait eu une vraie catastrophe!

1. Que croient les superstitieux à la vue d'une étoile filante?

   a. que c'est un désastre
   b. que c'est un signe de bonne chance
   c. que le temps va bientôt changer
   d. que quelque chose d'important va arriver

2. Qu'est-ce que c'est qu'un aérolithe?

   a. une masse tombant de l'espace céleste vers la terre
   b. une comète qui émet de la lumière
   c. un morceau de notre terre qui traverse le ciel
   d. une étoile brillante qui tombe du ciel

3. Qu'est-ce qui rend lumineuses les étoiles filantes?

   a. la chaleur du soleil
   b. la masse d'air qui nous environne
   c. la lumière du ciel
   d. la force de la gravité

4. D'ordinaire, que deviennent les étoiles filantes?

   a. Elles s'enfoncent dans la terre.
   b. Elles s'unissent les unes aux autres.
   c. Elles continuent leur vol vers une autre planète.
   d. Elles se détruisent.

5. Qu'est-ce qui arrive de temps en temps?

   a. Les étoiles filantes consument des villes.
   b. On observe ces "étoiles" qui filent lentement vers la terre.
   c. Les étoiles filantes arrivent à la terre.
   d. Les étoiles filantes sont composées de sable.

I

Un jour je voyageais en Calabre en compagnie d'un jeune homme. Calabre est un pays de gens qui en veulent surtout aux Français.

Dans les montagnes un chemin étroit et rude nous égara. Nous cherchâmes tant qu'il fit jour notre chemin à travers ces bois; il était nuit quand nous arrivâmes près d'une maison fort noire. Nous y entrâmes. Là nous trouvâmes toute une famille de charbonniers à table, où du premier mot on nous invita à dîner. Nos hôtes avaient bien mine de charbonniers; mais la maison, vous l'auriez prise pour un arsenal. Ce n'étaient que fusils, armes à feu, épées, couteaux. Tout me déplut, et je vis que je déplaisais aussi. Imaginez un peu! chez nos plus grands ennemis, si loin de tout secours humain!

Le souper fini, on nous laissa. Nos hôtes couchaient en bas, nous dans une chambre en haut. Mon camarade se coucha. Moi, j'étais déterminé à veiller. La nuit s'était déjà passée, quand j'entendis au-dessous de moi notre hôte et sa femme parler et se disputer. J'entendis le mari dire: "Eh bien! voyons, faut-il les tuer tous deux?" A quoi la femme répondit: "Oui," et je n'entendis plus rien. En quelle peine je me trouvais, imaginez-le, si vous pouvez.

Dès que le jour parut, toute la famille vint nous éveiller. On nous servit un déjeuner fort propre et fort bon. Deux poulets rôtis se trouvaient sur la table. En les voyant, je compris enfin le sens de ces terribles mots: "Faut-il les tuer tous deux?"

—D'après P. L. Courier

1. En général, quelle est l'attitude de habitants de Calabre envers les Français?
   a. Ils les estiment. *b.* Ils les plaignent.
   c. Ils sont jaloux d'eux. *d.* Ils ne les aiment pas.
2. Pourquoi les deux Français sont-ils entrés dans la maison?
   a. Ils cherchaient des renseignements. *b.* Ils s'étaient perdus.
   c. On les y avait invités. *d.* Ils avaient admiré l'extérieur de la maison.
3. L'auteur avait décidé
   a. de ne pas s'endormir *b.* d'écouter à la porte
   c. de partir tout de suite *d.* de se coucher tard
4. Qu'est-ce qui a étonné les deux voyageurs?
   a. l'air des charbonniers *b.* le bon souper
   c. l'intérieur de la maison *d.* leur chambre à coucher
5. Que prouve la fin de l'histoire?
   a. L'auteur s'était trompé. *b.* L'auteur rêvait.
   c. L'auteur avait trop bu. *d.* L'auteur avait raison.

J

Deux étudiants allaient à pied à l'Université de Salamanque. Se sentant las et ayant soif, ils s'arrêtèrent au bord d'une fontaine qu'ils rencontrèrent au bord de la route. Là, ils aperçurent par hasard auprès d'eux, sur une pierre par terre, quelques mots déjà effacés par les pieds des troupeaux qui venaient boire à cette fontaine. Ils jetèrent de l'eau sur la pierre pour la laver et ils lurent ces paroles: ICI EST ENFERMÉE L'AME DE PIERRE GARCIA.

Le plus jeune des étudiants dit en riant:

—Rien n'est plus plaisant. Une âme enfermée. Je voudrais savoir qui a pu faire une épitaphe si drôle.

En achevant ces paroles, il se leva pour s'en aller. Son compagnon, plus judicieux, dit en lui-même:

—Il y a là-dessous quelque chose de mystérieux; je veux demeurer ici pour en trouver la solution.

Sans perdre de temps, celui-ci se mit à creuser avec son couteau tout autour de la pierre. Il fit si bien qu'il l'enleva. Il trouva dessous une bourse de cuir qu'il ouvrit. Il y avait dedans cent ducats, avec une carte sur laquelle étaient écrites ces paroles: "Sois mon héritier, toi qui as eu assez d'esprit pour comprendre l'inscription."

L'étudiant, ravi de cette découverte, remit la pierre comme elle était auparavant, et reprit le chemin de Salamanque avec l'âme de Pierre Garcia.

—D'après Le Sage

1. Les deux étudiants
   a. se sentaient malades
   b. voulaient manger
   c. venaient de se rencontrer
   d. étaient fatigués

2. La pierre s'était usée à cause des
   a. soldats
   b. bêtes sauvages
   c. enfants
   d. animaux domestiques

3. Le plus jeune étudiant a trouvé l'inscription
   a. très agréable
   b. fort amusante
   c. pleine de sentiment
   d. effrayante

4. Pourquoi l'autre étudiant n'est-il pas parti avec son ami?
   a. Il voulait résoudre le mystère.
   b. Il était superstitieux.
   c. Il n'en pouvait plus.
   d. Il savait ce qui était caché sous la pierre.

5. A qui Pierre Garcia voulait-il léguer ses biens?
   a. à un pauvre
   b. à un homme religieux
   c. à une personne d'intelligence
   d. à un étudiant de l'université

K

J'imagine qu'un Parisien ne traverse jamais une petite ville de province sans envier le bonheur de ceux qui l'habitent. On sort d'une capitale bruyante où toutes les physionomies expriment la hâte, le trouble, et la fièvre; où tout le monde est dans la rue, faute de place dans les maisons; où l'on serre les coudes sur le trottoir, faute de place dans les rues; où chacun parle vite et court, au lieu de marcher, parce que le temps y vaut de l'or. On se voit transporté comme par miracle dans un pays différent, quoique voisin, et qui semble peuplé d'autres hommes. Les rues paraissent plus larges, parce qu'elles sont à moitié désertes; mieux aérées, parce que la foule ne s'y dispute pas une bouffée d'air. Les maisons ont beau être petites, mal bâties et incommodes dans le fond, on voit qu'on y vivrait plus à l'aise, par cela seul que les familles n'y sont pas entassées l'une sur l'autre, et que personne n'entend sur la tête le bruit des pas du voisin. La vie des habitants, ou du moins ce qu'on en voit, a quelque chose de calme, de reposé, de placide. Vous trouverez à la lenteur aisée de leurs mouvements que le ciel a fait pour eux des heures de cent et quelques minutes et des années de six à sept cents jours.

–D'après E. About

1. Selon cet auteur, quels gens sont heureux?

   a. ceux qui sont occupés
   b. les Parisiens
   c. les habitants des provinces
   d. ceux qui ont peu à faire

2. Pourquoi y a-t-il tant de personnes dehors dans la grande ville?

   a. On fait des emplettes.
   b. Tout le monde travaille dur.
   c. Les maisons sont trop petites.
   d. Les habitants de la ville aiment les places publiques.

3. On est toujours pressé dans la capitale

   a. parce que le temps est précieux
   b. parce qu'il y fait beau temps
   c. parce qu'il n'y a pas assez de place
   d. parce que le temps change subitement

4. Quel facteur contribue au confort des provinces?

   a. Les rues sont plus larges.
   b. Les familles sont moins serrées.
   c. Les voisins sont plus gentils.
   d. Les maisons sont mieux construites.

5. Le résultat des différences entre la ville et les provinces est que

   a. les habitants des provinces peuvent accomplir plus que ceux des villes
   b. les villageois visitent souvent les provinces
   c. les provinciaux gagnent peu d'argent
   d. la vie de province semble plus longue

L

Elle était grillée comme une cage de lions. Au fond, sous des quartiers de mouton, M. Lafolie sommeillait. Il avait commencé de travailler au petit jour et la fatigue amollissait ses membres vigoureux. Les bras nus et croisés, son fusil encore pendant à son côté, les jambes écartées sous le tablier blanc, taché de sang, il balançait lentement la tête. Sa face rouge étincelait et les veines de son cou se gonflaient sous le col de sa chemise rose. Il respirait la force tranquille. M. Bergeret disait de lui qu'il donnait quelque idée des héros homériques parce que son genre de vie ressemblait au leur et qu'il versait comme eux le sang des victimes.

M. Lafolie sommeillait. Près de lui sommeillait son fils, grand et fort comme lui. Le garçon dormait la tête dans ses mains sur le marbre. Dans une cage de verre, à l'entrée de la boutique, se tenait droite, les yeux lourds, gagnée aussi par le sommeil, Mme Lafolie, grasse, la chair tout imbibée du sang des animaux. Cette famille avait un aspect de royauté barbare.

—D'après Anatole France

1. M. Lafolie s'était mis au travail

   a. de bonne heure le matin
   b. la veille de ce jour-là
   c. tard dans l'après-midi
   d. le soir

2. Pourquoi disait-on que M. Lafolie ressemblait à un héros de l'antiquité?

   a. Il avait les muscles bien développés.
   b. Il avait l'air distingué.
   c. Il savait tuer.
   d. Il pouvait exécuter des ordres.

3. Le portrait de cette famille donne l'impression

   a. de tragédie
   b. de force brutale
   c. d'intelligence
   d. de bonheur

4. Dans ce magasin,

   a. tout le monde était accablé de fatigue
   b. il faisait chaud
   c. on voyait plusieurs cages d'animaux
   d. on venait de gagner beaucoup d'argent

5. Cette scène a lieu dans

   a. une boulangerie
   b. une pharmacie
   c. une épicerie
   d. une boucherie

M

Me voilà en route! La locomotive est déjà à cent cinquante kilomètres de Paris! . . . La vue des villages qui fuient devant moi ressuscite tout mon passé d'enfant. Maisonnettes coiffées de tuiles rouges, basses-cours où traînent de gros troncs d'arbres; jardinets plantés de soleils; barrières contre lesquelles les bébés appuient leurs nez crottés et leurs fronts pour regarder le train; cette simplicité, cette grossièreté, ce silence me rappellent la campagne où je buvais la liberté et le vent, étant tout petit.

Dans les femmes courbées aux champs, je crois reconnaître mes tantes, les paysannes; et je me lève malgré moi quand j'aperçois le miroir d'un étang ou d'un lac. Je regarde courir l'eau des ruisseaux et je suis le vol noir des corbeaux dans le bleu du ciel. Tout parle à ma mémoire: ce mur bâti de pierres posées au hasard; et ce bois sombre qui me rappelle la forêt de sapins où il faisait si triste et où j'aimais à m'enfoncer pour avoir peur!

Ah! je sens que je suis bien un morceau de toi, un éclat de tes rochers, pays pauvre qui embaume les fleurs, terre de vignes et de volcans! Ces paysans, ces paysannes qui passent, ce sont mes frères en veste de laine, mes sœurs en tablier rouge. . . .

—D'après J. Vallès

1. Le sentiment dominant de ce passage est

   a. la joie de voyager
   b. l'amour de la campagne
   c. l'amour de l'auteur pour son pays natal
   d. la honte de l'auteur d'être né dans cette région

2. On note dans le passage le souvenir ému de l'écrivain

   a. de son enfance
   b. du travail
   c. des chemins de fer
   d. des bébés

3. L'auteur exprime une chaude sympathie pour

   a. les ouvriers en général
   b. les touristes
   c. les pères de famille
   d. les habitants de sa terre

4. L'auteur est né dans une famille

   a. riche *b.* paysanne *c.* ambulante *d.* noble

5. Un des produits de la terre décrite par l'auteur est

   a. le beurre *b.* le vin *c.* la dentelle *d.* le cidre

N

Comme je sortais de mon église, une fillette que je ne connaissais point vint me chercher en toute hâte pour me mener auprès d'une pauvre vieille qui se mourait. Je fis monter l'enfant dans la voiture, après avoir cherché une lanterne, car je pensai ne pas pouvoir être de retour avant la nuit.

Le soleil se couchait et nous marchions depuis longtemps dans l'ombre, lorsque enfin ma jeune guide m'indiqua du doigt une maison que j'aurais cru inhabitée si je n'avais pas remarqué un peu de fumée qui s'en échappait. J'attachai le cheval à un pommier voisin, puis rejoignis l'enfant dans la pièce obscure où la vieille venait de mourir.

Une femme encore jeune était à genoux près du lit. Je lui demandai si la vieille avait des enfants. Alors, elle se releva, prit une chandelle et me montra, assise devant la cheminée, une fille d'une quinzaine d'années. —Cette fille aveugle, répondit-elle. La servante m'a dit qu'elle est une nièce. C'est tout ce qui reste de la famille, paraît-il. Il sera nécessaire de la mettre à l'orphelinage.

En entendant ces mots tristes, je décidai de prendre chez moi cette enfant malheureuse.

—D'après André Gide

1. La jeune guide
   a. était très pressée
   b. portait une chandelle
   c. était une amie du prêtre
   d. était la petite-fille de la vieille

2. Qu'est-ce qui indiquait que la maison était habitée?
   a. la cheminée *b.* la porte *c.* les fenêtres *d.* le jardin

3. A quoi le prêtre a-t-il lié la voiture?
   a. à une planche
   b. à un roc
   c. à un arbre
   d. à une porte de la maison

4. Quand les deux sont arrivés à la maison,
   a. la vieille n'était pas là
   b. la vieille était déjà morte
   c. la nièce de la vieille priait
   d. la vieille était sur le point de mourir

5. Pourquoi le prêtre plaignait-il la fille de quinze ans?
   a. Elle ne pouvait pas entendre.
   b. Elle pleurait à chaudes larmes.
   c. Elle n'avait plus de parents.
   d. Elle était bien malade.

O

Je revois avec une singulière précision une poupée qui, lorsque j'avais huit ans, s'étalait dans une méchante boutique de la rue de la Seine. Comment il arriva que cette poupée me plut, je ne sais. J'étais très fier d'être un garçon; je méprisais les petites filles et j'attendais avec impatience le moment (qui, hélas! est venu) où une barbe piquante me garnirait le menton. Je jouais aux soldats et, pour nourrir mon cheval à bascule, je ravageais les plantes que ma pauvre mère cultivait sur sa fenêtre. C'était là deux jeux mâles, je pense! Et pourtant, j'eus envie d'une poupée. Les Hercules ont de ces faiblesses.

Celle que j'aimais était-elle belle au moins? Non. Je la vois encore. Elle avait une tache de vermillon sur chaque joue, des bras mous et courts, d'horribles mains de bois et de longues jambes. Je me rappelle bien que, tout bambin que j'étais, je sentais à ma manière que cette poupée manquait de grâce, qu'elle était grossière. Mais je l'aimais malgré cela. Je la voulais. Mes soldats et mes tambours ne m'étaient plus de rien. Cette poupée était tout pour moi.

J'imaginais des ruses de sauvage pour obliger Virginie, ma bonne, à passer avec moi devant la boutique de la rue de Seine. J'appuyais mon nez à la vitre et il fallait que ma bonne me tirât par le bras. "Monsieur Sylvestre, il est tard et votre maman vous grondera." M. Sylvestre se moquait bien alors des gronderies. Mais sa bonne l'enlevait comme une plume, et M. Sylvestre cédait à la force.

J'étais malheureux. Une honte irréfléchie mais irrésistible m'empêchait d'avouer à ma mère l'objet de mon amour. De là mes souffrances.

–D'après Anatole France

1. Pourquoi le petit garçon aimait-il la poupée?

   a. L'auteur refuse de nous le dire.
   b. L'auteur en ignore la raison.
   c. L'auteur préfère ne pas en parler.
   d. L'auteur ne s'en souvient plus.

2. Quel jour le garçon souhaitait-il?

   a. le jour où il pourrait se raser
   b. le jour où il serait soldat
   c. le jour de son mariage
   d. le jour où il aurait un cheval

3. La poupée était

   a. délicate *b.* presque humaine *c.* jolie *d.* laide

4. Le garçon

   a. avait l'intention de voler la poupée
   b. avait peu de patience
   c. passait souvent devant la vitrine du magasin
   d. craignait les réprimandes

5. Pourquoi le garçon souffrait-il?

   a. Ses parents le grondaient souvent.
   b. La poupée coûtait cher.
   c. Sa bonne le battait.
   d. Il ne pouvait pas parler de la poupée à sa mère.

P

Son corps était de moyenne taille, un peu gros, épaissi par l'âge, sauf les mains fines et blanches, si jolies encore. Il était habillé d'un complet de grosse laine verdâtre, veston, gilet, culotte. On aurait dit que sa tête était de marbre blanc, coloré d'un peu de rose aux lèvres et de beaucoup de bleu pâle par les veines saillantes. Physionomie autoritaire, impatiente: un nez comme une figue, gros du bout; une bouche tirée en bas, et des plissures nombreuses. Il était de la vieille Angleterre, attaché à tout usage, à son rang, à son Église, parce que tout cela, pour lui, faisait partie de la Constitution. Il refusait une nouveauté, dès qu'elle lui semblait opposée à cet ensemble. Son amitié était fidèle, son inimitié également. On ne l'avait jamais vu pleurer. Dans les quelques circonstances douloureuses qu'il avait traversées, mort de sa mère, maladie grave de sa femme après la naissance de son second fils, sir George s'était enfermé dans ses appartements, il n'avait parlé à personne, et quand il était sorti enfin, on avait remarqué qu'il avait changé, maigri, pâli, et que la souffrance morale, par conséquent, avait prise sur ce cœur très caché.

—D'après René Bazin

1. Sir George était

   a. grand   *b.* mince   *c.* petit   *d.* ni grand ni petit

2. Quel trait visible le distinguait?

   a. Il était chauve.
   b. Il avait l'air sympathique.
   c. Il ne semblait pas vieillir.
   d. Il avait la peau rose.

3. Quelle attitude dominait sa vie?

   a. Il aimait le progrès.
   b. Il n'était ni conservateur ni radical.
   c. Il tenait à la tradition.
   d. Il était hostile aux institutions du passé.

4. Sir George

   a. n'avait pas d'ennemis
   b. savait conserver ses amis
   c. était sans amis
   d. avait plus d'amis que d'ennemis

5. Quant aux douleurs de sa vie,

   a. elles ont été nombreuses
   b. il les a souffertes en silence
   c. il s'en est moqué
   d. elles l'ont attendri

Q

A l'heure où j'écris ces lignes, en des jours difficiles, je ne puis dire que le monde et la vie m'aient abusé. Quand la vieillesse est arrivée, je l'ai trouvée incomparablement moins amère que vous ne le prétendiez. Je m'attendais à un sommet glacé, désert, étroit, noyé dans la brume; j'ai aperçu, au contraire, autour de moi, un vaste horizon qui ne s'était encore jamais découvert à mes yeux. Je voyais plus clair en moi-même et en chaque chose. Dans ma longue route, j'avais recueilli quelques vérités, qui, chaque jour, devenaient plus certaines.

Vous affirmez que les sentiments s'affaiblissent en vivant. Moi, je sens très bien que je vivrais un siècle, je ne m'accoutumerais jamais à ce qui me révolte aujourd'hui. Mensonges, défis à la justice, perversité tranquille, parce qu'elle se sent impunie, cela me sera aussi nouveau, aussi exécrable dans mille ans qu'aujourd'hui. De même les âmes belles que j'ai entrevues sur la terre ne s'effaceront jamais pour moi. Elles m'apparaîtront toujours telles que je les ai aperçues dans l'heure radieuse.

La vie humaine n'est point ce que vous dites; elle n'est pas une chute continue de la jeunesse à l'âge mûr, de l'âge mûr à la vieillesse. J'ai senti tout autrement l'existence. Ma jeunesse a été triste, mon âge mûr meilleur, ma vieillesse heureuse. La première lueur est devenue lumière; la lumière, vérité; la vérité, repos, paix, bonheur. Voilà quelles ont été pour moi les époques de la vie: une ascension vers la lumière.

–D'après Edgar Quinet

1. L'auteur compare la vie à

   a. un désert *b.* une montagne *c.* un glacier *d.* un nuage

2. A en croire l'opinion générale, la vieillesse serait une période où

   a. les sentiments sont presque éteints
   b. la vie devient moins amère
   c. s'ouvre un vaste horizon
   d. l'intelligence domine la vie

3. L'auteur dit qu'en vieillissant

   a. il se sent isolé au milieu des autres humains
   b. il a découvert que la vie est courte
   c. il a mieux compris les défauts des hommes
   d. il n'a pas changé d'idéal moral

4. L'auteur affirme

   a. qu'il est d'accord avec l'opinion générale à l'égard de la vie
   b. qu'on ne peut jamais trouver la vérité
   c. que l'âge mûr est préférable à la jeunesse
   d. que le repos et la paix sont nécessaires à tous les âges de la vie

5. Selon l'auteur, l'âge du bonheur est

   a. l'enfance *b.* la vieillesse *c.* l'adolescence *d.* la maturité

R

Ils sont venus. Les habitants, depuis deux jours, fuyaient. Les routes de l'ouest étaient encombrées de charrettes où ils avaient entassé plus de choses que le cheval n'en pouvait traîner, parce que toutes les choses sont précieuses quand on va les quitter. L'homme marchait à la tête du cheval, poussant quelquefois une vache, dont il frappait les reins avec le manche du fouet. Dans toutes les voitures il y avait de bons matelas, à plat sur les provisions et les meubles les moins lourds, et des enfants qui étaient assis dessus. Tout cela s'arrêtait des heures, au croisement des chemins, pour laisser passer des troupes, des trains de munitions et d'approvisionnement. Et on ne savait où on allait; toute la volonté était tendue vers ce seul objet: éviter d'être pris par l'ennemi. . . . Les femmes, assises, tournaient la tête, quelquefois, du côté où était Chaumecourt, à présent déjà loin et caché par d'autres collines. Elles cherchaient pour voir si une colonne de fumée n'allait pas monter de là.

—D'après René Bazin

1. Pourquoi ces habitants étaient-ils sur la route?

   a. Ils ne voulaient pas se laisser prendre.
   b. Ils n'avaient pas de quoi vivre.
   c. Leur village avait été détruit.
   d. Leur terre n'était plus labourable.

2. Ils portaient avec eux

   a. ce qu'il fallait pour subsister
   b. tout ce qu'ils avaient possédé
   c. tous leurs meubles
   d. tout ce qu'ils pouvaient

3. Qu'est-ce qui interrompait la marche continue de la caravane?

   a. les mauvaises routes
   b. des animaux fatigués
   c. le passage de matériel militaire
   d. la nécessité du repos

4. Que faisaient les femmes de temps en temps?

   a. Elles s'occupaient des provisions.
   b. Elles regardaient dans la direction de leur village abandonné.
   c. Elles aidaient les chevaux à traverser les collines.
   d. Elles regardaient la fumée qui montait.

S

Quand je devins rédacteur d'une feuille rurale, ce ne fut pas sans appréhension. Mais je me trouvais dans une situation qui me forçait à chercher un salaire. Le rédacteur habituel voulait partir en vacances; j'acceptai les offres qu'on me fit, et je m'installai à sa place.

J'éprouvai avec délices la sensation d'avoir de nouveau une occupation, et je travaillai toute la semaine avec un plaisir sans mélange. Nous mîmes sous presse et j'attendis toute la journée avec une anxiété, pour voir si mes efforts allaient attirer quelque peu l'attention.

Un jour, je vis entrer un vieux monsieur, porteur d'une barbe démesurée, à la physionomie distinguée et quelque peu sévère. Je l'invitai à s'asseoir; il prit un siège. Il semblait avoir quelque chose sur le cœur. Il étala un exemplaire du journal sur ses genoux; puis, il me dit:

—C'est vous le nouveau rédacteur en chef?

Je répondis que oui.

—Aviez-vous déjà rédigé un autre journal d'agriculture?

—Non. C'est mon coup d'essai.

—Je le crois sans peine. Avez-vous quelque expérience pratique en matière d'agriculture?

—Non, je ne pense pas.

—J'en avais comme un pressentiment, fit le vieux monsieur, mettant ses lunettes et me regardant par-dessus avec des yeux indignés. Voulez-vous que je vous lise ce qui m'a donné ce pressentiment? Écoutez, c'est cet article-là, et voyez si c'est bien vous qui l'avez écrit:

"Il ne faut jamais arracher les navets (turnips); ça leur est nuisible. Il est préférable de faire grimper quelqu'un et de lui faire secouer l'arbre."

Là-dessus, le vieux monsieur se leva brusquement, déchira le journal en petits morceaux, pulvérisa plusieurs choses à coups de canne, déclara que j'étais plus ignorant qu'une vache, puis sortit comme un furieux en fermant la porte avec un fracas épouvantable. Bref, il me parut qu'il était mécontent; mais ne sachant à quelle cause attribuer son agitation, je ne pus y porter remède.

—D'après Mark Twain

1. Mark Twain a accepté sa nouvelle responsabilité
   a. comme il avait accepté toutes ses autres responsabilités
   b. malgré lui
   c. avec un certain sentiment d'inquiétude
   d. avec assurance

2. Il a pris la nouvelle place
   a. pour oublier ses problèmes
   b. parce qu'il lui fallait de l'argent
   c. parce que sa vie était monotone
   d. pour pouvoir s'offrir des vacances

3. Qu'est-ce qui faisait croire au vieux monsieur que Twain ne se connaissait pas en agriculture?
   a. Twain était venu d'une grande ville.
   b. Twain avait fait une grosse faute.
   c. Twain avait menti de parti pris.
   d. Twain était à peine devenu rédacteur.

4. Qu'est-ce que le monsieur a fait avant de sortir?
   a. Il a brisé quelques objets.
   b. Il a changé d'avis.
   c. Il a fait ses excuses.
   d. Il a frappé Twain plusieurs fois.

5. Pourquoi Twain n'a-t-il rien fait pour améliorer la situation?
   a. Il était on ne peut plus obstiné.
   b. Il ne savait que faire.
   c. La conduite de l'homme l'avait découragé.
   d. Un rédacteur en chef doit toujours dire la vérité.

T

—Morbleu! lui dis-je un jour, c'est pour la troisième fois que je vous ordonne de m'acheter une brosse! Quelle tête! Quel animal!

Il ne répondit pas un mot; il n'avait rien répondu la veille à une pareille parole. "Il est si exact!" disais-je; je n'y concevais rien.

—Allez chercher un linge pour nettoyer mes souliers, lui dis-je en colère.

Pendant qu'il allait, je me repentais de l'avoir ainsi brusqué. Mon courroux passa tout à fait lorsque je vis le soin avec lequel il tâchait d'ôter la poussière de mes souliers sans toucher à mes bas; j'appuyai ma main sur lui en signe de réconciliation. "Quoi! dis-je alors en moi-même, il y a des hommes qui nettoient les souliers des autres pour de l'argent?" Ce mot d'argent fut un trait de lumière qui vint m'éclairer.

Je me ressouvins tout à coup qu'il y avait longtemps que je n'en avais point donné à mon domestique.

–Joannetti, lui dis-je en retirant mon pied, avez-vous de l'argent?

Un demi-sourire de justification parut sur ses lèvres à cette demande.

–Non, monsieur; j'ai dépensé tout ce qui m'appartenait pour vos petites emplettes.

Il sourit encore. Il se laissa maltraiter injustement plutôt que d'exposer son maître à rougir de sa colère. Que le ciel le bénisse!

–Tiens, Joannetti, tiens, lui dis-je, cours acheter la brosse.

–Mais, monsieur, voulez-vous rester ainsi avec un soulier blanc et l'autre noir?

–Va, te dis-je, acheter la brosse; laisse, laisse cette poussière sur mon soulier.

Il sortit; je pris le linge et je nettoyai délicieusement mon soulier gauche, sur lequel je laissai tomber une larme de repentir.

–D'après Xavier de Maistre

1. Pourquoi l'auteur est-il irrité contre son domestique?
   a. Le domestique n'a pas obéi à son ordre.
   b. Le domestique est paresseux.
   c. Le domestique ne lui répond pas.
   d. Le domestique a une mauvaise mémoire.

2. La colère du maître diminue
   a. quand Joannetti garde le silence
   b. quand le domestique ne se fâche pas
   c. quand le maître voit la diligence avec laquelle son domestique travaille
   d. quand Joannetti lui sourit

3. De quoi le maître se rend-il compte?
   a. de ce qu'il n'a pas payé son domestique
   b. de ce qu'il rougit de colère
   c. de la négligence de son domestique
   d. de ce que son domestique rit de lui

4. Pourquoi le domestique hésite-t-il à sortir?
   a. Il a trop d'autres choses à faire.
   b. Il n'a pas fini sa tâche.
   c. Son maître a été si bon pour lui.
   d. Il préfère se servir du linge.

5. Qu'est-ce que le maître fait à la fin?
   a. Il s'excuse auprès de son domestique.
   b. Il se sert de la brosse.
   c. Il regrette ce qu'il a fait.
   d. Il adresse une parole blessante à Joannetti.

A GUIDE TO THE COLLEGE BOARD ACHIEVEMENT TEST IN FRENCH

The scope of the College Board Achievement Test in French is a wide one. The questions are graded, ranging from easy to difficult. The test is designed to measure the candidate's mastery of both the spoken and the written language. Although the types of questions may vary from year to year, the following types illustrate what the candidate may generally expect.

SITUATION QUESTIONS

These questions are intended to test familiarity with the spoken language used in conversation or everyday situations.

In each of the sample situations below, choose the appropriate remark that is suggested by the initial statement.

1. Sachant qu'il allait revoir bientôt ses amis, il leur a dit en partant:

   (A) De rien. (B) A tout à l'heure. (C) D'aujourd'hui en huit. (D) A tout prix. (E) A la bonne heure.

2. La voisine a regardé l'enfant mignon. Puis elle a dit à la mère:

   (A) Ainsi soit-il. (B) Quel beau crépuscule! (C) Tant pis pour vous! (D) C'est un aspirateur. (E) Qu'il est sage!

3. Un voisin dont la maison a pris feu entre chez moi en criant:

   (A) Un peu à droite! Un peu à droite! (B) Aidez-moi, je vous en prie! (C) On n'est pas en retard? (D) Soyez le bienvenu. (E) Ce n'est rien, ça passera.

4. Heureuse de voir la belle piscine, elle a dit:

   (A) J'ai envie de danser toute la nuit. (B) Si nous allions à la nage? (C) Il y a longtemps que je n'ai mangé. (D) Allons faire une promenade tout de suite. (E) Que c'est joli, ce vêtement!

5. A la douane, le douanier nous a demandé:

   (A) Faut-il payer d'avance? (B) Et comme boisson, messieurs? (C) Avez-vous tout ce qu'il vous faut? (D) A quoi bon attendre? (E) Avez-vous quelque chose à déclarer?

6. Le petit était sur le point de traverser la chaussée. Par conséquent, sa mère lui a conseillé:

   (A) Fais attention aux voitures! (B) Ote le chapeau. (C) Marche dans les égouts. (D) Peigne-toi. (E) Fais la queue!

7. Après avoir déjeuné, M. Lebrun a appelé le garçon et lui a dit:

   (A) Ayez la bonté de me donner la paille. (B) Veuillez m'apporter des cendres. (C) Où est mon pourboire? (D) L'addition, s'il vous plaît. (E) Apportez-moi une nappe.

8. Puisque l'homme était sur le point de se noyer, il a crié:

   (A) Au feu! (B) Au plaisir! (C) Au secours! (D) De bonne heure! (E) A merveille!

9. La jeune fille s'approche timidement du guichet et demande:

   (A) Quel âge avez-vous? (B) A quelle heure peut-on déjeuner? (C) Est-ce que j'ai fait beaucoup de fautes? (D) Est-ce ici où l'on prend les billets? (E) Quelle est la leçon de demain?

10. J'étais enchanté de voir arriver le facteur, surtout quand il m'a dit:

    (A) Votre seau est maintenant vide. (B) Je vais toucher un chèque. (C) Il n'y a pas de chauffage central. (D) Cette maison est à vendre. (E) Voici votre courrier.

11. Nous attendions Guillaume pendant une heure. Tout à coup le téléphone a sonné, et j'ai reconnu la voix de Guillaume. Il a expliqué:

    (A) Je suis en panne. (B) Je n'ai pas de cuiller. (C) Je prends de l'embonpoint. (D) Je dois me moucher. (E) Je vous suis très reconnaissant.

12. Elle m'a passé le veau en disant:

    (A) Ce costume vous ira bien. (B) Comment trouvez-vous cette plante? (C) Servez-vous, je vous en prie. (D) Prenez garde à la peinture. (E) Lavez le plancher, s'il vous plaît.

13. Nous flânions sur le quai. J'ai demandé à un bouquiniste:

    (A) Avec quoi fait-on ce pain? (B) Avez-vous des chaussures noires à me montrer? (C) C'est combien ce pot de fleurs? (D) Pouvez-vous me vendre un paquet de cigarettes? (E) Puis-je regarder ce livre d'occasion?

14. Quand un train est sur le point de partir, on crie:

    (A) Déchirez les billets! (B) En voiture! (C) Baissez le store! (D) Entrez, s'il vous plaît. (E) Sauvez-vous!

15. Martin avait été très gentil envers moi. Je lui ai dit:

    (A) Je vous en veux. (B) Vous m'avez donc trahi! (C) Je vous en sais bon gré. (D) Sauve qui peut. (E) Comme vous êtes bête!

16. C'est la fin de l'entracte, et la pièce est très amusante. Vous dites à votre camarade:

    (A) La pièce va commencer tout de suite. (B) Qu'allons-nous faire maintenant? (C) Allons reprendre nos places. (D) Voulez-vous aller fumer une cigarette? (E) Si nous allions au cinéma?

17. Le monsieur, ayant porté son linge chez la blanchisseuse, lui a dit:

    (A) J'ai besoin d'une taille de cheveux. (B) Il faut laver ces chemises à l'eau tiède. (C) Nous aimons le fromage que vous vendez. (D) Cette montre ne marche pas bien. (E) Voulez-vous développer ces pellicules?

18. Quand elle a éternué, tout le monde a dit:

    (A) Encore des plaintes! (B) Ni nous non plus. (C) Ne dites pas de mensonges. (D) A vos souhaits! (E) Soyez la bienvenue!

19. Il est évident qu'elle n'en peut plus. Comment le savez-vous?

    (A) Elle tient à se reposer. (B) Elle veut aller chez le coiffeur. (C) Elle bavarde sans cesse. (D) Elle préfère sortir. (E) Elle mange de bon appétit.

20. L'homme ne peut pas atteindre le toit de sa maison pour le peindre. Il appelle son fils et lui dit:

    (A) Va me chercher une échelle. (B) Donne-moi ce balai. (C) Où est la pelle? (D) Apporte-moi un pinceau. (E) Amène-moi un témoin.

21. Le visiteur a regardé avec soin l'horaire. Il voulait savoir:

    (A) s'il allait pleuvoir. (B) le prix du repas. (C) pourquoi le moteur ne fonctionnait pas. (D) le nom du chef-d'œuvre. (E) l'heure de départ de son train.

22. Pendant les orages, la jeune fille se cachait en annonçant:

    (A) Je n'aime pas les foules. (B) La fumée me gêne. (C) Les éclairs me font peur. (D) Je ne veux pas prendre un coup de soleil. (E) Ces animaux m'effrayent.

23. Sa réponse m'a prouvé qu'il comprenait ce que j'avais expliqué. Voici ce qu'il a dit:

    (A) Je me moque de vous. (B) J'y suis. (C) Plaît-il? (D) Je peux m'en passer. (E) Je fais la sourde oreille.

24. Pourquoi ont-ils dû retourner à Paris?

    (A) Il était défendu de doubler. (B) Il n'y avait pas assez de carrefours. (C) Le pont n'était pas assez étroit. (D) Ils s'étaient trompés de chemin. (E) Il n'y avait pas de passage à niveau.

25. La dame est entrée dans un magasin pour acheter une paire de gants. Avant de lui montrer des gants, la vendeuse lui a demandé:

    (A) Avez-vous des vertiges? (B) Quelle est votre pointure? (C) Préférez-vous la natation? (D) De quelle couleur est votre menton? (E) Aimez-vous votre métier?

GRAMMAR QUESTIONS

These questions of correct usage test your ability to express yourself with reasonable accuracy in French. You are generally given an incomplete sentence in French and are asked to choose the correct answer. The completed sentence must correspond to the English equivalent given. Occasionally a whole sentence is to be translated.

1. We are leaving for Canada.

   Nous partons ______ Canada.

   (A) pour (B) au (C) pour le (D) en

2. I shall do it without his knowing it.

   Je le ferai sans ______.

   (A) qu'il le sait (B) qu'il le sache
   (C) le sachant (D) qu'il le saura

3. What happened?

   ______ est arrivé?

   (A) Qu'est-ce qui (B) Qu'
   (C) Qu'est-ce qu' (D) Qui est-ce qui

4. We shall dine as soon as she returns.

   Nous dînerons aussitôt qu'elle ______.

   (A) revienne (B) revient (C) soit revenue (D) reviendra

5. Whose hat is this?

   ______ est ce chapeau?

   (A) A qui (B) Dont (C) De qui (D) Duquel

6. If he were to do it, what would they say?

   S'il ______, qu'en diraient-ils?

   (A) était le faire (B) le ferait (C) le faisait (D) le fasse

7. He sees the skyscrapers of New York.

   Il voit les ______ de New-York.

   (A) gratte-ciel (B) grattes-ciel
   (C) gratte-ciels (D) grattes-ciels

8. Where is the house you had built?

   Où est la maison que ______?

   (A) vous avez faite construire (B) vous aviez construit
   (C) vous aviez à construire (D) vous avez fait construire

9. The merchant bought five hundred pens.

   Le marchand a acheté cinq ______ stylos.

   (A) centaines (B) cents (C) cent (D) centièmes

10. You should have seen her hat!

    Vous ______ voir son chapeau!

    (A) devez (B) avez dû (C) devriez (D) auriez dû

11. Butter costs four francs a pound.

    Le beurre coûte quatre francs ______ livre.

    (A) la (B) par (C) une (D) le

12. Do you know what we need?

    Savez-vous ______ nous avons besoin?

    (A) ce que (B) qu'est-ce que (C) ce dont (D) que

13. I have fewer than eleven.

    J'en ai moins ______.

    (A) d'onze (B) que onze (C) qu'onze (D) de onze

14. We are not the ones who spoke.

    Ce n'est pas nous qui ______ parlé.

    (A) aient (B) avons (C) ayons (D) ont

15. How long had you been studying?

    Depuis quand ______?

    (A) avez-vous étudié (B) étudiiez-vous
    (C) aviez-vous étudié (D) étudiez-vous

16. She has hardly any friends.

    (A) Elle n'a guère d'amis. (B) Elle a à peine d'amis.
    (C) Elle n'a pas à peine des amis. (D) Elle n'a guère des amis.

17. Here are the gifts that they sent each other.

    Voici les cadeaux qu'elles se sont ______.

    (A) envoyé (B) envoyés (C) envoyée (D) envoyées

18. I permitted her to sew.

    (A) Je l'ai permise de coudre. (B) Je lui ai permis de coudre.
    (C) Je lui ai permise de coudre. (D) Je l'ai permis de coudre.

19. We are always happy at home.

    On est toujours heureux chez ______.

    (A) lui (B) eux (C) soi (D) on

20. Most children like snow.

    ______ enfants aiment la neige.

    (A) La plupart des (B) Le plus d'
    (C) Le plus des (D) La plupart d'

21. Go away, Gerald.

    ______, Gérard.

    (A) Vas-en (B) Va-t'en (C) Va-t-en (D) Vas-t'en

22. The maid thanks them for it.

    La bonne ______ remercie.

    (A) leur en (B) le leur (C) les y (D) les en

23. I saw them smoking cigarettes.

    Je les ai ______ des cigarettes.

    (A) vus fumer (B) vu en fumant
    (C) vus fumants (D) vu fumer

24. We are looking for a child who writes well.

    Nous cherchons un enfant qui ______ bien.

    (A) écrit (B) écrira (C) écrive (D) écrivit

25. They finally left the country.

    Ils ont fini ______ quitter le pays.

    (A) de (B) par (C) à (D) après

Another type of grammar question has sometimes been included in the French examination. This question eliminates all use of English. It consists of a complete sentence in French with one or more words underlined. Of the five choices that follow, four may be substituted for the underlined words to form sentences that are grammatically correct but different in meaning from the original sentence. You are asked to choose the one answer that does *not* fit grammatically into the original sentence.

26. Nous avons beaucoup à faire ce matin.
 (A) mille choses (B) tant (C) des emplettes (D) rien du tout (E) une malle

27. Je suis enchanté qu'il arrive.
 (A) de vous revoir (B) qu'il ne pleut pas (C) des résultats (D) qu'elles soient arrivées (E) qu'ils parlent français

28. Dès que vous l'aurez fini, faites-le-moi savoir.
 (A) Lorsque (B) Si (C) Aussitôt que (D) Quand (E) Après que

29. Ma sœur a acheté une jolie robe.
 (A) de viande fraîche (B) des bas de nylon (C) trop de farine (D) plusieurs douzaines d'œufs (E) des petits pois

30. Nous y sommes arrivés en même temps.
 (A) ensemble (B) à temps (C) en retard (D) le lendemain (E) à la bonne heure

31. Ils lui ont dit de rester à la maison.
 (A) demandé (B) conseillé (C) prié (D) permis (E) commandé

32. Obéit-il à ses parents?
 (A) Répond-il (B) Ressemble-t-il (C) Écoute-t-il (D) Songe-t-il (E) Désobéit-il

33. Savez-vous ce dont il a besoin?
 (A) elle se servira (B) j'ai peur (C) elle se plaint (D) nous avons ri (E) il s'attendait

34. Il est possible qu'elle vende la voiture.
 (A) Il est probable (B) Son mari désire (C) Il faut (D) Nous regrettons (E) Il se peut

35. J'y vais.
 (A) suis (B) tenais (C) ai assisté (D) doute (E) jouerais

36. Nous préférons rester en ville.
 (A) Je devrai (B) Nous sommes bien aises (C) Sa mère l'a fait (D) Il vaut mieux (E) Elles espèrent

37. Il était deux heures.

(A) minuit moins quart (B) une heure précise (C) midi et demi (D) sept heures cinq (E) onze heures et quart

38. Georges danse chaque soir.

(A) tant bien que mal (B) de temps en temps (C) d'une façon magnifique (D) avec sa fiancée (E) davantage que moi

39. Je ne sais pas pourquoi il a échoué.

(A) ce qui est dans le tiroir (B) les routes françaises (C) patiner (D) la leçon pour aujourd'hui (E) qui a écrit cette lettre

40. C'était inutile.

(A) le meilleur (B) facile à faire (C) celle de Louis (D) poète (E) hier lundi

41. Philippe sait qu'il pleuvra ce soir.

(A) croit (B) espère (C) dit (D) doute (E) pense

42. Le matin il se levait tard.

(A) D'ordinaire (B) Le février (C) Le samedi (D) Quand il pleuvait (E) En hiver

43. Je viens de lui écrire une lettre.

(A) m'attends à (B) venais de (C) refuse à (D) n'ose (E) ne veux pas

44. Quand nous sommes sortis, il faisait chaud.

(A) nuit (B) du soleil (C) beau temps (D) doux (E) vent

45. J'ai commencé à lire le roman.

(A) Elle s'était amusée (B) Il a décidé (C) Je passerai l'après-midi (D) Tu as réussi (E) Je n'hésiterais pas

46. Espérez-vous qu'il le fasse?

(A) N'est-il pas évident (B) Souhaitent-ils (C) Pourquoi craignez-vous (D) Croit-elle (E) Doutent-ils

47. Je dois lui parler; elle désobéit toujours.

(A) Il vous faudra (B) On a beau (C) Il est impossible (D) J'ai à (E) Nous comptons

48. Qu'est-ce qui fait ce bruit?

(A) vous voulez dire (B) arrive (C) est tombé (D) se passait (E) les inquiète

49. Elles n'ont pas l'intention de le faire.

(A) honte de (B) assez d'argent pour (C) de quoi (D) envie de (E) temps de

50. Il ne sortira pas sans ses amis.

(A) faire ses adieux (B) argent (C) que je le voie (D) mangeant (E) l'avoir vu

VOCABULARY QUESTIONS

Although all questions are, in a sense, vocabulary questions, there are generally some questions that aim directly at testing mastery of vocabulary. Sometimes the candidate is asked to select an acceptable definition of a word; at other times, he or she is to select a word or phrase that completes a statement in a meaningful way.

Choose the correct definition.

1. ronfler

(A) satisfaire sa soif (B) faire du bruit en dormant (C) envahir un pays (D) bousculer une personne (E) punir beaucoup

2. poil

(A) éponge de mer (B) troupeaux d'animaux (C) esclave arabe (D) cheveux fins sur la peau des animaux (E) lieu où l'on fait le feu

3. méridional

(A) qui vient du Midi (B) saillant (C) qui s'éloigne peu à peu (D) entêté (E) qui mérite une récompense

4. verve

(A) carafe de cidre (B) grand immeuble (C) plante verte (D) chaleur d'imagination (E) punition sévère

5. drôle

(A) habile (B) élu (C) lointain (D) bizarre (E) pénible

6. nouer

(A) nier une dette (B) veiller sur (C) lier avec un nœud (D) enfoncer une porte (E) renoncer à quelque chose

7. vitre

(A) panneau de verre d'une fenêtre (B) coquille (C) ce qu'on mange (D) mauvais tour (E) exclamation de surprise

8. autrefois

   (A) au début (B) ailleurs (C) il y a bien longtemps (D) à cette heure (E) autrement

9. brouillard

   (A) branche d'un arbre (B) qui fait du bruit (C) brume (D) lampe de poche (E) toile de coton

10. volaille

    (A) explosion d'un volcan (B) avion moderne (C) action de prendre par force (D) distance qu'on parcourt en volant (E) oiseaux de basse-cour

11. équipage

    (A) hommes embarqués pour le service d'un navire (B) matériel (C) canotage (D) épée militaire (E) appareil cinématographique

12. interdire

    (A) parler sans cesse (B) échouer (C) refuser de faire quelque chose (D) défendre (E) interrompre

13. foudre

    (A) manque de savoir (B) instrument de musique (C) façade de maison (D) décharge électrique aérienne (E) beau papillon

14. vacarme

    (A) fromage de lait (B) bruit tumultueux (C) animal de ferme (D) costume de bal (E) exclamation de surprise

15. traîner

    (A) tirer après soi (B) fumer excessivement (C) attraper le train (D) essuyer avec une serviette (E) avaler

16. poumon

    (A) horloge (B) espèce de poisson (C) animal des forêts (D) organe de la respiration (E) wagon-lit

17. redouter

    (A) soupçonner (B) ne pas croire (C) craindre fort (D) avoir du doute (E) rebrousser chemin

18. épuisé

    (A) qui a des cornes (B) en forme de sphère (C) avec une expression douce (D) suivant (E) privé de ses ressources

19. auparavant

    (A) avant une autre chose (B) par conséquent (C) également (D) cependant (E) de parti pris

20. carnet

    (A) partie d'un meuble (B) viande (C) ouverture pour sortir (D) petit livre de notes (E) terreur soudaine

21. rosée

    (A) belle fleur (B) gouttelettes d'eau (C) trou profond (D) partie supérieure d'une salle (E) endroit pittoresque

22. naufrage

    (A) travail quotidien (B) perte d'un bateau en mer (C) tempête (D) petit manteau (E) instrument pour mesurer

23. teint

    (A) coloris du visage (B) abri portatif (C) nuance de couleurs (D) plus âgé qu'un autre (E) appliqué avec effort

24. désormais

    (A) de temps à autre (B) à peine (C) en revanche (D) à partir du moment actuel (E) d'une autre façon

25. frémir

    (A) venir de loin (B) éviter (C) trembler d'émotion (D) étouffer (E) fixer la valeur

Choose the word or phrase that completes the sentence in a meaningful way.

26. Puisqu'elle portait des vêtements noirs, nous savions qu'elle était en

    (A) nage (B) grève (C) ville (D) deuil (E) honte

27. Ils ont admiré les belles fleurs sans marcher sur la

    (A) pelouse (B) chair (C) ride (D) chaumière (E) nappe

28. Une personne qui se fâche se met en

    (A) nuage (B) orgueil (C) crainte (D) peur (E) colère

29. Pour prendre des billets, il faut faire la

    (A) place (B) queue (C) promenade (D) ligne (E) malle

30. Un rêve pénible est un

    (A) asile (B) œillet (C) matelas (D) cauchemar (E) oreiller

31. La pluie les a ______ de se promener sur l'avenue.

    (A) empêchés (B) évités (C) exigés (D) entourés
    (E) écrasés

32. La fenêtre ______ sur le jardin.

    (A) rend (B) donne (C) face (D) marche (E) porte

33. Si vous avez chaud, ______ ce tricot.

    (A) frottez (B) ôtez (C) mettez (D) habillez
    (E) chatouillez

34. Ce qui est évident ______ aux yeux.

    (A) jette (B) voit (C) monte (D) regarde (E) saute

35. Cette eau n'est ni chaude ni froide; elle est

    (A) raide (B) éteinte (C) maigre (D) tiède (E) foncée

36. Si elle n'a pas assez de sucre, elle peut m'en

    (A) prêter (B) lier (C) emprunter (D) gâter (E) lâcher

37. Mon frère a de la chance; il ______ hier soir.

    (A) l'a échappé belle (B) s'est ennuyé (C) a lavé la vaisselle
    (D) s'est peigné (E) a trempé ses vêtements

38. En me quittant, il m'a ______ la main.

    (A) apporté (B) empressé (C) serré (D) bouleversé
    (E) accablé

39. Au contraire, je l'aime bien; je ne lui en ______ pas.

    (A) peux (B) vois (C) tiens (D) hais (E) veux

40. Si tu comptes m'aider dans la cuisine, prends ce

    (A) poing (B) tablier (C) seuil (D) caillou (E) puits

41. En entendant ce chanteur remarquable, nous savions que l'oiseau était

    (A) une mouette (B) un pic (C) un rossignol (D) un moineau
    (E) un paon

42. Nous sommes entrés dans la charcuterie pour acheter des

    (A) aiguilles (B) saucissons (C) balais (D) puces (E) bagues

43. Les jeunes gens avaient décidé de dormir

    (A) à la belle étoile (B) à tout à l'heure (C) à travers champs
    (D) à l'envers (E) à perte de vue

44. En route, nous sommes descendus à ------ pour nous reposer.

(A) un coude (B) une bêtise (C) une auberge (D) un talon (E) une marée

45. Les souliers du petit étaient sales parce qu'il avait marché dans la

(A) peau (B) flèche (C) mairie (D) boue (E) ficelle

46. François n'aura pas de difficulté; il sait bien se ------ d'affaire.

(A) mettre (B) tirer (C) pousser (D) prendre (E) lever

47. Un ivrogne est un homme qui

(A) mange avec avidité (B) a la tête dépouillée de cheveux (C) mendie dans la rue (D) boit trop d'alcool (E) ne peut pas entendre

48. Le miel est produit par

(A) l'abeille (B) l'araignée (C) le homard (D) le matelot (E) la poule

49. On fabrique des machines dans cette

(A) averse (B) roue (C) ampoule (D) lutte (E) usine

50. Nous entendons constamment le bruit des camions parce que nous demeurons

(A) sur-le-champ (B) à l'abri du vent (C) au rez-de-chaussée (D) près de la plage (E) au-dessus des arbres

READING COMPREHENSION QUESTIONS

The reading passages are generally about 100 to 300 words in length. Each passage is followed by a series of questions. Some of the questions are factual, designed to test ability to extract the information given. Others deal with the total meaning of the passage or with a detail essential to full understanding of the author's point of view. Some questions may ask for inferences concerning mood, the author's attitude, or the feelings of the characters presented.

The passages may also be used to test *vocabulary in context*—idiomatic phrases or syntactical constructions that cannot be tested by ordinary grammar questions.

The first two reading passages that follow and questions 1–21 are reprinted with permission from *A Description of the College Board Achievement Tests*, published by the College Entrance Examination Board.

Par une ironie du sort, ce critique d'art qui s'était nourri, avec une admiration infatigable, de la magnificence du travail humain, devint l'esclave d'un péché tout contraire: la gourmandise. Le corps aussi a ses besoins. Flon, dont le peu de fortune et le goût du bric-à-brac lui imposaient un régime au rebours de ses goûts raffinés, avait tranché la question en allant tous les jours dîner en ville. Sa petite célébrité de connaisseur d'art à une époque où ce talent manquait, lui valait, aussi bien que son noble visage romain et son port majestueux, un couvert chez des gens pour qui le prix de vivres n'entrait pas en ligne de compte.

Mais ce qui n'avait été qu'un expédient devint bientôt une nécessité tyrannique et malsaine. Peu à peu les beaux traits devinrent flasques, l'allure d'empereur était parfois torturée par des crises de goutte. J'ose même assurer que Flon modifia parfois ces opinions sur l'art pour complaire à Mme la marquise, dont le faisan était renommé. Au début, le célibataire avait généreusement payé cette aumône gastronomique par ses propos savants, mais il n'avait pas suivi le progrès des arts avec le même intérêt qu'il accordait aux mets. Quand je l'ai connu, vers '58, ses opinions sur la peinture étaient vieux jeu. On attendait ses visites avec un manque d'impatience qui tournait à la froideur. Rien d'étonnant si, enfin, il se trouvait de plus en plus souvent dans la douloureuse obligation de prendre un pot-au-feu dans une gargote du quartier.

1. L'ironie consiste en ce que Flon

   (A) mourait de faim
   (B) oubliait l'heure des repas
   (C) a cessé de peindre
   (D) faisait seulement semblant d'aimer l'art
   (E) avait laissé son vice dominer sa personnalité

2. Flon avait un problème à résoudre parce qu'il

   (A) était trop intelligent
   (B) ne pouvait se payer les choses qu'il aimait
   (C) restait trop enfermé chez lui
   (D) avait mauvais appétit
   (E) ne savait pas faire la cuisine

3. Pour mettre fin à ses difficultés, Flon

   (A) avait décidé de se nourrir aux dépens des autres
   (B) avait vendu sa collection d'art
   (C) s'était marié avec une dame riche
   (D) était devenu connaisseur d'art
   (E) s'était mis au régime

4. L'inconvénient de la situation pour Flon, c'est que

   (A) Flon ne connaissait pas bien ses hôtes
   (B) ses hôtes voulaient qu'il fasse la cuisine
   (C) cette vie nouvelle devait l'asservir à son vice
   (D) les repas offerts n'étaient pas bons
   (E) Flon était traité avec trop de respect

5. Flon récompensait ses hôtes

   (A) en leur parlant d'art
   (B) en renonçant à sa carrière de peintre
   (C) avec le peu d'argent qu'il avait
   (D) en faisant leur portrait
   (E) en leur léguant sa collection

6. La vie mondaine de Flon

   (A) perfectionna son goût
   (B) le maintint en bonne santé
   (C) dura jusqu'à sa mort
   (D) lui assura les loisirs nécessaires à sa carrière
   (E) finit par détruire son intégrité professionelle

7. Avec le passage du temps, Flon

   (A) se plongea dans l'étude de l'art
   (B) perdit contact avec le monde de l'art
   (C) resta miraculeusement jeune
   (D) chercha les œuvres les plus rares
   (E) abandonna les marquises

8. Vers la fin de ce passage, l'auteur raconte que

   (A) les hôtes de Flon cherchaient en vain à l'éviter
   (B) les goûts de Flon devinrent plus simples
   (C) Flon se contentait de son travail
   (D) Flon fut oublié par les riches
   (E) Flon préférait les restaurants

Vous êtes venu de bien loin pour voir une ermite, me dit Mme S.; soyez le bienvenu. Je reçois peu d'étrangers, *un ou deux à peine* par année; mais votre lettre m'a plu, et j'ai désiré connaître une personne qui aimait comme moi Dieu, la nature, et la solitude. Quelque chose, d'ailleurs, me disait que nos étoiles étaient amies et que nous nous conviendrions mutuellement. Je vois avec plaisir que mon pressentiment ne m'a pas trompée, et vos traits que je vois maintenant et le seul bruit de vos pas, pendant que vous traversiez le corridor, m'en ont assez appris sur vous que je ne me repente pas d'avoir voulu vous voir.

9. *un ou deux à peine*

   (A) one or two with difficulty
   (B) one or two who are troubled
   (C) one or two nevertheless
   (D) not more than one or two
   (E) only one or two unfortunately

10. Mme S. a invité l'auteur

    (A) parce qu'elle le connaissait depuis longtemps
    (B) parce qu'elle avait souvent entendu parler de lui
    (C) parce qu'il était venu de loin
    (D) parce qu'elle avait deviné par sa lettre qu'il lui serait sympathique
    (E) parce qu'elle n'aurait pu faire autrement

11. Le pressentiment de Mme S. lui a dit

    (A) qu'ils étaient prédestinés à se plaire l'un à l'autre
    (B) que ses amies conviendraient à son visiteur
    (C) qu'elle allait recevoir une lettre de l'étranger
    (D) que l'auteur allait arriver
    (E) que son visiteur aimait Dieu, la nature, et la solitude

12. Avant de parler, l'auteur a déjà fait une bonne impression par la façon dont il

    (A) regarde Mme S.
    (B) est habillé
    (C) sourit
    (D) s'incline devant Mme S.
    (E) marche

13. On devine que ces deux personnes vont parler surtout

    (A) de l'astronomie
    (B) de la philosophie
    (C) de leurs amis
    (D) des voyages
    (E) des affaires

Je ne conçois qu'une manière de voyager plus agréable que d'aller à cheval, c'est d'aller à pied. On part à son moment, on s'arrête *à sa volonté,* on fait tant et si peu d'exercice qu'on veut. On observe tout le pays; on examine *tout ce qui nous flatte;* on s'arrête à tous les points de vue. Si j'aperçois une rivière, je la suis; un bois touffu, je vais sous son ombre; une grotte, je la visite. Partout où je me plais, j'y reste; à l'instant que je m'ennuie, je m'en vais. Je n'ai pas besoin de choisir des chemins tout faits, des routes commodes; je passe partout où un homme peut passer; je vois tout ce qu'un homme peut voir; et, ne dépendant que de moi-même, *je jouis de* toute la liberté dont un homme peut jouir.

J'ai peine à comprendre comment un philosophe peut se résoudre à voyager autrement, et s'arracher à l'examen des richesses que la terre prodigue à sa vue. Qui est-ce qui, ayant un peu de goût pour l'histoire naturelle, peut se résoudre à passer un terrain sans l'examiner, des cailloux sans chercher des fossiles?

Combien de plaisirs différents on rassemble par cette agréable manière de voyager! J'ai toujours vu ceux qui voyageaient dans de bonnes voitures bien douces, rêveurs, tristes, grondants et souffrants; et les *piétons* toujours gais, légers et contents de tout.

14. *à sa volonté*

(A) at the proper time
(B) to rest
(C) when one wishes
(D) at one's destination
(E) at one's goal

15. *tout ce qui nous flatte*

(A) everything that weighs upon us
(B) everything that surrounds us
(C) everything that strikes us
(D) everything that is visible to us
(E) everything that delights us

16. *je jouis de*

(A) I enjoy
(B) I need
(C) I use
(D) I realize
(E) I possess

17. *piétons*

(A) peddlers
(B) travelers
(C) pious ones
(D) pedestrians
(E) horsemen

18. L'auteur dit

(A) que la meilleure façon de voyager est à cheval
(B) qu'il ne monte jamais à cheval
(C) qu'il est agréable de voyager à cheval
(D) qu'il n'aime pas l'exercice
(E) qu'il fait peu d'exercice

19. Quand l'auteur voyage,

(A) il s'ennuie souvent
(B) il visite ce qui lui plaît
(C) il s'amuse partout
(D) il préfère les routes commodes
(E) il dépend d'un guide

20. En voyageant à pied,

(A) on n'a pas le temps de s'arrêter
(B) on observe peu
(C) on est souffrant
(D) on court beaucoup de risques
(E) on a l'occasion d'examiner le paysage

21. L'auteur a remarqué que

(A) les philosophes préfèrent rester chez eux
(B) les gens qui voyagent en voiture sont souvent de mauvaise humeur
(C) seulement les gens riches ont assez de liberté
(D) les voitures confortables font trop de bruit
(E) d'ordinaire les philosophes choisissent les chemins tout faits

SPECIAL VERB FORMS

IRREGULAR VERBS

INFINITIVE	PRESENT PARTICIPLE	PAST PARTICIPLE	PRESENT INDICATIVE	PASSÉ SIMPLE	FUTURE	PRESENT SUBJUNCTIVE
aller	allant	allé (*with* être)	je vais tu vas il va nous allons vous allez ils vont	j'allai	j'irai	j'aille tu ailles il aille nous allions vous alliez ils aillent
s'asseoir	s'asseyant	assis	je m'assieds tu t'assieds il s'assied nous nous asseyons vous vous asseyez ils s'asseyent	je m'assis	je m'assiériai je m'assoirai	je m'asseye
atteindre	(*See* peindre)					
avoir	ayant	eu	j'ai tu as il a nous avons vous avez ils ont	j'eus	j'aurai	j'aie tu aies il ait nous ayons vous ayez ils aient
battre	battant	battu	je bats tu bats il bat nous battons vous battez ils battent	je battis	je battrai	je batte

INFINITIVE	PRESENT PARTICIPLE	PAST PARTICIPLE	PRESENT INDICATIVE	PASSÉ SIMPLE	FUTURE	PRESENT SUBJUNCTIVE
boire	buvant	bu	je bois tu bois il boit nous buvons vous buvez ils boivent	je bus	je boirai	je boive tu boives il boive nous buvions vous buviez ils boivent
conduire	conduisant	conduit	je conduis tu conduis il conduit nous conduisons vous conduisez ils conduisent	je conduisis	je conduirai	je conduise
connaître	connaissant	connu	je connais tu connais il connaît nous connaissons vous connaissez ils connaissent	je connus	je connaîtrai	je connaisse
construire	(*See* conduire)					
courir	courant	couru	je cours tu cours il court nous courons vous courez ils courent	je courus	je courrai	je coure
couvrir	(*See* ouvrir)					

craindre	craignant	craint	je crains tu crains il craint nous craignons vous craignez ils craignent	je craignis	je craindrai	je craigne
croire	croyant	cru	je crois tu crois il croit nous croyons vous croyez ils croient	je crus	je croirai	je croie tu croies il croie nous croyions vous croyiez ils croient
décrire	(*See* écrire)					
devoir	devant	dû, due dus, dues	je dois tu dois il doit nous devons vous devez ils doivent	je dus	je devrai	je doive tu doives il doive nous devions vous deviez ils doivent
dire	disant	dit	je dis tu dis il dit nous disons vous dites ils disent	je dis	je dirai	je dise
dormir	dormant	dormi	je dors tu dors il dort nous dormons vous dormez ils dorment	je dormis	je dormirai	je dorme

INFINITIVE	PRESENT PARTICIPLE	PAST PARTICIPLE	PRESENT INDICATIVE	PASSÉ SIMPLE	FUTURE	PRESENT SUBJUNCTIVE
écrire	écrivant	écrit	j'écris tu écris il écrit nous écrivons vous écrivez ils écrivent	j'écrivis	j'écrirai	j'écrive
envoyer	envoyant	envoyé	j'envoie tu envoies il envoie nous envoyons vous envoyez ils envoient	j'envoyai	j'enverrai	j'envoie tu envoies il envoie nous envoyions vous envoyiez ils envoient
éteindre	(*See* peindre)					
être	étant	été	je suis tu es il est nous sommes vous êtes ils sont	je fus	je serai	je sois tu sois il soit nous soyons vous soyez ils soient
faire	faisant	fait	je fais tu fais il fait nous faisons vous faites ils font	je fis	je ferai	je fasse
falloir		fallu	il faut	il fallut	il faudra	il faille

joindre	joignant	joint	je joins tu joins il joint nous joignons vous joignez ils joignent	je joignis	je joindrai	je joigne
lire	lisant	lu	je lis tu lis il lit nous lisons vous lisez ils lisent	je lus	je lirai	je lise
mentir	(*See* sentir)					
mettre	mettant	mis	je mets tu mets il met nous mettons vous mettez ils mettent	je mis	je mettrai	je mette
mourir	mourant	mort (*with* être)	je meurs tu meurs il meurt nous mourons vous mourez ils meurent	je mourus	je mourrai	je meure tu meures il meure nous mourions vous mouriez ils meurent
naître	naissant	né (*with* être)	je nais tu nais il naît nous naissons vous naissez ils naissent	je naquis	je naîtrai	je naisse

INFINITIVE	PRESENT PARTICIPLE	PAST PARTICIPLE	PRESENT INDICATIVE	PASSÉ SIMPLE	FUTURE	PRESENT SUBJUNCTIVE
offrir	offrant	offert	j'offre tu offres il offre nous offrons vous offrez ils offrent	j'offris	j'offrirai	j'offre
ouvrir	ouvrant	ouvert	j'ouvre tu ouvres il ouvre nous ouvrons vous ouvrez ils ouvrent	j'ouvris	j'ouvrirai	j'ouvre
paraître	paraissant	paru	je parais tu parais il paraît nous paraissons vous paraissez ils paraissent	je parus	je paraîtrai	je paraisse
partir	partant	parti (*with* être)	je pars tu pars il part nous partons vous partez ils partent	je partis	je partirai	je parte

peindre	peignant	peint	je peins tu peins il peint nous peignons vous peignez ils peignent	je peignis	je peindrai	je peigne
plaindre	(*See* craindre)					
plaire	plaisant	plu	je plais tu plais il plaît nous plaisons vous plaisez ils plaisent	je plus	je plairai	je plaise
pleuvoir	pleuvant	plu	il pleut	il plut	il pleuvra	il pleuve
pouvoir	pouvant	pu	je peux (puis) tu peux il peut nous pouvons vous pouvez ils peuvent	je pus	je pourrai	je puisse
prendre	prenant	pris	je prends tu prends il prend nous prenons vous prenez ils prennent	je pris	je prendrai	je prenne tu prennes il prenne nous prenions vous preniez ils prennent
produire	(*See* conduire)					

INFINITIVE	PRESENT PARTICIPLE	PAST PARTICIPLE	PRESENT INDICATIVE	PASSÉ SIMPLE	FUTURE	PRESENT SUBJUNCTIVE
recevoir	recevant	reçu	je reçois tu reçois il reçoit nous recevons vous recevez ils reçoivent	je reçus	je recevrai	je reçoive tu reçoives il reçoive nous recevions vous receviez ils reçoivent
rire	riant	ri	je ris tu ris il rit nous rions vous riez ils rient	je ris	je rirai	je rie tu ries il rie nous riions vous riiez ils rient
savoir	sachant	su	je sais tu sais il sait nous savons vous savez ils savent	je sus	je saurai	je sache
sentir	sentant	senti	je sens tu sens il sent nous sentons vous sentez ils sentent	je sentis	je sentirai	je sente
servir	servant	servi	je sers tu sers il sert nous servons vous servez ils servent	je servis	je servirai	je serve

sortir	sortant	sorti (*with* être)	je sors tu sors il sort nous sortons vous sortez ils sortent	je sortis	je sortirai	je sorte
souffrir	(*See* offrir)					
suivre	suivant	suivi	je suis tu suis il suit nous suivons vous suivez ils suivent	je suivis	je suivrai	je suive
se taire	se taisant	tu	je me tais tu te tais il se tait nous nous taisons vous vous taisez ils se taisent	je me tus	je me tairai	je me taise
tenir	tenant	tenu	je tiens tu tiens il tient nous tenons vous tenez ils tiennent	je tins tu tins il tint nous tînmes vous tîntes ils tinrent	je tiendrai	je tienne tu tiennes il tienne nous tenions vous teniez ils tiennent
traduire	traduisant	traduit	je traduis tu traduis il traduit nous traduisons vous traduisez ils traduisent	je traduisis	je traduirai	je traduise

INFINITIVE	PRESENT PARTICIPLE	PAST PARTICIPLE	PRESENT INDICATIVE	PASSÉ SIMPLE	FUTURE	PRESENT SUBJUNCTIVE
valoir	valant	valu	je vaux tu vaux il vaut nous valons vous valez ils valent	je valus	je vaudrai	je vaille tu vailles il vaille nous valions vous valiez ils vaillent
venir	venant	venu (*with* être)	je viens tu viens il vient nous venons vous venez ils viennent	je vins tu vins il vint nous vînmes vous vîntes ils vinrent	je viendrai	je vienne tu viennes il vienne nous venions vous veniez ils viennent
vivre	vivant	vécu	je vis tu vis il vit nous vivons vous vivez ils vivent	je vécus	je vivrai	je vive
voir	voyant	vu	je vois tu vois il voit nous voyons vous voyez ils voient	je vis	je verrai	je voie tu voies il voie nous voyions vous voyiez ils voient

vouloir	voulant	voulu	je veux tu veux il veut nous voulons vous voulez ils veulent	je voulus	je voudrai	je veuille tu veuilles il veuille nous voulions vous vouliez ils veuillent

PATTERNS OF ORTHOGRAPHIC-CHANGING VERBS

INFINITIVE	PRESENT PARTICIPLE	PAST PARTICIPLE	PRESENT INDICATIVE	PASSÉ SIMPLE	FUTURE	PRESENT SUBJUNCTIVE
mener	menant	mené	je mène tu mènes il mène nous menons vous menez ils mènent	je menai	je mènerai	je mène tu mènes il mène nous menions vous meniez ils mènent
appeler	appelant	appelé	j'appelle tu appelles il appelle nous appelons vous appelez ils appellent	j'appelai	j'appellerai	j'appelle tu appelles il appelle nous appelions vous appeliez ils appellent
jeter	jetant	jeté	je jette tu jettes il jette nous jetons vous jetez ils jettent	je jetai	je jetterai	je jette tu jettes il jette nous jetions vous jetiez ils jettent

INFINITIVE	PRESENT PARTICIPLE	PAST PARTICIPLE	PRESENT INDICATIVE	PASSÉ SIMPLE	FUTURE	PRESENT SUBJUNCTIVE
espérer	espérant	espéré	j'espère	j'espérai	j'espérerai	j'espère
			tu espères			tu espères
			il espère			il espère
			nous espérons			nous espérions
			vous espérez			vous espériez
			ils espèrent			ils espèrent
employer	employant	employé	j'emploie	j'employai	j'emploierai	j'emploie
			tu emploies			tu emploies
			il emploie			il emploie
			nous employons			nous employions
			vous employez			vous employiez
			ils emploient			ils emploient
prononcer	prononçant	prononcé	je prononce	je prononçai	je prononcerai	je prononce
			tu prononces	tu prononças		
			il prononce	il prononça		
			nous prononçons	nous prononçâmes		
			vous prononcez	vous prononçâtes		
			ils prononcent	ils prononcèrent		
voyager	voyageant	voyagé	je voyage	je voyageai	je voyagerai	je voyage
			tu voyages	tu voyageas		
			il voyage	il voyagea		
			nous voyageons	nous voyageâmes		
			vous voyagez	vous voyageâtes		
			ils voyagent	ils voyagèrent		

AUDITORY COMPREHENSION

(QUESTIONS AND ALTERNATIVES)

After the reading of each paragraph by the Teacher, write the *number* of the alternative that best answers each question. Base your answers only on the content of the paragraph.

1. Pourquoi cette personne aime-t-elle écouter la musique de ce compositeur?
   1 On n'a pas besoin de se taire.
   2 Cette musique est très douce.
   3 Sa musique est brillante.
   4 C'est une musique qui semble lui parler.

2. Qu'est-ce qui irrite ces hommes?
   1 la circulation formidable de la capitale française
   2 les demandes indiscrètes des clients
   3 les conseils du Préfet de la Seine
   4 la pensée d'avoir à porter un costume spécial

3. Dans quel domaine cet homme a-t-il une aptitude spéciale?
   1 en peinture 2 en musique 3 en sport 4 en poésie

4. Pour quelle raison a-t-on applaudi?
   1 Le roi assistait à la célébration.
   2 Les princesses se joignaient au peuple.
   3 Les demoiselles portaient leurs robes royales.
   4 Les filles du roi dansaient avec grâce.

5. Où ce spectacle a-t-il lieu?
   1 au théâtre 2 au cirque 3 aux jeux Olympiques 4 au cinéma

6. Quelle difficulté ce jeune homme a-t-il?
   1 Il voudrait quitter son lycée pour chercher un emploi.
   2 Quand il parle à une jeune fille, elle ne lui répond pas.
   3 Il n'ose pas faire la connaissance d'une certaine personne.
   4 Il a une maladie de cœur.

7. Dans quelles conditions doit-on choisir ce sport?
   1 Si on est petit.
   2 Si on est nerveux.
   3 Si on est de nature lente.
   4 Si on n'est pas sûr de soi.

8. Comment ce jeune homme trouvait-il ses classes?
   1 Il ne les aimait pas.
   2 Il les trouvait faciles.
   3 Il devait y travailler dur.
   4 Il avait beau essayer, il ne réussissait pas.

9. Quel avantage ces cartes offrent-elles?
   1 Elles sont d'une beauté extraordinaire.
   2 Elles ne voleront pas.
   3 On ne peut pas les détruire.
   4 Elles sont plus faciles à lire.

10. Qu'est-ce qui dérangeait ce chien?
   1 l'odeur qu'il sentait
   2 ce qu'il voyait
   3 le bruit qu'il entendait
   4 l'espion derrière le rideau

11. Comment cette nouveauté aidera-t-elle le golfeur?
   1 Elle permettra au joueur de retrouver son sang-froid.
   2 Il se fâchera moins souvent.
   3 Le mauvais joueur pourra faire des progrès plus rapides.
   4 Elle épargnera au golfeur beaucoup d'effort.

12. Qu'est-ce qu'on peut dire au sujet de ces trois hommes?
   1 Ils se connaissent en agriculture.
   2 Ils se passionnent pour l'alpinisme.
   3 Ils manquent de courage.
   4 Ils aiment les températures froides.

13. A quoi cette salle de classe ressemble-t-elle?
   1 à un théâtre
   2 à un tribunal
   3 à une place publique
   4 à un château

14. Selon cet article, qu'est-ce que tout le monde devrait savoir?
   1 guérir un blessé
   2 appeler un agent de police en cas d'urgence
   3 prévenir un accident sérieux
   4 soulager la douleur de quelqu'un qui s'est fait mal

15. Qu'est-ce que ces quatre hommes essayaient de faire?
   1 de voler une nouvelle automobile
   2 d'emporter un appareil photographique
   3 de faire la connaissance d'un savant
   4 d'obtenir des renseignements secrets

16. Comment cet homme d'affaires a-t-il fait de la publicité pour son produit?
   1 Il a traversé un lac à la nage.
   2 Il a fait flotter un bouchon.
   3 Il a lancé son auto dans l'eau.
   4 Il a jeté quelque matière dans le lac.

17. Pourquoi fait-on ces recherches?
   1 pour retrouver un trésor perdu
   2 pour augmenter nos ressources industrielles
   3 pour mieux nourrir l'humanité
   4 afin de retrouver des hommes disparus

18. Qu'est-ce qu'il y a de différent dans la façon de vivre de ces animaux?
1 Des animaux domestiques s'accordent avec des animaux sauvages.
2 Ils n'ont pas de cages.
3 Toutes ces bêtes ont les mêmes habitudes.
4 Leur façon de vivre ressemble à celle de leur maître.

19. Quel moyen va-t-on utiliser pour résoudre ce problème?
1 la chaleur 2 la faim 3 la soif 4 l'extinction

20. Pourquoi y a-t-il tant de familles sans foyer dans ce village européen?
1 Une avalanche inattendue y est descendue.
2 Un vent violent a abattu leur logis.
3 Le village a été inondé.
4 Des incendies ont détruit leurs maisons.

21. A quoi sert cette nouvelle méthode?
1 à empêcher des accidents
2 à sauver des vies humaines
3 à exercer le corps humain
4 à remplacer le médecin

22. Qu'est-ce que cette femme a remarqué pendant son voyage?
1 que la vie aux États-Unis coûte cher
2 que les Américains sont tout à fait aimables
3 que le pays est plus grand qu'elle ne le croyait
4 que les touristes européens manquent souvent d'intelligence

23. Qu'est-ce qui a émerveillé la foule?
1 que le chien s'efforçait de chercher l'objet
2 que l'animal pouvait accomplir le fait en marchant
3 que la bête pesait si peu
4 que l'animal ne savait pas nager

24. Selon cet article, quelle est la récompense d'avoir obtenu le baccalauréat?
1 un emploi excellent
2 une vie joyeuse
3 un meilleur salaire
4 une vie plus longue

25. Qu'est-ce que cette innovation permettra au sportif?
1 d'avancer plus rapidement 3 de s'élever dans les airs
2 d'éviter les risques 4 de devenir plus expert

26. Pourquoi le directeur va-t-il commander deux de ces machines?
1 La machine est garantie pour longtemps.
2 Le directeur veut que tout le travail soit fait.
3 L'usine est vaste.
4 Le prix des machines est bien raisonnable.

27. A quel égard cet animal est-il anormal?
 1 Il a une maladie rare.
 2 Il sait bien nager.
 3 Il porte des vêtements.
 4 Il aime se baigner.

28. Que faisait ce jeune homme juste avant sa mort?
 1 Il conduisait une auto.
 2 Il pilotait son avion.
 3 Il participait à un match international.
 4 Il se lançait vers le soleil.

29. Quelle est l'importance de cette machine?
 1 On peut la reproduire facilement.
 2 Elle facilite le nettoyage des fenêtres.
 3 Elle vous aide à dormir.
 4 Elle empêche que la pluie vous dérange.

30. Qu'est-ce qu'on affirme dans cet article?
 1 que les femmes sont de meilleurs chauffeurs que les hommes
 2 que les hommes causent la plupart des accidents
 3 que les femmes ont peu de talent en ce qui concerne les automobiles
 4 que les femmes qui conduisent se moquent des hommes

31. Pour quelle raison a-t-on fermé cette école?
 1 Les clients s'en plaignaient.
 2 On s'y amusait trop.
 3 L'appareil nécessaire y manquait.
 4 La plupart des élèves échouaient à l'examen.

32. Quelle qualité de ce musicien se révèle tout de suite?
 1 sa méthode d'organisation
 2 son charme
 3 la façon dont il joue
 4 sa connaissance de toute sorte de musique

33. Qu'est-ce que cet homme souhaite faire?
 1 se faire instruire
 2 cultiver son jardin
 3 devenir boucher
 4 étudier l'agriculture

34. Pourquoi ce rêve dérange-t-il Lili?
 1 parce qu'elle perd de beaux cadeaux
 2 parce qu'elle croit entendre du bruit
 3 parce que la porte de sa chambre est souvent ouverte
 4 parce que le Père Noël laisse tomber ses colis

35. Que désire faire cette jeune fille?
 1 aller chez une amie
 2 rester seule dans sa chambre
 3 travailler dur
 4 avoir de l'indépendance

36. A quoi ces deux personnes doivent-elles leur rencontre?
1 à leur jeunesse
2 à un navire
3 à un sport
4 aux vagues de la mer

37. Pourquoi cette école jouit-elle d'une immense popularité?
1 parce que les élèves n'ont pas besoin d'étudier
2 parce que les classes sont petites
3 parce qu'on y trouve des activités variées
4 parce que les leçons sont fort intéressantes

38. Qu'est-ce qu'on voulait prouver dans cette expérience?
1 que ce nouveau produit ne se brise pas
2 que le cristal solide ne résiste pas à toutes sortes de forces
3 que le café est aussi bon dans un verre que dans une tasse
4 que le verre et le métal ont des qualités semblables

39. A quoi rêve chacun de ces jeunes gens?
1 à posséder un hôtel pareil
2 à passer du temps dans un bel appartement
3 à devenir acteur
4 à faire la connaissance d'une princesse

40. Pourquoi recommande-t-on ce plat?
1 parce qu'il évite le travail excessif
2 parce que même les malades le trouvent délicieux
3 parce que c'est bon marché
4 parce qu'on peut le préparer pour n'importe quel repas

41. De quoi cette jeune fille se plaint-elle?
1 de ne pas plaire aux garçons
2 de suivre des cours difficiles
3 d'avoir peu d'amies
4 de n'avoir pas assez d'argent

42. A quoi pourrait servir cet objet extraordinaire?
1 à nourrir une famille nombreuse
2 à bâtir des édifices dans le village
3 à vérifier l'heure exacte
4 à prévenir les accidents

43. Qu'est-ce que ce savant a découvert?
1 un moyen de faire pousser des plantes sans eau
2 une méthode d'augmenter la résistance des plantes à la chaleur
3 une façon de stimuler la croissance de grosses feuilles
4 une technique pour acclimater les plantes aux pays froids

44. Quelle considération a influencé cette décision?
1 le manque d'ouvriers
2 la vie de famille
3 le désir de la paix
4 l'abondance de travailleurs

45. Pourquoi cet oiseau est-il si recherché?
1 parce qu'il chante à merveille
2 parce qu'on peut lui enseigner à parler
3 parce que la couleur de ses plumes est magnifique
4 parce qu'il préfère manger des insectes

46. Qu'est-ce qui a mis en colère l'automobiliste?
1 qu'on l'a blessé
2 que le poisson s'est échappé
3 qu'il a perdu son pistolet
4 qu'on a failli le tuer

47. Quel problème grave nous confronte, selon cet article?
1 le grand nombre de fabriques démodées
2 la consommation d'énergie électrique
3 l'équilibre entre l'homme et la machine
4 la création de nouvelles machines

48. Qu'est-ce qui a retardé le départ de cet avion?
1 Il fallait réparer une aile de l'avion.
2 L'avion était en panne d'essence.
3 Le pilote a découvert un nid d'oiseau.
4 Des moineaux volaient devant l'avion.

49. Pourquoi Mme Laval n'est-elle plus inquiète?
1 Elle connaît sa visiteuse.
2 Elle est trop fatiguée.
3 Sa fille la protège.
4 Elle ne croit plus aux fantômes.

50. Quel est le but de cette entreprise?
1 de venir en aide aux malades
2 d'organiser les professions en France
3 d'encourager des recherches humanitaires
4 de lancer des jeunes gens dans leur métier préféré

FRENCH-ENGLISH VOCABULARY

abaisser, to lower, reduce
abeille (*f.*), bee
abord: **d'abord**, at first, first
abricot (*m.*), apricot
accueil (*m.*), welcome, reception
acheter, to buy
acier (*m.*), steel
acquérir (*p.p.* **acquis**), to acquire
actuellement, now, at the present time
addition (*f.*), check
adresse (*f.*), address
affaire (*f.*), affair, matter
affaires (*f. pl.*), business
agent (*m.*) **de police**, policeman
aigle (*m.*), eagle
aile (*f.*), wing
aimable, kind
ainsi que, as well as
aliment (*m.*), food
alimentation (*f.*), feeding, food
alimenter, to feed
Allemagne (*f.*), Germany
allemand, German
allumette (*f.*), match
alors, then
alouette (*f.*), lark
alpinisme (*m.*), mountain climbing
âme (*f.*), soul
amincir, to make thinner
amitié (*f.*), friendship
amour (*m.*), love
an (*m.*), year
ancien, ancienne, old, ancient, former
André, Andrew
âne (*m.*), donkey
Angleterre (*f.*), England
année (*f.*), year
anniversaire (*m.*), **de naissance**, birthday
Antoine, Anthony
appartenir, to belong
appeler, to call; **s'appeler**, to be called
apporter, to bring
apprendre, to learn
approcher: **s'approcher (de)**, to approach
après-midi (*m.*), afternoon
argent (*m.*), silver, money
armée (*f.*), army
armoire (*f.*), closet
arracher, to pull out
arrêter, to stop
arrivée (*f.*), arrival
arriver, to arrive; happen
ascenseur (*m.*), elevator
assez (de), enough
assiette (*f.*), plate
assis, seated
attendre, to wait (for)
attirer, to attract
attraper, to catch
au-delà de, beyond
aussitôt que, as soon as
autant (de), as much, as many
avant, before
avenir (*m.*), future
aveugle, blind
avion (*m.*), airplane
avis (*m.*), opinion
avocat (*m.*), lawyer

bagages (*m. pl.*), baggage
bague (*f.*), ring
bain (*m.*), bath
baisser, to lower
bal (*m.*), dance
balle (*f.*), ball
banc (*m.*), bench
barbe (*f.*), beard
bas (*m.*), stocking
bas, basse, low
bataille (*f.*), battle
bateau (*m.*), boat
bâtiment (*m.*), building
bâtir, to build
bâton (*m.*), stick
beau, bel, belle, beautiful, fine, handsome
beaucoup (de), much, many
beau-père (*m.*), father-in-law
beauté (*f.*), beauty
bébé (*m.*), baby
bénir, to bless
bergère (*f.*), shepherdess
beurre (*m.*), butter
bibliothèque (*f.*), library
bientôt, soon
bière (*f.*), beer
bijou (*m.*), jewel
billet (*m.*), ticket
blanchisserie (*f.*), laundry
blé (*m.*), wheat
blesser: **se blesser**, to get hurt
bœuf (*m.*), ox, beef
boire, to drink
bois (*m.*), wood
boîte (*f.*), box
bonbon (*m.*), candy
bonheur (*m.*), happiness
bonne (*f.*), maid
bonté (*f.*), goodness, kindness
bord (*m.*) **de la mer**, seashore
borner, to limit, form a boundary
bouche (*f.*), mouth
boucher (*m.*), butcher
boucherie (*f.*), butcher store
boulanger (*m.*), baker
boulangerie (*f.*), bakery
bouteille (*f.*), bottle
boutique (*f.*), shop
bras (*m.*), arm
brave, brave, fine
brebis (*f.*), sheep
briller, to shine

brique (*f.*), brick
brosse (*f.*), brush
brosser, to brush
bruit (*m.*), noise
brun, brown
bureau (*m.*), desk; office
bureau (*m.*) **de poste**, post office
but (*m.*), goal
butte (*f.*), mound, hillock

cadeau (*m.*), gift, present
calendrier (*m.*), calendar
camarade (*m.*), comrade
camion (*m.*), truck
campagne (*f.*), country
canapé (*m.*), sofa
canif (*m.*), penknife
cantique (*m.*), carol, hymn
car, for, because
carré, square
carte (*f.*), map, card, menu
cas (*m.*), case
casquette (*f.*), cap
casser, to break
casserole (*f.*), pot
causer, to chat, cause
cave (*f.*), cellar
Cendrillon, Cinderella
cercle (*m.*), club
cerise (*f.*), cherry
cesser, to stop
chambre (*f.*) **à coucher**, bedroom
champ (*m.*), field
chance (*f.*), luck
chanter, to sing, to crow
chapitre (*m.*), chapter
chaque, each
charbon (*m.*), coal
chasse (*f.*), hunting
chat (*m.*), cat
chauffer, to warm, heat
chaussette (*f.*), sock
chaussures (*f. pl.*), shoes, footwear
chef (*m.*), head, leader
chef-d'œuvre (*m.*), masterpiece
chemin (*m.*), road
chemin (*m.*) **de fer**, railroad
cheminée (*f.*), chimney, fireplace, mantelpiece
chemise (*f.*), shirt
chêne (*m.*), oak
chercher, to look for
cheval (*m.*), horse
cheveux (*m. pl.*), hair
chèvre (*f.*), goat
chien (*m.*) **de garde**, watchdog
chiffre (*m.*), number
choisir, to choose
choix (*m.*), choice
chose (*f.*), thing
chou (*m.*), cabbage
choux de Bruxelles, Brussels sprouts
chute (*f.*), fall
ciel (*m.*), sky, heaven
cigogne (*f.*), stork
cinéma (*m.*), movie theatre, movies
circulation (*f.*), traffic
cirque (*m.*), circus
citoyen, citoyenne, citizen
citron (*m.*), lemon
clair, light
clef (*f.*), key
client, cliente, customer
climatisé, air-conditioned
cloche (*f.*), bell
cochon (*m.*), pig
cœur (*m.*), heart
coiffe (*f.*), regional head-dress, peasant cap
coiffeur (*m.*), barber, hairdresser
coin (*m.*), corner
colis (*m.*), package, parcel
collier (*m.*), necklace
colline (*f.*), hill
combien (de)?, how much, how many
comme, like, as
complet (*m.*), suit
compris: **y compris**, including
compter, to count, to intend
comte (*m.*), count
concierge (*m.* or *f.*), superintendent, doorman
conduire, to lead, drive
confiance (*f.*), confidence
connaissance (*f.*), acquaintance
conseil (*m.*), advice
conte (*m.*), short story
content, glad, pleased
coq (*m.*), rooster
corbeille (*f.*), basket
corps (*m.*), body
corriger, to correct
côte (*f.*), coast
côté (*m.*), side
coton (*m.*), cotton
cou (*m.*), neck
coucher: **se coucher**, to go to bed, lie down, set
couler, to flow
couper, to cut
cour (*f.*), court, courtyard
courir, to run
courrier (*m.*), mail
cours (*m.*), course
court, short
couteau (*m.*), knife
coûter, to cost
coutume (*f.*), custom
couvrir, to cover
craie (*f.*), chalk
crier, to shout
crise (*f.*), crisis
croire, to believe
croix (*f.*), cross
croyance (*f.*), belief
cueillir, to gather
cuiller (*f.*), spoon
cuisine (*f.*), kitchen; cooking

cuisinier, cuisinière, cook
cuivre (*m.*), copper

dame, (*f.*), lady
debout, standing
début (*m.*), beginning
décerner, to award
déchiffrer, to decipher
défense de . . ., forbidden to . . ., no . . .
déjà, already
déjeuner (*m.*), lunch
demander, to ask, ask for
demeurer, to live
dent (*f.*), tooth
dépêcher: se dépêcher, to hurry
déranger, to disturb
derrière, behind
dès que, as soon as
désolé, very sorry, distressed
dessiner, to draw
devant, in front of
devenir, to become
devoir, to owe, have to
devoirs (*m. pl.*), homework
dictée (*f.*), dictation
dire, to say, tell
directeur (*m.*), principal
disque (*m.*), record
divertissement (*m.*), entertainment
doigt (*m.*), finger
domestique (*m.* or *f.*), servant
dos (*m.*), back
douche (*f.*), shower
douleur (*f.*), pain
doux, douce, sweet, mild, gentle
douzaine (*f.*), dozen
drapeau (*m.*), flag
dresser: se dresser, to rise
dur, hard

eau (*f.*), water
éclairer, to light
écolier, écolière, schoolboy, schoolgirl
écouter, to listen (to)
écraser, to crush
écrivain (*m.*), writer
effacer, to erase
effet (*m.*), effect, result; **à cet effet**, for that purpose
église (*f.*), church
électeur (*m.*), voter
élevage (*m.*), breeding (of animals)
élevé, high; bred
embouchure (*f.*), mouth (of river)
émouvant, moving, touching
empêcher, to prevent
emplette (*f.*), purchase
emprunter, to borrow
enchanté, delighted
encore, still, yet, again
endroit (*m.*), place, spot
enlever, to remove
ennuyer: s'ennuyer, to get bored
enseignement (*m.*), teaching, education
enseigner, to teach
ensemble, together
ensuite, next, afterwards
entendre, to hear
entrée (*f.*), entrance
envahir, to invade
envelopper, to wrap
envoyer, to send
épais, thick
épaule (*f.*), shoulder
épicerie (*f.*), grocery store
épicier (*m.*), grocer
épingle (*f.*), pin
épreuve (*f.*), test, quiz
épuiser, to exhaust
escalier (*m.*), staircase
escargot (*m.*), snail
espace (*m.*), space
espèce (*f.*), kind, sort
espérer, to hope
espoir (*m.*), hope
essayer, to try, try on
essence (*f.*), gasoline
est (*m.*), east
et . . . et . . ., both . . . and . . .
étage (*m.*), story, floor
étalage (*m.*), display
état (*m.*), state
été (*m.*), summer
étendre: s'étendre, to extend, stretch
étendue (*f.*), extent, stretch, expanse
éternuer, to sneeze
Étienne, Stephen
étiquette (*f.*), label
étoffe (*f.*), material
étoile (*f.*), star
étrange, strange
étranger, foreign
être (*m.*), being
étroit, narrow
étude (*f.*), study
explication (*f.*), explanation
expliquer, to explain

fabrique (*f.*), factory
fabriquer, to manufacture
fâcher: se fâcher, to get angry
façon (*f.*), manner, fashion
facteur (*m.*), postman
faible, weak
farine (*f.*), flour
faute (*f.*), mistake
fauteuil (*m.*), armchair
faux, fausse, false
féliciter, to congratulate
femme (*f.*), woman, wife
fer (*m.*), iron
ferme (*f.*), farm
fermier (*m.*), farmer
fête (*f.*), holiday, celebration
feu (*m.*), fire

feuille (*f.*), leaf, sheet (of paper)
fidèle, faithful
fier, proud
fièvre (*f.*), fever
figure (*f.*), face
filiale (*f.*), branch, subsidiary
fille (*f.*), daughter
fils (*m.*), son
fin (*f.*), end
flâner, to stroll
fleuve (*m.*), river
foi (*f.*), faith
foie (*m.*), liver
fois (*f.*), time
foncé, dark
fontaine (*f.*), fountain, spring
forêt (*f.*), forest
forgeron (*m.*), blacksmith
formidable, terrific, tremendous
fort, strong
foule (*f.*), crowd
fourchette (*f.*), fork
frais, fraîche, fresh, cool
fraise (*f.*), strawberry
François, Francis, Frank
Françoise, Frances
fréquemment, frequently
fromage (*m.*), cheese
front (*m.*), forehead
fumer, to smoke
funiculaire (*m.*), funicular, cable railway

gagner, to win, earn
gant (*m.*), glove
garder, to keep
gare (*f.*), railroad station
gargouille (*f.*), gargoyle
garnir, to adorn, decorate
gâteau (*m.*), cake
gâter, to spoil
Gautier, Walter
géant (*m.*), giant
geler, to freeze
genou (*m.*), knee
gens (*m. pl.*), people
gentil, gentille, nice, kind
glace (*f.*), ice, ice cream; mirror
glisser, to slip, slide
gloire (*f.*), glory
gomme (*m.*), eraser
gorge (*f.*), throat
goût (*m.*), taste
goûter, to taste
grâce à, thanks to
gras, grasse, fat
gratte-ciel (*m.*), sky-scraper
grave, serious
gris, gray
gronder, to scold
gros, grosse, big, stout
guérir, to cure
guerre (*f.*), war
guichet (*m.*), ticket window

habile, skillful
habiller: s'habiller, to dress (oneself), get dressed
habitant (*m.*), inhabitant
habiter, to live in
habits (*m. pl.*), clothes
habitude (*f.*), habit
haricots verts (*m. pl.*), string beans
haut, high, loud
haut-parleur (*m.*), loudspeaker
herbe (*f.*), grass
hiver (*m.*), winter
honte (*f.*), shame
horloge (*f.*), clock
hors de, outside (of)
hors-d'œuvre (*m.*), appetizer(s)
hôtel (*m.*) **de ville**, city hall
huile (*f.*), oil

idiotisme (*m.*), idiom
île (*f.*), island
image (*f.*), picture
immeuble (*m.*), apartment house
imperméable (*m.*), raincoat
infirmière (*f.*), nurse
ingénieur (*m.*), engineer
interrompre, to interrupt
inutile, useless
invité (*m.*), guest

jambe (*f.*), leg
jambon (*m.*), ham
jaune, yellow
Jeanne, Jean, Joan, Jane
jeter, to throw
jeu (*m.*), game
jeune fille (*f.*), girl
jeunesse (*f.*), youth
joue (*f.*), cheek
jouet (*m.*), toy
jour (*m.*) **de congé**, day off
journal (*m.*), newspaper
journée (*f.*), day
juge (*m.*), judge
jupe (*f.*), skirt
jus (*m.*), juice
jusqu'a, up to

kilogramme, kilo (*m.*), kilogram

là-bas, over there
laid, ugly
laine (*f.*), wool
laisser, to leave, let
lait (*m.*), milk
langue (*f.*), tongue, language
lapin (*m.*), rabbit
large, wide
laver, to wash; **se laver**, to get washed
lecteur (*m.*), reader
lecture (*f.*), reading
léger, legère, light
légume (*m.*), vegetable
lendemain (*m.*), next day
lever, to raise; **se lever**, to get up

lèvre (*f.*), lip
libre, free
lieu (*m.*), place
linge (*m.*), linen
lire, to read
lit (*m.*), bed
littoral (*m.*), coastline
livre (*f.*), pound
loi (*f.*), law
loin, far
loisir (*m.*), leisure, spare time; (*pl.*), diversions, pastimes
longtemps, a long time
lourd, heavy
lumière (*f.*), light
lune (*f.*), moon
lunettes (*f. pl.*), eyeglasses
lutte (*f.*), struggle
lycée (*m.*), high school

magasin (*m.*), store
magnifique, wonderful
main (*f.*), hand
mairie (*f.*), city hall, town hall
malade (*m.* or *f.*), patient
maladie (*f.*), sickness, illness
malheureux, malheureuse, unhappy
malle (*f.*), trunk
manière (*f.*), manner, way
manteau (*m.*), coat, wrap
marchand (*m.*), merchant, storekeeper
marché (*m.*), market; **bon marché**, cheap
marcher, to walk
mari (*m.*), husband
marine (*f.*), navy
marron (*m.*), chestnut
marteau (*m.*), hammer
massif (*m.*), mountain range
méchant, wicked, naughty
médaille (*f.*), medal
mêler, to mix
même, same, even, very
ménage (*m.*), household
mendiant (*m.*), beggar
mener, to lead
mensonge (*m.*), lie
menton (*m.*), chin
mer (*f.*), sea
merveille: à merveille, marvelously
métier (*m.*), trade, profession
métro (*m.*), subway
mettre, to put, put on; **se mettre (à)**, to begin
meubles (*m. pl.*), furniture
midi (*m.*), noon; south
milieu (*m.*), middle
minuit (*m.*), midnight
mœurs (*f. pl.*), customs
moins, less, fewer
mois (*m.*), month
moitié (*f.*), half
monde (*m.*), world
monnaie (*f.*), change
montre-bracelet (*f.*), wristwatch
morceau (*m.*), piece
mort (*f.*), death
mot (*m.*), word
motocyclette, moto (*f.*), motorcycle, motorbike
mouche (*f.*), fly
mouchoir (*m.*), handkerchief
moulin (*m.*), mill
mourir, to die
mousquetaire (*m.*), musketeer
mouton (*m.*), sheep
muet, muette, silent, mute
mur (*m.*), wall

nager, to swim
naissance (*f.*), birth
naître, to be born
nappe (*f.*), tablecloth
natation (*f.*), swimming
neige (*f.*), snow
neiger, to snow
nettoyer, to clean
neuf, neuve, new
neveu (*m.*), nephew
nez (*m.*), nose
nid (*m.*), nest
niveau (*m.*), level
Noël, Christmas
noir, black
nom (*m.*), name
nombre (*m.*), number
nommer, to name
nord (*m.*), north
note (*f.*), mark, bill
nouvelle (*f.*), item of news, novelette
nuage (*m.*), cloud

occasion (*f.*), opportunity
œil (*m.*), eye
œuf (*m.*), egg
œuvre (*f.*), work
oiseau (*m.*), bird
ombre (*f.*), shade, shadow
or (*m.*), gold
oreille (*f.*), ear
oreiller (*m.*), pillow
orphelin (*m.*), orphan
ôter, to take off, remove
oublier, to forget
ouest (*m.*), west
ouvrage (*m.*), work
ouvrier, ouvrière, worker

pain (*m.*), bread
paix (*f.*), peace
palais (*m.*), palace
panier (*m.*), basket
pantalon (*m.*), trousers
paquebot (*m.*), steamship, liner
Pâques, Easter
paquet (*m.*), package
paraître, to appear
parapluie (*m.*), umbrella
pardessus (*m.*), overcoat

paresseux, paresseuse, lazy
parfois, sometimes
parole (*f.*), word
partager, to share
partie (*f.*), part
partout, everywhere
passer, to pass, spend (time); **se passer,** to happen
patin (*m.*), skate
patiner, to skate
patrie (*f.*), fatherland
pays (*m.*), country
paysage (*m.*), landscape
paysan (*m.*), peasant
peau (*f.*), skin
pêche (*f.*), peach; fishing
pêcheur (*m.*), fisherman
peigner, to comb
peintre (*m.*), painter
pèlerinage (*m.*), pilgrimage
pendant, during
pendule (*f.*), clock
pensée (*f.*), thought
perdre, to lose
permettre, to permit
personne (*f.*), person
petit déjeuner (*m.*), breakfast
petit pain (*m.*), roll
petits pois (*m. pl.*), green peas
peu, little, few
peuplade (*f.*), small tribe
peuple (*m.*), people
peur (*f.*), fear
peut-être, perhaps, maybe
pharmacie (*f.*), drugstore
photographie, photo (*f.*), photograph
phrase (*f.*), sentence
pièce (*f.*), play; room; coin
pierre (*f.*), stone
Pierre, Peter
piller, to pillage, plunder
pire, worse
pis, worse
piscine (*f.*), swimming pool
place (*f.*), seat; place, public square
plafond (*m.*), ceiling
plage (*f.*), beach
plaisir (*m.*), pleasure
plancher (*m.*), floor
plein, full
pleurer, to cry
pleuvoir, to rain
plombier (*m.*), plumber
pluie (*f.*), rain
plusieurs, several
poche (*f.*), pocket
poésie (*f.*), poetry
poire (*f.*), pear
poisson (*m.*), fish
politesse (*f.*), courtesy
Pologne (*f.*), Poland
pomme (*f.*), apple
pomme (*f.*) **de terre,** potato
pont (*m.*), bridge
portail (*m.*), portal
portefeuille (*m.*), wallet
porter, to wear, carry; **se porter,** to feel
poste (*f.*), post office
poste (*m.*) **d'essence,** gas station
potage (*m.*), soup
poule (*f.*), hen
poulet (*m.*), chicken
poupée (*f.*), doll
pourboire (*m.*), tip
pousser, to push, grow
pouvoir, to be able
précis, sharp (of time)
premier ministre, prime minister
presque, almost
prêt, ready
prêter, to lend
prier, to pray
prix (*m.*), price; prize
prochain, next
profond, deep
projet (*m.*) **de loi,** bill
promenade (*f.*), walk, ride
promener: se promener, to take a walk
promettre, to promise
propre, clean; own
prune (*f.*), plum
puis, then, afterwards
puissant, powerful
pull(over) (*m.*), pullover, sweater
pupitre (*m.*), desk

quai (*m.*), pier, quay
quart (*m.*), quarter
quartier (*m.*), neighborhood, district
quel, quelle, which? what? what a . . . !
quelque, some, any
quelquefois, sometimes
quelques, some, a few
quelqu'un, someone
quête: en quête de, in search of
queue (*f.*), tail; line
quitter, to leave
quotidien, quotidienne, daily

raconter, to relate, tell
ramasser, to pick up, collect
ranger, to arrange, put in order
Raoul, Ralph
rappeler: se rappeler, to remember
ravi, delighted
récapitulation (*f.*), review
recevoir, to receive
récolte (*f.*), gathering, harvest
reconnaissance (*f.*), gratitude
reconnaître, to recognize
réfléchir, to reflect, think
regarder, to look (at)
règle (*f.*), rule; ruler
regretter, to be sorry

reine (*f.*), queen
relier, to connect, join
remarquer, to notice
remercier, to thank
remettre, to postpone
remonter, to date back
remplir, to fill
renard (*m.*), fox
rencontrer, to meet
rendez-vous (*m.*), appointment
rendre, to give back, return
renfermer, to contain, include
renseignements (*m. pl.*), information
rentrer, to go in again, return (home)
renverser, to overturn, overthrow
repas (*m.*), meal
repasser, to iron
rester, to stay, remain
retenir, to hold back, reserve
retourner, to go back, return
retrouver, to find (again)
réunion (*f.*), meeting
réussir, to succeed
rêve (*m.*), dream
réveille-matin (*m.*), alarm clock
réveiller: se réveiller, to wake up
revenir, to come back, return
revue (*f.*), magazine
rez-de-chaussée (*m.*), ground floor
rhume (*m.*), cold
rideau (*m.*), curtain
rire, to laugh
rive (*f.*), bank (of a body of water)
rivière (*f.*), river, stream
riz (*m.*), rice
roi (*m.*), king
roman (*m.*), novel
roman policier, detective story
rompre, to break
rôti (*m.*), roast
rougir, to blush
route (*f.*), road
royaume (*m.*), kingdom
ruban (*m.*), ribbon
russe, Russian

sable (*m.*), sand
sabot (*m.*), wooden shoe
sac (*m.*), bag
sacrer, to crown
saisir, to seize
saison (*f.*), season
sale, dirty
salle (*f.*) **de séjour**, living room, family room
salon (*m.*), formal parlor
saluer, to greet
sang (*m.*), blood
santé (*f.*), health
savant (*m.*), scientist
savon (*m.*), soap
sec, sèche, dry
secours (*m.*), help
séjour (*m.*), stay, sojourn; abode
sel (*m.*), salt
semblable, similar
serrurier (*m.*), locksmith
serviette (*f.*), napkin
servir, to serve; **se servir (de)**, to use
seulement, only
siècle (*m.*), century
siffler, to whistle
soie (*f.*), silk
soif: avoir soif, to be thirsty
soigner, to take care of
soin (*m.*), care
soirée (*f.*), evening party
sommeil: avoir sommeil, to be sleepy
son (*m.*), sound
songer (à), to think (of)
sonner, to ring
sortie (*f.*), exit
sot, sotte, foolish, silly
sou (*m.*), sou
souffler, to blow
souligner, to underline
sourd, deaf
sourire, to smile
souris (*f.*), mouse
sous, under
souvenir: se souvenir (de), to remember
souverain (*m.*), sovereign
stationner, to park
stylo (*m.*) **à bille**, ballpoint pen
sucre (*m.*), sugar
sud (*m.*), south
suivre, to follow
sûr, sure, certain
surtout, especially

tableau (*m.*), picture
tableau noir (*m.*), blackboard
tailleur (*m.*), tailor
taire: se taire, to be quiet
tant (de), so much, so many
tapis (*m.*), rug
tasse (*f.*), cup
tel, telle, such
tempête (*f.*), storm
temps (*m.*), time; weather
terre (*f.*), land, earth
timbre (*m.*), stamp
tiroir (*m.*), drawer
toile (*f.*), canvas
toit (*m.*), roof
tonnerre (*m.*), thunder
tort: avoir tort, to be wrong
tour (*f.*), tower
tour (*m.*), turn; trip
tourner, to turn
tousser, to cough
tout, all, whole, every
traduire, to translate
tramway (*m.*), streetcar
tranche (*f.*), slice
travail (*m.*), work

travailleur, travailleuse, industrious, hardworking
trésor (*m.*), treasure
tricot (*m.*), sweater
tristesse (*f.*), sadness
tromper, to deceive
trop (de), too, too much, too many
trottoir (*m.*), sidewalk
troubadour (*m.*), minstrel, troubadour
trouver, to find; **se trouver,** to be situated
T.S.F. (*f.*), radio

usine (*f.*) factory
utile, useful

vacances (*f. pl.*), vacation
vache (*f.*), cow
vague (*f.*), wave
veau (*m.*), veal
veille (*f.*), eve
vendange (*f.*), grape-gathering
vent (*m.*), wind
vérité (*f.*), truth
verre (*m.*), glass
vers, toward
vert, green
veston (*m.*), jacket
vêtement (*m.*), garment; (*pl.*), clothing
vêtir, to dress
viande (*f.*), meat
vide, empty
vie (*f.*), life
vieillard (*m.*), old man
vieillesse (*f.*), old age
vieux, vieil, vieille, old
vif, vive, lively
vigne (*f.*), vine
vin (*m.*), wine
visage (*m.*), face
vite, quickly
vitesse (*f.*), speed
vitrail (*m.*), stained-glass window (*pl.* **vitraux**)
vivre, to live
voisin, voisine, neighbor
voiture (*f.*), car, carriage
voix (*f.*), voice
voleur (*m.*), thief
vouer, to devote, dedicate
voyager, to travel
vrai, true
vue (*f.*), view

wagon (*m.*), car (of a train)

yeux (*m. pl.*), eyes

ENGLISH-FRENCH VOCABULARY

able: be able, pouvoir
abroad, à l'étranger
accompany, accompagner
acquaintance, la connaissance
active, actif, active
actor, l'acteur (*m.*)
actress, l'actrice (*f.*)
address, l'adresse (*f.*)
afternoon, l'après-midi (*m.*)
afterwards, ensuite
again, encore, encore une fois
ago, il y a
airplane, l'avion (*m.*)
all, tout, toute, tous, toutes
almost, presque
alone, seul
Alps, les Alpes (*f.*)
already, déjà
also, aussi
always, toujours
American, américain
ancient, ancien, ancienne
angry: get angry, se fâcher
announce, annoncer
answer, répondre (à); la réponse
apartment, l'appartement (*m.*)
appear, paraître
applaud, applaudir
apple, la pomme
arm, le bras
armchair, le fauteuil
around, autour de
as: as . . . as, aussi . . . que
as much (many), autant (de)
ask, ask for, demander
astonish, étonner
attentive, attentif, attentive
aunt, la tante
automobile, l'automobile (*f.*)
autumn, l'automne (*m.*)

bad, mauvais
badly, mal
baker, le boulanger
ball, la balle
beach, la plage
beautiful, beau, bel, belle
become, devenir
bed, le lit; **go to bed,** se coucher
before, avant
begin, commencer
believe, croire
bell, la cloche
belong to, être à
below, sous
best, le meilleur (*adj.*); le mieux (*adv.*)
bicycle, la bicyclette
big, grand; gros, grosse
bird, l'oiseau (*m.*)

birthday, l'anniversaire (*m.*) de naissance
black, noir
blackboard, le tableau noir
blue, bleu
blush, rougir
boat, le bateau
body, le corps
bore, ennuyer
born: **be born**, naître
borrow, emprunter
bottle, la bouteille
box, la boîte
bread, le pain
break, casser, rompre
bridge, le pont
bring, apporter
brown, brun
brush oneself, se brosser
build, bâtir
burn, brûler
bus, l'autobus (*m.*)
butcher, le boucher
butter, le beurre
buy, acheter

cake, le gâteau
call, appeler
candy, bonbons (*m. pl.*)
card, la carte
carry, porter
castle, le château
cat, le chat
cathedral, la cathédrale
ceiling, le plafond
certainly, certainement
chair, la chaise
chalk, la craie
charming, charmant
chat, causer
cheese, le fromage
child, l'enfant (*m.* or *f.*)
chocolate, le chocolat
church, l'église (*f.*)
city, la ville
classroom, la salle de classe
clean, nettoyer; propre
clock, l'horloge (*f.*), la pendule
close, fermer
coffee, le café
cold, froid
collect, ramasser
come back, revenir
come down, descendre
come in, entrer
come up, monter
complain, se plaindre
cool, frais, fraîche
correct, corriger
cost, coûter
count, compter
country, le pays; la campagne
cover, couvrir
cross, traverser; la croix
cruel, cruel, cruelle
cry, pleurer
cup, la tasse
cure, guérir
curious, curieux, curieuse
curtain, le rideau
cut, couper

dance, danser
dare, oser
daughter, la fille
dear, cher, chère
deceive, tromper
decide, décider
deep, profond
defend, défendre
desk, le bureau, le pupitre
dictation, la dictée
die, mourir
dirty, sale
disappear, disparaître
discover, découvrir
disobey, désobéir (à)
doctor, le médecin, le docteur
dog, le chien
dollar, le dollar
downstairs, en bas
downtown, en ville
dozen, la douzaine
drawer, le tiroir
dream, rêver; le rêve
dressed: **get dressed**, s'habiller
drink, boire
drive, conduire
dry, sec, sèche

each, chaque
early, de bonne heure
earn, gagner
easily, facilement
eat, manger
egg, l'œuf (*m.*)
elevator, l'ascenseur (*m.*)
empty, vide
enemy, l'ennemi (*m.*)
enjoy oneself, s'amuser
enormous, énorme
enough, assez (de)
erase, effacer
error, la faute, l'erreur (*f.*)
especially, surtout
European, européen, européenne
every, tout, toute, tous, toutes
everybody, tout le monde
everywhere, partout
examination, l'examen (*m.*)
exercise, l'exercice (*m.*)
expensive, cher, chère
explain, expliquer
eye, l'œil (*m.*); **eyes**, les yeux

face, la figure, le visage
fall, tomber
false, faux, fausse
family, la famille
famous, célèbre
far, loin
farm, la ferme
fat, gras, grasse; gros, grosse
favorite, favori, favorite
feather, la plume
few, peu (de); **a few**, quelques
fewer, moins (de)
fill, remplir
find, trouver
fine, beau, bel, belle

fire, le feu
first, premier, première; **at first**, d'abord
fish, le poisson
fishing, la pêche
flag, le drapeau
flower, la fleur
follow, suivre
foolish, sot, sotte
foot, le pied
foreign, étranger, étrangère
forget, oublier
franc, le franc
free, libre
Frenchman, le Français
fresh, frais, fraîche
full, plein
future, l'avenir (*m.*)

game, le jeu
garden, le jardin
gay, gai
general, général; le général
generally, généralement
generous, généreux, généreuse
gentle, doux, douce
gentleman, le monsieur
gently, doucement
George, Georges
German, allemand
gift, le cadeau
girl, la jeune fille
give back, rendre
glad, content
glass, le verre
glove, le gant
go away, partir, s'en aller
go back, retourner
go down, descendre
go in, entrer (dans)
go out, sortir
go up, monter
gold, l'or (*m.*)
gradually, peu à peu
grandfather, le grand-père
grass, l'herbe (*f.*)
gray, gris
green, vert

hair, le cheveu, les cheveux
hand, la main
handkerchief, le mouchoir
handsome, beau, bel, belle
happen, arriver, se passer
happy, heureux, heureuse
hard, dur
have to, devoir
head, la tête
hear, entendre
heart, le cœur
heavy, lourd
Helen, Hélène
help, aider
Henry, Henri
high, haut
hold, tenir
homework, les devoirs (*m. pl.*)
hope, espérer
horse, le cheval
hot, chaud
hotel, l'hôtel (*m.*)
hour, l'heure (*f.*)
how much (many)?, combien (de)
hurry, se dépêcher
hurt, blesser, faire mal (à); **to get hurt**, se blesser
husband, le mari

immediately, tout de suite, immédiatement
industrious, diligent
ink, l'encre (*f.*)
interesting, intéressant
interrupt, interrompre
Italian, italien

jewel, le bijou
Joan, Jeanne
John, Jean

keep, garder
key, la clef
kind, aimable; gentil, gentille
king, le roi
kitchen, la cuisine
knife, le couteau
know, savoir, connaître
know how, savoir

lady, la dame
lake, le lac
large, grand
last, dernier, dernière
late, en retard, tard
laugh, rire
lawyer, l'avocat (*m.*)
lazy, paresseux, paresseuse
lead, mener, conduire
learn, apprendre
leave, partir, sortir; laisser, quitter
left, gauche
lend, prêter
less, moins
library, la bibliothèque
lie, mentir
lie down, se coucher
life, la vie
lift, lever
light, léger, légère; clair; lumière (*f.*)
lightly, légèrement
like, aimer
listen (to), écouter
little, petit, peu
live, demeurer
live in, habiter
lively, vif, vive
long, long, longue
(a) long time, longtemps
look at, regarder
look for, chercher
lose, perdre
loud, haut
low, bas, basse

maid, le bonne
many, beaucoup (de)
map, la carte

mark, la note
market, le marché
maybe, peut-être
meal, le repas
meat, la viande
meet, rencontrer
memorize, apprendre par cœur
meter, le mètre
middle, le milieu
midnight, minuit (*m.*)
mild, doux, douce
milk, le lait
mistake, la faute, l'erreur (*f.*)
money, l'argent (*m.*)
month, le mois
moon, la lune
mountain, la montagne
movies, le cinéma
much, beaucoup (de)
mute, muet, muette

name, le nom
narrow, étroit
naturally, naturellement
naughty, méchant
near, près (de)
necessary, nécessaire
need, avoir besoin (de)
neighbor, le voisin, la voisine
nephew, le neveu
new, neuf, neuve; nouveau, nouvel, nouvelle
newspaper, le journal
next, prochain; ensuite
nice, gentil, gentille
night, la nuit
noon, midi (*m.*)
nose, le nez
notebook, le cahier
notice, remarquer

obey, obéir (à)
October, octobre (*m.*)
offer, offrir
often, souvent
old, vieux, vieil, vieille; ancien, ancienne
open, ouvrir
opportunity, l'occasion (*f.*)
overcoat, le pardessus
own, propre

package, le colis
palace, le palais
paper, le papier
Parisian, parisien, parisienne
park, le parc
patient, le (la) malade
pay, pay for, payer
peasant, le paysan, la paysanne
perfect, parfait
perhaps, peut-être
permit, permettre
Peter, Pierre
pick up, ramasser
picture, l'image (*f.*), le tableau
piece, le morceau
pity, plaindre
plane, l'avion (*m.*)
play, jouer
pleasant, agréable
pleased, content
pocket, la poche
polite, poli
poor, pauvre
pound, la livre
prefer, préférer, aimer mieux
present, le cadeau
pretty, joli
price, le prix
princess, la princesse
prize, le prix
promise, promettre
pronounce, prononcer
proud, fier, fière
punish, punir
put, put on, mettre

quarter, le quart
queen, la reine
quickly, vite, rapidement

rain, pleuvoir; la pluie
raise, lever
read, lire
ready, prêt
really, vraiment
receive, recevoir
recognize, reconnaître
red, rouge
reflect, réfléchir
relate, raconter
remain, rester
repeat, répéter
republic, la république
resemble, ressembler (à)
rest, se reposer
return, retourner, revenir, rentrer; rendre
return home, rentrer
rich, riche
ride, la promenade
ring, sonner
river, le fleuve
road, le chemin, la route
roll, le petit pain
round, rond
rug, le tapis
ruler, le règle
run, courir
Russian, russe

sad, triste
salt, le sel
say, dire
scold, gronder
sculptor, le sculpteur
sea, la mer
season, la saison
seated, assis
see, voir
seize, saisir
seldom, rarement
sell, vendre
send, envoyer
sentence, la phrase
serious, sérieux, sérieuse
serve, servir
several, plusieurs
shave (oneself), se raser
shine, briller
shoe, la chaussure

short, court
show, montrer
sick, malade
silent, muet, muette
silk, la soie
silly, sot, sotte
sing, chanter
sit down, s'asseoir
situated: **be situated**, se trouver
sky, le ciel
sleep, dormir
slow, lent
snow, neiger; la neige
so much (many), tant (de)
soldier, le soldat
someone, quelqu'un
something, quelque chose
sometimes, quelquefois
son, le fils
song, la chanson
soon, bientôt
south, le sud, le midi
Spanish, espagnol
spring, le printemps
stamp, le timbre
station, la gare
stay, rester
still, encore
store, le magasin
story, l'histoire (*f.*)
strange, étrange
street, la rue
strong, fort
succeed, réussir
suddenly, tout à coup
sugar, le sucre
summer, l'été (*m.*)
sure, sûr
sweet, doux, douce
swim, nager

take off, ôter
tall, grand
tea, le thé
teach, enseigner
tell, dire
than, que
then, alors, puis, ensuite
thick, épais, épaisse
thing, la chose
think, penser, réfléchir
throw, jeter
ticket, le billet
tie, la cravate
tip, le pourboire
tired, fatigué
together, ensemble
tonight, ce soir
too, aussi; trop
too much (many), trop (de)
tooth, la dent
toward, vers; envers
tower, la tour
translate, traduire
travel, voyager
traveler, le voyageur, la voyageuse
tree, l'arbre (*m.*)
trip, le tour, le voyage
truly, vraiment
trunk, la malle
truth, la vérité
try, **try on**, essayer
turn, le tour

ugly, laid
umbrella, le parapluie
uncle, l'oncle (*m.*)
under, sous
understand, comprendre
unfortunate, malheureux, malheureuse
unhappy, malheureux, malheureuse
United States, les États-Unis (*m. pl.*)
up: **get up**, se lever
upstairs, en haut
use, employer, se servir (de)
useful, utile
useless, inutile

vacation, les vacances (*f. pl.*)
vegetable, le légume
violin, le violon
visit, visiter, faire visite (à)
voice, la voix

wait, **wait for**, attendre
waiter, le garçon
wake up, se réveiller
walk, marcher; la promenade; **take a walk**, faire une promenade, se promener
wall, le mur
want, désirer, vouloir
war, la guerre
warm, chaud
wash, laver; **get washed**, se laver
watch, la montre
water, l'eau (*f.*)
weak, faible
wear, porter
week, la semaine
what?, **what a . . . !**, quel, quelle
which?, quel, quelle
white, blanc, blanche
whole, tout
wicked, méchant
wide, large
wife, la femme
win, gagner
wine, le vin
winter, l'hiver (*m.*)
without, sans
woman, la femme
wood, le bois
wooden shoe, le sabot
wool, la laine
work, travailler; le travail
world, le monde
write, écrire
writer, l'écrivain (*m.*)

year, l'an (*m.*), l'année (*f.*)
yellow, jaune
yet, encore